Frederick William Chapman

The Bulkeley Family

Or the descendants of Rev. Peter Bulkeley, who settled at Concord, Mass., in 1636.

Compiled at the request of Joseph E. Bulkeley

Frederick William Chapman

The Bulkeley Family
Or the descendants of Rev. Peter Bulkeley, who settled at Concord, Mass., in 1636. Compiled at the request of Joseph E. Bulkeley

ISBN/EAN: 9783337424718

Printed in Europe, USA, Canada, Australia, Japan

Cover: Foto ©ninafisch / pixelio.de

More available books at **www.hansebooks.com**

THE
BULKELEY FAMILY;

OR THE DESCENDANTS OF

REV. PETER BULKELEY,

WHO SETTLED AT

CONCORD, MASS., IN 1636.

Compiled at the request of JOSEPH E. BULKELEY.

BY

REV. F. W. CHAPMAN,

AUTHOR OF THE "CHAPMAN," "PRATT," "TROWBRIDGE," "BUCKINGHAM," AND "COIT" FAMILIES; MEMBER OF THE NEW ENGLAND HISTORICAL AND GENEALOGICAL SOCIETY, THE CONNECTICUT HISTORICAL SOCIETY, THE NEW HAVEN COLONY HISTORICAL SOCIETY, AND THE BUFFALO HISTORICAL SOCIETY.

HARTFORD:
THE CASE, LOCKWOOD & BRAINARD CO., PRINTERS.
1875.

[Let all read this Preface before examining the work.]

PREFACE.

ABOUT four years since, Mr. Joseph E. Bulkeley, of New York, who has a country seat in Rocky Hill, engaged the publisher to prepare a full and complete genealogy of the Bulkeley family in America, descended from the Rev. Peter Bulkeley, of Concord, Mass., who arrived in New England in 1634 or 1635. Most of the four intervening years have been faithfully devoted to this work. No pains have been spared to make out a correct list of all the descendants. The usual difficulties attending such an enterprise have been fully experienced. More than one thousand letters have been written to different members of the family. Two different circulars have also been sent to all whose residence has been known. The writer has also visited the offices of town clerks and clerks of probate, and examined church and parish records, searched burial-grounds, visited numerous families, and made as thorough investigation as practicable to include all of the race in the country. In order to gain all of historical interest that could be gathered, many days have been spent in the largest libraries of New York, Boston, New Haven, Hartford, and Worcester, the superintendents of which have afforded every facility in their power. The task of collecting materials for this memorial has of course been laborious beyond what any one can realize who has not been engaged in similar labors.

In multitudes of instances, no response has been given to letters repeatedly sent to individuals requesting dates and other important facts, which could be gathered from no other source. In some cases we have been obliged to address letters to professional men in the vicinity of the delinquents and offer them a compensation for gathering the needed information for us. The chirography of those who have returned answers, in cases not infrequent, has been such as was impossible to decipher, obliging us to write a second time, requesting an explanation. Many families have kept no record, but have forwarded lists from memory, and different members of the same family have often disagreed in the dates furnished. The history of the earlier generations has been made as complete as could be by a diligent search of public records, which are the principal sources of information respecting the earlier families; but all the facts sought were not recorded. Records in some instances have been lost; in others the desired items of information are omitted, and such records often disagree. In all such cases the writer has selected such names and dates as seemed sanctioned by the highest authority. The later generations have been collected mainly by examining family records and by correspondence with members of the various families now living. Great perplexity has been experienced from the fact that, until quite recently, there has been during the last hundred years unwarrantable neglect to register on public records the births, marriages, and deaths which have occurred in the various towns and parishes. These explanations are given, that those persons who do not find the account of their families as perfect as they expected, may understand that all reasonable effort has been expended to secure completeness and accuracy. The compiler has carefully examined all the records within his reach and the various manuscripts furnished him, and has diligently sought information from all available sources. It has been his constant aim to furnish a reliable record and history of the family in its numerous branches. For the errors of recorders and correspondents he cannot be held responsible. Manifest errors in the spelling of names have been corrected according to his best judgment, while some peculiarities in the earlier generations have been purposely retained. It is hardly possible in a work of this kind to avoid mistakes in deciphering and transcribing so many thousand names and dates, many of which are found in records and manuscripts scarcely legible. It is exceedingly difficult to avoid all errors in printing a volume containing so many dates and figures, even where the copy is complete. Although the sheets, as they have come from the press, have been carefully read before the last impression by some half dozen different individuals, some errors have escaped the notice of the compiler and his assistant proof-readers.

It is to be regretted that a few families have been so separated from their relatives that no trace of them and their descendants have been found. Still, with few exceptions, we think a full and accurate record has been given.

The thanks of the compiler are due to those members of the family who have aided him in his researches. He is under especial obligations to Mr. Joseph E. Bulkeley for records and historical matter relating to the family, collected by him in this country and in England, previous to his engagement with the author; to Mr. James H. Bulkeley, of Philadelphia, for the family records of descendants in Pennsylvania; to Miss Anna L. North, Checktowaga, N. Y., for assistance in tracing the descendants of Prescott and Lois Williams Bulkeley; to Mrs. M. S. Converse of Elmira, N. Y., for records of Benjamin, Brownell, and Francis Bulkeley; to Dr. Edward Bulkeley, of New Haven, for valuable statistics relating to the descendants of Edward and Diana Bunce Bulkeley; and especially to Miss Eliza Ann Bulkeley, of Southport, for aid in collecting the descendants of Thomas and Peter Bulkeley, sons of Rev. Peter Bulkeley, of Concord, and without whose assistance their records would unavoidably have been very incomplete; and to numerous other persons not connected with the family for the assistance they have rendered him in his investigations.

As the work will probably fall into the hands of some not extensively versed in genealogies, the author has endeavored to make it as free from intricacies as possible. The descendants of each child of the first settler who married and had offspring are distinctly traced by themselves, according to their generations, and are all numbered from the beginning. The marginal numbers give each descendant his place in the order of descent, while the head numbers in the middle of the page, corresponding to those in the margin, give the marriages of such as have entered the family relation, and as far as possible the names of their partners, with the dates of their marriage and decease.

A full index of the baptismal names of those whose surname is Bulkeley is furnished, the number of the individual being opposite to the Christian name on the left and the date of birth on the right; also an index of the descendants of other names than those of Bulkeley, with numbers and dates to correspond; and a list of those who have married into the Bulkeley family, with the number of their respective partners on the left and date of marriage on the right.

In conclusion, the volume is sent forth in the hope that it will be acceptable to the numerous living members of the family, and that it may stimulate the present and future generations to emulate the piety, the love of civil and religious liberty, and that devotion to the common welfare which characterized the early settlers of New England.

FREDERICK W. CHAPMAN.

Rocky Hill, Conn., December 1st, 1875.

TABLE OF CONTENTS.

	Page.
Earlier Notices of the Bulkeley Family, in England,	9
Bulkeley Pedigree,	18
Introductory History of the Family in America,	24
Will of Rev. Peter Bulkeley,	30
Genealogy of the Families in America,	35
Rev. Peter Bulkeley, the Puritan Settler,	35
Descendants of Rev. Edward Bulkeley,	38
Will of Joseph Bulkeley, of Littleton,	41
Descendants of Thomas Bulkeley, of Fairfield,	44
John Bulkeley and his descendants,	64
Will of John Bulkeley,	64
Will of Everard Faulkner,	68
Will of Elisabeth Faulkner,	70
Rev. Gershom Bulkeley, and descendants,	78
Will of Rev. Gershom Bulkeley, of Wethersfield,	81
Rev. John Bulkeley, of Colchester,	91
Exploits of Capt. Charles Bulkeley, of New London,	111
Untimely Death of Walter William Bulkeley,	123
Memoir of Dr. Sylvester Bulkeley,	127
Notice of Gurdon Bulkeley,	136
Memoir of Eleazer Bulkeley,	201
Index to Christian Names of those bearing the surname of Bulkeley,	255
Index to the Names of other descendants than those bearing the surname of Bulkeley,	269
Index to the Names of persons who have married into the Bulkeley family,	278
APPENDIX.—Life of Rev. Peter Bulkeley, by Rev. Cotton Mather,	247

THE BULKELEY FAMILY.

This family descended from remote antiquity. Its surname is derived from a ridge of mountains in the County Palatine of Chester. The name was spelled in the reign of John—1199 to 1216 and generations succeeding—Buclough, or larger mountain. In the 20th of Henry IV., and on the visitations of Edward IV., its designation was Bucclogh—Lord of Bulclogh in Cheshire; and of the manor of Eaton, Presland and Almon, Norbury and Steuben, and in the inquisitions of Post Mortem, of later dates, of Stoke and Mayfield.

Robert Bulclogh, Lord of Bulclogh.

Wm. Bulkeley, first son, 1302, married Miss Maud, daughter of Sir John Davenport and wife, Alice, and their descendants bore the manor of Norbury.

The following sketch of the Buckeleys is taken from Lyson's Magnalia of Great Britain:

The township of Bulkeley, or Buckley, lies about nine miles N. N. West from Nantwich; the manor was the inheritance of an ancient family of that name, the elder branch of which became extinct in the 4th century. After this period, we find two estates in this township, each called the manor of Bulkeley; one of these passed, by marriage, to Thomas Holford, Esq., of the body to King Richard II., and is now the property of George James, Earl of Cholmondeley, whose ancestor, Sir Hugh Cholmondeley, married the daughter and heir of Christopher Holford, Esq. The other passed, by marriage, from the family of Bulkeley to that of Calveley, and was purchased by Lord Cholmondeley in 1659, of Lord and Lady Byron, having been conveyed by Sir Hugh Calveley to Lady Byron—then Mrs. Elisabeth Booth—in 1646.

Robert Lord Cholmondeley, Thomas Bulkeley, and Edward

Bressey (or Brassay), are described as joint Lords of Bulkeley in a manuscript of 1662; the Brassays possessed their estates in Bulkeley by marriage with the heiress of Hadleigh, about the beginning of the 15th century. Webb, in his Itinerancy, written in the year 1662, speaks of a fair new house in this township, then belonging to Thomas Brassey, Gent. The mansion and its demesne still belong to the Brassey family. Thomas Bulkeley, the last male heir of that ancient family, resided in the township of Bulkeley, in an house now called Bulkeley Hall, which had been built by his father, till his death, which happened in 1802, at the advanced age of ninety-eight (98). This mansion passed, by bequest, to Mr. Thomas Orton, the present proprietor. Old Bulkeley Hall, the property of the Earl of Cholmondeley, is occupied by a farmer (Vide Lyson's Magnalia, Vol. 3. p. 681).

In Cheshire noblemen's seats is a seat of Lord Viscount Bulkeley, in right of his lady, the heiress of the Warrens. (Page 353.)

The Baskerayles, a younger branch of this family, settled at Bulkeley, by marriage with the heiress of Hadley, descended from a branch of the Bulkeleys. (Page 362.)

Richard Bulkeley was Sheriff of Chester in 1457. (Vide King's History of Chester, page 73.)

The Bulkeleys were Lords of Bulkeley in the reign of King John. Robert De Bulkeley, who was Sheriff of Cheshire in 1309, had three sons, William, common ancestor of most of the Cheshire branches; Thomas, whose posterity soon failed in the male line; and Peter, ancestor of the Bulkeleys of Ware in Shropshire, and the Bulkeleys of Boxton, who became extinct after three descents. William, above mentioned, had several sons, viz., William, who left an only daughter, married to Thomas Holford, in consequence of which match the Cholmondeleys of Vale Royal, by marriage with the heiress of Holford, are representatives of the elder branch of the Bulkeleys. Robert, the second son of William, settled at Eaton, in Devenham, and had two sons, Robert, ancestor of the Bulkeleys of Eaton, which family became extinct after six generations; and Richard, who married the heiress of Chedle and of Whatcroft in Devenham. The elder branch of these Bulkeleys removed to Beaumaris, in the Isle of Anglesea, and were ancestors of Lord Viscount Bulkeley, who has a seat in Cheshire, in right of his lady, as heiress of the Warrens. A younger branch of this house continued for some descents at Chedle. Roger Bulkeley, third son of William Bulkeley, above mentioned, settling at Nor-an early period in moities, between the families of Praers, succeeded by the Manwarings and that of Bulkeley in the reign of Henry VIII.

Thomas Bulkeley sold his estate in Ayton to the Breretons, who seem eventually to have been possessed of the whole Manor which before the year 1672 had passed, by successive sales, to the families of Lendsay and Cholmondeley. It is now the property of Thomas Cholmondeley, Esq., of Vale Royal, M. P. The Bulkeleys had a seat at Ayton. Bishop Gartrell mentions a monument, formerly in Davenham Church, for William Bulkeley, Esq., of Ayton, who died in the reign of Edward IV. Leland says that the two Bulkeleys, i. e. the Bulkeleys of Whatcroft and Ayton, contended either to be the Elder house of that name; he adds Bulkeley of Eaton Stakam to a daughter and Leftwich had her but Sir. Gul'. Breton of brought Eyton. (Vol. 3, p. 647. 1810.)

The township of Whatcroft lies three miles south-east of Norwich; the manor was for many generations in that branch of the Bulkeley family from which the present Lord Viscount Bulkeley is descended. This branch of the family had removed into North Wales before Leland's time but continued to possess Whatcroft till after the year 1756. (Page 650.)

In the sixth year of the reign of Edward II., David Bulkeley, Sergeant of the Peace, to Richard Sutton, presented the heads of two felons executed for burglary. (Page 686.)

A branch of the Bulkeleys resided at Hollyhurst in the seventeenth century. (Page 687.)

Roger, a younger son of William Bulkeley, having settled at Norbury, upon an estate given him by his father about the latter end of the thirteenth century, took the name of Norbury. (Page 687.)

In the parish church of Middlewich are two chapels which belonged to the Barons of Kinderton, one fitted up in 1615, the other in 1632, ornamented with the Arms and quarterings of that family. In the north-east chapel which was purchased of Sir Richard Bulkeley in 1858 are several memorials of Venables and Levera. (Page 688.)

In the parish church of Mothan are memorials of the Bulkeleys. (Page 696-7.)

On Page 262—and onward of Playfair's British Antiquity, published at London in 1809—is the following entry:

bury, his posterity assumed the name of Norbury, and became extinct in the elder branch, after four generations. The posterity of Richard, fourth son of William Bulkeley, settled at Prestland, near Bunbury, took the name of Presland, were for several descents of Wardle Hall in the same parish, and continued in the male line till the middle of the 17th century, if not later. *Thomas* Bulkeley, the fifth son, who was of Alpraham, left an only daughter, married to Thomas Arderne, whose heiress married Thomas Stanley of Elford.

David was the youngest son of William Bulkeley, Esq., by whose death this branch of the family became extinct in 1812. (Lyson, page 363.)

Lawrence Wright, Esq., who became thus possessed of Offerton about the year 1600, was grandson of Thomas Wright, of Nantwich, whose pedigree is traced a few descents higher to Thomas Wright, *alias* Bulkeley. (Page 369.)

The Prestlands, descended from a younger branch of the Bulkeley family, were for many generations of Wordle in Bunbury. They became extinct in the early part of the 17th century. (Page 472.)

The manor of Austersan, or Alstanton, was at an early period the property of the Alstantons, from whom it passed by successive female heirs to the families of Bulkeleys, Weterhall, Praers, and Bromley. (Page 477.)

A free school was founded at Wrenbury by Mr. Ralph Bulkeley in 1605. It is endowed with the interest of £230, the interest of which is appropriated to bind their apprentices. (Page 515.)

The other moiety of the manor of Timperly was held, at a very early period, under the Barony of Durham Massay, by the Cheadles and their representatives, the Bulkeleys of Cheadle. This estate belonged to Lord Bulkeley in 1702. (Page 552.)

The Township of Wardhull, or Wardle, lies about five miles north-west from Nantwich. The Manor is the property of the Earl of Dysart, by inheritance from the Wilbraham family. Sir Thomas Wilbraham, who was possessed of this Manor in the middle of the seventeenth century, purchased the Hall which is now a farm-house, from the Prestlands, who had been settled there for several descents from a younger branch of the Bulkeley Family. (Page 552.)

The township of Eaton, or as it was anciently written, Ayton, lies near three miles south by west of Norwich; the Manor was at

Sir Robert Bulkeley of Beaumaris and Chedd, the eldest son, was knighted in 1576; represented the county of Anglesey in several Parliaments, in the reigns of Queen Mary and Queen Elizabeth, to the latter of whom he proved an excellent soldier and faithful subject on many occasions. He was also chamberlain of North Wales. He was married to his first wife, Margaret, daughter of Sir John Savage of Rock Savage and Clifton, in Cheshire, Knight, and to his second, Agnes, daughter of Thomas Needham, of Shavington, in Shropshire, Esq., and had, by her, eight sons and two daughters.

Dr. Launcelot Bulkeley, the sixth son of Sir Richard, was admitted a commoner of Brazen Nose College, Oxford, in 1587, the eighteenth year of his age, and taking his degree of A. M. in 1593, was, on the 13th of November in that year, ordained deacon, and the same day inducted to the rectory of Llandyffran, to which was added, on the 4th of March following, the rectory of Llandegvaine, otherwise Beaumaris, of which Lord Bulkeley is patron. On the 25th of March, 1594, he was admitted into priest's orders; after which, being Archbishop of Dublin, he took the degree of D.D. in that University, and by letters patent, August 11th, 1619, was promoted to the Archepiscopal See, soon after which, he was sworn of the privy council, and on the 15th of April, 1624, appointed one of the commissioners for the preservation of the peace in the provinces of Leinster and Ulster, during the deputy Lord Falkland's absence to visit the new plantations in the north. He died at his palace of Tallayht, September 8th, 1650, in the 82d year of his age. He married Alice, daughter of Rowland Bulkeley, of Beaumaris, and had issue by her of two sons and two daughters.

William Bulkeley, D.D., Archbishop of Dublin, at Miltown, which, with many other houses and castles belonging to the Protestant nobility and gentry in the counties of Dublin and Wicklow, were burnt in 1641, to prevent the English from planting any garrisons in those parts. He was a person of great virtue and piety, one who made it his chief occupation to serve the church, and his amusement to improve and adorn his estate with plantations, whereby from a rude, desolate, and wild land he brought it to be a most delightful patrimony. He married Elisabeth, daughter of Henry Manwaring of Kilkenny, Esq., one of the masters in the high court of chancery in Ireland, by whom he had three sons and three daughters. Sir Edward, the eldest son, who

Viscount Bulkeley in Ireland.

This ancient and noble family appears, by a curious illuminated pedigree in his Lordship's possession, to be descended from Robert Bulkeley, Esq., Lord of the manor of Bulkeley in the County Palatine of Chester, in the reign of King John, who was succeeded in his estates by his son William, who had five sons.

Robert Bulkeley of Bulkeley, Esq., the eldest son, married a daughter of Thomas Butler, Baron of Warrington in Cheshire, by whom he had two sons and four daughters. William, the oldest son and heir, was living at Bulkeley in the year 1302, and twice married, 1. To Maud, daughter of Sir John Davenport Knight. 2. To Alice, daughter of Vigan St. Piere. By the latter wife he had one son, Richard, to whom he gave the manor of Prentland, in Cheshire, whereupon he assumed that name which his descendants continued to use. The issue of the former (marriage) was five sons.

Robert Bulkeley, 2d son of William, became seated at Eaton in Cheshire, which he had of his father's gift. He was sheriff of the County in 1341, and married Isabel, daughter of Philip Edgerton of Malpas in Cheshire, and had by her a daughter, Cecily, who married Thomas Weaver, of Cheshire, and had two sons. Robert, from whom the Bulkeleys of Calemand Burgate in Cheshire are descended, and Richard, ancestor to Lord Bulkeley. Richard married Agnes, daughter and co-heiress to Roger Chidel, of Chidel, in Cheshire, and had with her that estate in which he was succeeded by his only son William Bulkeley, Esq., of Chidel, who, in the reign of Henry VI., being Constable of Beaumaris in the Isle of Anglesy, prevented the Duke of York from landing there on his return from Ireland to join the Earl of Warwick against the King. He married Ellen, daughter of Gwilliam ap Griffith of Pentrie Esq., by whom he had six sons and four daughters. Rowland Bulkeley, of Beaumaris, Esq., the eldest son, married Alice, daughter and heiress to William Beconsal, of Beconsal in Lancashire, Esq., and had issue five sons and two daughters.

Sir Richard Bulkeley, the eldest son, succeeded his father Rowland at Beaumaris; was honored with knighthood and made chamberlain of North Wales in 1534. He married Catharine, daughter of Sir William Griffith, Jun., of Penrhyn, in the county of Carnarvon, chamberlain of North Wales, and had, by her, four sons and two daughters.

Davenport of Bromhall, in Cheshire, Knight, and, second, to Mary, daughter of William Lord Borough of Gainsborough, in Lincolnshire. By the former he had one son and one daughter; by the second, two sons and four daughters.

Thomas, first Viscount, the younger son, was seated at Barnhill, near Beaumaris ; and being a person of great merit and strict loyalty to King Charles I., was advanced. by patent under the privy seal, dated at Oxford, June the 6th, 1643, to the dignity of Viscount Bulkeley of Cashel, in the Kingdom of Ireland. He married Blanche, daughter of Robert Coytmore of Coytmore, in Carnarvonshire, Esq., and, secondly, the daughter of Robert Cheadle, who was some time his Lordship's steward. By the latter he had five sons and four daughters.

Robert, 2d Viscount Bulkeley, the eldest surviving son and heir, was sheriff of the county of Anglesey, in 1658, and served for that county, in the Parliament which restored King Charles II., continuing to be its representative, till his death, which happened Oct. the 16th, 1688. He married Sarah, daughter of Daniel Harvey, of Coombe, in Surrey, Esq., and had issue three sons and six daughters.

Richard, the 3d Viscount, was born in 1658. He represented the county of Anglesey in Parliament, from 1680 until his death, and in 1701 was appointed Vice Admiral of North Wales. He married 1st, Mary, daughter of Sir Philip Egerton, of Egerton and Duddin, Knight.

Richard, 4th Viscount, who succeeded his father Aug. 9th, 1704, was representative for the county of Anglesey, from 1705 till his death, the constable of Beaumaris castle and constable of North Wales, on the 2d of Nov., 1713, was made constable of Carnarvon castle, and died at Bath, June 4, 1724, having always distinguished himself by a steady adherence to principles of loyalty, and disinterested zeal for the good of his country, and the strictest regard to every social virtue. He married Lady Bridget Bertie, eldest daughter of James, Earl of Abingdon, and by her left issue two sons and four daughters.

Richard, 5th Viscount, born in 1708, was, in March, 1730, elected member of Parliament, for Beaumaris, and was re-chosen at the next general election ; he was likewise Governor of Beaumaris castle and chamberlain of North Wales. On the 12th of Jan., 1731, his Lordship married Jane, daughter and heiress of Lewis Owen, of Penairth, in Merionithshire, Esq., but, dying without issue, succeeded to Old Bawne, was also seated at Dunlaven, in the county of Wicklow. He was created a Baronet of Ireland by patent, December 9th, 1682. In 1650 he married, first, Catharine, daughter and co-heiress of John Byhe, Esq., chief baron of the exchequer in Ireland, and by her, who died in 1624, had two sons, and his second wife was Dorothy, daughter of ——— Whitfield, Esq., by whom he had no issue. He died in 1635, and was succeeded by Sir Robert Bulkeley, Bart., and their oldest son and heir, who had his education in the Universities of Oxford and Dublin, and took the degree of A.B., May 21st, 1680. He was a person of good understanding and reason, which in many respects were set off by the imperfect symmetry, or rather deformity, of his body. In the course of his childhood his faculties were so extraordinary that in a few years he acquired a very great share of learning, and, being blessed with a great memory, his knowledge and learning were therein most securely treasured up. At sixteen years of age he had a large stock of human learning, with talents that have rarely been equalled, wit, fancy, and ready apprehension, with a memory almost miraculous. Yet with all this fund of reason and literature, he was strangely deluded and led away by the absurd ravings of a set of enthusiastic pretenders to prophecy, who first appeared among the French Camisards and Huguenots. With these he engaged so deeply that not only his estate partly supplied their extravagance, but he prostituted his excellent pen in defense of their phrenzy and misapplied his great capacity and good sense by endeavors to support their groundless delusions, and was only prevented by death, from selling his estate to distribute amongst them. He married Lucy, daughter of Sir George Downing of Hatley, in Cambridgeshire, Baronet, and leaving no issue, the title became extinct, for his brother John Bulkeley, who died July 18th, 1699, left by Elisabeth, his wife, daughter of Henry Whitfield, Esq., an only daughter, Hesther, who became heiress to the estate and was married April 15th, 1702, to James Worth Tynte, Esq., younger son of Mr. Baron Worth, and died August 9th, 1723.

Sir Robert Bulkeley, eldest son of Sir Richard Bulkeley, of Beaumaris, by his first wife, Margaret Savage, received the hono of Knighthood, and by King James I. instructions to Wm. Lord Compton, President of Wales, dated November 12, 1617, was appointed one of the council of his Lordship, for that principality He died June the 28th, 1621, and was buried at Beaumaris, having been twice married, first, to Catharine, daughter of William

March the 15th, 1738, the title descended to his brother, James, 6th Viscount, who on the 19th of April was elected representative in Parliament for Beaumaris ; was also constable of the castle there and chamberlain for North Wales. In August, 1747, he married Emma Isle, daughter and heiress of Thomas Rowland, of Cærn, in the Isle of Anglesey, Esq., by whom he had two daughters, and also a posthumous son.

Thomas James, 7th Viscount Bulkeley of Ireland, and 1st Lord Bulkeley, Baron of Beaumaris, in the Isle of Anglesey, was born on the 12th of Dec., 1752. At the general elections in the years 1774 and 1780 his Lordship was chosen representative, for the county of Anglesey ; was created a peer of Great Britain by the title of Lord Bulkeley, Baron of Beaumaris in the Isle of Anglesey, by patent dated May the 14th, 1784, and was likewise Lord Lieut. and Custos Rutulorum of the city of Carnarvon. His Lordship on the 27th of April, 1777, was married to Elizabeth Harriet, only daughter and heiress of Sir George Warner, Knight of the Bath, but has no issue. He made the grand tour in conjunction with the Marquis of Buckingham.

NOTE.—Thomas James Warner Bulkeley, Baron Bulkeley of Beaumaris, in the county of Anglesey, also Viscount Bulkeley of the kingdom of Ireland, Lord Lieut. of Carnarvon, third chamberlain of North Wales and hereditary constable of Beaumaris' castle, May 14, 1784.

THE BULKELEY PEDIGREE.

Prepared for the Genealogical Register by Miss H. A. BRAINBRIDGE, of London.

THE Bulkeley, or Bulkley, or, as it is sometimes spelt, Buckley, family, is of very ancient origin, and thrived in Cheshire for many years. They were afterwards scattered far and wide; several branches taking other names.

William Bulkeley, one of the early lords of Bulkeley, who married the daughter of Sir John Davenport, had six sons: the eldest William, took a share of Bulkeley; Robert took Eaton and Alstanton; Roger assumed the name of Norbury and took that estate: Richard took Prestland, and assumed that name; Thomas married a daughter of Matthew de Alpraham, and seems to have taken Alpraham; and David took a share of Bulkeley.

From these sprang the lords Bulkeley; the Bulkeleys of Ireland, Beaumaris, Davinham, Haughton, Cheadle, Burgate, Porthamel, Wore (or Woore), Broxton, Stanlow, Odell, and America.

A paragraph in Neal's *History of the Puritans* relative to Peter Buckeley of Odell, afterwards of America, reads thus:—

"But notwithstanding this prohibition, numbers went to New England this summer [1635]; and amongst others the Reverend Mr. *Peter Bulkley*, B. D., fellow of St. John's College, Cambridge. He was son of Dr. *Edward Bulkley* of Bedfordshire, and succeeded him at Woodhill or Odell in that county. There he continued above twenty years, the Bishop of Lincoln conniving at his nonconformity; but when Dr. *Laud* was at the helm of the church and the Bishop of Lincoln in disgrace, *Bulkley* was silenced by the vicar-general, Sir Nathaniel Brent; upon which he sold a very plentiful estate and transported himself and his effects to New England, where he died in the year 1658–9, and in the seventy-seventh of his age. He was a thundering preacher and a judicious divine, as appears by his treatise *of the Covenant*, which passed through several editions and was one of the first books published in that country."[1]

As regards Edward, the father, the registers at Woore, where he was born, are not perfect. He was the son of Thomas, and was curate of St. Mary's, Shrewsbury, in 1550; afterwards prebend of Chester, then of Lichfield, and minister at Odell, where he died.

---

[1] The *Gospel Covenant* by Rev. Peter Bulkley, though preached as a sermon at Concord, N. E., was not printed in this country. The first edition appeared in London in 1646, and the second in 1651.—ED.

PEDIGREE OF BULKELEY OF CHESHIRE AND IRELAND, WALES, SALOP, AND BEDFORD.

Corrected from Lodge, Burke, the Harleian and Additional MSS., Wills, Drs. Commons, etc.

ROBERT BULKELEY= Lord of Bulkeley, Co. Cheshire.

Emma. | Letitia. | William de Bulkeley= | Felicia. | Leuka.

Robert de B.= . . . dau. of Butler of Bewsey, Warrington. son and heir.

Peter de B. | William de B.=Maude, dau. of Sir John Davenport. 1302. | Thomas B.= See Pedigree A. | a dau.=Griffith Vychan, ap Jer Griffith, ap Jer Goch.

William B., living 1372, of Osworth.= . . . dau. of Robin Offerton | Robert B.=Agnes. had Eaton in Davenham and Alstanton. | Richard B.= assumed name of Prestland. | Roger B.= assumed name of Norbury. | Thomas B.=dau. of Matt. de Alpraham. | David B.=Ellen, heres . . . de Bickerton. See Pedigree B.

Alice = Thos. Holford. | 4 William B. of Bulkeley, co. Cheshire. | 2 Richard B.=Agnes, dau. and co-heiress of Roger Cheadle. ancestor of Lords Bulkeley of Beaumaris. | 3 Peter B. of Haughton.=Nicola, dau. and heiress of Thos. Bird, by whom he had lands in Alpraham. See Pedigree C. | Cicely = . . Wever. | 1 Robert B. of Eaton, 1341, son and heir.=Isabel, dau. of Sir Phil. Egerton of Malpas. See Pedigree D. | Elizabeth = Thos. Wever. | Ellen = Sir Thos. Arderne of Aldford.

Richard B. of Cheadle.=Alice, dau. of Sir Ralph Bostock. | Clementia. Alice. | Sir Lawrence Warren of Poynton, Cheshire.=Margery.

William B. of Cheadle, Constable of Beaumaris 1484.=Ellen, dau. of Guillim, ap Griffith of Petrie.

Ellen=Rt. Merydyth. | Jenet=Hugh Lewellin. | Alice. Agnes. | Rowland B. of Beaumaris.=Alice, dau. of Sir Wm. Besconal, co. Lancaster. | Hugh. | Richard. | Edward. d. y. | William of Burgate in Hants.= . . dau. and heiress of Sir John Popham.

Ellen=Sir Wm. Norreys of Espeche in Lancashire. | Margaret=Geo. Booth of Durham, Cheshire. | Robert. Thomas. John. | William B. of Porthamel, Isle of Anglesea=Ellen, dau. of Rich ap Merydyth, ap Thomas of Porthamel. | Hugh. Henry. | Sir Rich. B. Kt. eld. son, Kt. of Beaumaris and Cheadle, Chamberlain of N. Wales, 1534.=Catherine, dau. of Sir William Griffith of Penrhyn. | Robert B.=Anne, dau. of John Pointz of Acton, co. Gloucester.

BULKELEY FAMILY.

[This page contains a complex genealogical chart/family tree that cannot be meaningfully rendered in markdown. The chart shows multiple generations of the Bulkeley family with numerous branches, marriages, and descendants. Key names visible include:]

- Rowland B., s. and heir = Alice, dau. of John Conway of Portrnathan.
- Rowland B. = Margaret, dau. of Wm. Lloyd.
- Rowland B. = Jane, dau. of Rt. Bulkeley of Grynlyn.
- Rowland B. living at Porthamel 1603.
- Catherine = John Owens of Llandaginan. Rowland ap Rhyswin of Llansdovo.
- Sir Richard B., eld. son, Kt. of Beaumaris and Cheadle, k'd 1570 = 1w. Margaret, dau. of Sir Richard Savage of Rocksavage, co. Chester. = 2w. Anne, dau. of Thos. Needham, Esq. of Shenton.
- Thomas, William, of Lanvechall. Laurechall. Anne
- Ellen = Daniel, son of Sir Richard Bulkeley.
- Anne = Thos. Dalton of Carnarvon.
- Robert. Eleanor Jane Thomas. John Ardeno. Mauriee Gloyn.
- Robert B. = Joan, dau. of Wm. Gascoigne of Carrington. 1565.
- William B., ancestor of Burgat Family.
- Catherine – Gaflield ap John Griffith of Lyn.
- William, Thomas.
- Charles, s. p.
- Jane. R't ap Hugh Craythln.
- John. Margaret. Elizabeth. Penelope Sir Edwin Sandys.
- Richard, Robert, Hugh, John, all d. s. p.
- Margaret, Thomas, John, s. p.
- William, Hugh, Henry.
- Ellen, Mary, Margaret, Elizabeth.
- Catherine, dau. of Sir Wm. Davenport of Broomhall, Co. Chester.
- Sir Richard B. of Beaumaris, Kt.
- Mary, dau. of Wm. Lord, Borough of Gainsboro'.
- Elizabeth of Cheadle, d. v. p.
- Richard Catherine, dau. of Geo. Needham.
- John B. = Margaret, dau. of . . Morgan. Charles. Margaret.
- Sir Richard B. = Anne, dau. of Thomas Welford.
- Daniel B. = Ellen, dau. of Rowland Bulkeley.
- Ellen – Owen Holland.
- Margaret, Elizabeth unmarried.
- Richard. Rowland. Ellen Sir Thomas Porter.
- Margaret = Geo. Shellot of Heath, Yorkshire.
- William B. = Mary, dau. of Dr. Lancelot Bulkeley, arch. of Dublin.
- Thomas Viscount Bulkeley. See Burke.
- Dorothy. Lucy. Catherine.
- Richard – Dorothy, dau. of Sir Wm. Hopkins.
- Francis B. of Porthamel. d. s. p.
- Dorothy – Richard Connell.
- Mary – Michael Boyle.
- Frances. d. unm.
- Peter, Humphrey.
- Francis, Capt. in Virginia.
- Edward, d. s. p.
- Alice – Rev. Stephen Vaughan of Kilkenny.
- Dorothy – Henry Ayloffe.
- Lancelot B., a son. d. s. p. celebs.
- Rowland B. = Margaret, Jane, Alice.
- Grisolda = Robert Lloyd of Placeanryt. d. s. p.
- Peter, cœlebs. Robert.
- Margaret = John Rodyehan.
- Anne – Dr. Robert Lloyd.
- Richard = . . Hill.

A—PEDIGREE OF THOMAS BULKELEY.

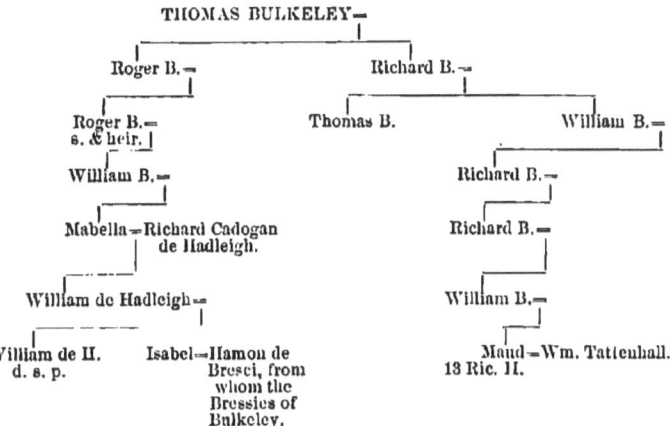

B—PEDIGREE OF DAVID BULKELEY.

DAVID BULKELEY=Ellen, dau. of De Bickerton.
|
Robert Bulkeley=
|
William B.=
13 Edw. III.
|
Richard B. of=
Bulkeley and
Bickerton.
|
David B.=Alicia.
of Bulkeley and
Bickerton, d.
1439.
|
John Bulkeley=a dau. of Fisher
temp. Hen. VII. | of Broxton, Co.
 Cheshire.
|
John B. of=——, dau. of —— Dod
Bulkeley. | of Chester.
|
Robert B.=Helena, dau. of Thos. Booth of
3 & 4 Q. Mary. | Cholmondeley, Co. Chester.
|
Thomas B.=Cicely, dau. of Humphrey Wittingham
of Bulkeley. | of Moseborrow.
|
Thomas B.=Elizabeth, dau. of Thomas Roe=Elizabeth, dau. of Randell
 | of Tissington. | Hopley of Everton.
|
Robert B.=   a dau.=Thomas Brassey.
|
Thomas B. of Bulkeley,=——, dau. of —— Whitfield.
left his estates to his nephew, |
Thomas Horton, Esq.
|
Robert=Lydia Higgonson.
d. s. p.
|
Elizabeth=John Barnaby of
heiress. Brockhampton.

22 BULKELEY FAMILY.

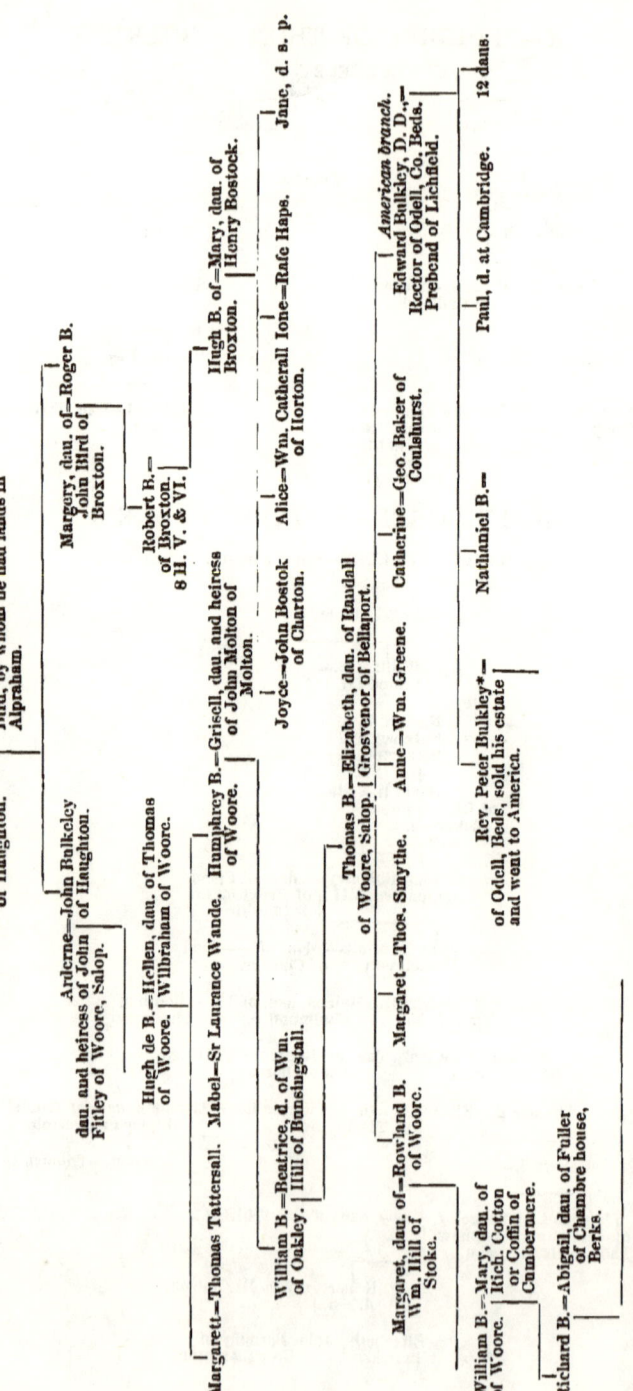

C.—PEDIGREE OF BULKLEY OF HAUGHTON.

D—PEDIGREE OF BULKLEY OF EATON.

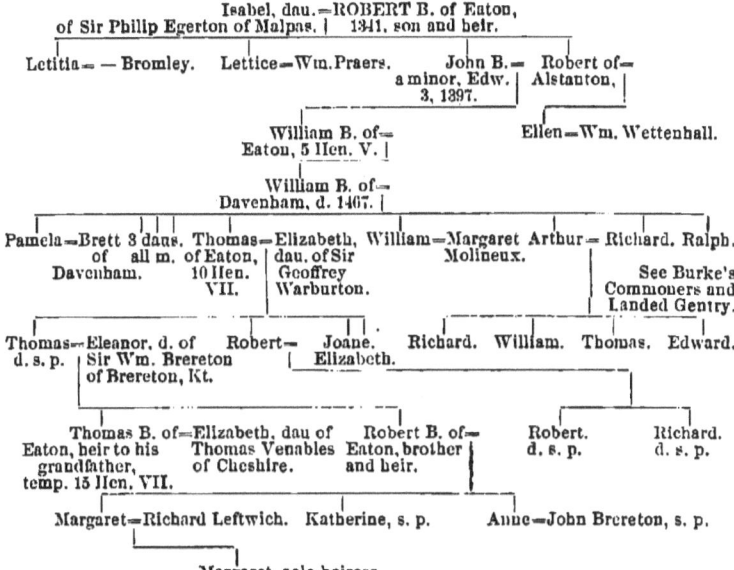

INTRODUCTORY HISTORY OF THE BULKELEY FAMILY IN AMERICA.

As the Rev. Peter Bulkeley was one of the organizers and the first pastor of the church of Concord, Mass., and was identified with the town in all its interests, we have deemed it fitting to extract from Shattuck's History the following :—

This church was organized at Cambridge, July 5th, 1636, and was the thirteenth established in the colony. The meeting was called by the Rev. Peter Bulkeley* and the Rev. John Jones who, with others, had previously begun the settlement of Concord. The Governor and Deputy Governor were invited to be present on the occasion, but because they supposed there was an informality in the invitation, at variance with their over-precise notions of etiquette, they did not attend. They sent word three days before, to the Governor and Deputy, to desire their presence, but they took it in ill-part, and thought not fit to go, because they had not come to them before, as they ought to have done, and as others had done before, to acquaint them with their purpose.

On the 6th of April, 1637, the church kept a day of humiliation at Cambridge, preparatory to the ordination or installation of Mr. Bulkeley, whom they chose teacher, and of Mr. Jones, whom they chose pastor. Delegates were present from most of the churches in the colony to assist in the ordination, but, says Winthrop, "the Governor and Mr. Cotton and Mr. Wheelright, and the two ruling elders of Boston, and the rest of that church which were of any note, did none of them come to this meeting. The reason was conceived to be because they counted there as legal preachers, and therefore would not give approbation to their ordination."

---

* The name is also spelt Bulkley, Bulkly, and Buckly. The Rev. Peter and his family wrote it Bulkeley, and the leading families among his descendants write it Bulkeley.

The ordination, however, proceeded. Shattuck continues his narrative. "I have a long letter before me, written by Mr. Bulkeley, before his ordination, to the Rev. Mr. Cotton of Boston, in which this subject is discussed in his usual style. Its great length prevents its insertion here. In a Postscript he says, 'I should have acquainted you yesterday that the *ordination of the elders of the church of Concord* is to be on Wednesday, come seven, night. It is to be here at Newtown. I pray take notice of it. If it be necessary to give any other notice to other persons, or in any other way, we would not be wanting therein for avoiding of offense, and I have spoken also to Mr. Wilson.' The distinguished reputation of Mr. Bulkeley, of noble family—a man of wealth, a scholar and divine—might have excited the envy of his fellow clergymen. He, however, received their approbation and, on the 30th of the following August, was chosen one of the moderators of the first great ecclesiastical council or synod of the colony, which was then held in Cambridge. Winthrop mentioned the Rev. Mr. Hooker as also a moderator. This assembly was attended by nearly all the clergy and magistrates, and many other distinguished laymen of the colony. It continued in session twenty-four days, and examined and condemned eighty-two opinions which had crept into the churches, "some blasphemous, others erroneous, and all unsafe."

"Litchford's Plain Dealing" mentions the church in Concord as the first one in the colony which had adopted the practice of catechising children. Mather says this was one of the constant exercises of the Sabbath. All the unmarried people were required to answer questions, after which expositions and applications were made by Mr. Bulkeley to the whole congregation. This exercise was, however, soon adopted in the other churches. The church was unanimous soon after its organization, and continued some time in harmony. But the unexpected pecuniary difficulties of the town, occasioned by its peculiar local situation, and its condition at that time, induced many to remove, which rendered it difficult for the remainder to support two ministers, Mr. Bulkeley's salary as teacher being £70 per annum. Some difficulties arose in the church on this account. The subject of a separation was often discussed, and on the 28th of July, 1642, some of the elders went to Concord, being sent for by the church there, to advise with them about the maintenance of their elders, and they found them wavering about removal, not finding their plantation answerable to their expectation, and the maintenance of two elders too heavy a burden for them. The elders' advice was, that they should continue, and wait upon God, and be helpful to their elders in labor, and what they could, and all to be ordered by the deacons (whose office had not been formerly improved this way amongst them), and that the elders should be content with what means the church was able, at present, to afford them, and if either of them should be called to some other place, then to advise with other churches about their removal.

"The advice of this council was followed a short time; but about October, 1644, a separation took place, and Mr. Jones removed to Fairfield, Conn." Thomas Bulkeley, the second son of the Rev. Peter by his first wife, having married a daughter of Mr. Jones, and Peter, Jun., youngest child by his second wife, removed to Fairfield, and are the ancestors of the numerous families of the name in Fairfield County. Cotton Mather, who has written an outline of the life of Mr. Bulkeley in his Magnalia, gives the following account of this affair in his own peculiar style:

"Upon Mr. Bulkeley's pressing a piece of charity, disagreeable to the will of the ruling elder, there was occasioned an unhappy *discord* in the church of *Concord*, which was at last healed by their calling in the help of a council, and the ruling elder's (Mr. Jones) abdication. Of the temptations which occurred on these occasions, Mr. Bulkeley would say, he thereby came: 1. To know more of God. 2. To know more of himself. 3. To know more of men. Peace being thus restored, the small things in the church there increased in the hands of their faithful Bulkeley, until he was translated into the regions which afford nothing but *concord* and *glory*, leaving his well-fed flock in the wilderness under the pastoral care of his son, Mr. Edward Bulkeley. The Rev. John Jones was born, educated and regularly ordained as a preacher of the gospel in England, but at what place is not known. He arrived in New England, October 2d, 1635, with the Rev. Mr. Shepard, afterwards of Cambridge, and the Rev. John Wilson of Boston. After remaining as the colleague pastor of the church in Concord about eight years, he removed with a part of his society to Fairfield and there undertook the charge of a newly organized church, where he spent the remainder of his life. He attained an age exceeding "three score years and ten," and died about 1664. Few records are preserved concerning this early devoted friend to the cause of Christian liberty, or concerning his family. Tradition gives him a highly respectable character. He left six children. John was graduated at Harvard College in 1643, and Eliphalet, born January 9th, 1640, who studied divinity and was the first minister of Huntington, L. I., where he died aged about 100 years. One daughter, Sarah, married Thomas Bulkeley, second son of Rev. Peter, as already stated.

After Mr. Jones' removal the whole care of the church of Concord devolved on Mr. Bulkeley for the remaining 14 years of his life. At this time according to Johnson it contained about seventy communicants. The following letters of Mr. Bulkeley are deemed worthy of publication :

"To his dear and loving friend Mr. Shepard, pastor, of the Church at Cambridge."

Dear Sir—I hear the Lord hath so far strengthened you as that you were the last Lord's day at the assembly. The Lord go on with the work of his goodness towards you. Being that now the Lord hath enabled you, thus far, I desire a word or two from you what you judge concerning the teacher in a congregation, whether the administration of discipline and sacraments do equally belong unto him with the Pastor, and whether he ought therein equally to interest himself. I would also desire you to add a word more concerning this, viz : What you mean by the execution of discipline, when you distinguish it from the power. We have had speech sometimes concerning the church's power, in matters of discipline, wherein you seemed to put the power itself into the hands of the church, but to reserve the execution to the eldership. Here also I would see what you comprehend under the word *execution*. I would gladly hear how the common affairs of the churches stand with you. I am here shut up and do neither see nor hear.* Write me what you know. Let me alsoe understand which way Mr. Phillips doth incline, whether towards you or otherwise, and which way Mr. Rogers is like to turn, whether to stay in these parts or goe into Conticote (Connecticut). I wrote to you not long agoe advising you to consider *quid valent humeri*. I know not whether you received that letter. The Lord, in mercy, bless all our labors, to his churches' good. Remember my love to Mrs. Shepard with Mrs. Harlakenden. Grace be with you all.

Yours in Christ Jesus,
P. BULKELEY.

Feb. 12, 1639.

* Mr. Bulkeley often laments his situation. In a letter to the Rev. Mr. Cotton, dated Dec. 17, 1640, he says: I lose much in this retired wilderness in which I live, but the Lord will, at last, lighten my candle. In the meanwhile, help us with some of that which God hath imparted unto you.

"To his reverend and loving friend, Mr. Cotton, teacher of the church at Boston :

Reverend in the Lord. These are to desire you to convey this letter in one of your own to Boston. I do the rather send it to you, because, I suppose those you commit your letters to, will be careful of the delivery, and this letter concerns matters of some moment, in regard whereof I desire you to take the more notice of it, and convey it by a safe hand. If the business concerning Virginia be finished, I desire to know how it stands; or if not finished what is intended or thought upon. My wife hath been ill ever since our coming home, but now I thank the Lord, begins to recover. This day she began to go down into the house. Remember her in your prayers and us all. And so with both our loves to yourself and Mrs. Cotton, I leave you with all yours to the Lord's rich goodness and grace, resting yours ever on him.

Pet. Bulkeley.

Sept. 26, 1642.

To the Reverend, his honored friend, Mr. Cotton, Teacher of the church at Boston, give these.

Reverend in the Lord.

* * * * Some other things I am full of, but will not write with paper and ink; only in a word, I bless God for what I hear, —how the Lord doth fill your ministry with abundance of grace, life, and power, to the exceeding joy of those that are true hearted towards the Lord. But with all, I stand amazed and wonder at God's forbearance, considering what I hear in another kind; which I do also believe to be true in some parts: true, I mean, as done and spoken by some, though untrue in respect of any cause given on your part. Truly, sir, it is to me a wonder that the earth swallows not up such wretches, or that fire comes not down from heaven to consume them! The Lord hath a number of holy and humble ones here amongst us (in the country generally) for whose sake He doth spare and will spare long; but were it not for such a remnant, we should see the Lord would make quick work amongst us. Shall I tell you what I think to be the ground of all this insolency which discovers itself in the speech of men? Truly I cannot ascribe it so much to any outward thing as to the putting of too much liberty and power into the hands of the multitude, which they are too weak to manage, many growing conceited, proud, arrogant, self-sufficient as wanting nothing. And I am persuaded that except there be some means used to change the course of things on this point, our churches will grow more corrupt day by day and tumult will arise, hardly to be stilled. Remember the former days which you had in Old Boston, where though (through the Lord's blessing upon your labors,) there was an increase daily added to your Church, yet the number of professors is far more here than it was there. But answer me, which place was better governed? Where matters were swayed there by your wisdom and counsel matters went on with strength and power for good. But here, where the heady or headless multitude have gotten the power into their hands there is insolency and confusion. And I know not how it can be avoided, in this way, unless we should make the doors of the church narrower. This we have warrant for from the Word, which course if it should be taken, would bring its inconveniency also in another kind. But of these things no more. Only I pray the Lord to heal the evil of the places and times we live in and remove that woful contempt of His gospel which doth abound. Oh, what mischief doth one proud, lofty spirit that is in reputation for understanding among a number of others that are weak! and some of both such there are in every place. But our comfort is God's end and work shall go forward. Some shall be converted, some hardened. The God of mercy carry on His work in our hearts and hand to the glory of His rich grace in Christ Jesus. I pray remember my hearty love to good Mrs. Cotton, thanking her for her kind remembrance of my little ones. I pray God give us both to see His grace increasing in those that He hath continued toward us. Farewell, dearly beloved and honored in the Lord, comfort yourself in Him who is most ready to be found in time of need. In Him I rest.

        Yours ever,

          Pet. Bulkeley.

April 4, 1650.

"I could wish you would write to Mr. Goodwin to deal with those that are in place of authority in England to take care that the Scripture may be printed more truly. I have a Bible printed 1648, which hath (little and great) above 100 faults in the printing of it. And I have an old Bible printed 1581 which hath but one or two, and those very small ones. I intend to write to my nephew St. John about it. A word from yourself to Mr. Goodwin, who is a man of so much respect there, would do much good."

The following is a copy of his will.

WILL OF PETER BULKLEY.

I PETER BULKLEY, Minister of the Word, being now in the seventy-sixth year of my age, and ready to go the way of all flesh, do make this my last will and testament, as followeth: first I do hereby testifie unto all that I do dy in the fayth of that doctrine which I have here preached in Concord, among my hearers, testifying and sealing the same with this my last confession, that it is the saveing truth of God, and therefore do humbly desire of God that those who have opposed and gain-sayed may in time bethink themselves and repent, that they may find mercy with the Lord in that behalfe, even the same mercy as I desire unto myne own soul, desireing also that though I have manifested much weakness in my dispensacion yet the hearers would labor to express the power of what they have received so that both I and they may rejoice together in the day of Christ. Now as touching my worldly estate, which is now very little in comparison of what it was when I first came to this place, I do dispose thereof as followeth: *first*, I do give unto my sonne Edward Bulkley, (to whom I did at the time of his marriage give such a portion as I was then able to give,) if he continue and stay in this land, these books following hereafter to be set down in a schedule annexed to this my will, or if he should remove from this country to England then (instead of ye books) before expressed, in *gen'all* and to be particularly named in the schedule, I give unto him five pounds of English money, to be paid him there in England, by my sonne John. Item, I do give unto my daughter-in-law, the widow of my son Thomas, deceased, the vallue of one kow, to be payd unto her by my executor hereafter named, only with this exception, that if her necessity do require the same to be payd unto her while I am liveing, then that so given in my life time shall be instead of the other here before named, to be payed by my executor, and my executor to be discharged of that legasy.

Item. I do give to my sonne Eliezer, either the farme which is now used by Widow Goble and her sonne Thomas Goble, adjoining to Mrs. Flent's farme, or my mill here in the town, or the hunded acres of land be the same more or less, which lies at the nearer end of the great meadow, liing towards the further end of the great meadow, beyond the poynt of upland, which *shooles* down into the meadow towards the River, one of these three, namely, either the farm or the mill, or the hundred acres of land, with the twenty acres of meadow. I do here give unto my said sonne

Eliezur, but which of the three to settle upon him I do not at present resolve, but, I leave the considerecion thereof to my executor and the overseers of this my will hereafter named, desiring them to let him have that which will be most usefull and profitable to him when he is fit to make use thereof. Item, I do give and bequeath to my sonne Peter, the next in vallew of these three things before named so that when Eliezur's portion is set out, then the next in worth to be for Peter, and the third of the three to remayne to those that shall inheritt mine house in which I do now live. Item, I do give to my Sonne John, Mr. Cartwright upon the Rhemish Testament and Willett Synopsis. Item, to my son Joseph, Mr. Wildersham upon the one and fiftieth psalme and ye history of the Council of Trent in English, and Cornelius Tacitus in English and Mr. Bolton on Gen. 6: concerning a Christian walking with God. Item, I do bequeath to my Lord Oliver St. John, Lord Chief Justice of the Common Please, my great English Bible, in folios which hath the letters of his name (O. G.) upon the cover of it; intreating him to accept this small token of my due love which I owe unto him and as a testimony of my thankful acknowledgement of his kindness and bounty towards me, his liberality having been a great help and support unto me in these my later times and many straytes. Item, I do give unto my cousin, Mr. Samuel Haugh, Dr. Twiss, in folio, against the Arminians. Item, I do give to my daughter Dorothy, the hundred and fifty pounds of English money, which I have in England, in the hands of my sonne John, the most part thereof came to me and my wife by the death of one of my wife's sisters. I mencion here £150 be the same more or less,—and though I suppose it is some what more, but what it is in just and exact amount I do not know but whatsoever it is, to my daughter Dorothy I give it which being lesser than to suffice for her suteable disposall in marriage I do therefore desire my wife, when God shall take her to himself, to add something more to the £150, as God shall enable her, and in the mean time I will that if my sonne do make any profit thereof, that then not only the said £150, be it more or less, but the profit of it also shall be reserved to the increase of my daughter's portion. The rest of my estate unbequeathed before, whether moveables or unmoveables, as, namely, my house, land, whether granted me first by the town or bought by money from others, cattle or money, or household stuff, or plate or whatsoever, I do give unto my dear wife, and her heirs by me begotten, giving her power hereby to dispose by sale, or otherwise, to her benefit of any part of the lands I have in the town (except before bequeathed and given) to her own benefit as her need shall require. And in case any of my children before named by me in this my will to whom I have bequeathed the legacies named, should prove disobedient to their mother, or otherwise vicious and wicked (which God of his mercy prevent), then I will that the legacy before bequeathed to any of them, so proving disobedient and wicked, shall be wholly in the power of my said wife, their mother, to deal with them therein as shee herself in Christian wisdom shall think meet, either to give them their legacy, or to keep it to herselfe, and my will further is, that if any the three children before named, Eliezer, Peter or Dorothy, should dy before their legacyes be paid them, that then the legacy of the deceased shall go to the other two surviveing, if my wife do not stand in need of it, but if she do stand in need thereof, for her necessary maintenance, then she shall have power to take it to herself. It may perhaps be expected that I should bequeath something to the publique use of the country, which practice I wish were observed more than it is by those that are of ability. But were my estate better than now it is, I suppose I may be therein excused, in regard to what I have done formerly, in the beginning of these plantations, wherein what I have done, some few do know, but I will here be sparing therein. This only I know and may say, that which I did then was an help to the weake beginning, which then were, more than what was then done, I do not thinke God requires of me now, considering my wasted estate, which I have here consumed, haveing little to leave to the children *what* God hath given me and to pretious wife whose unfeigned piety, and singular grace of God shining in her, doth deserve more than I can do for her. Her and her children by me, I do now leave to the goodness, and mercifull providence and care of God, my mercifull father in Christ Jesus beseeching him that as he hath given them to me so he wont take them again as a gift from my hands, owneing them as his owne, being a father to the fatherlesse and a Judge unto the widow: to defend her case, in case any should go about to do her wrong. And of this my will and testament. I do make my loveing wife mine only Executrix, desireing my loving Bretheren Robert Merriam and Luke Potter, the faythfull Deacons of our church, and William Hunt and Timothy Wheeler to be overseers of this my will, and to assist my said wife in any thing wherein shee shall stand in need of their help.

giving to Robert Merriam Mr. Rutherford's treatise upon the Wonders of Canaan, to Luke Potter Mr. Rutherford's upon the Dying of Christ on Jno. 12th. To William Hunt. Mr. Cooper on the 8th chapter to the Romans, and to Timothy Wheeler Mr. Dike on Jeremiah 17th concerning the deceitfulness of man's heart, which small tokens though they be unanswerable to the care or paynes they may meet with upon these occasions, yet my hope and confidence is that they will afford there helpe herein more out of conscience toward God, than out of respect of reward from man. And to this my last Will and testament I have set my hand and seal this 14th day of April in the year one thousand six hundred and fifty-eight—1658. By me, Peter Bulkeley, a seal and 17th of Feb'r in the same year.

An addition to this my Will, added Jan. 13, 1658. Be it known also that as a part of my will now written, I do add this, namely, that whereas I have agreed for a sixteenth part of the mill and for a like sixteenth part in the Iron Works which is now in frameing, I do give all my interest in both these unto my beloved wife.

PETER BULKELY, Jan. 13: 1658.

A request to the overseers of this my will and testament. These I do earnestly intreate not to suffer any materiall or substantiall part or point of my Will to be changed, on any pretence whatsoever, especially if it do concern my dear wife, whose interest and welfare I do cheifely respect, so that be the pretence either color of law or matter of conscience, yet I desire them to retain the substance of my Will as I have set it downe as being that I have herein discharged my duty to each one so farr as my weake decaied estate will beare.

In Witness whereof I have here subscribed my name this 26th of Feb'r, 1658.

By me, PETER BULKELEY

Witness hereof—
    JOHN JOANES,
    THOMAS BATEMAN,
    THOMAS BROWN.

The names of the books which I bequeathe to my sonne Edward:

1. I give him all Piscator's Commentaries on the Bible.
2. D. Willett on Exodus and Levitt., on Sam. 1 and 2, and on Daniell.

3. Tarnovious, in 2 Vollums, upon Prophetæ Minores.
4. Dr. Owen against the Arminians, in 4°.
5. I give him one part of the English annotations upon the Bible, the other part to be to my son Gershom, these my two sons shall divide the books between themselves, and, if they desire to have the whole they may join together in buying the whole, and then they may divide those two as they have done these of mine and so each of them may have the whole worke.
6. Mr. Aynesworth's Notes upon the 5 Books of Moses and upon the Psalmes.

Item, whereas I above bequeathed the vallew of one kow to my daughter-in-law, the widow of my son Thomas. I do hereby discharge mine Executor of that legacy, I haveing already disposed the vallew expressed to her use and benefitt.

PETER BULKLEY.

The witnesses above written gave upon oath to the truth of this will the 30th day of the 4th mo., 1659. Before me,

SIMON WILLARD.

Entered and Recorded, June 21, 1659.

By Thomas Danforth, Recorder

COMMONWEALTH OF MASSACHUSETTS.
MIDDLESEX, ss.

In Probate Office, March 3d, 1649.

I hereby certify that the foregoing is a true copy of the last will and testament of Peter Bulkely, deceased, as by record appears in the first volume of Records, in said Office, Page 201.

ISAAC FISKE,
Reg. of Probate.

GENEALOGY OF THE FAMILIES IN AMERICA.

FIRST GENERATION.

The REV. PETER BULKELEY, B. D., was of honorable and noble descent. He was of the tenth generation from Robert Bulkeley, Esq., one of the English barons, who in the reign of King John (who died in 1216) was Lord of the Manor of Bulkeley in the County Palatine of Chester.* He was born at Woodhill,† in Bedfordshire, Jan. 31, 1583. His father, the Rev. Edward Bulkeley, D. D., was a faithful minister of the Gospel, under whose direction his son received a learned and religious education suited to his distinguished rank. About the age of sixteen, he was admitted a member of St. John's College at Cambridge, of which he was afterwards chosen fellow, and from which he received the degree of Bachelor of Divinity. He succeeded his father in the ministry, in his native town, and enjoyed his rich benefice and estate; where he was a zealous preacher of evangelical truth about twenty years, and, for the most part of the time, lived an unmolested non-conformist. At length, his preaching meeting with distinguished success, and his church being very much increased, complaints were entered against him by Arch-bishop Laud, and he was silenced for

---

* The names of the lineal descendants from Robert, furnished by Charles Bulkeley, Esq., of New London, a grandson of Gershom, gathered from the previous sketch on the names and titles of nobility, were 1. William; 2. Robert; 3. Peter, who married Nicholaus Bird of Hampton. 4. John, who married Andryne, daughter and heir to John Colley of Ward and died 1450. 5. Hugh, who married Hellen Wilbriham, of Woodley; 6. Humphrey, who married Cyle, daughter and heir of John Matten; 7. William, who married Beatryce, daughter and heir to William of Bulansdale; 8. Thomas, who married Elizabeth, daughter of Randelle Grovenor; 9. Edward, D. D., of Woodhill, who married Olive Islby of Lincolnshire; 10. Peter of Concord. He had two brothers, Nathanael and Paul. The latter died fellow of Queen's College, Cambridge. From William a brother of Peter of the third generation, were also many ennobled descendants among whom are recorded in the Irish Peerage seven Viscounts in succession. Other branches have been much distinguished. The motto adopted in the Family Coat of Arms was "*Nec temere nec timide*"—*Neither rashly nor timidly*, and contains a beautiful sentiment characteristic of the eminent father of the American family.

† Odell, in the hundred of Willey.

his non-conformity to the requirements of the English Church. This circumstance induced him to emigrate to New England, where he might enjoy liberty of conscience.*

He arrived in Cambridge in 1634 or 1635† and was the leader of those resolute men and self-denying Christians who soon after "went further up into the woods and settled on the plantation at Musketaquid Concord." Here he expended most of his estate for the benefit of his people; and after a laborious and useful life died March 9th, 1659, in his 77th year.

Mr. Bulkeley was remarkable for his benevolence. He had many servants, on whom, after they had lived with him several years, he bestowed farms, and then received others to be treated in a like benevolent manner. By great familiarity of manners he drew around him persons of all ages; and his easy address, great learning, and eminent piety, rendered his society pleasing and profitable to all. Persons seldom separated from his company, without having heard some remark calculated to impress the mind with the importance of religion. Though sometimes suffering under bodily infirmities, he was distinguished for the holiness of his life, and a most scrupulous observance of the duties of the Christian ministry. He avoided all novelties in dress and wore his hair short. Being strict in his own virtues, he was occasionally severe in censuring the follies of others. He was considered as the father of his people, and addressed as father, prophet, or counsellor by them, and all the ministers of the country. Had the scene of Mr. Bulkeley's labors been in Boston, or its immediate vicinity, and not, as he expresses it, "shut up" in this remote spot, then difficult of access, his name would have appeared more conspicuously in the published annals of the country. He was a thorough scholar; an elevated devotional Christian; laborious in his profession; and, as a preacher, evangelical, faithful, and of remarkably energetic and persuasive eloquence. He often wrote a series of sermons on a particular

---

* Savage in his Genealogical Dictionary says "He came in the Susan and Ellen, 1635, his age at the Custom House called 50 (and for more perfect deception of the Government Spies, his wife Grace, 33, appears to be embarked in another ship and son John 15, some weeks earlier, besides Benjamin 11, and Daniel 9, (which two though not names of his sons yet may stand for them,) all these in the same ship with himself, but set down at intervals in the record, both of time and space, and of course his clerical character does not appear or he would have been stopped."

† The Rev. Edward Bulkeley, his son, was admitted *Freeman* May 6, 1635, and from the Cambridge Records it seems probable that Mr. Bulkeley came to **America in 1634.**

book or passage of Scripture. One of these series on Zachariah 9: 11, was published as "The first born of New England," and passed through several editions. The latest edition bears the following title, "The Gospel Covenant, or The Covenant of Grace Opened," wherein are explained—1. The difference between the Covenant of Grace and Covenant of Works. 2. The different administration of the Covenant before and since Christ. 3. The benefits and blessings of it. 4. The conditions. 5. The properties of it. Preached at Concord in New England by Peter Bulkeley, sometime fellow of St. John's College in Cambridge. (Here follow quotations; Gen. 17: 1–7, and Isaiah 55: 3–7). The second edition was much enlarged and corrected by the author. And the chief heads of things which were omitted in the former distinguished into chapters. London, printed by Matthew Simmins, dwelling in Aldersgate Street, next door to the Golden Lion, 1651, pp. xvi, and 442 Quarto. It was dedicated "to the Church and Congregation at Concord;" and to his nephew "The Rt. Honorable Oliver St. John, Lord Embassador extraordinary from the Parliament of the Commonwealth of England, to the High and Mighty Lords, the States General of the United Provinces of the Netherlands; and Lord Chief Justice of the Common Pleas."

It is a work of great merit for that age, and considering it was preached in the remote ends of the earth, "the Church of God," says the Rev. Mr. Shepard of Cambridge, "is bound to bless God for the holy, judicious, and learned labors of this aged, experienced, and precious servant of Christ." After reading this book, President Stiles observes: "He was a masterly reasoner in theology, and equal to the first characters in all Christendom and in all ages.

Two of Mr. Bulkeley's manuscripts are preserved in the Library of the American Antiquarian Society. One contains answers to several theological questions, and is addressed to the Rev. Mr. Phillips of Watertown. The other is on the character and government of the Church. The following analysis is given at the close of this work: "Part 1. The visible Church is: 1.—For the efficient cause, called of God. 2.—For the material cause, a number of visible saints and believers in the judgment of men. 3.— For the formal cause, union by an explicate and implicate covenant together. 4.—For the final cause, to set out God's praises. Part II. The Church's government: 1.—Is originally in the people's hands. 2.—Which people are to elect their own offiers, teachers, elders, and deacons. 3.—By which officers they are to rule and govern,—by admitting fit members, and by watching over, admonishing, and casting out those that be bad." This is a most able defence of Congregationalism in opposition to Episcopacy, and touches with the author's peculiar power and clearness the ecclesiastical questions in discussion at that period.

Mr. Bulkeley was twice married. 1. To *Jane Allen*, daughter of Thomas Allen of Goldington, whose nephew was Lord Mayor of London. By her he had twelve children, ten sons and two daughters. He lived eight years a widower, and then married 2d, *Grace Chetwood* (or Chitwood). By her he had four children. She survived him and removed to New London, where she bought a house in 1663, and died April 21, 1669.

SECOND GENERATION.

CHILDREN OF REV. PETER BULKELEY BY HIS FIRST MARRIAGE.

2. Edward, born June 17, 1614, at Odell, England.
3. Mary, baptized Aug. 24, 1615; died in a few months.
4. Thomas, born April 11, 1617.
5. Nathanael, " Nov. 29, 1618; died at 9 years of age.
6. John, " Feb. 17, 1620.
7. Mary, " Nov. 1, 1621; died at 3 years of age.
8. George, " May 17, 1623; not known to have been married.
9. Daniel, " Aug. 28, 1625.
10. Jabez, " Dec. 20, 1626; died under 3 years of age.
11. Joseph,
12. William,
13. Richard,

CHILDREN BY THE SECOND MARRIAGE.

14. Gershom, born Dec. 6, 1636.
15. Eliezer, " probably 1638; died without issue.
16. Dorothy, " Aug. 16, 1640.
17. Peter, " June 12, 1643.

THIRD GENERATION.

2.

Rev. EDWARD BULKELEY, son of Rev. Peter and Jane Bulkeley, born at Odell, England, June 17 1614, where he was chiefly educated; emigrated to this country; was admitted a member of the

First Church in Boston, in 1634. Having acquired a professional education, under the instruction of his father, he was licensed to preach the Gospel, and ordained at Marshfield, Mass., in 1642 or 1643. On the death of his father, in 1659; he was dismissed and installed over the Church in Concord, as his successor, with an annual salary of £80. He died in the 53d year of his ministry, at Chelmsford, Jan. 2, 1696, probably on a visit to his grandson, and was buried in Concord, aged 82.

Few records are preserved concerning his ministry or himself. He is represented, by tradition, to have been lame and of a feeble constitution. He was however greatly reputed for his talents, acquirements, irreproachable character, and piety. He preached an election sermon in 1680, from 1 Sam. 2: 30, and one before the Ancient and Honorable Artillery Company in 1679 from 1 Pet. 2: 11. He also preached one in 1676 in commemoration of the safe return of Capt. Thomas Wheeler and his associates, after the Battle of Brookfield. The duties of his office increasing with the growth of the town, assistance was judged necessary and the Rev. Joseph Estabrook was ordained as his colleague in 1667. His salary was also £80, of which £40 was to be paid in money, and £40 in grain, wheat to be estimated at 5s., rye at 4s., and corn at 3s., per bushel.

March 12, 1681, the town voted "That every householder that hath a teame, greater or lesser, shall carry yearly one load of wood to the minister, and every other householder or votable person shall cut wood one day for the minister, and that the wood be equally divided to the ministers, as the selectmen shall appoint." The arrangement which the following vote specifies was made March 5, 1694. "Whereas the Rev. Pastor, Mr. Edward Bulkeley, is under such infirmities of body by reason of great age, that he is not capable of attending the work of the ministry as in times past, being also sensible of the obligations the town is under to afford him a comfortable maintenance during the term of his natural life, that thereby the people may testifie their gratitude for his former services in the Gospel, they do hereby oblige the town to pay Mr. Bulkeley, yearly, during his natural life, the sum of £30 in lieu of his former salary." This proposition was assented to by Mr. Bulkeley, on condition that he should have liberty to preach or not as he please.

Mr. Bulkeley married and had a family, but the date of his marriage and the name of his wife has not been ascertained.

CHILDREN.

18. Peter,   born Nov. 3, 1641, at Concord.
19. Elizabeth, "   married (1.) Rev. Joseph Emerson, Dec. 7, 1665. (2.) John Brown, Esq.,
20. John,   died young at Marshfield; buried Feb. 26, 1658.
21. Jane,   m. Ephraim Flint.

FOURTH GENERATION.

18.

HON. PETER BULKELEY, oldest son of Rev. Edward Bulkeley, born Nov. 3, 1641, graduated in 1660. He settled in Concord, and in 1673 and the four subsequent years represented the town in the General Court of Massachusetts. In Feb., 1676, he was chosen speaker of the house of Deputies; and in August of the same year was appointed with the Hon. William Stoughton, Agent to England, on the complaints of Georges and Mason, and re-appointed in 1682. They sailed on the first mission, Oct. 30, 1676. On the 27th of February, 1679, he was re-appointed by King Charles the II, with Stoughton as agent to England, respecting the Naragansett country. They returned Dec. 23, 1679. In 1677 he was chosen one of the Judges, or Court of Assistants, and re-elected eight years. He was also one of the commissioners of the United Colonies the greater part of that time. On the 8th of October, 1685, he was appointed by King James the Second, one of the counsel of which Joseph Dudley, Esq., was President, which constituted the government of the Colonists, after the charter was forfeited. In 1680, the militia of the county was divided into two regiments and Major Peter Bulkeley appointed to command one of them. This was an office in those days of great distinction. In all these and other important offices he acquitted himself with honor and general acceptance. He was one of twenty who in 1683 made the "million" purchase, in New Hampshire, and had several special grants of land for public services. He died May 24th, 1688, aged 44, and "was buried," says Judge Sewall, the "27th, because he could not be kept, word of which was sent to Boston the same day to prevent any going in vain to his funeral. He married Rebecca Wheeler, only daughter of Lieut. Joseph Wheeler, April 16, 1667. After his death, his widow, Mrs. Rebecca Bulkeley, married Jonathan Prescott, as his third wife.

CHILDREN OF PETER AND REBECCA BULKELEY.

22. Edward,   born   Mar. 18, 1669.
23. Joseph,   "   Sept. 7, 1670; m. (1.) Widow *Rebeccah Minot*, 1696 ; (2.) *Silence Jeffrey*, 1713.
24. John,   "   July 10, 1673.
25. Rebecca,   "   1681 ; m. *Jonathan Prescott*, June.

19.

ELIZABETH BULKELEY, daughter of Rev. Edward Bulkeley, married 1, *Rev. Joseph Emerson*, in 1665. Mr. Emerson died Jan. 3, 1680. 2. *John Brown, Esq.*

Mr. Emerson preached for some time at Wells, and was ordained the first minister of Meriden about 1667, and continued there until the destruction of the town in Philip's war, when he removed to Concord and there remained until his death. He had three sons who were progenitors of a long list of clergymen.

CHILDREN.

26. Peter *Emerson*, born   m. Miss Brown.
27. Edward,   "   m. *Mary Moody*.
28. Joseph,   "

FIFTH GENERATION.

23.

JOSEPH BULKELEY, son of Hon. Peter and Rebecca *Wheeler* Bulkeley, born Sept. 7, 1670, married 1, Widow *Rebeccah Minot*, daughter of John Jones, 1696. She died July 17, 1712. 2, *Silence Jeffrey*. He made his will previous to his death, which is found on the records of Middlesex, Mass., as follows.

CHILDREN BY THE FIRST MARRIAGE.

29. Rebecca,   about 1697, m. *Joseph Hubbard.*
30. Dorothy,   about 1699, m. *Samuel Hunt.*
31. John,   about 1703, died in 1772.
32. Jane,   about 1703, m. —— Dwight of Sutton, Mass.
33. Silence,   about 1705, m. —— Davis, Harvard.

In the name of God, Amen. I, Joseph Bulkeley of Littleton, in the county of Middlesex, in the Province of Massachusetts Bay,

New England, gentleman, being of a disposing mind and memory and in usual health, but calling to mind my frailty and being desirous to dispose of my worldly estate, do make this my last Will and Testament, recommending and committing my soul to God, who gave it, and my body to the earth, to be decently buried, at the discretion of my executors, hereafter named. As to my worldly estate, I dispose of the same as follows:—

I give unto my beloved wife *Silence Bulkeley*, all my moveable estate within doors forever, to be improved and disposed of by her as she shall think best, and also the liberty of dwelling in and improving a room in my dwelling house, in said Littleton, with a chamber over it, as she shall choose, and so much of the cellar room as she shall need during her widowhood, all to be improved by her; also firewood brought to the door and cut fit for the fire, bread, corn, rye, and Indian, meat, malt, cider, and all manner of provisions, to be procured and provided for her from time to time and yearly, as she shall need, during her widowhood, by my son Peter Bulkeley hereafter named, or otherwise I allow and give to her the free use and improvement of the one-third of my lands at Littleton in the room of said provisions, with the improvement of said house room during her being my widow as she shall chose.

2. I give to my son John Bulkeley of Groton, five shillings old tenor, he having had already his part of my estate.

3. I give to my daughter Rebecca Hubbard, of Concord, five shillings old tenor, she having had before her part of my estate.

4. I give to the children of my daughter *Dorothy Hunt*, of Littleton, deceased, five shillings old tenor among them, she having had her part in my estate.

5. I give to my daughter *Jane Dwight*, of Sutton, five shillings old tenor, she having had her part in my estate.

6. Item. I give to my daughter *Silence David*, of Harvard, five shillings old tenor, she having had her part in my estate.

7. I give to my son *Joseph Bulkeley*, his heirs or assigns, the sum of two hundred pounds old tenor, to be paid by my son Peter Bulkeley within a year after my decease. Also I give the sum of one hundred pounds old tenor, to my son *Charles Bulkeley*, his heirs or assigns, to be paid by said Peter Bulkeley within a year after my decease, in which time, also, the aforesaid small sums are to be paid to my daughters and the children above named by said Peter Bulkeley. Also I give to my son *Peter Bulkeley* aforesaid, his heirs and assigns forever, my dwelling house and barn, together

with all my lands, in said Littleton, as also my stock of creatures and moveables abroad, as husbandry tools, and also I give to said Joseph and Charles Bulkeley, their heirs or assigns forever, all those rights of land that may belong to be my right in any town or place whatever, excepting Concord. And my will is that said Peter Bulkeley, besides the legacies above mentioned, pay all my just debts and likewise pay the cost and charges of my funeral, and I make him, said Peter, the sole executor of this my Last Will, desiring that James Minot, of Concord, Esq., would give his advice and assistance to my said executor. It may be needful also that I give to said Peter those debts which may be due to me at my decease, if any there should be. Allowing this and no other to be my Last Will and Testament. In witness whereof I have hereunto set my hand and seal this 17th day of December, 1744, in the 18th year of his majestie's reign.

JOSEPH BULKELEY, *Seal*.

Signed, sealed and delivered by the
said Joseph Bulkeley, as his last
Will and Testament, in the
presence of the subscribers.

THOMAS JANNE,
TIMOTHY MINER,
ISRAEL CHEEVER.

CHILDREN BY THE SECOND MARRIAGE.

34. Joseph, born 1715.
35. Peter, " 1717.
36. Charles, " 1719. Never married. He made a Will, signed by his name in the presence of Wm. Ramsdell, Samuel Lincoln and Samuel Proctor, dated August 1, 1757, in which he gives his property to his brother, Peter, as follows:

" In the name of God, Amen. I, Charles Bulkeley, of Littleton, in the Province of Massachusetts Bay, in New England, Captain of a company of Rangers in his Majestie's service, in the forces commanded by his excellency the Earl of Loudon that is going on the present expedition, being of sound mind and body, do, in consideration of the uncertainty of human life, make this my Last Will and Testament in the following manner:— .

I commend my soul to the author of my being, trusting in the merits of Christ Jesus, my Redeemer, for its salvation and the pardon of all my sins. But as to the interment of my body I must leave that to the humanity and discretion of those that are about, at the time of my decease, and as to my worldly estate, both real and personal, with everything I may be possessed of or entitled to, at that period, I give, devise and bequeath unto my beloved brother and friend, *Peter Bulkeley*, of the town and Province aforesaid, hereby appointing him the sole executor of this my last Will and Testament, revoking and making void all other and former wills by me made. In witness whereof I have hereunto set my hand at Halifax, Nova-Scotia, the 1st day of August, Anno Domini one thousand seven hundred and fifty-seven, and in the thirty-first year of his Majesty's reign.

CHARLES BULKELEY, *Seal.*

Signed, sealed, published and deliv-
    ered by the testator as his last
    Will and Testament, in presence
    of, as witnesses,
WM. RAMSDELL,
SAMUEL LINCOLN,
SAMUEL PROCTOR.

SIXTH GENERATION.

31.

JOHN BULKELEY, son of Joseph Bulkeley, born about 1703, married and had one child, and perhaps others. He held a colonel's commission, and died in Groton in 1772, aged 69.

37. John,   born 1748,   Graduated at Harvard in 1769, and died was a lawyer and died Dec. 16, 1774, aged 26.

THIRD GENERATION.

4.

THOMAS BULKELEY, son of Rev. Peter and Jane Allen Bulkeley, born in England April 11, 1617, was made a freeman March 13, 1639. He married Sarah Jones of Concord, Mass., daughter of Rev. John Jones. He had by her five children, of whom the name of one is recorded on the Concord Records, and the rest are found at Fairfield, Ct. Lands are recorded there in 1653, bounded by land of Thomas Bulkeley. The precise date of his death is not known. It was previous to Feb. 26, 1658, for his father, in his Will of that date, gives property to "his daughter-in-law, the widow of his son, Thomas Bulkeley." An inventory of Thomas Bulkeley's estate was presented to the Court of Probate the 4th day of June, 1658. After his death his widow married *Anthony Wilson*, by whom she had no children. Mr. Wilson died in 1662, leaving a good estate to his only child, Sarah, by his former wife. After his death, Mrs. Wilson gave, by Will of April 26, 1667, lands to her two sons, John and Joseph Bulkley, besides books and other property, and to her daughter Sarah, the wife of Eleazer Brown, Rebecca, wife of Joseph Whelpley and daughter Hannah (probably unmarried), books and other property.

CHILDREN.

38.	Sarah,	born Aug. 12, 1640;	m. Eleazer Brown.
39.	John,	" about 1642;	
40.	Joseph,	" " 1644;	
41.	Rebeccah,	" " 1646;	m. *Joseph Whelpley.*
42.	Hannah,	" " 1648;	

FOURTH GENERATION.

38.

SARAH BULKELEY, daughter of Thomas and Sarah Jones Bulkeley, born Aug. 12, 1640, married *Eleazer Brown*, son of Francis Brown, of New Haven.

CHILDREN.

43.	Eleazer *Brown*, born	Jan. 6, 1663.
44.	Gershom " "	Oct. 9, 1665.
45.	Daniel " "	Jan. 16, 1668.

39.

JOHN BULKELEY, son of Thomas and Sarah *Jones* Bulkeley, born about 1642, had lands granted him by his mother, and also by the town of Fairfield, as appears by the records of that town:—"Dec.

10, 1669, John Bulkeley hath received three parcels of land following, due to him as his portion from his mother, Sarah Wilson, to be to him and his heirs forever, these parcels as followeth:—One home lot, being in quantity two ackers and a half, being more or less bounded on the south with an highway, on the north-east with the land of Henrich (?), on the north-west with land now in possession of said Sarah, on the south with the highway. Also a third part of the meadow before the house, being in quantity one acker, more or less, bounded on the north-east with the land of Will Ward, on the south-west with the land of said Sarah, on the north-west with an highway. Also one third part of the meadow in the Middle Meadow, being in quantity two acres, being more or less, bounded on the north-east with the lands of George Squire, on the south-east with the Creek, on the south-west with the land of the said Sarah, on the north-west with the Old Field ditch.

Also two acres of land lying over the Creek, more or less, being in quantity bounded on the north-east with the land of Mr. Gold, on the south-west with the land of John Odell, on the southeast with an highway.

Also one parcel of land in Sascoe field, being in quantity one acre, more or less, bounded on the north and south with highway, on the east with the land of Jacob Gray, on the west with the land of Mr. Wakeman." Feb. 15, 1672, The Town hath granted to John Bulkeley one parcel of land in the Sascoe field, being in quantity an hundred and twenty-two rods, more or less, bounded on the south-east, north and south-east with highways, on the south-west with the lands of Francis Bradley, on the north-east with the land of John Hide.

There are also several other deeds of gift from the town, and also deeds of purchase of land from individuals.

He married Eliza——, the surname not known. He died in February, 1709. An inventory of the estate, which was quite large for the times, was presented to the Court Feb. 7, 1709. He being intestate, Sarah Bulkeley, his oldest daughter, and Joseph Whelpley, were appointed administrators. The estate was divided between his five daughters.

CHILDREN.

46. Sarah, born
47. Ester, "
48. Harriet, "
49. Elisabeth, "
50. Olive, "
51. Gersham, baptized Sept. 13, 1796 ; died young.

40.

JOSEPH BULKELEY, son of Thomas and Sarah *Jones* Bulkeley, born 1644, married *Martha Beers* of Fairfield. The Fairfield Records show that he was a large land-holder, as was his brother John. The following are some of the entries:—Feb. 15, 1672, Joseph Bulkeley hath received three parcels of land due to him, as his portion of his mother, Sarah Wilson, to be to him and his heirs forever.

The lands are as followeth:—

One home lot, being in quantity two and a half acres, being more or less bounded on the south-east with the land of John Bulkeley, on the south-west with the highway, on the north-west with the lands of his mother Wilson, on the north-east with the land of (Henrich ?) and George Squire, so much of the orchard as falls to his lot. Also a third part of her meadow before the house, being in quantity more or less bounded on the north-east with the land of his mother Wilson, on the south-west with the lands of George Squire, on the north-west with the highway, on the south-east with the seaboard. Also a third part of the meadow in the Middle Meadow, being in quantity two acres, being more or less bounded on the north-east with the land of his said mother, on the south-east with the Creek, on the south-west with the land of George Squire, on the north-east with the highway. Also a parcel of land in Sascoe field, being in quantity one acre and a half, more or less, bounded on the south-west with the land of Thomas Bennet, on the south-east with a highway, on the north-east with the salt marsh, on the north-west with the land of said Sarah, his mother. Also one parcell of meadow in Sascoe north, being in quantity half an acre-more or less, bounded ye north-east with a highway, on the south-east with the land of Joshua Knowles, on the south-west with the land sometime pertaining to George Godwin, deceased, on the north-east with the land of Thomas Beers. The first parcel above mentioned, viz., ye home lot, was given to Mr. Thomas Bulkeley, deceased, by the last Will and Testament of his brother, Daniell Bulkeley, deceased. There appears also on the Records an agreement between John and Joseph Bulkeley in regard to property left by their mother, Sarah Wilson, Oct. 29, 1688.

CHILDREN.

52.	Thomas,	born		1678;	m. *Abigail* ———
53.	Daniel,	"		1680;	m. *Hannah Bartram*.
54.	Joseph,	"	May 9, 1682;	m. *Esther*.

55.	Peter,	born	May 21, 1684;	m. *Abigail.*
56.	Sarah,	baptized	Sept. 23, 1684;	
57.	John,	"	May 22, 1701;	m. *Martha.*
58.	Rachel,	"	Mch. 23, 1706;	
59.	Grace,	"	May 27, 1711;	

41.

REBECCAH BULKELEY, daughter of Thomas and Sarah Jones Bulkeley, born about 1646, married *Joseph Whelpley.*

CHILDREN.

60. Sarah *Whelpley,* born
61. Rebeccah "   "
62. Joseph   "   "

FIFTH GENERATION.

52.

THOMAS BULKELEY, son of Joseph and Martha Beers Bulkeley, born 1678, in Fairfield, Conn., married *Abigail,* who died April 5, 1765. He died May 25, 1756.

CHILD.

63. Abigail,   born   ; married *John Osborn,* Jr., of Fairfield.

53.

DANIEL BULKELEY, son of Joseph and Martha *Beers* Bulkeley, born in Fairfield, in 1680, married *Hannah Bartram.*

CHILDREN.

64.	Daniel,	baptized June 15, 1718;	died June 9, 1797.
65.	Jabez,	"	Feb. 28, 1719-20; died young.
66.	Martha,	"	July 2, 1721; m. *Calvin Wheeler,* of Redding, Ct.
67.	Nehemiah,	"	Nov. 15, 1724.
68.	Jabez,	"	March 16, 1729.

54.

JOSEPH BULKELEY, son of Joseph and Martha Beers Bulkeley, born in Fairfield, May 9, 1682; married *Esther* ———, and died May 6, 1750.

CHILDREN.

69.	Sarah,	baptized Sept. 23, 1694 ; died young.
70.	Gershom,	"	Sept. 13, 1696.
71.	John,	"	March 22, 1701.
72.	A son,	"	March 9, 1711.
73.	Esther,	"	Dec. 30, 1713 ; m. *John Hill*, Jan. 27, 1729.
74.	Nathan,	"	Jan. 16, 1718.
75.	Joseph,	"	Nov. 22, 1719.
76.	Samuel,	"	March 1, 1726.
77.	Sarah,	"	Feb. 23, 1729.
78.	Ebenezer,	"	Dec. 5, 1731.

55.

PETER BULKELEY, son of Joseph and Martha *Beers* Bulkeley, born in Fairfield, Conn., May 21, 1684. He married *Abigail* ———. She was born in 1703. He died in 1753. She died June 12, 1795.

CHILDREN.

79.	Abigail,	baptized April 13, 1729 ; m. *Peter Burr*.
80.	Jonathan,	"	Sept. 12, 1731 ; died April 13, 1789.

57.

JOHN BULKELEY, son of Joseph and Martha *Beers* Bulkeley, baptized in Fairfield, March 22, 1701; married *Martha*. He was received into the church, April 5, 1735.

CHILDREN.

81.	Seth,	baptized Nov. 2, 1735.
82.	Rebecca,	"	Dec. 11, 1737; died in infancy.
83.	Rebecca,	"	March 23, 1739.
84.	Martha,	"	March 4, 1741.
85.	Josiah,	"	March 18, 1743 ; m. *Abigail Beers*.
86.	Peter,	"	May 29, 1745.
87.	Esther,	"	Jan. 20, 1746; m. Dec. 25, 1771.
88.	Joseph,	"	Dec. 31, 1748; m. *Elizabeth Lewis*.

SIXTH GENERATION.

63.

ABIGAIL BULKELEY, daughter of Thomas and Abigail Bulkeley; born ———; married *John Osborne*, son of John Osborne, of Fairfield.

CHILDREN.

89. Mary Osborne, born April 23, 1742.
90. Ebenezer Osborne, " Jan. 19, 1747.

64.

DANIEL BULKELEY, son of Daniel and Hannah *Bartram* Bulkeley; baptized June 15, 1718; married *Hannah Hill*, who was born in 1727, and died Oct. 7, 1809. Mr. Bulkeley died June 9, 1797.

CHILDREN.

91. Joseph, born Aug. 1759; d. Oct. 17, 1848.
92. Mabel, " Jan. 17, 1768; m. Joseph Nichols Nov. 22, 1778; died Jan. 16, 1819.
93. Esther, m. 1, *Chapman Hull*; 2, *Gould Nichols*.
94. Ruth, " 1773; m. *Wm. Henry Peabody*, Feb. 19, 1795: died Oct. 11, 1853.

73.

ESTHER BULKELEY, daughter of Joseph and Esther Bulkeley; born Dec. 20, 1713; married *John Hill*, Jan. 27, 1729.

CHILDREN.

95. Jonathan *Hill*, born Oct 9, 1731.
96. Esther " " April 21, 1738.
97. Sarah " " April 28, 1742.
98. Isaac " " Sept. 25, 1745.
99. Joseph " " May 2, 1752.
100. John " " Dec. 17, 1759.

74.

NATHAN BULKELEY, son of Joseph and Esther Bulkeley; born Jan. 16, 1718; in 1763 he was a deacon, a prominent man in the Congregational Church. He married *Sarah Perry*, April 15, 1756. She was born Jan. 30, 1728. Mr. Bulkeley died in 1763. Mrs. Bulkeley died in 1798.

CHILDREN.

101. Nathan, born Jan. 16, 1757.
102. Sarah, " Jan. 30, 1758.
103. Esther, " Aug. 1, 1763; m. *Daniel Judson*, of Stratford.
104. Sarah, " Jan. 26, 1768.

BULKELEY FAMILY. 51

75.

JOSEPH BULKELEY, son of Joseph and Esther Bulkeley, born in Fairfield Nov. 22, 1719; married *Ruth*.

CHILDREN.

105.	John.	
106.	Nathan.	
107.	Samuel.	
108.	Ebenezer,	died Jan. 3, 1800.
·109.	Esther.	
110.	Sarah,	m. Sept. 20, 1749, *Ebenezer Middleton*.

76.

SAMUEL BULKELEY, son of Joseph and Esther Bulkeley; born March 1, 1726; married *Beulah Henry*, daughter of Samuel Henry, Sept. 2, 1754.

CHILDREN.

111.	Esther,	born Dec. 7, 1755; m. Dr. *John Williams*.
112.	Samuel,	" Dec. 19, 1758. Will made May 2d, 1814.
113.	Deborah,	" Jan. 25, 1761; m. *David Davis*.
114.	Hannah,	" April 4, 1763; m. *David Parsons*.
115.	Mindwell,	" April 22, 1765; m. *John Davis*.

78.

EBENEZER BULKELEY, son of Joseph and Esther Bulkeley; born in Fairfield, Conn., Dec. 5, 1731; married *Hannah Maltbie*, of New Haven, Dec. 11, 1765.

CHILDREN.

116.	Ebenezer,	born Nov. 19, 1766.
117.	Hannah,	" Oct. 14, 1768; m. Elijah Morehouse March 18, 1789.
118.	Maltbie,	" Dec. 3, 1770; m. *Parthenia Morehouse*.
119.	Sarah,	" May 2, 1773; m. *Abram Morehouse* Feb. 3, 1781.
120.	Mary,	" May 14, 1775; m. *Silas Beach*.
121.	John,	" Oct. 28, 1778; died in 1872. Unmarried.
122.	Abigail,	" March 16, 1781.
123.	George,	" Aug. 2, 1784.

83.

JONATHAN, son of Peter and Abigail Bulkeley, born Sept. 21, 1731, married *Hannah Hoyt*, daughter of James Hoyt, of Norwalk, Ct., June 21, 1762. He died April 13, 1789.

On the 7th of July, 1776, Gov. Tryon, with his army, sailed

from New Haven to Fairfield, and the next morning disembarked upon the beach. The Hessians who accompanied Tryon were his incendiaries. To them he entrusted the wielding of the torch, and faithfully they obeyed their master. When the people fled from the town, not suspecting that their homes would be burned, they left most of their furniture behind. The distress was, consequently, great, for many lost every earthly possession. Among the buildings saved was that of Mr. Bulkeley. Tryon made it his headquarters. The naval officer who had charge of the British ships, piloted them to Fairfield, was Mrs. Bulkeley's brother, and he had requested Tryon to spare the house of his sister. Tryon acquiesced and, feeling his indebtedness to her brother, the general informed Mrs. Bulkeley that if there was any other house she wished to save she should be gratified. After the enemy left, the enraged militia under Captain Sturges placed a field piece in front of the dwelling, and then sent Mrs. Bulkeley word that she might have two hours to clear the house and leave it, or they would blow her to atoms. She found means to communicate a notice of her situation to General Silliman, who was about two miles distant. He immediately went to the town and found one hundred and fifty men at the Common. By threats and persuasions, he induced them to withdraw. The next day Col. Benjamin Talmadge, with his regiment, arrived from White Plains and, encamping on the smoking ruins, made Tryon's quarters his own. Mrs. Bulkeley was not a friend of the enemy.

According to her testimony under oath, she was badly treated by the soldiery, notwithstanding she had a protection from General Garth, the second in command. They plundered her house, stripped the buckles from her shoes, tore a ring from her finger, and fired the house five times before leaving it."

(See Field Book of the Revolution.)

CHILDREN.

124.	Peter,	born	April 3, 1765.
125.	Jonathan,	"	March 9, 1767.
126.	Abigail,	"	Aug. 30, 1769.
127.	Thomas,	"	Nov. 23, 1771.
128.	Hannah,	"	Sept. 1, 1773.
129.	Henry Stanley,	"	March 18, 1776.
130.	James Chester,	"	May 24, 1779.

81.

SETH BULKELEY, son of John and Martha *Beers* Bulkeley, born in Fairfield, Ct., Nov. 9, 1735. Married ——.

CHILDREN.

131.	Sally,	baptized	Sept. 7, 1783.
132.	Daniel,	"	March 28, 1785; died Oct. 31, 1860.
133.	John,	"	July 1, 1788; died Mch. 17, 1859.
134.	Stephen,	"	

85.

JOSIAH BULKELEY, son of John and Martha *Beers* Bulkeley, born March 18, 1743. Married *Abigail Beers*.

CHILDREN.

135.	Abigail,	baptized	May 20, 1787.
136.	Abel,	"	Sept. 28, 1789.
137.	Lucretia,	"	Sept. 18, 1791.
138.	Polly,	"	July 13, 1794.

88.

JOSEPH BULKELEY, son of Joseph and Martha *Beers* Bulkeley, born in Fairfield, Dec. 31, 1743. Married *Elisabeth Lewis*, March 4, 1776.

CHILDREN.

139.	Joseph,	born ——	
140.	Morehouse,	"	died unmarried.
141.	Adad.		
142.	Medad.		
143.	Lewis.		
144.	Elizabeth.		m. *David Penfield* of Black Rock, Ct.
155.	Esther.		m. *David Patchen*.

SEVENTH GENERATION.

91.

JOSEPH BULKELEY, son of Daniel and Hannah *Hill* Bulkeley, born in Fairfield, Ct., Aug. 21, 1759. Married *Ellen Hubbell*. She died Jan. 18, 1819, aged 56. He died Oct. 17, 1859.

CHILDREN.

156. Ellen, born, Oct. 3, 1779; m. *Philo Ruggles* of New Milford, died Feb. 25, 1865.
157. Uriah, " Aug. 12, 1782; died Aug., 1874, aged 92.
158. Wm. Samuel, " Oct. 7, 1786; " 1797.
159. Wm. Henry, " Oct., 1796; " 1840, in New York.

94.

RUTH BULKELEY, daughter of Daniel and Hannah *Hill* Bulkeley, born in 1773. Married Wm. *Henry Peabody*, son of Asa Peabody, Feb. 19, 1795. Mr. Peabody was born in 1769. Mrs. Peabody died Oct. 11, 1853.

CHILDREN.

160. Catharine Maria *Peabody*, born Aug. 17, 1796.
161. Henry Bulkeley " " Dec. 19, 1797.
162. Charlotte " " June 25, 1799.
163. Mary " " April 7, 1801.
164. Lucy " " March 13, 1803.
165. William " " May 20, 1805.
167. George " " Jan. 29, 1807.
168. Charles Alfred " " July 29, 1810.
169. John B. " " March 7, 1812.
170. Augustus " " July 3, 1814.
171. Frederick Gideon " " May 6, 1818.

106.

NATHAN BULKELEY, son of Joseph and Ruth Bulkeley, born, married, and had children. The name of his wife, the date of marriage, and the dates of children's birth, have not been ascertained.

CHILDREN.

172. John.
173. Nathan.
174. Samuel.
175. Hester.

113.

EBENEZER, son of Ebenezer and Hannah *Maltbie* Bulkeley, born in Fairfield, Nov. 19, 1766. Married *Diana Williams*.

CHILDREN.

176. Lydia. born 1798; unmarried.
177. Sarah, " 1800;
178. John, " 1805;

118.

MALTBIE BULKELEY, son of Ebenezer and Hannah *Maltbie* Bulkeley, born in Fairfield, Dec. 3, 1770. Married *Parthenia* Morehouse.

CHILDREN.

179.	Andrew, born ——	Died Oct., 1873; unmarried.
180.	Ruth, "	Jan. 9, 1800; m. *Daniel Beach* of Trumbull, March 18, 1832.
181.	Clarissa, "	July 8, 1804; m. *Henry Seeley at Stratfield*, Ct.
182.	Charity, "	m. *Thomas Wheeler.*
183.	John, "	Jan. 22, 1808; m *Catharine Morehouse*, June 19, 1836.

123.

GEORGE BULKELEY, son of Ebenezer and Hannah *Maltbie* Bulkeley, born Aug. 2, 1784. Married *Ruth Barnes* and removed to Ohio, where he died, aged 80.

CHILDREN.

184.	John,	
185.	Hannah,	m. *Enoch Esterling.*
186.	Stephen,	m. *Sarah Wakeman.*
187.	Maria,	m. *Henry Vanderburgh.*
188.	Annie,	
189.	Mary,	m. *Orlando Myers.*
190.	George,	m. *Eunice Howland.*
191.	Annie,	m. *Allen Haines.*
192.	Andrew,	m. *Mary A. Varstres.*
193.	Emeline,	
194.	Ada.	

129.

HENRY STANLEY BULKELEY, son of Jonathan and Hannah *Hoyt* Bulkeley, born March 18, 1776. Married, 1, *Sallie Durrin*; 2, *Mary Feller.*

CHILD BY FIRST MARRIAGE.

195. Charles,   born

CHILDREN BY SECOND MARRIAGE.

196.	Abby Hannah,	born		m. *Samuel Walruth.*
197.	Sarah Ann,	" May	1, 1812;	m. *Joseph Wakeman*, May 1, 1834.
198.	James Stanley,	"	1814;	died in infancy.
199.	Catharine A.,	" April,	1815;	m. *Townsend Parrish* of Catskill.
200.	Lucina,	"	1817;	m. *George Downer* of Illinois.
201.	Mary M.,	"	1819;	m. *Silas Way* of Batavia, Ill.
202.	John,			died young.

BULKELEY FAMILY.

203.	Caroline,	born	1823; m. *Wm. Donelson*, Kingston, Ca.
204.	Hannah,	"	1825; m. *Wm. Smith*, St. Catharine, Ca
205.	William,		died young.
206.	Jane,	"	1829.

132.

DANIEL, son of Seth Bulkeley, born March 28, 1785, married *Sarah*, who was born March 2, 1786, and died Nov. 11, 1868. Mr. Bulkeley died in Newtown, Conn., Oct. 31, 1860.

CHILDREN.

207.	Parmelia,	born	April 25, 1808; m. *Lord Northrop*, a farmer, resides in Stockton, California; has had eleven children, three now living.
208.	Bronson,	"	April 6, 1811; m. *Polly Bennet*.
209.	Julia,	"	June 21, 1818; m, Dec. 6, *John Homer Merwin*, is a farmer in Brookfield, Ct.

133.

JOHN BULKELEY, son of Seth Bulkeley, born at Fairfield, July 1, 1788, married, Feb. 25, 1813, *Lucinda Elwood*, who was born March 4, 1795, died June 22, 1820. Mr. Bulkeley died March 17, 1859.

CHILDREN.

210.	Stephen E.,	born	Nov. 12, 1824.
211.	Anna Lorinda,	"	Sept. 25, 1826; died Feb. 1, 1834.
212.	Miranda,	"	Sept. 25, 1827; m. *Samuel Fairchild*, 1855.
213.	Leman Lee,	"	Aug. 25, 1829; died July 18, 1832.

134.

STEPHEN, son of Seth Bulkeley, born, married, and had a son.

CHILD.

| 214. | Daniel, | b. ——— |

139.

JOSEPH, son of Joseph and Elisabeth *Lewis* Bulkeley, born in Fairfield, married *Chloe Hubbell*, April 27, 1812, and his widow married *Wm. Kennedy*, June 17, 1836.

CHILDREN.

215.	Caroline Silliman,	baptized	1813; died May 4, 1818.
216	Morehouse,	"	June 18, 1815;
217.	Adad,	"	Mch. 21, 1816.
218.	Henrietta,	"	Nov. 29, 1817; m. *Wakeman Burr.*
219.	Lewis,	"	May 18, 1823; m. ———— *Harding.*
220.	Caroline,	"	died at Savannah, unmarried, Dec. 17, 1845.
221.	Nathanael Silliman,	"	Feb. 3, 1828; m. *Martha Dimon.*

EIGHTH GENERATION.

172.

JOHN, son of Ebenezer and Diana *Williams* Bulkeley, born in 1805, married *Emily Mallory*, and removed to Brooklyn, L. I. He is a member of the Board of Education.

CHILDREN.

233.	Hattie,	born	1835; unmarried.
234.	Emily,	"	1838; m. *Eaton*, of Williamsburgh.

182.

URIAH BULKELEY, son of Joseph and Ellen Hubbell Bulkeley, born at Greenfield, Ct., Aug. 12, 1782, married *Jane Sayre,* who was born April 20, 1788, and died Feb. 10, 1831. Mr. Bulkeley died at Dobbs Ferry, Westchester County, New York, July 23, 1874, aged 92.

CHILDREN.

222.	Elisabeth Lois,	born	1807; m. *George Ufford* of Stratford; died Nov. 24, 1861.
223.	Jane Mildred,	"	Feb. 2, 1809; m. *Rufus Nichols*, and died Sept. 19, 1862.
224.	Francis Samuel,	"	June 3, 1811; d. March 30, 1853.
225.	John Sayre,	"	Mch. 17, 1813; died Sept. 5, 1869.
226.	James Denney,	"	July 29, 1817; died, 1839.
227.	Wm. Henry,	"	Mch. 30, 1819; m. *Sarah Lee*, at Rye, N. Y.
228.	Hettie Julia,	"	1821; m. *Henry Gordon Harrison,*
229.	Mary Eunice,	}	
230.	George Frederick,	}	died young.
231.	Mary Eunice,	}	
232.	Marion,	"	Mch., 1831; m. *Joseph Nelson*, and died July 30, 1858.

180.

RUTH BULKELEY, daughter of Maltbie and Parthenia Bulkeley, born Jan. 9, 1800; married *Daniel Beach* of Trumbull, March 18, 1832.

181.

CLARISSA BULKELEY, daughter of Maltbie and Parthenia Morehouse Bulkeley, born July 8, 1804; married *Henry Seeley* of Stratfield, Ct.

182.

CHARITY BULKELEY, daughter of Maltbie and Parthenia Morehouse Bulkeley, born ——; married *Thomas Wheeler.*

183.

JOHN BULKELEY, son of Maltbie and *Parthenia Morehouse* Bulkeley, born Jan. 22, 1808; married *Catharine Morehouse*, June 9, 1834.

CHILDREN.

235.	Matilda,	born	1835; unmarried.
236.	Mary,	"	May, 1837; m. *Henry Sturges*, Nov. 29, 1870.

185.

HANNAH BULKELEY, daughter of George and Ruth *Barnes* Bulkeley, born ——; married *Enoch Esterting.*

186.

STEPHEN BULKELEY, son of George and Ruth *Barnes* Bulkeley, born ——; married *Sarah Wakeman.*

187.

MARIA BULKELEY, daughter of George and Ruth *Barnes* Bulkeley, born ——; married *Henry Vanderburgh.*

189.

MARY BULKELEY, daughter of George and Ruth *Barnes* Bulkeley, born ——; married *Orlando Myers.*

190.

GEORGE BULKELEY, son of George and Ruth *Barnes* Bulkeley, born ——; married *Eunice Howland.*

191.

ANNE BULKELEY, daughter of George and Ruth *Barnes* Bulkeley, born ——; married *Allen Haines*.

192.

ANDREW BULKELEY, son of George and Ruth *Barnes* Bulkeley, born ——; married *Mary A. Varstres*.

196.

ABBY HANNAH STANLEY, daughter of Henry and Mary *Zeller* Stanley, born ——; married *Samuel Walruth*.

197.

SARAH ANN STANLEY, daughter of Henry and Mary *Zeller* Stanley, born May 1, 1812; married *Joseph Wakeman*, May 1, 1834.

CHILDREN.

237.	Jane L. *Wakeman*,	m. *Brenan P. Bacon*.
238.	Andrew C., "	m. *Cornelia Burr*.

198.

CATHARINE A. STANLEY, daughter of Henry and Mary *Zeller* Stanley, born April, 1815, married *Townsend Parrish*, of Catskill.

CHILD.

239. Carrie *Parrish*,   born   ——

200.

LUCINA STANLEY, daughter of Henry and Mary *Zeller* Stanley, born in 1817, married *George Downer*, of Illinois.

CHILDREN.

240.	Henry *Downer*,	married.
241.	George "	"
242.	John Melville,	
243.	Martha,	m. —— Lee.

201.

MARY M. STANLEY, daughter of Henry and Mary *Zeller* Stanley, born in 1819, married *Silas Way*, of Batavia, Illinois.

CHILD.

244. Ella *Way*,   born   ——

203.

CAROLINE STANLEY, daughter of Henry and Mary *Zeller* Stanley, and granddaughter of Jonathan and Hannah *Hoyt* Bulkeley, born in 1823, married *Wiliam Donnelson*, of Kingston.

CHILDREN.

245. William *Donelson*, born ——
246. Jeannette, "   "   "
247. Anne "   "   "
248. Harry "   "   "
249. Frederick "   "   "
250. Catharine "   "   "

204.

HANNAH STANLEY, daughter of Henry and Mary *Zeller* Stanley and granddaughter of Jonathan and Hannah *Hoyt* Bulkeley, born ———, married *William Smith*, of St. Catharine's, Canada.

CHILD.

251. Stanley *Smith*, born ——

207.

PAMELIA BULKELEY, daughter of Daniel and Sarah Bulkeley, born April 25, 1808; married *Lord Northrop*, a farmer, resides in Stockton, California; has had eleven children, of which three are now living.

208.

BRONSON BULKELEY, son of Daniel and Sarah Bulkeley, born in Newtown, April 6, 1811, married *Polly Bennet*, daughter of Philo and Hannah Bennett of Monroe.

CHILDREN.

252. Susan *Bulkeley*, born April 10, 1831; m. *Henry E. Beebe*, of Norwalk, Conn., confectioner, resides in Bridgeport, Ct.
253. George B., " Aug. 6, 1836; served with honor in the late war as volunteer in the 1st Connecticut Cavalry, and was at the battle of Gettysburgh.
254. William H., " June 16, 1838; unmarried.
255. Eugene, " Nov. 11, 1844.

210.

STEPHEN BULKELEY, son of John and Lucinda *Elwood* Bulkeley, born Nov. 12, 1824, married, 1. *Harriet Rockwell*, of Danbury, Conn.; 2. *Sarah Woodruff*; 3. —— *Rockwell*, sister of the first wife.

CHILDREN.

256.	Ann,	born	Jan. 3, 1836; m. Davis.
257.	Caroline,	"	Dec. 4, 1837; died Feb. 15, 1840.
258.	Frederick,	"	Aug. 21, 1840; died Feb. 18, 1841.
259.	Mary,	"	Jan. 24, 1846.
260.	Ira,	"	Feb. 4, 1848.
261.	Alford,	"	May 10, 1849.
262.	Jerome,	"	Feb. 24, 1852.

212.

MIRANDA BULKELEY, daughter of John and Lucinda *Elwood* Bulkeley, born Sept. 25, 1822, married *Samuel Fairchild*, in 1855, of Newtown, Conn.

CHILDREN.

263.	Mary E.,	born	1856; died Oct. 26, 1857.
264.	Sarah Jane,	"	April 29, 1858.

216.

MOREHOUSE BULKELEY, son of Joseph and Chloe *Hubbell* Bulkeley, born June 18, 1815, married *Sarah Raynor*.

CHILDREN.

265..	Elizabeth,	born	died unmarried.
266.	Letetia Ann,	"	"
267.	Morehouse,	"	
268.	Joseph,	"	m.; lived in Norwalk.
269.	Stephen Raynor,	"	m., 1, Adeline Humphrey; 2, Caroline Davis.
270.	William,		died in Mexico, at the convent of Santa Clara.

217.

ADAD BULKELEY, son of Joseph and Chloe *Hubbell* Bulkeley, born March 21, 1816, married *Harriet Hubbell*.

CHILDREN.

271.	Elisabeth,	born	died young.
272.	Harriet,	"	m. *Milton Roof*.
273.	Henry Lewis,	"	
274.	Charles Hubbell,	"	

BULKELEY FAMILY.

218.

HENRIETTA BULKELEY, daughter of Joseph and Chloe *Hubbell* Bulkeley, born Nov. 29. 1817, married *Wakeman Burr*.

220.

CAROLINE BULKELEY, daughter of Joseph and Chloe Hubbell Bulkeley, born May 18, 1823, married Mr. *Harding*.

221.

NATHANAEL SILLIMAN BULKELEY, son of Joseph and Chloe *Hubbell* Bulkeley, born Feb. 3, 1828, married *Mary Dimon*, May 25, 1851.

CHILD.

275. Elisabeth, born

NINTH GENERATION.

222.

ELISABETH LOIS BULKELEY, daughter of Uriah and Jane *Sayre* Bulkeley, born in 1807, married *George Ufford*, of Stratford, and died Nov. 24, 1861.

223.

JANE MILDRED BULKELEY, daughter of Uriah and Jane *Sayre* Bulkeley, born Feb. 2, 1809, married *Rufus Nichols*, and died Sept. 19, 1862.

225.

JOHN SAYRE BULKELEY, son of Uriah and Jane *Sayre* Bulkeley, born March 17, 1813, married *Ann May*.

CHILD.

276. Elisabeth Julia, born April 28, 1842; m. *Frederick Dwight Stoddard of West Troy, N. Y.*

227.

WILLIAM HENRY BULKELEY, son of Uriah and Jane *Sayre* Bulkeley, born March 30, 1819, married *Sarah Lee Riggs*, June 13, 1841. Her mother's name was Lee. He is a book-seller in Louisville, Kentucky, where he now resides.

CHILDREN.

277.	Sarah Lee Riggs,	born	April 12, 1842; died April 9, 1851.
278.	Harriet Winslow,	"	Sept. 11, 1844; m. Dr. *John Larrabee* of Gorham, Maine.
279.	Joseph,	"	Mch. 24, 1846.
280.	Mary Riggs,	"	Jan. 24, 1848; m. *John Brent Fishback* of Garrard County, Kentucky.
281.	Ellen Rebecca,	"	May 10, 1850; died April, 1869.
282.	James Sayre,	"	Nov. 25, 1852; died Aug. 6, 1871.

228.

HETTIE JULIA BULKELEY, daughter of Uriah and Jane Sayre Bulkeley, born in 1821, married *Henry Gordon*, of Harrison, New York.

232.

MARION BULKELEY, daughter of Uriah and *Jane Sayre* Bulkeley, born March, 1831, married *Joseph Nelson*, and died July 30, 1858.

272.

HARRIET BULKELEY, daughter of Adad and Harriet Hubbell Bulkeley, born ——, married *Milton Roof*.

273.

HENRY LEWIS, son of Adad and Harriet *Hubbell* Bulkeley, born ———, married ———.

CHILDREN.

283.	Elisabeth,	born
284.	Henry,	"

274.

CHARLES HUBBELL BULKELEY, son of Adad and Harriet *Hubbell* Bulkeley, born ———, married *Julia Smith*.

CHILDREN.

285.	Lewis,	born	drowned at Maul Main.
286.	Harriet Elisabeth,	"	m. *William Crane* of Brooklyn, L. I.
287.	Anna Roof,	"	

TENTH GENERATION.

278.

HARRIET WINSLOW BULKELEY, daughter of William Henry and Sarah Lee *Riggs* Bulkeley, born Sept. 11, 1844, married Dr. *John Henry Larribee*, of Gorham, Maine.

CHILD.
288. John Albert Sayre *Larribee.*

279.

JOSEPH BULKELEY, son of Wm. Henry and Sarah Lee Riggs Bulkeley, born March 21, 1846, married. Sept. 11. 1872, *Agnes Marshall.*

280.

MARY RIGGS BULKELEY, daughter of William Henry and Sarah Lee *Riggs* Bulkeley, born Jan. 24, 1848, married *John Brent Fishback*, of Garrard County, Kentucky.

CHILDREN.

289.	Ella May *Fishback*,	born Aug.,	1869.
290.	William Brent "	" June 11,	1871.

THIRD GENERATION.

6.

JOHN BULKELEY, son of Rev. Peter and Jane Bulkeley, born Feb. 17, 1620, graduated in 1642, at Harvard College. He returned to England and had a living at Fordham, whence, being ejected in 1662, he removed to Wapping, near London, and practiced physic with good success, and died Jan. 28, 1689, old style, or according to the present computation, Jan. 28, 1690. His will, which was probated in the Prerogative Court at Canterbury, bears date Oct. 11, 1689. In said will he names his wife *Avis*, and three children, as follows:—

291. Elisabeth, born m. *Edward Falkner.*
292. Edward, } " There is no evidence that these
293. Thomas, } " two had any descendants. They were, when young men, engaged abroad, in the service of the East India Company, and probably never returned to England.

WILL OF JOHN BULKELEY.

Recorded in the Records of the Prerogative Court, of Canterbury, England. Copy procured by Horatio G. Somerby, Esq.

The last Will and Testament of John Bulkeley, of the Precincts of St. Katharines, near the tower of London, Gent., made and ordained this 11th day of October, 1689, Witnesseth and declareth as followeth : Imprimis that I, the said John Bulkeley, having first resigned my Imortal soul into the gracious hands of him that gave it, with good hope and humble confidence, founded on the Scripture of faith, through the sole merits of Jesus Christ, that blessed and only mediator between God and man, who is himself both true God and true man, in one person, received and applied, by the renewing work of the Holy Spirit, that he will receive it into his everlasting glory.

As for my mortal body after its decease, I leave it to the care of my executor and joint executresses, hereafter named, to be decently buried, in such place and manner as by special direction, in a small schedule, under my hand given, shall be by me hereafter ordered, only having long observed the general dislike of and complaint against late burials. As to the time of my bodie's interment, my express will is that, if it shall happen in the winter, or when the daies are shorter than the nights, that then the said interment be actually made, at the furthest by half an hour before sunset. If in the summer, when the daies are longer than the nights, that it be at the furthest by six o'clock in the afternoon. As to the portion of worldly goods, which God, of his free bounty, hath bestowed upon me, my just debts and funeral charges being first paid and, that as soon as may be, I give and bequeath the same, in manner and form following.

Imprimis, I give and bequeath unto my loving wife *Iris* over and above what is and was settled upon her by speciall covenant and agreement, by me, to and with her, had and made before our inter-marriage, the sume of thirty pounds of good and lawful money of England, to be to her paid by, five pounds a quarter, within eighteen callendar months next after my decease. Moreover, I hereby give and grant unto her my said wife the possession and use during her natural life of all of those rings, necklaces, jewels, pieces of plate, and other household stuffs, which she had before, and brought with her at our said inter-marriage, or hath been by me since given, willing with all, and desiring that her best diamond ring be, immediately after her decease, given, taken by or delivered to my loving daughter Elizabeth, the now wife of Edward Falkner, Grocer, for her sole proper use and dispose, if she shall happen to be then living, otherwise to be and come to her sole and eldest daughter, if she leave any. But if she my said daughter shall happen to decease before my said wife, and leave no daughter of her own surviving, then my mind and will is that the said best diamond ring, with the rest of the said rings, necklaces, jewells, &c., be sold and equally divided between my two sons, *Edward* and *Thomas Bulkeley*, and their brother-in-law, my son-in-law before named.

Item. I give and bequeathe unto my loving sister, Mrs. Eleanor Frye, the sum of five pounds, and unto my brother and sister Vicaridge, if at my decease surviving, and to every of their children, then living, the sum of ten shillings apiece, and also to my late nephew, Trye Vicaridge, his eldest son, the like legacy of ten shillings.

Item. In like manner I give and bequeathe unto my three brothers, in New England, Vizt., Edward, Gershom and Peter twenty shillings apiece, if then living. As above, the sons of my deceased brother Thomas, if to be heerd of and then living, to my nephew, Edward Bulkeley, here in England, and to my nephew, Thomas Trye, the son of my late brother-in-law, Mr. Wm. Trye, the sum of ten shillings apiece, if then living, to be to them and every of them respectively, paid as soone as may be after my decease, and as for the remainder of my personal estate, my mind and will is that it be forthwith sold and turned into money, and to equally divide between my sonnes and son-in-law, Edward, Thomas and Everard, afore mentioned, and in case of any of their personal decease before me, my mind and will then is that the part of the said dividend which should have come to such said child, son or son-in-law, shall be and come to his or their oldest child, respectively, if any such shall be then living. If any of them shall decease before me, then the said dividend to be proportionably to the then survivors.

As to the land in Kings Hall, Suffolk, settled upon me and my heirs, after my wife's decease, my mind and will is that that also be forthwith sold, and that of the product thereof, within two months of the said sale, two hundred pounds of good and lawful money of England be paid to my son Falkner as the full remainder of his present wive's portion by me before marriage, promised, and as for the remainder of said product, my mind and will is that it be equally divided between my two *sons Edward* and Thomas aforesaid, only in case either of them happen to decease before the said last dividend made, and shall leave lawful issue behind them, my will is that their respective parts thereof do and shall come and be to the use and behoof of such issue, and accordingly to them or their guardian paid within six months after the said sale, and the money thence arising received, or else to be otherwise put out upon good security for the benefit of the said issue as my executor shall think safest and best. All other of my estate, whether reall or personal, together with my seal ring (which I hereby particularly exempt and reserve from all foregoing bequests), I give and bequeath fully and wholly to my son Edward, whome, together with my said wife, Avis, and my daughter Elisabeth Falkner, I hereby nominate, ordaine, and appoint joynt executor and executresses of and to this my last Will and Testament, revoking and disannulling hereby all former wills whatever. Written with my own hand this eleventh day of October, 1689, in the first year of our sovereign Lord and Lady William and Mary, by the wonderful grace of God, of England, Scotland, France and Ireland, King and Queen whome God of his mercy to those nations grant long to live and continue their sovereign blessings thereunto. Amen.

JOHN BULKELEY.

Signed, sealed and delivered to be the last will of me, the within said named John Bulkeley, in the presence of

ISAAC HEATH, JOHN HAND, AND WILLIAM HODGES.

Probatum fuit humor testamentum apud London, veneribili viro domino Thomas Pinfold milite legam doctor surrogate venerabilis et egregii viri domini. Richardi James, milites legam etiam doctoris civia, Prerogativæ Caulnonensis Magii Custodis sine commissary otiam, constituti visessimo Octavo die mensis, January, Anno Domini Millessimo sex centi Octogessimo novo juvamento Edwardi Bulkeley, Avis Bulkeley, et Elisabetha Faulkner, executorum in humori, et, testamento quibus com missa fuit, administratio omnium et singalorum bonorum jurium, et creditorum, dicti defuncti de bene et fidelites Administrando ad Sancta Dei evangelia juret. Office copy.

Court of Probate.

FOURTH GENERATION.

27.

Elizabeth Bulkeley, daughter of John and Avis Bulkeley, born . married *Everard Faulkner*, of England. They had no children. They had large estates, which were disposed of by will as follows:

WILL OF EVERARD FAULKNER.

Extracted from the Principal Registry of her Majesties Court of Probate,

In the Prerogative Court of Canterbury.

In the name of God, amen, I, Everard Faukner, citizen and grocer of London, being of sound and perfect mind and memory, thanks be to God for it, do make and declare this to be my last will and Testament, as followeth: And first, I give my soul into the hands of my Almighty Creator, resting myself on the hopes of His infinite mercy, through the merits of Christ my Redeemer. As to my body, I commit it to the earth, to be decently interred at the discretion of my executors herein after named and, as to what worldly estate I have of what nature, kind or qualitye soever the same is, I dispose of in manner following, that is to say,

Imprimus, my will and mind is that my debts be duly paid and satisfied.

Item. I give, devise and bequeathe to my dear and loving wife Elisabeth Faukner, all my goods, house hold stuffe, debts due to me, moneys and plate, jewells, chattels and personal estate, whatsoever, to her own sole use and disposing.

Item. I give, devise and bequeathe to my said dear wife, Elisabeth Faukner, all my reall free and Copy hold messuages, lands, tenements and hereditaments whatsoever and wheresoever the same are or is or shall hereafter be. To have and hold the same and every part thereof to her, the said Elisabeth Faukner, her heirs and assigns forever, to her and their own use.

Item. All the rest, residue and remainder of my estate (if any there is or if any hereafter shall arise or come to me,) and of what nature, kind or quality soever, either real, personal or otherwise, the same is or hereafter shall be, I give, devise and bequeathe the same to my said dear wife Elisabeth Faukner, and to her executors and assigns forever. And I do hereby constitute, nominate and appoint my said dear and loving wife, Elisabeth Faukner, sole executrix of this my last will and Testament. And I do herewith appoint and direct my said wife that she make provision that, at her death such of my relations as are hereinafter named may have such moneys as are herein after expressed, if my or her estate will at such her death bear and pay the same. To wit, that she provide for and give to Everard Faukner, the son of my brother John Faukner, three hundred pounds, and to all the other children of my said brother John, borne or to be borne, that shall be living at my decease, two hundred pounds apiece, and in case any of them die in their minority, the same to go to the survivors, Everard included, and that share and share all alike, and if my said wife shall think fit at any time to advance, dispose or pay any sume or sumes of money, for the benefit or placing out of any or either of such child, or children.

Then what monies she shall soe advance, disburse or pay to be deducted from the part or sume limited or hereby intended, to any such child or children whose receipt the minor shall be a valid discharge, in Law, to my said wife. And I do hereby declare and also appoint that if any of the children of my said brother John Faukner, or if my said brother John, prosecute, sue or trouble my said wife in any court of law or equity for touching or concerning this my will, or such monies or legacies as I have hereby devised my said dear wife to give them or any of them, at the time of her death or otherwise. That then every such child or children so prosecuting, sueing or troubling my said wife, either by him, her or themselves, or any person in his or her or their behalf, be prevented and excluded from the money or legacy hereby intended to him, her or them, in like manner as if he, her or they were not the child or children of my said brother John or had not been herein named or mentioned, any aforesaid to the contrary notwithstanding. And I do hereby revoke and annull all other wills by me at any time heretofore made, and do declare and appoint this writing as and for my only last will and Testament. In witness whereof I, the said Everard Faukner, have unto this my last will set my hand and seal the tenth day of December, in the fourth year of the reigne of our Sovereign, Lady Anne, by the grace of God, Queen of England, Scotland, France, and Ireland, Defender of the Faith, &c.

EVERARD FAUKNER.

Anno Domini 1705.

Signed, sealed, published, and declared in the presence of us,
 J. Shepard, Lidia Ketle, John Grant, James Marten.

Faulkner:
 Probatum fuit humor testamentum Apud London coram virili et egregio Viro Domino Ricardo Raines Milite Legum

Doctore curia Prerogitiva Cantabriensis magistro custode sine commissario legitimo constituto tricessimus die mensis July Anno Domini malissimo septengissimo septimo juramento Elisabethe Faulkner relicte dicti defuncti et executricio in dicto testamento nominat cui commissa fuit administratio omnium et singulorum bonorum Jurium et creditorum dicti defuncti de bene et fideliten administrando eadem et Sancta Dei Evangelia.

Vigore commissionis jurat,
   Office copy Court of Probate,   J. J. B.
(164 Paley. 10 forum.)

WILL OF ELISABETH FALKNER.

Extracted from the Principal Registry of her Majestees Court of Probate.

In the Prerogative Court of Canterbury.

In the name of God, Amen. This fourth day of June, in the sixth year of the reign of his Majesty King George, over Great Britain, France, and Ireland, Annoque Domini 1720, I, Elisabeth Faulkner, of Epsom als Elisham, in the county of Surrey, widow, being weak in body, but of sound and disposing mind and memory, praised be God for the same, and being desirous to settle my affairs, do make this my last Will and Testament, in manner following: First and principally I resign my soul into the hands of Almighty God, my Creator, looking and believing in and thro' the atonements of Jesus Christ, my only Lord and Savior, to obtain everlasting happiness in his eternal kingdom. My body I commit to the earth from whence it was taken, in faith of a joyful resurrection, willing the same to be decently buried at the discretion of my executors, hereinafter named, with and by my late indeared husband, Mr. Everard Faulkner, deceased, and inasmuch as he now lies crowded, or liable to be, in the church of Epsom aforesaid, my will and mind is, and I do hereby direct my executors, to prepare and provide with all convenient expedition after my decease a fit and proper vault, in the church-yard of Epsom aforesaid, or some other fitting and convenient place, and thereunto to remove and lodge the corps of my said husband together with my own, the arrangement of which together with my funeral, I leave unto my executors, so as they lay out therein a sum not exceeding six hundred pounds. And as to such temporal good and estate as it hath pleased God to bestow upon me, I give and dispose thereof in manner following, that is to say, I give, devise, and bequeath, all those my lands, tenements and hereditaments, scituate and lying in the Town and Parish of Epsom aforesaid, held by Copy of Court Roll of the Manor of Epsom aforesaid, and which I have surrendered to the use of my will, (except a small piece of land or ground, (parcel of the premises,) by me allotted and set out or agreed and intended to be allotted and appropriated for the erecting thereon, a meeting place for religious worship, and also all other my copy Hold and customary estate in England, unto my nephew, *Thomas Bulkely*, now or late Factor at Fort St. George, in the East Indies, and the heirs of his body lawfully begotten, or to be, together or for want of such issue, I give and devise the same premises (except before excepted) unto Stanley West, of London, Gent', and the Revd. William Harris, of London aforesaid, minister of the gospel, my executors hereinafter named, and their heirs upon trust, to make absolute sale thereof, for such price as can be reasonably obtained for the same, and to bring in and add all such money as shall arise unto my personal estate, to the end and intent the same may go with, and be applied in like manner, as the surplus and residuum of my personal estate is herein by me willed and appointed. Also I give and devise the aforesaid piece or parcel of ground so allotted, designed, or intended, for the building thereon such an erection as aforesaid for religious worship, unto the said Stanley West and William Harris, and their heirs in trust, to devise, surrender, convey, and settle the same for the use and purpose aforesaid for such term of years, or other estate as they or the survivor of them shall see meet. And I do desire and direct my said nephew, Thomas Bulkely, and the heirs of his body, to confirm and corroborate the same estate by such waies and manners as my said Trustees or their counsel, learned in the law, shall reasonably advise. Item. I give and bequeathe all my share and interest (being one thousand pounds nominal stocks) in the capital stock or fund of the Bank of England, and the growing dividends and profits thereof, and all benefit and advantage of the same unto my executors herein after named and appointed in trust, to permit and suffer my cousin, Edward Bulkly, and his assigns, to take and receive to his and their own proper use, the interest, dividends, or profits of my said stock for and during the term of his natural life, and from and after his decease to permit and suffer my cousin, Sarah Bulkeley, now wife of the said Edward Bulkly, and her assigns, to take and receive to her and their use one moiety or equal half part of the dividends, or interest, or profits of my said stock, for and during the time of her natural life, and as to the same moiety from and immediately after the decease of the said Edward Bulkeley, and all the dividends, profits, and proceeds thereof.

In trust for Elisabeth Bulkeley, daughter of the said Edward and Sarah Bulkeley. Nevertheless if the said Elisabeth Bulkeley shall happen to die or depart this mortal life before she shall attain her age of one and twenty years, or day of marriage, then my will and mind is and I do hereby provide that my executors and the survivor of them, and the executors and administrators of such survivor, shall stand and be possessed of and entitled to my said stock, and all the dividends, profits, and proceeds thereof, in trust for such person or persons who, at the time of the decease of the said Elisabeth Bulkley, shall be the heir at law of me, the said Elisabeth Falkner, and the executors and administrators of the same heir at law forever and upon their further trust, nevertheless, and I do hereby will and provide that my said executors and trustees, and the survivor of them, shall and may by and with the privity and consent of my said cousins, Edward Bulkeley, Sarah Bulkeley, and Elisabeth Bulkeley, or the major part of them, or of the survivors or survivor of them, at any time after my decease, absolutely sell and transfer my said stock, or any part thereof, at such price as they can reasonably obtain for the same, and take and receive all or any part of my said capital stock, and likewise shall and may place at and dispose of the moneys thereby accruing upon such securities, or in or for such purchasers of houses, lands, annuities, or other public stocks as they in their discretion shall think fittest, and settle, or cause the same to be settled, upon the like trusts as are herein before mentioned and declared of and concerning my said stock, any thing contained to the contrary thereof in any wise notwithstanding. Item, I give and bequeath unto the said Elisabeth Bulkeley, if and when she shall attain her age of one and twenty years, or day of marriage, the sum of five hundred pounds, to be paid unto her without interest at her attainment of the said age or day of marriage first happening. Item, I give and appoint unto my nephew, Everard Fawkner, four hundred pounds, and to my three neices, his sisters, Sarah, Jane, and Susannah, three hundred pounds a piece, which said last mentioned summes make together the summe of one thousand and three hundred pounds, and is the sum directed, intended, and appointed them, in and by the last Will and Testament of my said late husband, and is the whole amount and in full of what my said husband so in-

tended or appointed them. But inasmuch as I have already paid
and advanced, and may yet advance and pay unto or for them respectively, several sums of money in part of such their said intended
gifts or legacies, and hereby expressly provide and do direct my
executors to deduct and take from the same gifts and legacies respectively all such sum and summes of money as by receipts or
otherwise shall appear to have been by me at any time or times in
my life time advanced or paid unto or for them, my said nephew
and neices, the Fawkners, or any of them respectively, for or in
respect of all or any moneys or legacies given, appointed, or intended them, or any of them, in and by my said late husband's
will or otherwise, and if they are grateful and quiet under his and
my will, (and not otherwise,) I further bequeath of my own free
gift unto each and every one of them, my said nephew and nieces,
the Fawkners, the further sum of three hundred pounds. Item.
I give and bequeath unto my cousin, Mary Rotherain, one hundred
pounds. To my brother-in-law, William Bradenall, fifty pounds,
and to him and his wife forty pounds for mourning; to the lady
Catharine Taylor, one hundred pounds; to the Revd. Mr. Thomas
Valentine, of Epsom aforesaid, one hundred pounds, and ten
pounds more for mourning; to Mrs. Reddall, of Northtoneshire,
twenty pounds; to Mrs. Martha Barrow, daughter of my cousin,
Thomas Barrow, fifty pounds; to my said cousin, Edward Bulkeley,
and his wife and daughter, every said nephew and neices, the
Fawkners, ten pounds a piece for mourning; to Mr. ——— Barrow and Mrs. Elisabeth Barrow, ten pounds a piece for mourning,
and to the Bishop and his lady ten pounds a piece for mourning.
Item, I give unto the Revd. Mr. Woodford, minister of Epsom
aforesaid, ten pounds; to Mr. Anderson, of the same place, twenty
pounds; to Mrs. Drury, five pounds, to whom I also remit four
pounds of the debt she owes me; to Jane Furness, ten pounds; to
my God daughter, Elisabeth Herkins, twenty pounds, and do will
and appoint my executors to pay unto or for the benefit of Mrs.
Elisabeth Herkins, wife of John Herkins, the sum of ten pounds,
for her separate and peculiar use, apart from her said husband,
whom I will shall not meddle therewith, nor shall the same be subject to his control or debts; and the receipt or direction in writing
of the said Mrs. Herkins I will shall be a sufficient discharge to
my said executors for the same. Item, I give unto Izan Patrick
ten pounds; to my maid, *Susannah Fletcher*, twenty pounds, together
with mourning at the discretion of my executors, and to John Stone

Street five pounds. *Item*, I give unto my said executors one hundred pounds in trust and to the intent, that they or the survivor of them, or the executors and administrators of such survivor, shall pay and apply the same for and towards the building of the aforesaid house or place for the religious worship of the dissenting congregation at Epsom aforesaid, when and as they shall see fit. *Item*, I will and direct my executors to give and distribute the sum of one hundred pounds sterling, to and amongst twenty such dissenting preachers or teachers in the county as they or the survivor of them shall see fit. *Item*, I give and bequeath unto such the children and grandchildren of my uncles, *Edward Bulkeley*, Peter *Bulkeley*, and Gershom Bulkeley, late of New England, as shall be living at the time of my decease, the sum of five hundred pounds sterling, in such parts and proportions, at such times, and in such manner, as my executors, or the survivor of them, or the executor and administrater of such survivor shall see meet. *Item*, I give to his grace, the Archbishop of Canterbury, and his lady, twenty shillings a piece for rings; to Mrs. Hester Vicarage, fifty pounds; to Rachel Dent, of Coleman Street, ten pounds; to the Revd. Mr. Joshua Bayes, five pounds; to the lady Ward and her four daughters each a ring of twenty shillings value; to Mrs. Poyston and her two eldest daughters, and Mr. Thomas Wooley and his wife, and their two daughters, each a ring of twenty shillings value, and to Mrs. Elizabeth Dirton, Mrs. Casey, Mrs. Bridges and her nephew, John Bridges, and his sister, twenty shillings a piece for rings. Item, I give unto my coachman, George, his livery, together with a mourning (suit), at the discretion of my executors, and do will that they pay him half a years wages from my death, and permit him to live that half year at my house at Epsom, clear of all charges for board and diet; and my will is that all my aforesaid money legacies to be paid at the end of six callendar months next after my decease, or as soon as conveniently may be and not before, save only those given for mourning and rings, and as to such plate, jewells, rings, goods, or other things, whereon I have or shall write, or by any note under my hand or of my own hand writing, I shall signify to whom I would have the same respectively go, my will is and I do hereby desire my executors to give and devise the same over accordingly. And my will is and I do hereby direct that my said cousin, Edward Bulkeley, and his said wife and daughter, and the survivors and survivor of them, do inhabit in my present dwelling house in Epsom aforesaid, while and until my said nephew,

Thomas Bulkeley, shall arrive in England, or my executors have certain advices of his death, and that they take care to keep my said house and the gardens and appurtenances thereto belonging in the mean time in good repair and condition, and the charges and expenses thereof I will to be paid out of my estate by my executors, together with such the provision for my said cousins, Edward and wife, and daughter, during their abode here, as my said executors or the survivor of them shall from time to time adjudge, or think fitting, necessary, or reasonable, and all the rest and residue of all and singular, my monies, securities for money, goods, chattels, and personal estate, that shall be and remain after my debts, funeral charges, be paid and discharged. I give and bequeath unto my executors hereinafter named and appointed in trust for my said nephew, Thomas Bulkeley, if and in case he shall be living at the time of my decease, equally to be divided between, (if more than one,) part and share alike, and if but one of them, in trust for that one, so that such child or children live to attain the age of one and twenty years. Then in trust to pay to my said nephew and nieces, the Fawkners, or such of them as shall be then living, the sum of sixteen hundred pounds sterling, in equal parts and shares, and upon further trust to pay unto such of the children of the said sister, Vicarage, except he, that is the Chirurgeon, as shall be then living, the sum of fifty pounds a piece, and upon further trust to pay unto the child or children, or grandchild, or grandchildren of my said late uncle, Edward, Peter and Gershom Bulkeley, as shall be then living, one-half part of the then remaining surplus of my said personal estate, in such parts and proportions, at such times and in such manner as my executors, or the survivors of them, or the executors or administrators of such survivor, shall think fit; and upon further trust to pay unto every legatee in this my will named, (other than and except my said relations, the Fawkners and Bulkeleys, and the legatees for mourning and rings,) the like sums of money and legacies by way of addition, as I have ordered by this my will, give, allot, or intend, unto or for them respectively, and as to all the rest and residue of the said overpluss in one residuum of my said personal estate upon the further trust and to the intent and purpose. That my said executors and trustees, and the survivor of them, shall pay, apply, and dispose of the same, and every part thereof, unto such person or persons, and to and for such charitable uses, intents and purposes, in such proportions, at such time, and in such manner, as I have or shall direct them, or as they or the survivor of them, or the executors or administrators of the survivor of them shall see fit, and to, for, and upon no other use, intent, or purpose whatsoever. And I do earnestly desire and entreat my good and faithful friend, Stanley West, to take upon him the burthen of being one of my executors, and I do name, ordain, and appoint him, the said Mr. Stanley West, and the said Mr. William Harris, executors of this, my last Will and Testament, having an entire confidence in their integrity, and as a token of my respect unto them for their care and trouble to be had and taken therein, I do give unto each of them two hundred pounds sterling; and I do desire and direct my said executors in the first place to pay all my just debts as I shall truly owe at the time of my decease, according to equity and good conscience; and I do hereby give full power and authority unto my said executors and the survivors of them, and the executors and administrators of such survivor, to make such occupation and to give such discharge for any debts or sums of money as at the time of my decease shall be due, owing, and payable unto me as they in their discretion shall think fit. And I do hereby also empower and direct my executors either to sell or continue my stock, subscription, or interest in the South Sea Company, as they shall think fittest; and my will and desire is that my said nephew, Thomas Bulkeley, and other my legatees who may be concerned therein, do entirely acquiesce in what they, my said executors, or the survivor of them, shall see meet to do in and about the same, and I do hereby declare my express will and mind to be, and do provide that it shall and may be lawful to and for my said executors, their executors and administrators, and each and every of them, in the first place to satisfy and reimburse him and themselves by and out of my estate, and the several devises and legacies herein before given and made unto them, all such costs, charges, and expenses, as they either or any of them shall reasonably lay out and expend in the execution of this my will and performance of the trusts hereby in them reposed, and that they either or any of them shall not be charged or chargeable with, or answerable for any part of my estate, save what shall actually be in or come into their respective hands, or be actually received by them respectively by their respective express orders. Nor shall either or any of them be answerable for the defaults, neglects, or misdoings of the other of them, nor shall either or any of them be answerable for any monies they shall place out at interest, or otherwise dispose of by virtue and in pursuance of this my will. If the same shall hereby happen to be lost in part or in all, so that it be done with the joint consent and concurrence of both my said executors during their joint lives, and so that in the writings or securities taken for the same, or by some indorsement thereon, or other writing made and executed at the time of taking such securities, it be from time to time expressed that the same is or are taken in trust for or for the account or benefit of my legatees interested therein, some one of them respectively. And lastly, I do hereby revoke and make void and null all former and other wills by me made, and do publish and declare this present writing, contained in eleven sheets of paper, including this present sheet, all of them written on one side only, to be and contain my last Will and Testament. In witness whereof I, the said Elisabeth Fawkner, the testatrix, have to every of the said sheets set my hand and seal, and also put my seal to the top of the first sheet, the day and year above written. ELISABETH FAWKNER.

Signed, sealed, published, and declared by the said Elisabeth Fawkner, as and for her last Will and Testament, on the day and date thereof, in the presence of us who have hereunto subscribed our names as witnesses, in the presence and at the request of the said Testatrix.

JOHN WILDMAN.
JNO. NARDEN, at Blacksmiths' Hall.
GABLE BRADFORD, Clerk to
Mr. Wildman.

DESCENDANTS OF REV. GERSHOM BULKELEY.

THIRD GENERATION.

1·1.

Rev. GERSHOM BULKELEY, son of Rev. Peter Bulkely, the Puritan settler of Concord, Mass., and his second wife, Grace Chetwood Bulkeley, born Dec. 6, 1636, graduated at Harvard College in 1655, before completing his nineteenth year. He married *Sarah Chauncey*, daughter of President Chauncey of Harvard, the emigrant ancestor of the name, Oct. 26, 1659. She was born in Ware, England, June 13, 1631, and was admitted to the church in Cambridge Dec. 10, 1656. She died June 9, 1669. In the year 1661, Mr. Bulkeley located at New London as the second minister of the church in that place. The following entry in regard to him is in Miss Caulkin's History of New London (page 131): "The year 1661 presents us with a new minister, Mr. Gershom Bulkeley of Concord, in the Bay Colony, who, having preached several months in the place, entered into a contract to become the minister of the town. This was merely an engagement for a term of years, and contained no reference to a settlement or ordination. The town pledged a salary of £80 yearly, for three years; and afterwards more, if the people found themselves able to give more, or as much more as God shall move their hearts to give, and they do find it needful to be paid." It was to be reckoned in provisions or English goods, and for the first three years he was to have all such silver as weekly contributed by strangers, to help towards the buying of books. The town was to pay for the transportation of himself, family, and effects from Concord, provide him with a dwelling house, orchard, garden, and pasture, and with upland and meadow for a small farm ; and supply him with firewood for the use of his family, and do their endeavors to suit him with a servant or youth and a maid, he paying for the time. Finally, if Mr. Bulkeley should die during the continuance of his ministry, his wife and children should receive from the town the full and just sum of £60 sterling." The contract was afterward modified, to obviate some difficulty which occurred in building the parsonage. Mr. Bulkeley proposed to provide himself with a house and free the town from an engagement to pay £60 to his family in case of his decease for the sum of £80 in hand. To this the town consented, on condition that he remained with them seven years; but they added this clause: "In case he remove before the seven yeer, he is to return the 80 £ agen, but if he stay the 7 yeere out, the 80 £ is wholly given him, or if God take him away before this time of 7 yeeres, the whole is given his wife and children."

Mr. Bulkeley, after having freed the town from their engagement to build a parsonage, purchased the homestead of Samuel Lothrop, who was about to remove to the new settlement of Norwich. The house is said to have stood beyond the bridge over the mill brook, on the east side of the way toward Mohegan. Here Mr. Bulkeley dwelt during his residence in New London, probably where the Hallam house now stands.

The following entries are found on the records of the town:

"15th Jan. 63–4. James Rogers, Levt. Smith, Cary Latham, John Smith, and William Hough are appoynted to go to Mr. Bulkeley for the settling him amongst us."

* "25 Feb. Old Mrs. Bulkeley's request be read."

"Mr. Buckley, for enlarging maintenance yt he may keep a man, and also take the geting wood into his own hand—if not, let 10l. more be added to our town rate for wood cutting and carting, and 4l. for raising the pulpit."

"At a town meeting, Feb. 25, 1664-5:

"The town having desired to declare their myndes concerning Mr. Bulkeley, it was propounded whether they were willing to leave Mr. Bulkeley to the libertye of his conscience, without compelling or enforcing him to anything in the execution of his place and office contrarye to his light, according to the laws of the Commonwealth. Voted to be their myndes."

This is the first intimation of any uneasiness between Mr. Bulkeley and the people. There are no church records reaching back to this period, and his reasons for leaving are but obscurely intimated. He had not been settled, and no great formality was necessary to his departure.

"At a town meeting, June 10, 1665:

---

* Mrs. Bulkeley, the mother of Rev. Gershom Bulkeley, removed to New London, and resided there after the decease of her husband, Rev. Peter Bulkeley, of Concord, Mass.

"The town understanding Mr. Buckley's intention to go into the Bay, have sent James Morgan and Mr. Douglas to desire him to stay untill seacond day come seven night, which day the town have agreed to ask againe Mr. Fitch to speak with him, in order to know Mr. Buckley's mynde fullye whether ha will continue with us to preach the gospell."

The overtures made to him seem to have proved unsuccessful. A vote, however, was passed, showing that no embittered feeling had grown up between Mr. Bulkley and the people. Though he had ceased to be considered as their minister, he remained in town and occupied the pulpit with acceptance until a successor was obtained. The following vote appears on the town records:

"It is voted and agreed that Mr. Bulkeley, for his time and paines taken in preaching the Word of God to us since the time of his yere was expired, have thirty pounds to be gathered by a rate."

Mr. Bulkeley is supposed to have removed from New London to Wethersfield in the early part of the year 1667. He was installed pastor of the church in Wethersfield the same year of his removal, as successor to Rev. John Russel, who had removed to Hadley, Mass. He continued the pastor there about ten years, when he was dismissed in the year 1677. He then devoted himself to the practice of medicine and surgery. He was appointed by the General Court, in 1675, surgeon to the army that had been raised against the Indians, and Mr. Stone was directed to supply his place in his absence. In 1676, while the party to which he was attached was in pursuit of the enemy, he was attacked by a number of Indians near Wachuset Hill, in Massachusetts, and received a wound in his thigh. As a clergyman, he stood at the head of his profession, and ranked among the first in medical science. He devoted much time to chemistry, with its useful researches, and to philosophy as a cardinal branch of medical knowledge. He was master of several languages, among which were the Latin, Greek, and Dutch. He was famous as a surveyor, pre-eminent, in his time, as a chemist, and highly respected as a magistrate. His sympathies were not always on the popular side. He was a man of peace; but was, at the same time, one who expected unqualified obedience to authority. At least, as a politician, he was opposed to the assumption of the government by the Colonial authorities in 1689, after the time of Sir Edmund Andross. His political sagacity and foresight enabled him to foresee that the course the colonists were pursuing would finally lead to the triumph of those democratic principles which they all disavowed, and consequently he set his face against them. In 1689, he published at Philadelphia, a pamphlet on the Affairs of Connecticut; but no copy is known to exist of it in this country. The same year he wrote an elaborate work, with the curious title: "*Will and Doom, or the Miseries of Connecticut, by and under an usurped and arbitrary power, being a narrative of the first erection and administration of Government in their Majesties Colony of New England, in America.* 1689."

The work was never printed, but was sent to England by the Governor of New York, some dozen years after, as the most reliable account of New England to be found.* At a subsequent period, a copy elegantly transcribed was procured, and may be seen in the State Library at Hartford, Conn. He died at Wethersfield Dec. 2, 1713, aged 77 years and 11 months old. On his monument is the following testimonial: "He was honorable in his descent; of rare abilities, extraordinary industry, excellent learning, master of many languages; exquisite in his skill in divinity, physick and law, and of a most exemplary and Christian life. "In certam spem beate resurrectiones repositas."

Soon after Mr. Bulkeley's devoting himself to the practice of medicine, he located on the east side of the river, in what is now Glastonbury, and became quite a landowner.

During the year previous to his decease, he made his will, of which the following is a copy:

The last will and testament of Gershom Bulkeley, of Wethersfield (alias G. Bulkly of Glastenbury), in the county of Hartford, in her Majesties Colony of Ct., in New England, Practitioner of Physick, made on the 26th day of May, in the year of our Lord 1712, and in the eleventh year of the reign of our Sovereign Lady Anne, by the grace of God Queen of Great Britain, France, and Ireland, and of the Dominions thereto, Defender of the Faith, &c., is as follows: The said Gershom Bulkely having much more than twenty years walked upon the very mouth of the grave, under so great infirmity that I cannot but wonder how I have all this while escaped falling into it, have not been wholly unmindfull of that which nature and common prudence calls for in such cases. But in the mean time, sorrowful changes from the Most High have

---

* This work has recently been published by Mr. Charles J. Hoadly, the State Librarian, but unfortunately the printing office took fire when it was about printed, and two copies only are preserved.

passed over me, and some that I had hoped would have survived me, have prevented me and left me behind them, whereby together with some incident considerations, I am moved to alter some things which otherwise I should not have done. And therefore remaining, tho' very weak in body, yet (through divine mercy) of sound mind and memory, I do now make this (I hope) my Last Will and testament, hereby unmaking and annulling all former wills whatsoever made by me. In the first place, casting myself upon the riches of Sovereign Grace (if God hath wrought any truth in my most deceitful heart), I commit my sinful soul into the merciful hands of my most gracious Lord and Savior Jesus Christ, whom God hath exalted by and at his own right hand to be a Prince and a Savior, to give repentance and remission of sins unto Israel. To him, therefore, I fly for both, with that humble and comprehensive petition of the Publican: 'God be merciful to me a sinner;' and my body I commit to the dust as it was, to be (as near to my late dear wife as, conveniently, may be) decently but obscurely buried, without much cost or ceremony. I neither deserve nor desire those things, yet desire a part in the first and better resurrection of the just.

In the next place I will that all my just debts, due from me (which I thank God are now and I hope shall be very few and small, if any) be well and duly paid, by my executor hereafter named, and as for those poor children which I shall leave behind me in a most sinful calamitous world to grapple with difficult times, the best bequest I have for them is Luther's short, but significant and pertinent prayer, "To domine nutri servatore": To him, therefore, I commend and give them all, humbly beseeching him that he will graciously accept them and theirs; and make them all his own and faithful to the death, and be their portion a God and father to them, in Christ his son, from generation to generation. Amen. As for that little real estate which I had, I have already, by acts executed in my own life time, disposed of it, some to others and the rest of it among my sons or, to their use and behoof, respectively, as occasion hath required, and some also part of my personal estate I have bestowed upon my children already; the remnant thereof of my personal estate I dispose of as follows: Imprimis to my son Charles his daughter, *Hannah Goodrich*, (not to say what I have already done for her since her marriage which she knows, yet to her) or to the next Representative or Representatives I give and bequeath eight pounds in current money of Connecticut or equivalent thereto, to be paid by my executor hereafter named, as soon as conveniently he may after my decease, except only, that in case her occasion should require, and I live to pay the same or any part thereof myself; that then my executor shall be discharged of so much as I shall pay or cause to be payed.

Item, to my good daughters in law, *Hannah Avery* and *Rachel Wolcott*, I give each of them a golden Ducat (or ten shilling piece) if I happen to have a couple.

Item, to my son Edward's present wife, Dorothee, I give a golden guinea (or twenty shilling piece) if I happen to have one.

Item, to my brother Peter's children (Gershom, Peter, Grace, Margaret and Dorothee) I give each of them ten shillings in current money of Connecticut or equivalent thereto, and if any of them happen to owe me anything at my decease not exceeding ten shillings, I will that it be remitted to the debtor, and in particular to the said Grace, I give my great red rugg which was once her mother's, provided that she the said Grace do survive me.

Item, to my son Edward, I give and bequeath the clock, now standing in its case in his house as also my Seal Ring, the great gilt spoon, the least of my two silver porringers and all the books and manuscripts that I have touching matters of law, except the notes which I had at some time written out of Coke's 1st, 2d, 3d and 4th Institutes, which notes I formerly gave to my son, and which tho now in my hand; my will is that he shall have them again, if they may be of use to him. I give my son Edward also, my whip saw, tension saw and timber chain, being of use for his mill.

Item, to my son John, aforesaid, besides what I have otherwise done for him, to the utmost of my ability (and I wish I could have done as well for the rest of his brethren) I have already given the greatest part of my books and my silver pocket watch (which last I mention that my executor may not be at a loss what is become of it) but besides, there are some other parcels needless to be mentioned and besides what I may and shall yet do for him, if God give me life and further ability I give and bequeath to him all the rest of my books which I now have and also my manuscripts, written by my grandfather, my father, or others, I say all such my books and manuscripts, as concern only divinity and other learning, except the law (which books and manuscripts I have given to Edward as aforesaid), and except also medicine and chymistry and some few other books, which with those that concern medicine and chymestry I shall otherwise dispose of by and by.

Item, to my grandson Richard Treat, (the son of Thomas and Dorothy, I give and bequeath all my books and manuscripts, which any way concern medicine and chymestry, among which I include all Glaubus and Boyle's Books* which I have, whether in Latin or English as also Georgics, Agricola, De Re Metallica and Lazarus, each retranslated by St. John Pettus, called Fleeta Minor, or the art &c. of Metalls ; and the same St. John Pettus, his Fodine Regales, and such like books, and also Littleton's Dictionary, for the Latin tongue, and my Dutch Grammar for the Dutch language, together with my manuscript Dutch Dictionary, which may help him to read and understand Hehwart's Degerend, &c., i. e., the Day Spring, a new resurrection of the art of Medicine, which book is in the Dutch language, and together with all my vessels and instruments usefull thereabout, of glass, brass, or copper, iron, stone or earth. All these I give to him provided he hold and pursue his inclination to that study, but if by death or otherwise he be diverted or depart from it, then I give them all to the next of his brethren, that will apply himself to the study, but if none of them then I give them all to his mother (my daughter Dorothy) to dispose of at her discretion or to his father, in like manner, if he survive her.

Item to my daughter Catharine Treat (now deceased), I have already given a competent portion in proportion to my tenuity, yet her only child and daughter *Catharine Treat*, I give and bequeath my lesser silver tankard, my lighter silver cucurbite to be distinguished by its weight from that which I have already given to my daughter Dorothe, (tis not that which belongs to the silver retort but is much better and bigger than that), I give her also the silver salt sellers and the small silver dram cup, all which I had intended for her mother, had she survived me, and which are (I doubt not) worth at least twenty pounds in money. Yet I reserve and give liberty to my daughter *Dorothy*, to redeem any of the silver vessels aforesaid for the full value thereof if she desire so to do. This Legacy I will to be paid to the said Catharine Treat, at her age of eighteen years, or day of marriage which of them shall first happen, but if neither of them happen, then, at her decease, to her father, (my grandson in Law, Richard Treat) if he be then living, but if not then this legacy to be divided equally, in value, between my son Charles, his daughter *Hannah Goodrich* aforesaid and my daughter Dorothy Treat aforesaid or their next legal representatives, by nature and blood respectively.

* Bulkeley's copy of Georgics Agricola and of Glaubus and other medical books are now in the library of Trinity college.

Lastly to my daughter, *Dorothy Treat*, aforesaid, who as yet hath had but little and what she hath had is not now to be accounted for (to her), I give and bequeath all the rest of my personal estate, whatsoever it be, without mentioning or apprizeing of particulars, whether it be in my own hands or in the hands of others, or due and owing from others to me; except only that if there shall be any poor widow or widows or other truly poor persons not able to pay their debts to me, my will is that my executor shall remit it and not trouble them for it,—which I must leave to his discretion, yet with this advertisement, that by poor I mean such as are indeed poor, at least by divine Providence, not by idleness, nor such as may say they are poor and yet can find wherewith to drink, swell, and swagger, and make themselves poor and others, too.

And in particular, To her, my said Dorothy Treat, I give and bequeath my negro maid Hannah, willing and solemnly requiring that into whose hands soever she may happen to come they use her well, and consider that she hath a soul to save as well as wee, and is a Christian; and therefore that they make conscience to promote her in her reading, catechism, and all Christianity, that she may profit and grow in religion and godliness, and attain the end of baptism to the glory of God; and this I earnestly require on her behalf, as they will answer the neglect thereof before God.

To conclude, there is a manuscript of my own concerning the Divinity of the Scriptures, which I did not intend to be included among the theological manuscripts above given to my son John, tho' I forgot particularly to except it there, and therefore I do except it here; and this manuscript I give and bequeath to all my children, Edward, John, and Dorothy, for the good of themselves and their's for whose sakes I principally wrote it (not excluding but including Hannah Goodrich, aforesaid, and Catharine Treat, aforesaid also), that they may know whom and what they believe, and especially such of them as have not these other (and possibly better) helps, which my said son John hath or may have. But the trust and custody of it for the use of them all I commit to my said daughter, Dorothy Treat, to whom all the rest may resort for that end as their behoof and desire shall move and direct them. Finally, for the execution of this my Last Will and Testament, I nominate, constitute, and appoint my loving and trusty son-in-law, *Thomas Treat*, to be my sole and only executor, and in testimony and confirmation of all the premises, I have to these presents put

my hand and seal, in Glastonbury, aforesaid, on the day and year first above written.
                    GERSHOM BULKELEY.   (A Seal.)

Signed, sealed, and published, and declared to be the last Will and Testament of the said Gershom Bulkeley, in the presence of these witnesses,
                    JOHN HOLLISTER,
                    SAMUEL BROOKS,
                    DANIEL ANDREWS, (a) his mark.

P.script. An addition and confirmation of this my last will and testament here above written. For as much as it hath pleased God to take away my son, Thomas Treat, before me, whom I had made my sole executor, my will is and I do hereby ordain my daughter, Dorothy Treat, his widow, to be my sole executrix of this my last will, and this was always my will in that case, so that there is no change or revokation on my part. In testimony whereof I hereunto put my hand and seal, in Glassenbury, in the county of Hartford, on the twenty and fourth day of Nov., Anno Domini, 1713, Gershom Bulkeley. This addition, dated and on the date aforesaid, was by the said Gershom Bulkeley, the testator, signed, sealed, and declared, and published to be his addition and to be his last Will and Testament in presence of,
                    SAMUEL BROOKS,
                    JOSEPH EASTON,
                         her
                    SARAH (8) BROOKS.
                         mark.

CHILDREN.

294.	Catharine,	born about 1660; m. *Richard Treat*.
295.	Dorothy,	" 1662; m. Thomas Treat, July 5, 1693.
296.	Charles,	" 1663.
297.	Peter,	" 1664; m. Rebeccah Talcott.
298.	Edward,	m. Dorothy.
299.	John,	m. *Patience Prentice*.

FOURTH GENERATION.

294.

CATHARINE BULKELEY, daughter and eldest child of Rev. Gershom and Sarah *Chauncey* Bulkeley, born about 1661; married *Richard Treat*, August 20, 1704, by whom she had one child; she died soon after. Mr. Richard Treat died May 7, 1713.

CHILD.

300. Catharine *Treat*, born Aug. 26, 1706; m. Samuel Deming, of Wethersfield, June 16, 1726.

295.

DOROTHY BULKELEY, daughter of Rev. Gershom and Sarah *Chauncey* Bulkeley, born about 1662 or 1663; married *Thomas Treat*, July 5, 1693. He was son of Richard Treat and brother of Richard, the husband of her sister Catharine. He is known in the records as "Thomas Treat, at Nayaug; married the daughter of the Rev. and Hon. Garsham backly" (Bulkeley). He appears to have been lieutenant of the train-band. He was one of the petitioners for the incorporation of Glastonbury, and died Jan. 17, 1713, aged 44. He was appointed executor of his father-in-law, Gershom Bulkeley's, will, but died about eleven months before him, whereupon Mr. Bulkeley, by a codicil, left the settlement of his estate to his daughter, Dorothy Treat, who survived him. Mrs. Dorothy Treat died in 1757.

CHILDREN.

301.	Richard	*Treat*,	born May 14, 1694; supposed to have m. Susanna Woodbridge, daughter of the Rev. Timothy Woodbridge, of Hartford, Aug. 7, 1728.
302.	Charles	"	" Feb. 28, 1696; m. *Sarah Gardner*, 1727.
303.	Thomas	"	" May 3, 1699; m. *Mary Hopson*, Colchester.
304.	Isaac	"	" Aug. 5, 1701; m. *Rebecca Bulkeley*, Dec. 10, 1730, daughter of Edward.
305.	Dorotheus,	" twins,	" Aug. 25, } m. widow *Hannah Benton*, Dec. 18,
306.	Dorothy,		1704; } not known to have married. [1754.
307.	Sarah,	"	" Jan. 21, 1707; m. *Joseph Tryon*, jun., March 13, 1729.
308.	Mary,	"	" Jan. 9, 1710; m. *Joseph Stevens*.

296.

Dr. Charles Bulkeley, born about 1663. Studied medicine, probably with his father. The following entry is found in the court records of New London county:—" 1687. This court grants liberty unto Mr. Charles Bulkeley to practice physick in this county, and grants him license according to what power is in them so to do." He married and had one child, but died young. The family name of his wife is not known, nor the date of marriage. He died before his father, Rev. Gershom Bulkeley, as appears from the following instrument, contained in the sixth volume of the New London Records, page 203:

To all people to whom this present writing shall come, greeting: Whereas I, Gershom Bulkley, Late of New London, in the county of New London, in her Majesties Colony of Connecticut, in New England, in America, and now resident in Glassenbury, in the county of Hartford, in the Colony aforesaid, practitioner in physic, have formally, by my deed of gift under my hand and seal, enfeoffed my son, Charles Bulkley, late of New London, aforesaid, of all my land and tenements in the same New London, to have and to hold the same, with all privileges and appurtenances to the same belonging, to him, the said Charles, and to his heirs and assigns forever; which deed of gift is also acknowledged good before the Honorable John Allyn, esq., late of Hartford, aforesaid, in or about as I remember, the year 1688, to the end that the said deed might be recorded according to law, but am now informed the said deed of Gift is since the decease of my said son Charles, casually burnt in the burning of the house wherein it was and is not to be ffound on record. Now know ye that in consideration of the premises, and to the end that no inconveniences may grow by means of the loss of the said deed of gift, I, the said Gershom Bulkley, do by these presents acknowledge and allow the said deed of gift made by me to my said son Charles, and that I allowed his entry into and possession of the said lands and tenements in New London, afforesaid; and that he was lawfully seized thereof in fees, and for the more full assurance thereof, I, the said Gershom Bulkley, have ratified, approved, and confirmed, and do by these presents ratify, approve, and confirm, my sd son Charles in his entry into and possession of the said land and tenements, together with the rights lawfully accruing thereupon, as particularly the right of dower to his rellict, and the right of inheritance descended upon his heir;

accordingly have ratified, approved, and confirmed, and do by these presents ratify, approve, and confirm, to my said son Charles, his only child, daughter, and heir, Hannah, now *Hannah Goodrich*, of Glassenbury, aforesaid, the estate of inheritance in fee which the said Hannah by law and right hath in the said lands and tenements, with the privileges and the appurtenances of the same. That is to one messuage which I bought of Samuell Lathrop, late of New London, aforesaid, as by his deed of sale on record may appear, with the house and orchard thereupon. Item: one other piece of land which I purchased of Jacob Waterhouse, late of the same New London, as by his deed of sale on record may appear. Item: one other small strip of land which was granted me by the town of New London, aforesaid, lying betwixt the Mill Brooke and the streete upon which streete the messuage aforesaid abutts south-westward, which grant may appear by the Register of the said town, to have and to hold the said lands and tenements and every part and parcel thereof, of the same and of every of them, with all priveledges and appurtenances to the same and to every of them belonging, or any wise appertaining to her, the said Hannah Goodrich, and to heirs, that is to say true and right heirs, according to the due course of the common law of England, and to her assigns and to her and their and every of their owne only and proper use and behoofs forever, as fully and absolutely to all intents and purposes: as if the said deed of gifts to her father, now extant and on Record, or as if the same deed had been made immediately to herself only, reserving to her mother her right of dower during her natural life, accordingly to the law; and also advertising that whereas I observe that the Register that then was hath omitted the abatements of ye south-eastward end butts upon the neck and uppermost mill-dam, and not upon the lower dam, and so it abuts upon the streete also which in that place passeth over the said dam. And advertising also that this said strip of land must be no detriment or incumbrance to the proprietors or occupiers of the mill, but they may at all times raise the water to what height they can and will, without denyall or disturbance from the said Hannah or her heirs or assigns. And in testimony of the premises, I have to these presents put my hand and seale, in Glassenbury aforesaid, on the second day of December, in the eighth year of the reigne of our Sovereign Lady Ann, by the Grace of God Queen of Great Britain, France, and Ireland, and of the dominions thereto belonging, defender of the faith, &c., &c. Annoque Domini Dei, ᵣ1709.

GERSHOM BULKLEY,
Jany the 27, 170 9/10.

Signed, sealed, and
delivered in presence
of us,
THOMAS KIMBLY,
DOROTHE TREATE.

Mr. Gershom Bulkeley, of Glassenbury, personally appeared before me and acknowledged the above instrument to be his free act and deed before me,
ROBERT WELLES,
Justice of the Peace.

Extracted out of the Original and recorded April the 5, 1710.
DANIEL WETHERELL, Recorder.

CHILD OF DR. CHARLES BULKELEY.

310. Hannah, born   ; married *Richard Goodrich*, May 18, 1709.
(See Goodwin, page 75.)

297.

PETER BULKELEY, son of Rev. Gershom and Mrs. Sarah *Chauncey* Bulkeley, born in 1664; married *Rachel Talcott* in 1687, and was lost at sea at the age of 37 years, and left but one

CHILD.

310½. John,   born about 1689.

298.

EDWARD BULKELEY, son of Rev. Gershom and Mrs. Sarah *Chauncey* Bulkeley, born in 1673; married *Dorothy Prescott*, daughter of Jonathan Prescott, of Concord, Mass., and died at Wethersfield, Aug. 27, 1748.

CHILDREN.

311. Charles,   born March 27, 1703; m. *Mary Sage*, of Middletown.
312. Elisabeth,   " Jan. 24, 1705; m. *Joseph Smith*.
313. Sarah,   " Feb. 8, 1707; m. *Joseph Stow*.
314. Rebecca,   " Feb. 22, 1709; m. *Isaac Treat*.

315.	Peter,	born Mch. 19, 1711;	died in infancy.
316.	Peter 2d,	" Mch. 11, 1712;	m. *Abigail Curtis.*
317.	Gershom,	" July 29, 1714;	m. *Thankful Belding.*
318.	Dorothy,	" Sept. 11, 1716;	m. *Thomas Curtis*, of Rocky Hill.
319.	Jonathan,	" , 1718;	m. *Abigail Williams.*
320.	Abigail,	" , 1720;	m. John Marsh.
321.	Lucy,	" , 1723;	m. Charles Butler.

299.

REV. JOHN BULKELEY, son of Rev. Gershom and Sarah *Chauncey* Bulkeley, born   ; married *Patience Prentice*, daughter of John and Sarah Prentice, in 1701, and was the father of twelve children. He graduated at Harvard College in 1699. Studied divinity, and was ordained as pastor of the church in Colchester, Ct., Dec. 20, 1703, and took a high rank among the clergymen of his time. He wrote "*A preface to R. Wolcott's Meditations;* an election sermon in 1713, entitled " *The Necessity of Religion in Societies.*" In 1724, he published an "Inquiry into the Right of the Aboriginal Natives to the Land in America." In 1729, he published another tract, " An impartial account of a late Debate at Lyme, upon the following points: *Whether it be the will of God that the Infants of Visible Believers should be baptized; Whether sprinkling be lawful and sufficient; and whether the present way of maintaining ministers, by a public rate or tax, be lawful.*"

Dr. Chauncey thus writes concerning him: "Mr. John Bulkeley I have seen and conversed with, though so long ago that I formed no judgement of him from my own knowledge. Mr. Whittlesey, of Wallingford, Mr. Chauncey, of Durham, and others I could mention, ever spoke of him as a first rate genius; and I have often heard that Dummer and he, who were classmates in college, were accounted the greatest geniuses of that day. The preference was given to Dummer in regard of quickness, brilliancy, and wit; to Bulkeley, in regard of solidity of judgement and strength of argument. Mr. Gershom Bulkeley, father of John, 1 have heard mentioned as a truly great man and eminent for his skill in chemistry; and the father of Gershom, and grandfather of John, Mr. Peter Bulkeley, of Concord, was esteemed in his day as one of the greatest men in this part of the world. But by all that I have been able to collect, the Colchester Bulkeley surpassed his predecessors in the strength of his intellectual powers. Mr. Bulkeley was classed by the Rev. Dr. Chauncey, in 1768, among the three most eminent for strength of genius and powers of mind, which New

England had produced. The other two were Mr. Jeremiah Dummer and Mr. Thomas Walter." He was regarded, by the men of his time, as a famous casuist and a sage counsellor. The following anecdote in regard to him is well authenticated:

"A church in the neighborhood had fallen into unhappy division and contentions which they were unable to adjust among themselves. They deputed one of their number to the venerable Bulkeley, for his advice, with the request that he would send it to them in writing. It so happened that Mr. Bulkeley had a farm in the extreme part of the town, upon which he had located a tenant. In superscribing the two letters, the one for the church was, by mistake, directed to the tenant, and the one for the tenant, to the church. The church was convened in order to hear the advice which was to settle all their disputes. The moderator read as follows: '*You will see to the repair of the fences that they be built high and strong, and you will take special care of the old black bull.*' This mystical advice puzzled the church very much at first, but an interpreter among the more discerning ones, was soon found who said, 'Brethren, this is the very advice we most need; the direction to repair the fences is to admonish us to take good heed in the admission and government of our members; we must guard the church by our Master's laws, and keep out strange cattle from the fold. And we must in a particular manner set a watchful guard over the devil, the old black bull, who has done so much harm of late.' All perceived the wisdom and fitness of Mr. Bulkeley's advice, and resolved to be governed by it. The consequence was that all the animosities subsided, and harmony was restored to the afflicted church. What the subject of the letter received by the tenant was, we are not informed, and what good effect it had upon him the story does not tell."

Among the land deeds of the town of Colchester, are several to Mr. Bulkeley, which show him to be one of the largest owners of that kind of real estate in town.

He died without having made a will, and the following joint agreement was entered into by his children, as appears on the Probate Records:

"Articles of agreement made this 17th day of July, Anno Domini 1733, by and between John Bulkeley, Gershom Bulkeley, Charles Bulkeley, and Peter Bulkeley, on ye one part, and Sarah Trumble, Dorothy Bulkeley, and Patience Bulkeley, on the other part, witness that all the above named persons, being children and co-heirs of the late Rev'd Mr. John Bulkeley, of Colchester, deceased, taking into our consideration the necessity of a speedy distribution of our Honored Father's estate, who died Intestate, we, under the present situation of affairs, according to the late law of this government enacted for the settlement of such estates, cannot be claimed, do covenant and agree among ourselves that the said estate shall be distributed in manner and form following:

1st. Imprimis that our honored mother shall have the one-half of our father's personal estate, as all ye Negro Man Cæsar.

2d. That John Bulkeley shall have our father's Library, as also one tract of land lying between land of Peletiah Bliss and John Dolbear, being about 30 acres, together with such lands as he the said John Bulkeley hath lately laid out, or in time to come may lay out, on the common right that did belong to our father.

3d. That Gershom Bulkeley shall have all the land in ye lane on which he has erected his house, with the mill and the appurtenances whatsoever.

4th. That Charles shall have the land lying on the road to Glastenbury and adjoining to land of Mrs. Woodbridge, being about 150 acres, together with twenty acres in addition to such tract, to be set off to it by ye said John Bulkeley, on the northerly side of said Charles' land, in good form.

5th. That Peter shall have all the land that lyes between land of William Douglass and Col. Brown's heirs, and adjoining east on land of Mr. Thatcher.

6th. That the several sums of £36 s3 d8, now delivered to us the said Sarah Trumbull, Dorothy Bulkeley, and Patience Bulkeley, respectively, in personal estate, together with what we have received in good bonds well executed of our bretheren John Bulkeley, Gershom Bulkeley, Charles Bulkeley, Peter and Oliver (Bulkeley), shall be in full of our respective portions; that we said Sarah, Dorothy, and Patience shall have no further claim on our father's estate, either real or personal. In witness and confirmation whereof we have hereunto set our hand and seal, this 17th day of July, 1733.

	JOHN BULKELEY,	(O & Seal.)
	GERSHOM BULKELEY,	(O & Seal.)
In presence of	CHARLES BULKELEY,	(O & Seal.)
Nathanael Foot,	PETER BULKELEY,	(O & Seal.)
Sarah Mayhill, alias Prentice,	OLIVER BULKELEY,	(O & Seal.)
Daniel Gillett,	SARAH TRUMBLE,	(O & Seal.)
Sam'l Tilden,	DOROTHY BULKELEY,	(O & Seal.)
Silas Phelps.	PATIENCE BULKELEY,	(O & Seal.)

N. B. It is to be understood that Charles is to have such physical Books as are in the English tongue, as witness my hand ye day within mentioned.

JOHN BULKELEY.

At a Court of Probate held in Colchester, for the District of East Haddam, present John Bulkeley, Judge of said Court, and Nathanael Foot, Esq., was desired to assist, before which court Sarah Wells called in this agreement, Sarah Trumble, Dorothy Bulkeley, and Patience Bulkeley, and also Peter Bulkeley, and acknowledged the within agreement to have been signed by them, and it was and is their free act and deed.   ye Court of Probate and me,

NATHANAEL FOOTE, *Justice of Peace.*

Court of Probate, Aug. 5, 1753. Personally appeared Oliver Bulkeley, and acknowledged ye within written instrument to be his free act and deed.

Attest,   ALEX. PHELPS, *Clerk.*

At a Court of Probate held at Colchester, July 25, 1754, present Joseph Spencer, Esq., Judge, personally appeared Major Charles Bulkeley and resigned his guardianship of Eliphalet and Mary Bulkeley, minors and children of John Bulkly, Esq., late of Colchester, and at the same court Mr. William Adams, of New London, was appointed guardian of the said Eliphalet and Mary Bulkeley, and Lucy Bulkeley, a minor, and gave bond according to law, and on file.

At said court Epaphras Lord, Esq., administered on ye estate of John Bulkeley, Esq., deceased, and exhibited an addition to ye Inventory of said deceased's estate.

Attest,   ALEX. PHELPS, *Clerk.*

CHILDREN OF REV. JOHN AND PATIENCE PRENTICE BULKELEY.

322.	Sarah,	born April 8, 1702; m. 1, *Jonathan Trumbull*; 2, *John Wells.*	
323.	Another daughter,	" May 6, 1704, and died about three hours after.	
324.	John,	" April 19, 1705; m. 1, *Mary Gardiner*, Oct. 29, 1738; 2, *Abigail Hastings*, April 16, 1751.	
325.	Dorothy,	" Feb. 28, 1706.	
326.	Gershom,	" Feb. 14, 1709.	
327.	Charles,	" Dec. 26, 1710.	
328.	Peter,	" Nov. 21, 1712.	
329.	Patience,	" May 21, 1715.	
330.	Oliver,	" July 29, 1717; died Jan. 1, 1779.	
331.	Lucy,	" June 29, 1720.	
332.	Irene, } Twins,	" Feb. 10, 1722;	died Feb. 20, 1722.
333.	Joseph,		died Feb. 25, 1722.

FIFTH GENERATION.

300.

CATHARINE TREAT, only child of Richard and Catharine Bulkeley Treat, born Aug. 20, 1706, was married to *Samuel Deming*, Jr., son of Samuel and Sarah Deming, June 16, 1726.

CHILDREN.

334. Treat *Deming*, born Sept. 28, 1727.
335. Sarah   "   " Mar. 10, 1730.
336. Katharine "   " Jan. 18, 1733.
337. Samuel   "   " Dec. 10, 1735.
338. Rebecca   "   " Oct. 10, 1738 ; died July 6, 1758.
339. Mabel   "   " Aug. 24, 1743.
340. Deliverance "   " Dec. 3, 1746.
341. Richard   "   " April 11, 1755.

310.

HANNAH BULKELEY, daughter and only child of Dr. Charles Bulkeley, of New London, married *Richard Goodrich* of Wethersfield, May 18, 1709. They settled in Glastonbury, Conn., but, by a deed from him to Thomas Wells, dated in 1725, it appears that they were then residing in Middletown, Conn. Probably in Upper Houses, so called.

Mrs. Hannah Goodrich died Sept. 23, 1720.

CHILDREN.

342. Ann *Goodrich*, born March 6, 1710.
343. Richard   "   " July 13, 1712; died Sept. 1, 1714.
344. Sarah   "   " July 6, 1715.
345. Gershom   "   " May   5, 1717.
346. Richard   "   " July 23, 1719.

311.

CHARLES BULKELEY, son of Edward and Dorothy *Prescott* Bulkeley, born March 25, 1703. Married *Mary Sage*, of Middletown.

CHILDREN.

347. John,   born 1725; m. *Honor Francis*, July 15, 1750.
348. Giles,   "   m.
349. Benjamin,   "   m. 1, Susannah Kirby, Nov. 3, 1757 ; 2, *Elisabeth Brownwell*, of Compton, R. I., Feb. 6, 1776.
350. Charles,   "   m. *Mary Griswold*.

351. Edward,   born   ; m. 1, *Rachel Pomeroy* ; 2, Prudence Wells.
352. Prescott,   "   1744 ; m.
353. Mary,   "   m. *David Webb*.
354. Catharine, "   m. *Cadwell*.
355. Sarah,   "   m. *Cephas Smith*, Aug. 5, 1756.
356. Olive,   "   m. *James Deming*.

312.

ELIZABETH BULKELEY, daughter of Edward and Dorothy *Prescott* Bulkeley, born Jan. 24, 1705. Married Ensign *Joseph Smith*, Dec. 20, 1726. They resided at Middletown, where he died Jan. 17, 1769, and she died Oct. 20, 1761.

CHILDREN.

357. Martha   *Smith*, born April 15, 1728.
358. James   "   "   Jan. 2, 1730.
359. Elisabeth   "   "   Dec. 31, 1733.
360. Joseph   "   "   Mar. 16, 1736 ; died Oct. 6, 1741.
361. John   "   "   Mar. 26, 1738.
362. Nathaniel "   "   June 25, 1741.
363. Joseph   "   "
364. Edward   "   "

313.

SARAH BULKELEY, daughter of Edward and Dorothy *Prescott* Bulkeley, born Feb. 8, 1707, married *Joseph Stowe*.

She died at Upper Middletown, now Cromwell, April 3, 1783.

314.

REBECCA BULKELEY, daughter of Edward and Dorothy *Prescott* Bulkeley, born Feb. 22, 1709, married her first cousin, *Isaac Treat*, in 1730.

316.

PETER BULKELEY, son of Edward and Dorothy *Prescott* Bulkeley, born March 11, 1712, married (1.) *Abigail Curtis*, April 2, 1741. She died Nov. 27, 1762. (2.) *Christian Smith*, Jan. 26, 1769. He was appointed Justice of the Peace for Hartford County, May, 1775. Mr. Bulkeley died April 4, 1776.

CHILDREN.

365. Joseph,   born Jan. 28, 1742 ; m. *Mary Williams*, May 3, 1776.
366. Abigail,   "   April 13, 1743 ; m. *Nathanael Miller* of Rocky Hill.
367. Oliver,   "   Dec. 5, 1744 ; m. and died at sea in 1776.
368. Solomon,   "   March 21, 1747 ; m. *Martha Williams*, June 6, 1776.
369. Dorothy,   "   July 17, 1749 ; died in infancy, July 28, 1749.
370. Justus,   "   Dec. 24, 1752 ; m. 1, *Mabel Boardman*, March 22, 1781 ; 2, *Lucretia Churchill* ; 3, Mehetable Culver.

317.

GERSHOM BULKELEY, son of Edward and Dorothy *Prescott* Bulkeley, born July 29, 1714, married *Thankful Belding*, Feb. 17, 1743.

CHILDREN.

371. Thankful,	born May 20, 1744.	
372. Jehiel,	" Oct. 23, 1745; m. *Mary Robbins*, March 2, 1775.	
373. Gershom,	" Dec. 3, 1746.	
374. Mabel,	" May 2, 1750.	
375. Ruth,	" May 17, 1752.	
376. William,	" Sept. 2, 1754.	
377. Hosea.		
378. Chloe,	" Sept. 24, 1765.	

318.

DOROTHY BULKELEY, daughter of Edward and Dorothy *Prescott* Bulkeley, born Sept. 11, 1716, married *Thomas Curtis*, Jan. 8, 1741.

CHILDREN.

379. Dorothy *Curtis*, born Dec. 5, 1741.		
380. Josiah	" " May 11, 1744.	
381. Charles	" " Mar. 7, 1746.	
382. Rachel	" " April 9, 1748.	
383. Wait	" " Jan. 1, 1751.	
384. Eleazer	" " Mar. 4, 1753.	
385. Mary	" " Oct. 6, 1755.	

319.

JONATHAN BULKELEY, son of Edward and Dorothy *Prescott* Bulkeley, born Sept. 11, 1716, married *Abigail Williams*, Nov. 13, 1746. He died.

CHILDREN.

386. Eleanor,	born Nov. 11, 1747.
387. Stephen,	" Dec. 19, 1749; m. 1, Susan Riley; 2, Prudence Williams; 3, Marsh.
388. Edmund,	" Dec. 7, 1751.
389. Jonathan,	" Nov. 3, 1753; died July 11, 1770.
390. Frederick,	" Aug. 27, 1755; died Jan. 20, 1777.
391. A son,	" June 25, 1758.
392. Jonathan 2d,	" May 10, 1759; m. Mary Edwards, June 16, 1787.
393. Lydia,	" May 9, 1761.
394. A daughter,	" May 4, 1762. Still born.
395. Moses,	" Feb. 7, 1764.
396. Dorothy,	" April 8, 1766; died Aug. 18, 1766.
397. Burrage,	" Aug. 9, 1767.
398. Dorothy,	" June 17, 1770.

320.

ABIGAIL BULKELEY, daughter of Edward and Dorothy *Prescott* Bulkeley, born —— 1720, married *John Marsh*, Jan. 17, 1749.

CHILDREN.

399. Mary *Marsh*, born Sept. 22, 1749.
400. Martha   "   "   Nov. 10, 1751.
401. John   "   "   Sept. 25, 1753; m. *Ann Grant*, Dec. 6, 1775.
402. Rebecca   "   "   Nov. 2, 1755.

321.

LUCY BULKELEY, daughter of Edward and Dorothy *Prescott* Bulkeley, born in 1723; married *Charles Butler*.

CHILDREN.

403. Stephen *Butler*, baptized October 21, 1764.
404. John   "   "   March 30, 1766.
405. Dorothy   "   "   October 2, 1768.
406. Sarah   "   "   June 16, 1771.

322.

SARAH BULKELEY, eldest child of Rev. John and Patience *Prentice* Bulkeley, born April 8, 1702. She was twice married—1, to *Jonathan Trumbull*; 2, *John Wells*, January 29, 1738.

324.

HON. JOHN BULKELEY, son of Rev. John and Patience *Prentice* Bulkeley, born April 19, 1705; graduated at Yale College in 1725; studied law and became eminent in his profession. In 1753 was elected an assistant, and onward for a period of ten years. He was judge of probate, and held many important offices of trust. He was twice married—1, to *Mary Gardiner*, October 29, 1738. She died December 4, 1750. 2, to *Abigail Hastings*, April 16, 1751. He was, in addition to his many civil offices, also colonel of militia. He died very suddenly, July 21, 1753, being found dead in his bed. The following inscription is copied from Judge Bulkeley's monument:

"The Hon. Judge Bulkeley, Esq., of Colchester, who for a number of years was a great honor to an uncommon variety of exalted stations in life. *Morte subitanæ corripuit Julii 21, A. D. 1753, Anno Ætates sua 49.*

> Beloved and 'fear'd for vertues Sake,
> Such vertue as the great doth make.

BULKELEY FAMILY. 99

CHILDREN BY THE FIRST MARRIAGE.
407. Lydia, born October 21, 1739; married Captain Robert Latimer.
408. Mary, " May 27, 1741; died June 1st, 1741.
409. John, " May 20, 1742; died November 13, 1742.
410. Mary 2d, born November 15, 1743; married *George B. Hurlburt*, and died childless.
411. Eliphalet, born August 8, 1746; married *Anna Bulkeley*, of New London.
412. Lucy, " August 2, 1749; married Captain *John Lamb*, of Groton.
413. Charles, " May 22, 1752.

326.

GERSHOM BULKELEY, son of Rev. John and Patience *Prentice* Bulkeley, born February 4, 1709; married *Abigail Robbins*, November 28, 1733. He was a prominent citizen of Colchester, and held many important offices of trust.

CHILDREN.
414. Sarah, born January 10, 1735; married Joseph Isham, January 17, 1765.
415. John, " August 23, 1738; married *Judith Worthington*, January 11, 1757.
416. Joshua, born February 24, 1741; married *Lois Day*, November 9, 1761.
417. Daniel, " May 13, 1744; married *Dorothy Olmsted*, August 16, 1764.
418. Eunice, " May 14, 1747; married *Elisha Lord*, May 25, 1767.
419. David, " July 18, 1749; married Hannah Beckwith.
420. Roger, " September 14, 1751; married *Jerusha Root*.
421. Ann, " May 11, 1758.

327.

CHARLES BULKELEY, son of Rev. John and Patience *Prentice* Bulkeley, born December 26, 1710; married *Ann Latimer*, October 8, 1741. They removed to New London, and lived and died there. He died November 22, 1762.

CHILDREN.
422. John, born October 7, 1744.
423. Anna, " April 14, 1747.
424. Patience, born April 23, 1749.
425. Charles, " December 19, 1753.

328.

PETER BULKELEY, son of Rev. John and Patience *Prentice* Bulkeley, born November 21st, 1712; married twice—1, *Lucy Avery*, January 13, 1742. She died August 21st, 1752. 2, *Susannah Newton*, December 16, 1756.

CHILDREN BY THE FIRST MARRIAGE.
426. Peter, born February 3, 1744; married *Hannah Breed*, of Stonington.
427. William, married *Polly Champion*.
428. Lucy, married *John Breed*.

CHILDREN BY THE SECOND MARRIAGE.

429. James, born September 7, 1757.
430. Susannah, born November 23, 1759.
431. Israel,   " January 22, 1762.
432. Charles,   " December 17, 1763.

329.

PATIENCE BULKELEY. daughter of Rev. John and Patience *Prentice* Bulkeley, born March 21, 1715; married *Ichabod Lord*, December 14, 1743. He died December 18, 1761.

CHILDREN.

433. Abigail *Lord*, born November 22, 1744.
434. Patience "   " February 2, 1746.
434½. Mary   "   " May 12, 1748.
435. Sarah   "   " November 28, 1749.
436. Elisabeth"   " October 7, 1751.
437. Anna   "   " September 19, 1753.
438. Jerusha "   " February 5, 1755.
439. Lydia   "   " July 4, 1756; died January 18, 1759.

330.

OLIVER BULKELEY, son of Rev. John and Patience *Prentice* Bulkeley, born July 29, 1717; married *Sarah Wells*.

CHILDREN.

440. Joseph, born January 9, 1740.
441. Chauncey, born October 22, 1741.
442. Noah,   " June 20, 1744.
443. Sarah,   " December 4, 1745.

331.

LUCY BULKELEY, daughter of Rev. John and Patience *Prentice* Bulkeley, born January 29, 1720; married *Epaphras Lord*. They had a family of fourteen children. Mr. Lord died November 25, 1742.

CHILDREN.

444. Epaphras *Lord*, born December 22, 1743.
445. Elisha   "   " March 18, 1745.
446. Dorothy   "   " April 27, 1746; died May 26, 1752.
447. Theodoret "   " May 18, 1747.
448. Luce   "   " August 26, 1748.
449. Jerusha   "   " November 7, 1749.
450. Bulkeley "   " June 15, 1751; died June 25, 1751.
451. Dorothy 2d "   " June 16, 1752; " April 16, 1753.
452. John   "   " November 5, 1754.
453. Eunice   "   " July 26, 1756.
454. Caroline "   " March 2, 1758.

455. Lydia *Lord*, born November 14, 1759.
456. Abigail   "   " January 3, 1761.
457. Ichabod   "   " June 12, 1762.

SIXTH GENERATION.

347.

JOHN BULKELEY, son of Charles and Mary *Sage* Bulkeley, born in 1725; married *Honor Francis*, July 17, 1750.

CHILDREN.

458. John, born November 10, 1750; married *Sarah Wright*.
459. Honor, " March 14, 1753; married Sylvanus Brown.
460. William, born   1754. Lost at sea.
461. Elisabeth, "   1755; married *John Mygatt*.
462. Francis,   "   1757; m., 1, *Rhoda Griswold*; 2, *Elisabeth Fosdick*.
463. Benjamin, "   1761; died young.
464. Sarah,   "   1765; died young.
465. Edward,   "   1767; married *Dina Bunce*.
466. Sarah 2d, "   1770; married   Bostwick.

348.

GILES BULKELEY, son of Charles and Mary *Sage* Bulkeley, born   ; married

CHILDREN.

467. Levi, baptized September 30, 1764.
468. David,   "   August 30, 1766.
469. Abigail, "   October 22, 1769.
470. Daniel, "   June 28, 1772.
471. Hetty,   "   April 15, 1781.

349.

BENJAMIN BULKELEY, son of Charles and Mary *Sage* Bulkeley, born   ; married twice—1, *Susannah Kirby*, daughter of John Kirby, of Middletown, November 3, 1757. She died May 27, 1776. 2, *Elisabeth Brownwell*, February 6, 1777.

CHILDREN BY THE FIRST MARRIAGE.

472. Thomas, born October 2, 1758; married *Bathsheba Sage*.
473. Lucy,   " September 18, 1760; married *Joseph White*.
474. George, " November 28, 1762; married
475. Huldah, " October 1, 1764; married *John Francis*, November 7, 1792.

476. James,   born September 11, 1766; married *Caroline Hallam*.
477. Stephen,   "   November 8, 1768; married *Margaret Fanning*.
478. Abigail,   "   December 30, 1770; married *Jasper Lacy*.
479. Martha,   "   April 26, 1773; married *George Webster*.
480. Hannah,   "   June 25, 1775; married *Amos Woodruff*.

CHILDREN BY THE SECOND MARRIAGE.

481. Benjamin, baptized May 13, 1784.
482. Samuel,   "   "   "
483. Brownell, born February 16, 1782; baptized September 24, 1786.
484. Betsey,   "   "   "

350.

CHARLES BULKELEY, son of Charles and Mary *Sage* Bulkeley, born ———; was married to *Mary Griswold*.

CHILDREN.

485. Charles, born March 9, 1760; married *Eunice Robbins*, October 15, 1782.
486. Mary, baptized June 15, 1764; married *Elisha Wetherell*.
487. Elisabeth, "   January 25, 1766.
488. Daniel,   "   August 14, 1769.
489. Eunice,   "   December 11, 1774.
490. Nancy,   "   April 27, 1777; married Joshua Goodrich.
491. Chester,   "   February 25, 1781; married *Hannah Buckerts*, October 5, 1806.
492. Polly,   "   October 30, 1783.

351.

EDWARD BULKELEY, son of Charles and Mary *Sage* Bulkeley, born ———; was twice married; 1. To *Rachel Pomeroy*, Oct. 27, 1771; she died Aug. 14, 1774. 2. *Prudence Williams*, Nov. 2, 1775. Mr. Bulkeley died June 30, 1787.

CHILDREN BY THE FIRST MARRIAGE.

493. Roxa,   baptized Oct. 25, 1772; m. *Selah Francis*.
494. William,   "   Nov. 2, 1773; washed overboard and drowned, July 23, 1788.

CHILDREN BY THE SECOND MARRIAGE.

496. Rhoda,   baptized Aug. 11, 1776.
497. Fanny,   "   April 29, 1781, m. *Elihu Frisbie*, of Albany, N. Y., Oct. 29, 1813.
498. Rachel,   "   Feb. 16, 1783.
499. Pamela,   "   June 6, 1784.
500. Rodney,   "   June 13, 1784; died Sept. 22, 1786.
501. Prudence,   "   April 1, 1787.
502. Oliver Pomeroy,   "   April 8, 1787.
503. Edward Rodney,   "   July 5, 1789.

352.

PRESCOTT BULKELEY, son of Charles and Mary *Sage* Bulkeley, born ——; married *Lois Williams* in 1774, and had children baptized at Rocky Hill. Mr. Bulkeley died Sept. 10, 1791, aged 47.

CHILDREN.

504.	Simeon,	baptized	Aug. 21, 1774; died in West Indies, unmarried, aged 18.
505.	Horace,	"	Oct. 10, 1779; died in Leyden, N. York, in 1813.
506.	Nancy,	born	Oct. 1, 1781; m. *Nathan North*, of Exeter, N. H., Aug. 4, 1805.
507.	Laura,	baptized,	March 21, 1784; died, unmarried, March 23, 1841, at Leyden, N. Y.
508.	Louisa,	born	Jan. 31, 1786; m. *John G. Post*.
509.	Lydia,	"	Feb. 24, 1788; m. *P. Irwin*.
510.	Belinda,	"	June 5, 1790; m. *Dr. Samuel Bass?*

353.

MARY BULKELEY, daughter of Charles and Mary *Sage* Bulkeley, born about 1744; married *David Webb*.

CHILDREN.

511.	William *Webb*,	baptized	Feb. 17, 1765.
512.	Abigail,	"	" Dec. 21, 1766.
513.	Martha,	"	" March 5, 1769.

354.

CATHARINE BULKELEY, daughter of Charles and Mary *Sage* Bulkeley, born ——; married *M. Caldwell*. No record of children has been found.

355.

SARAH BULKELEY, daughter of Charles and Mary *Sage* Bulkeley, born ——; married *Cephas Smith*, Aug. 5, 1756. Nothing further has been ascertained.

356.

OLIVE BULKELEY, daughter of Charles and Mary *Sage* Bulkeley, born ——; married *James Deming*.

365.

JOSEPH BULKELEY, son of Peter and Abigail *Curtis* Bulkeley, born Jan. 28, 1742; married *Mary Williams*, daughter of Moses Williams, May 3, 1776. She was born Jan. 3, 1756, and died

Dec. 23, 1848, aged 92. Mr. Bulkeley was an extensive merchant in Rocky Hill; for many years Justice of the Peace, and represented his town in the State Legislature.

CHILDREN.

514.	Mary,	born	Dec. 18, 1778; m. *Joseph Butler.*
515.	Rhoda,	"	Jan. 21, 1781; m. *Wyllis Williams.*
516.	Ralph,	"	Sept. 14, 1783; m. *Elizabeth Bradford.*
517.	John,	"	Oct. 28, 1785; died June 5, 1806.
518.	Edmund,	"	Dec. 6, 1787; m. *Nancy Robbins.*
519.	Joseph,	"	Oct. 28, 1789; graduated at Yale College in 1810; studied law, and practised in New York City from 1815 until his death, which transpired at Rocky Hill, March 21, 1851. He was never married.
520.	Henry,	"	June 11, 1793; m. *Martha Tucker.*
521.	Walter Williams,	"	Sept. 15, 1797; m. *Lucy Robbins.*

366.

ABIGAIL BULKELEY, daughter of Peter and Abigail *Curtis* Bulkeley, born April 13, 1743; married *Nathanael Miller*, of Rocky Hill, in the year 1762; he was born April 9, 1737, and removed to Brookfield, New York, where he died, July 20, 1808. She died April 14, 1834.

CHILDREN.

522.	Mercy *Miller,*	died young, at Wethersfield, Conn.
523.	Abigail *Miller,*	m. —— *Lamb.*
524.	Caleb *Miller,*	born Feb. 6, 1767; m. *Dorothy Butler;* died in Lodi, New York, Sept. 26, 1850.
525.	Amos *Miller,*	" Feb. 3, 1769; died at sea; left two sons.
526.	Nathanael *Miller,*	" April 26, 1773; died Nov. 4, 1840.
527.	Rebeccah *Merrill,*	" Jan. 7, 1776; m. *George Button.*
528.	Elijah Bulkeley *Miller,*	" July 22, 1783; m. *Ruth Hall.*

368.

SOLOMON BULKELEY, son of Peter and Abigail *Curtis* Bulkeley, born March 21, 1747; married *Martha Williams*, daughter of Moses Williams. Mr. Bulkeley died suddenly, March 4, 1790, aged 43.

CHILDREN.

529.	Sally,	born ——
530.	James,	"
531.	Oliver,	"
532.	George,	"
533.	Martha,	"
534.	Nancy,	"

370.

JUSTUS BULKELEY, son of Peter and Abigail *Curtis* Bulkeley, born Dec. 24, 1752; was three times married; 1. To *Mabel Boardman*, March 22, 1781; she died Sept. 11, 1804. 2. To widow *Ackley Riley*, June 19, 1805; she died Sept. 12, 1826, aged 75. 3. To widow *Mehitable Culver*, Nov. 12, 1826. Mr. Bulkeley died March 22, 1829, aged 77.

CHILDREN.

535.	Sophia,	baptized	Oct. 16, 1782.
536.	Chesterfield,	"	Nov. 7, 1784.
537.	An infant—without name,		died Oct. 19, 1786.
538.	Lora,	"	Nov. 4, 1790.
539.	Clarissa,	"	May 1, 1791.
540.	Betsey,	"	Aug. 1, 1793.
541.	Justus,	"	Sept. 23, 1795; died young.
542.	William,	"	April 4, 1799.
543.	Harriet,	"	Oct. 11, 1801.
544.	Justus,	"	Nov. 13, 1803.

372.

JEHIEL BULKLEY, son of Gershom and Thankful *Belding* Bulkeley, born October 23, 1745; married *Mary Robbins*, March 2, 1775.

CHILDREN.

545. An infant, died without name, April 29, 1781.
546. Chauncey, baptized September 8, 1782; married *Nancy Hart*, August 27, 1805.

373.

REV. GERSHOM BULKLEY, son of Gershom and Thankful *Belding* Bulkeley, born December 3d, 1746. Graduated at Yale College in the class of 1770. Studied theology, and settled at Cromwell in June, 1778, and was dismissed in 1808, after having served the church thirty years, and died at Cromwell, April 7, 1832, aged 86. He married *Hope Huntington*.

CHILDREN.

547. Betsey, born in 1781; died August 21, 1863, aged 82. Never married.
548. Sally,   "   1783; died December 10, 1831, aged 48. Never married.
549. Leonard,   married *Polly Warner*.

376.

WILLIAM BULKELEY, son of Gershom and Thankful *Belding* Bulkeley, born September 2, 1754; married *Olive Williams*, January 31, 1776. He was washed overboard from a vessel and drowned, July 23, 1788.

CHILD.
550. William, baptized March 25, 1781; died February 14, 1790, aged 10.

377.

HOSEA BULKELEY, son of Gershom Bulkeley, born ; married *Abigail Griswold*, May 1, 1781. She died August 28th, 1823, aged 63.

CHILDREN.
551. Amelia, born April 24, 1782.
552. Ursula,   "   June 8, 1783; died March 27, 1863.
553. John G., "   January 3, 1785.
554. Sylvester," June 1, 1787.
555. Gershom, " February 11, 1789.
556. Mabel,   "   November 13, 1792.
557. Olive,   "   September 1, 1794.
558. Abigail, "   September 17, 1795; died June 8, 1798.
559. Abigail S., born January 20th, 1799.

378.

CHLOE BULKELEY, daughter of Gershom and Thankful *Belding* Bulkeley, born September 24, 1765; married *Frederick Boardman*, July 28, 1790.

CHILDREN.
560. William Bulkeley *Boardman*, baptized June 5, 1791; died July, 1793 aged 3.
561. William Bulkley,   "   June 29, 1794.

387.

STEPHEN BULKELEY, son of Jonathan and Abigail *Williams* Bulkeley, born December 19, 1749. He was twice married—1, to *Martha Marsh*. She died April 26, 1804. 2, to Susan Riley, September 16, 1805. Mr. Stephen Bulkeley died May 1813, aged 69.

CHILDREN BY THE FIRST MARRIAGE.
562. Honor, born May 5, 1774; married Daniel Edwards, Jr., of Middletown, November 16, 1795.
563. Stephen, born April 18, 1776; died young, September 29, 1779.
564. Catherine, born October 15, 1778; died October 11, 1799.
565. Cate,   "   September 2, 1780; married *Zenas Edwards*, December 7, 1800.
566. Stephen 2d, born March 30, 1783.
567. Allen,   "   July 19, 1786.
568. Frederick, " June 1, 1792.
569. A daughter, " December 18, 1796.

CHILDREN BY THE SECOND MARRIAGE.
570. Burrage, born December 22, 1805.
571. Wait,   "   March 4, 1807; married, 1,   ; 2, Charlotte Whitmore.

388.

EDMUND BULKELEY, son of Jonathan and Abigail *Williams* Bulkeley, born December 7, 1751; married *Prudence Williams*, November 2, 1773.

CHILDREN.

572. Rhoda, baptized August 11, 1778.
573. Fanny, " August 29, 1781.
574. Rachel, " February 16, 1783.
575. Pamela, " June 6, 1784.
576. Rodney, "

392.

JONATHAN BULKELEY, JR., son of Jonathan and Abigail *Williams* Bulkeley, born November 3, 1753; married *Mary Edwards*, January 16, 1787.

CHILDREN.

577. Sally, baptized December 2, 1787; m. Elisha Goodrich, July 30, 1821.
578. Nabby, born 1792; married Isaac Stevens, of Portland, April 20, 1819.
579. Prescott, born February 8, 1797.

401.

REV. JOHN MARSH, son of John and Abigail *Bulkeley* Marsh, born September 25, 1753. He graduated at Yale College in the class of 1774, studied divinity, settled as pastor of the church in Wethersfield soon after graduation, and received subsequently the title of D. D. He was dismissed from his charge about 1816, and died September 13, 1821. He married *Anna Grant*, December 6, 1775. Widow Marsh died November 13, 1838, aged 90.

CHILDREN.

580. Ebenezer Grant *Marsh*, born February 2d, 1777; died November 16, 1803.
581. Ann " " November 17, 1778.
582. Mary " " May 29, 1782.
583. Abigail " " May 24, 1784.
584. Lydia " " February 28, 1786.
585. John " " April 2, 1788. He was pastor of the Congregational Church, of Haddam, for many years, and afterward secretary of the American Temperance Union until his death, about 1872.

407.

LYDIA BULKELEY, daughter of Hon. John and Mary *Gardner* Bulkley, born October 21, 1739; married *Captain Robert Latimer*. No record of children has been found.

408.

MARY BULKELEY, daughter of Hon. John and Mary *Gardiner* Bulkeley, born Nov. 15, 1743; married *George B. Hurlburt*, and died without issue.

411.

ELIPHALET BULKELEY, son of Hon. John and Mary *Gardiner* Bulkeley, born Aug. 8, 1746; married *Anna Bulkeley*, of New London, Sept. 16, 1767.

CHILDREN.

586.	Lydia Ann,	born	May 18, 1768; m. *Col. Daniel Watrous.*
587.	Mary Adams,	"	June 25, 1770; m. *James Worthington.*
588.	John Charles,	"	Aug. 8, 1772; m. *Sally Taintor.*
589.	Patience,	"	Dec. 1774; m. *Charles Chapman.*
590.	Jonathan,	"	July 8, 1777; m. *E. Simons.*
591.	Pettis,	"	April 30, 1780.
592.	Eliphalet,	"	April 22, 1782; not married; died some years since, near Austin, Texas.
593.	Sarah Chauncey,	"	July 24, 1784; m. *James Bolton.*
594.	Fanny,	"	April 6, 1787; m. *Henry Lamb.*
595.	Orlando,	"	Jan. 19, 1793.
596.	Julia,		m. *Steuben Butler.*

412.

LUCY BULKELEY, daughter of Hon. John and Mary *Gardiner* Bulkeley, born August 2, 1749; married Capt. *John Lamb*, of Groton.

414.

SARAH BULKELEY, daughter of Gershom and Abigail *Robbins* Bulkeley, born January 10, 1735; married *Joseph Isham*, Jan. 17, 1765, by whom she had four children, and died January 9, 1773. After her decease, Mr. Isham married *Esther Taintor*, August 18, 1774.

CHILDREN.

597.	Alfred,	born Feb. 20, 1766; died Oct. 12, 1768.
598.	David,	" Aug. 18, 1767; died Aug. 31, 1767.
599.	Alfred, 2d,	" Aug. 30, 1769.
600.	Sarah,	" Nov. 23, 1771.

415.

JOHN BULKELEY, son of Gershom and Abigail *Robbins* Bulkeley, born Aug. 23, 1738; married *Judith Worthington*, Jan. 11, 1759.

CHILDREN.

601.	John,	born Oct. 7, 1759; m. *Theodora Foote.*
602.	William,	" Aug. 30, 1761; m. *Mary Champion.*
603.	Gershom,	" Oct. 3, 1763.
604.	Elijah,	" Jan. 29, 1766; m. *Pamela Loomis.*
605.	Nabby,	" Dec. 30, 1769; m. *Roger Taintor.*
606.	Joshua Robbins,	" Nov. 2, 1771; m. *Sally Taintor.*
607.	Mary,	" Feb. 2, 1774; m. *Aaron Buckland.*
608.	Judith,	" Jan. 30, 1775; m. *Solomon Taintor.*
609.	Gurdon,	" March 15, 1777; m. 1. *Fanny Wright*; 2. *Nancy Porter.*
610.	Gad,	" Feb. 20, 1779; m. *Orra Barstow.*
611.	Lydia,	" April 25, 1781; m. 1. *John Worthington*; 2. Dr. *William Mason.*
612.	Dan,	" March 20, 1784; m. *Phebe Burnet.*
613.	Harriet,	" Jan. 22, 1787; m. *Samuel Moseley.*

116.

JOSHUA BULKELEY, son of Gershom and Abigail *Robbins* Bulkeley, born Feb. 24, 1741; married *Lois Day*, Nov. 9, 1761. Said Lois was born March 13, 1744. Joshua Bulkeley died Jan. 22, 1821, aged 80. Mrs. Lois Bulkeley died July 8, 1812.

CHILDREN.

614.	Gurdon,	born July 1, 1764; died June 26, 1776.
615.	Anna,	" Oct. 18, 1770; died July 5, 1776.
616.	Sarah,	" Oct. 9, 1779.

117.

DANIEL BULKELEY, son of Gershom and Abigail *Robbins* Bulkeley, born May 13, 1744; married *Dorothy Olmsted*, Aug. 16, 1764. Capt. Daniel Bulkeley died July 20, 1810.

CHILDREN.

617.	A son,	born and died, Feb. 23, 1765.
618.	Daniel,	" Aug. 19, 1766.
619.	Ichabod,	" Sept. 23, 1769; died ——
620.	Eunice,	" April 14, 1772; m. *Roger Foote.*
621.	Dorothy,	" Oct. 8, 1774; died Nov. 17, 1776.
622.	Oliver,	" Jan. 24, 1776; m. *Sophia Foote.*
623.	Joshua,	" June 5, 1778.
624.	Dorothy, 2d,	" July 11, 1780.

118.

EUNICE BULKELEY, daughter of Gershom and Abigail *Robbins* Bulkeley, born May 14, 1747; married *Elisha Lord*, May 25, 1769.

She died April 2. 1796, and Mr. Lord married *Sarah Olmsted*, Nov. 12, 1797.

CHILDREN.

625.	Abigail Robbins *Lord*,	born July 14, 1770.
626.	Elisha, } twins,	" " Feb. 12, 1773.
627.	Eunice,	
628.	Lucy,	" " Aug. 16, 1775.
629.	Gershom,	" " Oct. 27, 1777.
630.	Russell,	" " June 3, 1780.
631.	Amasa,	" " Feb. 22, 1783.
632.	Alfred,	" " Sept. 13, 1785.
633.	Ralph,	" " March 6, 1790.
634.	Oliver,	" " May 6, 1792.
635.	Jervis, } twins,	" " Dec. 24, 1794. died Sept., 1795.
636.	Ogden,	died Dec. 24, 1795.

419.

DANIEL BULKELEY, son of Gershom and Abigail *Robbins* Bulkeley, born July 18, 1749; married *Hannah Beckwith*, Dec. 18, 1781, and had one child, and perhaps others.

CHILD.

637. David, born about Sept. 24, 1783; m. *Sally Chapman.*

420.

ROGER BULKELEY, son of Gershom and Abigail *Robbins* Bulkeley, born September 14, 1751. He was three times married—1, to *Jerusha Root*. She died July 27, 1788. 2, to *Rhoda Loomis*, who died June 15, 1807. 3, to *Polly Bulkeley*, widow of William Bulkeley, *nee Polly Champion*, November 15, 1808. Mr. Roger Bulkeley died August 1, 1819.

CHILDREN BY THE FIRST MARRIAGE.

638.	Benjamin Root, born August 25, 1772; died October 25, 1776.
639.	Asa,	" April 24, 1774; married Sophia Loomis.
640.	Benjamin Root 2d, born September 2, 1776.
641.	Roger,	" May 4, 1778; died September 22, 1785.
642.	George,	" March 8, 1780; married Sophia Loomis.
643.	Gershom,	" May 19, 1783; died November 1, 1783.
644.	Roger 2d,	" May 6, 1786.
645.	Gershom 2d,	" May 14, 1788.

425.

CHARLES BULKELEY, son of Charles and Ann *Latimer* Bulkeley, born December 19, 1752. The following historical sketch was published in the *New London Morning News* at the time of his decease, February 25, 1848:

CAPTAIN BULKLEY.

"Captain Charles Bulkley, an aged citizen of this place, recently deceased, was born in Colchester, 19th of December, 1752, and at the time of his death was 95 years and 2 months old. Longevity appears sometimes to be an inheritance. His mother died in 1811, at the age of 90 years.

"His father, Major Charles Bulkley, was son of Rev. John Bulkley, of Colchester, a divine of great eminence in his day, and grandson of Rev. Gersham Bulkley, the second minister of New London, and afterwards minister of Wethersfield. The mother of Major Charles Bulkley was Patience, daughter of Captain John Prentis, of New London. Major Bulkley himself married Ann, daughter of Jonathan and Borradil Latimer, of New London, and removed to this place from Colchester when his son, Charles, was about two years of age. Here he purchased of Deacon Thomas Fosdick the property on Bank Street, both sides of the way, which, with some addition, has ever since continued in the family. He went into business in this town, and was honored with several offices of public trust, but was suddenly removed by death in the year 1762, when he was about 52 years of age. He is interred in our old burial ground, where a moss-covered stone shows the place of his rest.

"His son, Charles, went early to sea, and was an expert and thorough seaman when the war of the revolution broke out. Many pages might be written, full of romantic interest, and yet literally true, relating to the adventures of our townsmen at that period. They were a community of mariners—all the young men went to sea—and were early inured to bear and defy every kind of peril that could beset them upon the broad ocean. Along this coast and in the sound during the eight years of warfare many hard conflicts took place, and many brilliant exploits were performed, which, though only of local and minor importance in the result, are worthy of being rescued from oblivion. They show, at least, the hardihood of our people at that time, the fortitude with which they endured suffering and exposure, and the patriotic devotion to the cause of liberty, which often led them into combat against fearful odds and brought them off victorious.

"Perhaps none of our townsmen at that period met with more wild and perilous adventures than Charles Bulkley. In the spring of 1775 a sloop from New London, which had been on a peaceful trading voyage to the West Indies, was rounding Montauk Point, and had almost arrived in sight of home, when an armed vessel bore down upon her, fired a shot athwart her course, and demanded her surrender. The sloop being unarmed, and totally unprepared for defence or escape, was, of course, given up. The armed vessel was a tender from the British frigate Rose, commanded by Captain Wallace, who was then stationed on this coast, and who afterwards became notorious for his bombardment of Stonington, and for plundering and annoying the inhabitants on the sea-coast to the eastward. The nephew of Captain Wallace came on board the sloop with four men, took possession, and informed the Americans that a battle had been fought at Lexington, and, of course, war had commenced. He transferred the crew of the sloop to the tender, with the exception of the captain, mate, and Charles Bulkley, who was a seaman on board. These he retained to navigate the vessel, and ordered them to shape their course for Boston, where he should take his prize.

"Not long after this change was accomplished a boat from the neighboring shore with two men in it approached the vessel. Wallace armed his men with such weapons as he could find, (harpoons and hand spikes,) and ordered the men in the boat to keep off, which they did. He could not fire upon them, for it happened that there was but one gun on board, and in the first moments of capture Bulkley, with quick foresight, had secreted the powder and ball. As the boat pushed off a bold expedient rushed into Bulkley's mind, which was executed as soon as conceived. He ran along on the boom, plunged into the ocean, got into the boat, and imparting his spirit and activity to the other two men, they pulled for Block Island, and were soon safe on shore. Here he found a small body of militia engaged in taking off some cattle to secure them from the plunder of the British. He made known to the commander a plan he had formed to wrest from the enemy their prize, and was readily furnished by him with two row-boats and a number of men and arms, with which he set out in chase of the sloop. He was so fortunate as to get possession of her without bloodshed. The next day she was towed into New London and delivered up to the owners, and young Wallace and his men were consigned as prisoners to the civil authority.

"Soon after this we find Charles Bulkley a midshipman in the newly-formed American navy, and sailing in the fleet fitted out at New London under Commodore Hopkins. This little fleet had been a source of much solicitude and expense to Congress. It was intended to annoy the British armed vessels that infested the coasts of the Southern States, and much was expected from its gallantry. It left New London harbor in fine style, the stars and stripes on its flag—*thirteen stars and thirteen stripes*—streaming out on the wind. Yet this fleet accomplished nothing but the plunder of the island of Providence, and the chief officers were afterwards censured by Congress for their inactivity. On the homeward voyage, however, just eastward of Montauk Point, they had a sharp engagement with the British frigate Glasgow, which was considerably injured, and only escaped by the skill and tact of its commander. In this action, fought very near the spot where less than a year before he had displayed such signal energy and adroitness, young Bulkley was distinguished for the cool intrepidity with which he stood at his gun.

"He remained several years in the navy, was soon made a sailing master, and then advanced to a lieutenancy. He made one cruise with the valiant Paul Jones, and was afterwards transferred to the Alfred, commanded by Captain Elisha Hinman. This vessel being overtaken by a superior force, and basely deserted by her consort, was taken, and the crew carried prisoners to England. Lieutenant Bulkley, with others, was confined in Falkland Prison, where he suffered a weary confinement, and was subjected to great privations and indignities. He at length made his escape, by secretly digging, with great labor and perseverance, a trench under ground, leading beyond the outward wall, and succeeded in getting to France, from whence, after some delay, he returned to America.

"On reaching home, without waiting to repose or recruit, he took command of a privateer, and hurried again to sea. In this capacity he made several voyages, and brought a number of valuable prizes into port. After the conclusion of the war he gladly returned to the peaceful merchant service, in which he continued for a long term of years. It would be interesting to know the number of voyages which a man of so much activity in the course of so long a life had made. We may safely say that they must be estimated by hundreds.

"This is but an imperfect tribute to the memory of a brave man, a skillful navigator, an estimable and venerable citizen, one who for almost a century has walked these streets, and sailed on these waters. It is one of the penalties of longevity to outlive old friends and time-endeared acquaintances, and often too the cherished companion of the household and hearthstone. Captain Bulkley had great afflictions of this kind for his portion. Not only neighbors and friends, and a generation of townsmen, and the companions of his youth went before him, but he lived to see most of his children laid in the grave. He leaves behind no descendants but one only son.—F. M. C."

CHILD.

646. Leonard, born . He was a bachelor, and died leaving a large fund by will for the establishment of an academy at New London, which should go into operation when it should amount to $50,000. The academy is now in operation.

426.

PETER BULKELEY, JUN., son of Peter and Lucy *Avery* Bulkeley, born Feb. 3, 1744; married *Hannah Breed*, of Stonington, March 9, 1768.

CHILDREN.

647.	Peter,	born July 22, 1770.
648.	Prentice,	" June 11, 1772.
649.	Hannah,	" Aug. 25, 1775.
650.	Lucy,	" March 9, 1778.

427.

WILLIAM BULKELEY, son of Peter and Lucy *Avery* Bulkeley, born ——; married *Polly Champion*, Dec. 18, 1788.

CHILDREN.

651.	A son,	born and died, 1790.	
652.	Henry,	} twins, " June 16, 1791.	
653.	Epaphroditus,		died Jan. 26, 1807.
654.	Mary,	" July 13, 1793.	
655.	William,		died May 11, 1801.

SEVENTH GENERATION.

458.

JOHN BULKELEY, son of John and Honor *Francis* Bulkely, born Nov. 10, 1750; married *Sarah Wright*. He had by her, two children, who were baptized after his death.

BULKELEY FAMILY. 115

CHILDREN.

656. John, baptized Nov. 30, 1783; m. —— *Daggett.*
657. Elizabeth? (Patty), " Nov. 30, 1783; m. *James Goodrich.*

459.

HONOR BULKELEY, daughter of John and Honor *Francis* Bulkeley, born March 14, 1753; married *Sylvanus Brown.*

CHILDREN.

658. William   Brown.
659. Austin   "
660. John Bulkeley "
661. George Washington "
662. A daughter—name unknown.
663. A daughter—name unknown.

461.

ELIZABETH BULKELEY, daughter of John and Honor *Francis* Bulkeley; married *John Mygatt.*

CHILD.

664. Thomas Mygatt, born —— m. *Miss Gay.*

462.

FRANCIS BULKELEY, son of John and Honor *Francis* Bulkeley, baptized July 31, 1757; married, 1. *Rhoda Griswold*, Jan. 18, 1781. She died March 6, 1795; and he married, 2. *Elizabeth Fosdick*, Jan. 5, 1797. He died Nov. 11, 1803, on board the brig Ontario, Capt. Timothy Stillman, master, of Wethersfield, Conn.

CHILDREN BY THE FIRST MARRIAGE.

665. William,   born Nov. 11, 1781; died in 1802, on board brig Ontario, T. Stillman, master.
666. Clarissa,   " March 20, 1784; m. *Charles Noyes.*
667. Harriet,   " April 13, 1786; died in infancy.
668. Francis,   " Nov. 6, 1788.
669. Chauncey,   " June 12, 1790; died in infancy.
670. Harriet, 2d, " Feb. 4, 1795; died in infancy.

CHILDREN BY THE SECOND MARRIAGE.

671. Chauncey,   born Jan. 16, 1798. The following notice of him appears in the obituary record of Yale College: "Chauncey Bulkeley died in Philadelphia, May 23, 1860, in his 62d year. He was born in Wethersfield, Conn., Jan. 16, 1698, being a son of Francis Bulkeley, of that town, and a descendant of Rev.

Peter Bulkeley, of Concord, Mass. After graduating, he taught school in Philadelphia for about a year, and then for three years he was an instructor in the college at Germantown, Penn. He studied law with Charles Chauncey, Esq., of Philadelphia, was admitted to the bar May 20, 1822, and resided in that city engaged in practice. In 1832 and 1833 he was Secretary and Treasurer of the Germantown and Morristown Railroad Company. From 1845 to 1850, he was one of the Aldermen of the city of Philadelphia. After this, he resumed the practice of his profession until his death."

At a meeting of the bar, May 25, 1860, Col. J. Gooshman was called to the chair, and Henry Paul Bush appointed Secretary, when Gen. Horatio Hubbell submitted the following resolutions, after an address, in which a brief outline of the character of the deceased and his professional standing was communicated to the meeting.

Resolved, That we have heard with deep regret of the sudden death of Chauncey Bulkeley, Esq., a member of this bar.

Resolved, That we have always recognized Mr. Bulkeley as an accomplished scholar, an upright counsellor, and honest man.

Resolved, That we will attend his funeral, and wear crape upon the arm in respect for his memory, thirty days.

Resolved, That a committee be appointed to convey to the family of the deceased a copy of the foregoing resolutions, which were ordered to be published.

A committee was accordingly appointed.

672. James Henry, born July 23, 1799; m. *Adaline Alexander.*
673. Charles, " April 27, 1801.

465.

EDWARD BULKELEY, son of John and Honor *Francis* Bulkeley, born in 1767; married *Diana Bunce*, in 1794.

CHILDREN.

674. Honor Francis, born 1795; m. *Joel Chaping*, 1823.
675. John Bunce, " 1797; died at Port au Prince, in 1822, unmarried.
676. Eliza, " 1799; m. *Richard Green.*
677. Edward, " 1801; m. *Lucy Mansfield.*
677½. Wealthy, " 1804; m. *Jesse St. John.*

BULKELEY FAMILY.   117

466.

SARAH BULKELEY, daughter of John and Honor *Francis* Bulke, born in 1770; married Mr. *Boskwick.*
Nothing further is known.

472.

THOMAS BULKELEY, son of Benjamin and Susannah *Kirby* Bulkeley, born October 2, 1758; married *Bathsheba Sage.*

CHILDREN.

678. George.
679. Laura.
680. Fanny.
681. Henry.
682. Sophia.

473.

LUCY BULKELEY, daughter of Benjamin and Susannah *Kirby* Bulkeley, born Sept. 18, 1760; married *Joseph* White, of Whitesborough, New York, April 4, 1782.

683.	Susan	*White,*	born Feb. 6, 1783.
684.	Lucy	"	" July 22, 1784; m. 1. *Orran Clark,* of Farmington, Conn.; 2, *Jesse Stanley.*
685.	Huldah	"	" April 19, 1786; died in infancy.
686.	Henry	"	" Feb. 8, 1788; m. *Julia Bidwell.*
687.	Abigail	"	" Aug. 26, 1789; m. *Samuel Wilcox.*
688.	Bulkeley	"	" March 10, 1791; died in infancy.
689.	Bulkeley	"	" May 2, 1793; died in infancy.
690.	Joseph	"	" Dec. 10, 1794; m. ——
691.	Thomas Bulkeley	"	" Feb. 3, 1797; m., and had a family.
692.	Eliza	"	" Nov. 8, 1798; m. *Reuben Wilcox.*
693.	Mary	"	" 1800; m. *Henry Cooley.*

474.

GEORGE BULKELEY, son of Benjamin and Susannah *Kirby* Bulkeley, born Nov. 28, 1762; married *Martha Webster.*

475.

HULDAH BULKELEY, daughter of Benjamin and Susannah *Kirby* Bulkeley, born Oct. 1, 1764; married *John Francis,* Jun., of Wethersfield, Nov. 8, 1792.

CHILDREN.

694.	Caroline	*Francis,*	born April 21, 1794.
695.	Huldah	"	" Jan. 16, 1796.

696.	John	*Francis,*	born July 30, 1797.
697.	James Bulkeley	"	" June 9, 1799.
698.	William	"	" March 12, 1801.
699.	Stephen	"	" Dec. 14, 1802.
700.	Albert	"	" Dec. 5, 1808.

476.

JAMES BULKELEY, son of Benjamin and Susannah *Kirby* Bulkeley, born Sept. 11, 1766; married *Caroline Hallam*, ——; died in Charleston, S. C. She is said to have died without children.

477.

STEPHEN BULKELEY, son of Benjamin and Susannah *Kirby* Bulkeley, born Nov. 8, 1768; married Miss *Margaret M. Fanning*, of Charleston, S. C. After a prosperous mercantile career, he purchased the Charter Oak place, in Hartford, Conn., and resided there many years, until his death, in 1840.

CHILDREN.

701. George.
702. Caroline,   m. *I. W. Stuart.*

478.

ABIGAIL BULKELEY, daughter of Benjamin and Susannah *Kirby* Bulkeley, born Dec. 30, 1770; married *Jasper Lacy*, and removed to ——, Ohio.

Nothing further is known.

479.

MARTHA BULKELEY, daughter of Benjamin and Susannah *Kirby* Bulkeley, born April 26, 1773; married *George Webster*, of Whitesboro, New York.

No further returns have been received.

480.

HANNAH BULKELEY, daughter of Benjamin and Susannah *Kirby* Bulkeley, born June 25, 1775; married *Amos Woodruff*, of Stockbridge, Mass.

The names of children have not been received.

481.

BENJAMIN BULKELEY, JUN., son of Benjamin and Elisabeth *Brownwell* Bulkeley, baptized May 13, 1784; married *Sarepta Woodruff*, daughter of Solomon Woodruff, of Farmington, Conn.

CHILDREN.

704.	Martha,	born
705.	Lucy,	"
706.	Samuel,	"
707.	Julia,	"

482.

SAMUEL BULKELEY, son of Benjamin and Elisabeth *Brownwell* Bulkeley, born June 6, 1784; married Mrs. *Eliza P. Harkin*, (nee Hough,) Oct. 19, 1814. He died July 8, 1867, aged 83. She died Nov. 9, 1872, aged 90.

CHILDREN.

708.	William Foster,	born Sept. 5, 1816; m. *Mary F. Stacy.*
709.	Samuel Francis,	" Aug. 8, 1818; m. *Mary F. Sanger.*
710.	Nancy Hough,	" Sept. 3, 1820; m. *Joshua H. Poole.*
711.	Mary Saunders,	" March 10, 1822; m. *Abijah Peabody.*
712.	Albert Harkin,	" July 9, 1825; m. *Angeline Augusta Clark.*

483.

BROWNWELL BULKELEY, son of Benjamin and Elisabeth *Brownwell* Bulkeley, baptized Feb. 16, 1786; married *Dolly North*, of Farmington, Conn., and removed to Coventry, Chenango County, N. Y.

CHILDREN.

713.	George,	born Nov. 20, 1814; m. *Esther Pendleton.*
714.	Francis,	" April 16, 1819; m. *Grace Joella Adams.*

484.

BETSEY BULKELEY, daughter of Benjamin and Elisabeth *Brownwell* Bulkeley, born about 1787; married *Philo Yale*, and died childless, in July, 1864.

485.

CHARLES BULKELEY, son of Charles and Mary *Griswold* Bulkeley, born March 9, 1760; married *Eunice Robbins*, Oct. 15, 1782. They reside in Wethersfield, Conn.

CHILDREN.

715.	Mary,	born April 8, 1785; m. *Thomas Selden*, of E. Haddam.
716.	Augusta,	" Jan. 26, 1787; never married; died in New York City, April 18, 1859.
717.	Henry,	" March 7, 1789; m. *Betsey Dodd*, April 15, 1812.

120   BULKELEY FAMILY.

718. Archibald,	} twins,	m. *Wealthy Ann Burr*, Sept., 1815.
719. Ashbel,		born April 6, 1792.
		m. *Ann Eliza Fanning*, May 25, 1816.
720. Erastus,	} twins, "	m. *Mary Wallbridge*, Sept. 2, 1824.
		Nov. 6, 1798.
721. Emeline Mehitable,		m. *S. H. P. Hall*, May 14, 1826.

486.

MARY BULKELEY, daughter of Charles and Mary *Griswold* Bulkeley, baptized June 15, 1764; is supposed to have married *Elisha Wetherell*, Jan. 26, 1785.

CHILDREN.

722. Daniel Bulkeley *Wetherell*,	baptized Aug. 4, 1785; died Dec. 27, 1786.
723. Harriet "	" May 6, 1787.
724. Polly, "	" Sept. 6, 1789.

490.

NANCY BULKELEY, daughter of Charles and Mary *Griswold* Bulkeley, baptized April 27, 1777; married *Joshua Goodrich*, October 25, 1800.

CHILDREN.

725. Walter Bulkeley *Goodrich*,	baptized May 22, 1803.
726. Oliver Butler "	" May 27, 1804.
727. George Williams "	" April 27, 1806.
728. Martha Elvira "	" April 16, 1809.
729. Eli "	" Sept. 22, 1811.
730. Jerusha "	" Aug. 27, 1815.

491.

CHARLES BULKELEY, son of Charles and Mary *Griswold* Bulkeley; married *Hannah Buckerts*, of Wethersfield, Oct. 5, 1806.

493.

ROXA BULKELEY, daughter of Edward and Rachel *Pomeroy* Bulkeley; baptized Oct. 25, 1772; was married to *Selah Francis*, of Wethersfield, Feb. 25, 1793.

CHILDREN.

731. Selah *Francis*.
732. Roxa "

497.

FANNY BULKELEY, daughter of Edward and Prudence *Williams* Bulkeley, born April 29, 1781. He was married to *Elihu Frisbie*, of Albany, N. Y., October 29, 1813.

CHILDREN.

733. Fanny *Frisbie.*
734. Elihu "

501.

PRUDENCE BULKELEY, daughter of Edward and Prudence *Williams* Bulkeley, baptized April 1, 1787; married Ebenezer Parker, of Boston, Mass., August 9, 1812.

CHILD.

735. Ebenezer *Parker.*

506.

NANCY BULKELEY, daughter of Prescott and Lois *Williams* Bulkeley, born October 1, 1781; married Dr. *Nathan North*, of Farmington, Conn., August 4, 1805. He died April 28, 1860.

CHILDREN.

736. Alfred *North*, born March 10, 1807, at Exeter, N. H. He married *Minerva Bryan.*
737. Henry *North*, " 1811; died October, 1814.
738. Charles, " " 1813; died October, 1814.
739. Theresa Orne Bulkeley *North*, born July 22, 1815; married *Ezra Sterling Ely*, February, 1843.
740. Laura Bulkeley *North*, born January 18, 1818.
741. Lydia *North*, born January 20, 1820; died September, 1829.
742. Anna Langdon *North*, born July 30, 1823. Unmarried, and resides at Cheektowaga, N. Y.

508.

LOUISA BULKELEY, daughter of Prescott and Lois *Williams* Bulkeley, born January 31, 1786; married *John G. Post*, of Pompton, N. J., May 6, 1806, and died at Booneville, N. Y., April 22, 1863.

CHILDREN.

743. A son born and died in 1807.
744. Mary *Post*, born July 20, 1809.
745. Louisa " " May 23, 1811.
746. Gerrit Prescott *Post*, " November 9, 1812; married *Ruth Keith.*
747. Peter Bulkeley " born July 25, 1817.
748. Sophia *Post*, " November 3, 1820.
749. John Williams *Post*, " December 16, 1822; died at Booneville, April 26, 1842.
750. George Ryerson *Post*, " May 1, 1824.

509.

LYDIA BULKELEY, daughter of Prescott and Lois *Williams* Bulkeley, baptized February 24, 1788; married *Peter Irwin*, of New Jersey, in 1808; died at Booneville, N. Y., July 12, 1811.

CHILDREN.

752. A daughter, born in 1809; died in infancy.
753. Cornelius Bulkeley *Irwin*, born June 7, 1811; married *Maria North*.

511.

BELINDA BULKELEY, daughter of Prescott and Lois *Williams* Bulkeley, baptized August 29, 1790; married Dr. *Samuel Bass*, January 1, 1811, and died at Leyden. N. Y., March 12, 1841.

CHILDREN.

754. Louisa Bulkeley *Bass*, born October 26, 1812; died May 25, 1815.
755. Charles North " " August 30, 1816; married *Juliette Burnham*.

514.

MARY BULKELEY, daughter of Joseph and Mary *Williams* Bulkeley, born December 18, 1778; married *Joseph Butler*, May 23, 1803.

CHILDREN, BAPTIZED AT ROCKY HILL.

756. Mary Williams *Butler*, May 14, 1806.
757. Juliana " May 21, 1809.
758. Cornelia " November 15, 1812; married Benjamin Smith.
759. Eunice Robbins " September 10, 1814.
760. Joseph Henry Bulkeley *Butler*, August 2, 1818.
761. Nancy " June 18, 1820.

515.

RHODA BULKELEY, daughter of Joseph and Mary *Williams* Bulkeley, born June 21, 1781; married *Wyllis Williams*, June 19, 1799.

CHILDREN.

762. George Lewis *Williams*, baptized August 11, 1801; died July 31, 1803.
763. Ralph Henry " " April 24, 1803; died young.
764. Mary Bulkeley " " June 16, 1805; married John Edwards.
765. Lorenzo Lewis " " April 24, 1808.
766. Ralph Wyllis " " November 10, 1811; married *Sarah Arnold*, December 7, 1836.

516.

RALPH BULKELEY, son of Joseph and Mary *Williams* Bulkeley, born September 14, 1783; married *Elisabeth Bradford*, January 21, 1808.

518.

EDMUND BULKELEY, son of Joseph and Mary *Williams* Bulkeley, born Dec. 6, 1787; married *Nancy Robbins*, April 18, 1811.

CHILDREN.

767. Joseph Edmund, born Feb. 9, 1812; m. *Mary Lawrence Bicknell*.
768. Justus Robbins, " June 15, 1813; m. *Mary K. Adams*.
769. Julius Huntington, " March 9, 1815; died at Washington, N. C., July 30, 1833.
770. Susan Mansfield, " April 30, 1825; died of cholera, in New York, Sept. 30, 1832.

520.

HENRY BULKELEY, son of Joseph and Mary *Williams* Bulkeley, born June 11, 1793; was for many years Town Clerk of Rocky Hill; represented the town in the Legislature of the State, and held other important offices of trust. He married *Martha Tucker*, May 16, 1847. He died June 10, 1860.

CHILDREN.

771. Henry Williams, born June 30, 1847.
772. Martha Robbins, " Dec. 31, 1848.
773. May, " Feb. 23, 1850.
774. Joseph, " Oct. 16, 1851.
775. Walter, " June 1, 1853.
776. John, " Feb. 6, 1855.
777. Laura, " Nov. 22, 1856.
778. Julia, " Nov. 13, 1857.

521.

WALTER WILLIAMS BULKELEY, son of Joseph and Mary *Williams* Bulkeley, born Sept. 15, 1797; married *Lucy Robbins*, daughter of Levi Robbins, June 17, 1830. Was a merchant in Rocky Hill, Conn. Being in feeble health, he went South, and spent the winter of 1834, and lost his life on his return passage, March 2, 1834, by the burning of the steamboat on the Delaware river, near Philadelphia. An account of his unfortunate death is thus given by an aged member of the Bulkeley family:

In the winter of 1834, the steamboat Pennsylvania, of the Philadelphia and Baltimore passenger line, took fire on the passage up the Delaware river, was run on to the flats below the Navy Yard, Philadelphia, and burned to the water's edge. Among the passengers was a gentleman, in delicate health, returning to his home from a sojourn in the South, who threw overboard sundry settees, and committed himself to their buoyancy as a means of safety. This gentleman was rescued by some boats at hand completely wet through and chilled, and unfortunately taken into a low grogery, known as the Khouli Khan tavern, in Chestnut, above Front street.

Here in the course of the evening this gentleman died from the effects of this severe exposure upon his debilitated frame. A gentleman present had heard him say his name was Bulkeley, and speaking of his black silk neckerchief, also said, that it contained something valuable. These facts this gentleman communicated to Charles, J. H., and Chauncey Bulkeley, who immediately sought the aid of the then mayor, Hon. John Swift, in the matter. The party proceeded at once to the tavern spoken of; found deceased there, and the cravat missing. The mayor, addressing himself to a female present, (whom he denominated a "Meg Merrilies" in aspect,) asked her for the missing article. She was then told (after denying knowledge of it) to produce the cravat forthwith, or the whole household would be marched to the lockup in short order. The missing neckerchief was found stowed away under the counter, unfolded, and found to contain several hundred dollars in bank notes. These the mayor took charge of, and the deceased was found to be the above Walter W. Bulkeley, of Rocky Hill, (Stepney, Conn.) Chauncey Bulkeley took charge of the remains, placed them in the care of an undertaker, notified the family, and Mr. Ralph Bulkeley, of New York, went to Philadelphia, identified and removed them to Rocky Hill, with the funds found.

CHILDREN.

779. Amelia, m. Rev. *Horace Williams.*
780. Susan M., m. *Hiram H. Webb*, of Rockingham, N. C., Oct. 8, 1855.

523.

ABIGAIL MILLER, daughter of Nathanael and Abigail *Butler* Miller, born ———; married *Asa Lamb*.

CHILDREN.

781. Abigail Lamb, born ———
782. Bushrod W. "   "
783. Melinda "   "

524.

CALEB MILLER, son of Nathanael and Abigail *Bulkeley* Miller, born Feb. 6, 1767; married *Dorothy Butler*, Oct. 15, 1795. They resided in Lodi, New York, where he died, Sept. 26, 1850; and she died April 27, 1853.

CHILDREN.

784. Mercy *Miller*, born Nov. 28, 1796, in Brookfield, New York;
m. *Braddock G. Brand*, April 27, 1815.

785.	Amanda	*Miller,*	born Oct. 13, 1798, in Brookfield, N. Y.; died at the age of six years.
786.	Urben Butler	"	" Dec. 31, 1800; m. *Anna Rees,* May 23, 1822.
787.	Solomon Bulkeley	"	" Sept. 12, 1803, in Brookfield, N. Y.; m. *Fanny Burton,* Dec. 26, 1828.
788.	Sylvester	"	" Nov. 24, 1806, in Brookfield, N. Y.; a lawyer; never married; died March 11, 1865.

525.

AMOS MILLER, son of Nathanael and Abigail *Bulkeley* Miller, born Feb. 3, 1769; married ——; died at sea, leaving two sons, names not known.

527.

REBECCA MILLER, daughter of Nathanael and Abigail *Bulkeley* Miller, born Jan. 7, 1776; married *George Button,* of Brookfield, Madison County, New York. Mr. Button died Oct., 1864. She died in Feb., 1812.

CHILDREN.

789.	Emery	*Button,*	born	
790.	Thankful	"	"	m. *Wm. Knapp,* Jan. 27, 1820.
791.	George	"	"	
792.	Fanny	"	"	
793.	Nancy	"	"	July 8, 1837; m. *Ariel T. Alderman.*
794.	Emy	"	"	
795.	Elijah	"	"	died at 21 years of age.

528.

ELIJAH BULKELEY MILLER, son of Nathanael and Abigail *Bulkeley* Miller, born July 22, 1783; married *Ruth Hall,* Jan. 21, 1808.

CHILDREN.

796.	Amanda	*Miller,*	born Feb. 15, 1809; m. *Horace Hall,* Dec. 25, 1828.
797.	Harriet	"	" August 28, 1812; died at 4 weeks of age.
798.	Adaline C.	"	" Nov. 3, 1814; m. Rev. *C. D. Burlingham,* Sept. 7, 1834.
799.	Hannah H.	"	" Jan. 30, 1819; m. *Charles Todd,* Oct. 13, 1844.
800.	Nathanael W.	"	" Oct. 9, 1820; m. *Juliaett Kenyon,* July 22, 1848.
801.	Charles V.	"	" April 27, 1825; died at 10 years of age.
802.	Hiram C.	"	" June 25, 1834; m. *Mary Canfield.*

530.

JAMES BULKELEY, son of Solomon and Martha *Williams* Bulkeley, born ——; married *Hannah Myears,* Feb. 14, 1802.

BULKELEY FAMILY.

CHILDREN.

803.	Sarah M.,	born Sept. 4, 1803; m. *Sylvester Goodrich.*
804.	Harriet,	" Nov. 30, 1805; m. *Rodolphus Griswold.*
805.	Julia,	" July 3, 1807; m. *Daniel Small.*
806.	James,	" Aug. 30, 1811; m. *Julia Risley.*
807.	George W.,	" Sept 6, 1814; m. *Lucy Sperry.*
808.	Eliza,	" Dec. 15, 1816; m. *Isaac Sperry.*
809.	Nancy,	" June 2, 1818; m. *Edward Risley.*
810.	Jane E.,	" April 7, 1822; m. *Joseph Latham.*
811.	William R.,	" April 7, 1825; m. *Emma S. Freeman.*

544.

JUSTUS BULKELEY, JUN., son of Justus and Mabel *Boardman* Bulkeley, born Nov. 18, 1803; married ——.

CHILDREN.

812.	Maria,	born	m. *Lyman Wilson.*
813.	Walter,		never married.
814.	Edwin.		
815.	Mary Amelia,		m. *Francis Chambers.*
816.	Harriet,		m. *Lester* ——.

546.

CHAUNCEY BULKELEY, son of Jehiel and Mary *Robbins* Bulkeley, baptized Sept. 8, 1782; married *Nancy Hart*, Aug. 27, 1805.

549.

LEONARD BULKELEY, son of Rev. Gershom Bulkeley; married *Polly Warner*, and resided at Cromwell. He died Feb. 20, 1826.

CHILDREN.

817.	Hannah,	m. *Charles Arnold*, of Hartford, Conn.
818.	William.	
819.	John.	

551.

AMELIA BULKELEY, daughter of Hosea and Abigail *Griswold* Bulkeley, born April 24, 1782. Was married to *Allen Robbins*, October 17, 1804.

CHILDREN.

820.	Thomas Stanley,	born October 17, 1805; m. 1, *Martha C. Sears*; 2, *Marabah M. Conner.*
821.	Chloe W.,	" January 9, 1808; m. *Frederick Marsh.*
822.	Mary A.,	" July 13, 1810. Unmarried.
823.	Allen A.,	" May 15, 1816; married *Abby Ann Goodrich.*
824.	Abigail U. B.,	" January 19, 1819; m. *Rev. Joshua L. Maynard.*
825.	Emily Webster,	" January 14, 1823; married *Robert Sugden, Jr.*

553.

JOHN G. BULKELEY, son of Hosea and Abigail *Griswold* Bulkeley, born January 3, 1785; married *Abigail Hart*, November 25, 1804. 2, Widow Mary Hubbard, January 12, 1830.

CHILDREN.

825¼.	William,	baptized July 26, 1818.			He was never married.
826.	Amelia Ann,	"	"	"	"	married *Norman Butler*.
827.	Ursula Bull,	"	"	"	"	married *Josiah Button*.
828.	John,	"	"	"	"	died unmarried at the age of 22.
829.	Hosea,	"	"	"	"	married
830.	Caroline Hart,	"	"	"	"	married *Philip Butler*.
831.	Benj. Griswold,	"	"	"	"	
832.	Frances,	"	"	"	"	married William Clark.

554.

DR. SYLVESTER BULKELEY, son of Hosea and Abigail *Griswold* Bulkeley, born June 1, 1787. He was twice married—1, to *Mary Johnson*, of Lyme. She died at Cromwell, March 2, 1824, aged 36. 2, To Nancy Bradford, of Rocky Hill, May 1, 1825. He died in 1857. The following obituary notice of him was prepared by Dr. Rufus W. Griswold:

DR. SYLVESTER BULKLEY.

"Sylvester Bulkley was the second son of Hosea Bulkley, of Rocky Hill, formerly a part of Wethersfield, in which place he was born in 1787. He was prepared for college by Rev. Calvin Chapin, D. D., of Rocky Hill, entered Yale in 1806, and graduated in 1810. The following winter he taught school in Wethersfield, meantime pursuing the study of medicine under the instruction of Dr. Daniel Fuller, of Rocky Hill. He then attended lectures in the medical department of Dartmouth College, Hanover, N. H., and received the degree of M. D. at that institution in 1812. Dr. Bulkley first commenced the practice of his profession in Haddam, where he remained about eight years, when he disposed of his business to a Dr. Munger, and went to Chester. There he remained but a short time, when he returned to that part of Haddam known as Higganum, in professional connection with Dr. Munger. A more favorable offer presenting itself, Dr. Buckley located in Upper Middletown, (now Cromwell,) where he remained in successful practice for about twelve years. He then relinquished his business in that place, and after spending a few months in New York and its neighborhood, availing himself of the facilities for acquiring medical knowledge there afforded, he returned and settled in Berlin. In that town he continued until 1848, when Rocky Hill being left without a resident physician, by the removal of Dr. A. W. Barrows to Hartford, Dr. Bulkley returned to his native place. Here he continued in the practice of his profession until within a few days of his death, though age and its consequent infirmities restricted the amount of his business for the latter part of the time.

"Dr. Bulkley was of a robust habit of body, and of vigorous constitution, and had good health, with the exception of attacks of rheumatism, which is hereditary in his family. In consequence, probably, of exposure and over exertion in visiting a patient in the severe weather of the season, he was taken sick the twenty-seventh of January last, and died the first of February, in the seventieth year of his age. His disease was an acute inflammation of that portion of the peritoneum covering the liver, which probably extended to the liver itself. For the first three days of his illness Dr. Bulkley expected to recover, and his physician thought him improving, but after this he passed into a state of total insensibility, and sank rapidly. He was attended by Dr. A. S. Warner, of Wethersfield, and once seen by Dr. E. K. Hunt, of Hartford, and myself. Dr. Bulkley was a member of the Hartford County Medical Society at the time of his decease, and had always felt a lively interest in all efforts for the promotion of the profession.

"Dr. Bulkley was an honest man, upright and straight forward in his dealings, an active and excellent member of society, of high moral character and correct habits of life, enjoying the esteem of his neighbors and acquaintances, and a sincere professing Christian. He became a member of the Congregational Church in Berlin during his residence in that town, and continued his connection there till his death, though an attendant on divine worship at Rocky Hill after his removal thither.

"As a physician Dr. Bulkley enjoyed a liberal patronage in the several localities where he resided. He stood well in the estimation of his brethren of the medical profession, and was on particularly confidential terms and often in consultation over the sick-bed with the late Drs. Richard Warner, of Cromwell, and Archibald Welch, of Wethersfield. Naturally of a strong mind and independent character, he had little disposition to yield to the foolish whims of his patients, when he saw that yielding would be prejudicial to their recovery; and his refusal to gratify them in this respect some times made enemies of those who should have had the greater regard for him for his firmness of purpose in their behalf. Considerations of policy, which often stand men instead of sound medical knowledge; subterfuge in conversation, which is a cover for professional ignorance; suavity of manner, which hides defects in the practice of medicine—upon these Dr. Bulkley did not altogether rely to gain the esteem of the families in which he practiced. He expected to benefit his patients rather by the potency of his remedies than by the grace of his bow; by the efficacy of his prescriptions, rather than by the ease of his conversation. Consequently, those who call a physician more for the purpose of having their diagnosis confirmed, and their views of the proper treatment supported by him, than for the sake of his medical advice and care, and who dislike him in proportion as he disagrees with their notions, often complained of Dr. Bulkley, when they would have done better to listen willingly to his counsel, and adhere trustingly to his orders. With quacks and quackery he had no patience, and quite as little with those who followed them. Of 'steam doctors,' 'consumption doctors,' and other like empyrics, he entertained a great abhorrence and contempt; and with the various isms in medicine that from time to time spring up to have a mushroom existence, he would have nothing to do. Correctly considering a proper medical education as indispensably necessary to the proper practice of the profession, and that the science must have a stable theory, based upon known facts for its foundation, in order to be deserving confidence, Dr. Bulkley had no part with those who 'take up' the trade without a thorough training in the various fundamental branches of the profession, and would have no counsel with interlopers, who had no other title to be called doctors than that bestowed by themselves alone.

"Dr. Bulkley lived to a ripe old age, in the enjoyment of respect and esteem, performing his duties, as a man and a physician, capably, faithfully, and honestly, and was gathered to his fathers in peace, like a shock of wheat fully ripe for the harvest.

Rocky Hill, April 28, 1857."

CHILDREN.

833. Sylvester, born ; died young at Cromwell.
834. William, " ; married *Lurania Belden.*
835. Mary Ann, " ; married *John Brandegee.*

555.

GERSHOM BULKELEY, son of Hosea and Abigail *Griswold* Bulkeley, born Feb. 11, 1789; married *Laura Goodrich*, July 4, 1816.

CHILD.

836. Martha G., born Dec. 11, 1826; m. *Lucius Beaumont*.

556.

MABEL BULKELEY, daughter of Hosea and Abigail *Griswold* Bulkeley, born Nov. 13, 1792; married *Ira Beaumont*, of East Hartford, Oct. 10, 1811.

CHILDREN.

837.	Edmund	born Sept. 2, 1812; m. *Elisabeth Church*.
838.	Ira O.,	" 1814; m. *Sarah Ann Douglass*.
839.	Lucius M.,	" Dec. 4, 1816; m. *Martha G. Bulkeley*.
840.	Charles G.,	" Dec. 24, 1818; m. *Mary Pratt*.
841.	Laura,	" March 30, 1820; m. *Alfred Smith*.
842.	Olive,	" 1822; died young.
843.	Thomas,	" ; m. *Josephine Peckwell*.
844.	Emeline,	" ; m. *Joseph McFarland*.
845.	Harriet L.,	" ; m. *John Lockwood*.

557.

OLIVE BULKELEY, daughter of Hosea and Abigail *Griswold* Bulkeley, born Sept. 1, 1794; married *Revilo Chapman*, May 29, 1823. Mr. Chapman was a merchant. They resided at Rocky Hill, Conn., where he died, Feb. 15, 1866, aged 72.

CHILDREN.

846. Henry B., born Jan. 25, 1825; died Aug. 4, 1842.
847. Amelia M., " Feb. 16, 1827; unmarried.
848. Sarah J., " Dec. 4, 1829; died June, 1874.

559.

ABIGAIL S. BULKELEY, daughter of Hosea and Abigail *Griswold* Bulkeley, born Jan. 20, 1799; married *Davis Smith*, March 18, 1819. Mr. Smith was for many years an Innkeeper in Haddam, and finally removed to Rocky Hill, Conn., where he resided as a farmer. He died in the Spring of 1875.

CHILDREN.

849. Abigail G., born Dec. 7, 1819, at Haddam; died April 25, 1821.
850. Abigail R., " Nov. 7, 1821, " m. *Moses Williams*.
851. Martha G., } twins, " Nov. 5, 1823, " died Sept. 25, 1826.
852. Mary I., } m. *Ambrose Wolcott*.

853.	Sarah Jane,	born March 9, 1826, at Haddam; died Aug. 25, 1826.	
854.	Henry Davis,	" Nov. 25, 1827,	" died Nov. 2, 1828.
855.	Henry Horace,	" Dec. 1, 1829,	" m. *Philippa Hubbard*.
856.	Martha Amelia,	" Feb. 11, 1832,	" m. *Walter S. Wilcox*.
857.	Margaret Ursula,	" Nov. 23, 1835, at Rocky Hill.	
858.	Caroline Eliza,	" July 1, 1838.	

562.

HONOR BULKELEY, daughter of Stephen and Martha *Marsh* Bulkeley, born May 5, 1774; married *David Edwards*, of Middletown, Nov. 16, 1795.

567.

ALLEN BULKELEY, son of Stephen and Martha *Marsh* Bulkeley, born March 30, 1783; married *Eliza Riley*.

CHILDREN.

860.	Ebenezer,	born	; m. *Anastasia Crittenden*. Several children.
861.	Harriet Abbot,	"	; m. *Henry Roberts*.
862.	Joseph,	"	; died in California, unmarried.
863.	Mary Jane,	"	; m. *William Spear*.

568.

FREDERICK BULKELEY, son of Stephen and Martha *Marsh* Bulkeley, born June 1, 1792; married *Nancy Riley*, Oct. 6, 1814. He died Sept. 24, 1850. She died Dec. 24, 1857.

CHILDREN.

864.	Martha,	born Oct. 15, 1815. She died unmarried, April 1, 1870.	
865.	Julia,	} twins,	unmarried.
866.	Jane,	" Jan. 2, 1819.	m. *Walter Edwards*.
867.	Nancy R.,	" Dec. 30, 1822; m. *Benjamin H. Turner*, Jan. 3, 1865. No children.	
868.	Stephen,	" May 6, 1825 ; m. *Prudence Warner*.	
869.	Kate E.,	" April 23, 1834.	

570.

BURRAGE BULKELEY, son of Stephen and Susan *Riley* Bulkeley, born   ; married *Caroline Miller*. They resided in the southeast part of Rocky Hill, in that section of the town called Dividend. He died Feb. 26, 1874.

CHILDREN.

870.	Henry W.,	born Sept. 25, 1833.
871.	Burrage,	" Jan. 15, 1836; lived 3 days.
872.	Albert,	" Jan. 26, 1838.
873.	Mary D.,	" Sept. 19, 1840; unmarried.
874.	Joseph A.,	" Nov. 3, 1843 ; m. *Emma Jane Whitmore*.
875.	Carrie M.,	" March 4, 1846; m. *Franklin E. Davenport*.

571.

WAIT BULKELEY, son of Stephen and Susan *Riley* Bulkeley, born March 4, 1807; was twice married, 1. To   ; 2. To *Charlotte Whitmore.*

CHILDREN.

876. Edward.
877. Mary.
878. Lucy.

577.

SALLY BULKELEY, daughter of Jonathan and Mary *Edwards* Bulkeley, baptized Dec. 2, 1787; married *Elisha Goodrich*, July 31, 1821.

CHILDREN.

879. Mary Eborn *Goodrich,*   born Oct. 1, 1822.
880. Henry B.,   "   " Nov. 10, 1824.

578.

NABBY BULKELEY, daughter of Jonathan and Mary *Edwards* Bulkeley, baptized in 1782; married *Isaac Stevens*, April 20, 1819.

CHILDREN.

881. Norman B.   *Stevens,*   born Jan. 25, 1820.
882. Frederick M.   "   " May 17, 1824.
883. Joseph H.   "   " Jan. 5, 1828.
884. George O.   "   " May 5, 1835.

579.

PRESCOTT BULKELEY, son of Jonathan and Mary *Edwards* Bulkeley, born Feb. 8, 1797; married *Penelope Tryon*, Sept. 15, 1822. Mr. Bulkeley died at the house of his daughter, Mrs. Martha E. Tyler, South Glastonbury, Dec. 16, 1874. Mrs. Penelope Bulkeley died about 10 years before her husband.

CHILDREN.

885. Lucy,   born June 17, 1823; m. *Hamilton Horton*, Aug. 1, 1844.
886. Laura,   " Feb. 8, 1825; m. *George Smith.*
887. Martha Edwards, " Jan. 8, 1827; m. *William Tyler*, Dec. 29, 1850.
888. Mary.
889. Mary.
890. Horace.
891. Walter,   m. *Electa Hunt*, in 1852.
892. Ellen Louise,   m. *Samuel Abbey*, May 15, 1866.
893. Harriet Griswold,   m. *Lyman Kellum*, Sept. 25, 1865.
894. Abby Jane,   m. *Henry Hutchinson.*
895. Noah Edwards,   born March 3, 1843; unmarried.
896. Imogene Lawrence,   " Nov. 7, 1851.

586.

LYDIA ANN BULKELEY, daughter of Eliphalet and Anna Bulkeley, born May 18, 1768; married *Daniel Watrous*. He died June 6, 1828.

CHILDREN.

897. Daniel Ellsworth *Watrous*, born June 22, 1792.
898. A daughter, born and died January 11, 1794.
899. Frederick Augustus *Watrous*, born November 25, 1795; died at New Orleans, where he had a family.
900. Nancy Bulkeley *Watrous*, born April 16, 1797.
901. John Charles " " July 30, 1800; died August 4, 1800.
902. John Charles 2d, " August 1, 1801; married . He had no children. He was a United States senator. He died in a state of mental imbecility.
903. Mary Jerusha *Watrous*, born August 9, 1803.
904. Nathanael Huntington *Watrous*, born February 13, 1808; died in Texas unmarried.

587.

MARY ADAMS BULKELEY, daughter of Eliphalet and Anna Bulkeley, born June 25, 1770. She was married to *Joseph Worthington*, of Colchester, September 10, 1791.

CHILDREN.

905. Nancy *Worthington*, born July 1, 1792.
906. Joseph " " September 6, 1795.
907. Eliphalet " " September 1, 1797.
908. Maria " " February 28, 1800.

588.

JOHN CHARLES BULKELEY, son of Eliphalet and Anna *Bulkeley*, born August 8, 1772; married *Sally Taintor*, December 22, 1798.

CHILDREN.

909. Charles Edwin, born October 16, 1799.
910. John Taintor, " October 3, 1801.
911. Eliphalet Adams," June 20, 1803.

589.

PATIENCE BULKELEY, daughter of Eliphalet and Anna Bulkeley, born December 17, 1774; married *Charles Chapman*, of Wilkesbarre, Penn., and died in Ohio.

590.

JONATHAN BULKELEY, son of Eliphalet and Anna Bulkeley, born July 8, 1777; married *Elisabeth Simons*, daughter of Joseph Simons, February 8, 1823. She was born March 28, 1806. He was a midshipman in the United States Navy about 1800, under Commodore Jewett, and assisted in the capture of Touissant, in the island of San Domingo. He was sheriff of Lucerne County, Pennsylvania, in 1824 or 1825. He died at Wilkesbarre, March 1, 1867, aged nearly 90.

CHILDREN.

912. Dr. J. E. A., born November 16, 1823; married *Clara C. Stark*.
913. Mary Ann, " March 24, 1826; died August 18, 1828.
914. Elisabeth, " May 1, 1828; died October 21, 1850.
915. Frances, " March 10, 1832; married *A. R. Brundage*, September 22, 1855.
916. Julia, " November 13, 1837; died August 30, 1838.
917. Charles L., " January 15, 1843. He is a lawyer and alderman of the city of Wilkesbarre, Penn.

593.

SARAH C. BULKELEY, daughter of Eliphalet and Anna Bulkeley born July 24, 1784; married *James Bolton*.

594.

FRANCES or FANNY BULKELEY, daughter of Eliphalet and Anna Bulkeley, born April 6, 1787; married *Henry Lamb*, of Wilkesbarre, Penn.

596.

JULIA BULKELEY, daughter of Eliphalet and Anna Bulkeley, born ——; married *Steuben Butler*, of Wilkesbarre, Penn.

CHILDREN.

918. William *Butler*.
919. George "
920. Edward "
921. Frances "
922. Gertrude "
923. Ellen "

600.

JOHN BULKELEY, son of John and Judith *Worthington* Bulkeley, born October 7th, 1759; married *Theodora Foote*, April, 1787, and he died October 10, 1788.

CHILD.

924. Roxy, born May 14, 1788; married *James M. Goodwin*, of East Hartford, December 21, 1809.

602.

WILLIAM BULKELEY, son of John and Judith *Worthington* Bulkeley, born August 30, 1761; married *Mary Champion*, December 18, 1788, and died May 11, 1801.

BULKELEY FAMILY.   135

CHILDREN.
925. An infant, born   ; died April, 1790.
926. Henry,   } married in Middle Haddam.
        twins, born June 16, 1791 ;
927. Epapbraditas,   } died January 26, 1807.
928. Mary, born July 13, 1793; married Charles Hurd, of Middle Haddam.

603.

GERSHOM BULKELEY, son of John and Judith *Worthington* Bulkeley, born October 3, 1763; married Widow Noble, and removed to Williamstown, Mass.

CHILDREN.
929. George, a lawyer who lived in Kinderhook.
930. William. He has had one child, and lived and died in New York.
931. Gershom.
932. Harriet; died unmarried.
933. Judith; married Platt Talcott, of Lanesborough.
934. Mary; died unmarried.

604.

ELIJAH BULKELEY, son of John and Judith *Worthington* Bulkeley, born January 29, 1766; married *Pamela* Loomis, April 22, 1787. He died July 31, 1842, aged 76.

CHILDREN.
935. John W., born January 22, 1788; died March 12, 1850. He was never married.
936. Richard, born December 26, 1789; married Aurel Chapman.
937. Celinda, " August 23, 1793; married, 1, *Alanson Porter*, of Williamstown; 2, *Russel Chapman*.
938. Emeline U., born September 12, 1806; married *Pomeroy Hall*.
939. Clarissa Pamela, born May 8, 1809; married *John T. Bulkeley*.
940. Sophia Maria, " November 15, 1811; married *Jonathan Chapel*.

605.

ABIGAIL or NABBY BULKELEY, daughter of John and Judith *Worthington* Bulkeley, born December 30, 1769; married *Roger Taintor*, December 6, 1789.

CHILDREN.
941. Clarissa, born September 19, 1790; died September 27, 1794.
942. John A. Taintor, April 22, 1800.

606.

JOSHUA ROBBINS BULKELEY, son of John and Judith *Worthington* Bulkeley, born November 2, 1771; married *Sally Taintor*, September 7, 1793. They lived and died in Williamstown, Mass.

136   BULKELEY FAMILY.

CHILDREN.
943. Clarissa, born   ; married *Job Pierson.*
944. Mary,   "   ; married *Parker Hall.*
945. John,   "   . He lived in Williamstown unmarried.
946. Abby,   "

610.

GAD BULKLEY, son of John and Judith *Worthington* Bulkeley, born February 20, 1779; married *Orra Barstow,* and settled in Canterbury, Conn.

CHILDREN.
947. Adaline, born   ; married *Jared Warner Fitch.*
948. John Worthington, born ; married, 1, *Adalaide Hillard;* 2, *Eliza Tracy;* 3, *Widow Helen Reynolds.*
949. Samuel Barstow, born January 21, 1813; married Mary Elisabeth Roath.
950. Simon Spalding, " November 11, 1815. Never married.

607.

MARY BULKELEY, daughter of John and Judith *Worthington* Bulkeley, born Feb. 2, 1774; married *Aaron Buckland.* She survived her husband, and lived with her sister Morcley, where she died, leaving no children.

608.

JUDITH BULKELEY, daughter of John and Judith *Worthington* Bulkeley, born Jan. 30, 1775; married *Solomon Taintor.*

CHILDREN.
951. Bulkeley *Taintor,*   lives in Brookfield, Mass.
952. Henry G.   "   lives in Hampton, Conn.

609.

GURDON BULKELEY, son of John and Judith *Worthington* Bulkeley, born March 15, 1777; married twice, 1. *Fanny Wright,* Nov. 22, 1798. She died Dec. 24, 1819. 2. *Nancy Porter,* Sept. 10, 1820. She died July 7, 1859. Mr. Bulkeley died June 13, 1845; the last survivor of eight brothers. His early life was passed at a time of great spiritual declension and worldliness in that vicinity, where no special efforts were made for the conversion of children, and yet he was, from a child, the subject of many serious impressions, and when in early manhood, he, with the wife of his youth, united with the Congregational church of Colchester, they were regarded as very young members.

In 1806 he removed to Williamstown, Mass., where, during a residence of nearly forty years, he exemplified the virtues of a sincere and active piety, by a zealous coöperation with his pastor, in private counsel, in social religious converse and prayer, going from house to house, and in the varied forms of usefulness presented by that series of revivals which signally blessed that region. The Rev. Ralph Welles Gridley, who was for some eighteen years his pastor, used to remark that Mr. B. was his right-hand man. Though a layman of moderate acquirements, he treasured up a large fund of practical religious knowledge, which, united with a happy faculty of winning the unconverted, often rendered his persuasions effectual upon more cultivated minds. They sought and improved occasions of private interview with the students of Williams College, and other young persons, when with great earnestness and force he urged the necessity of personal piety. He thought much of the conversion of children, and passed whole nights in prayer for the conversion of his own, whom he taught and governed with the faithfulness of a Christian father. To great firmness and energy of character he united a habit of great personal industry, literally doing with his might what he found to do. During his last illness from dropsy, he was for seven months an example of Christian patience, the happy result of his settled confidence that the anchor of his hope was cast within the vale. He so familiarized himself with the bright scenes in prospect, that his conversation and prayers evinced an ardent desire to depart and be with Christ. Without a struggle he fell asleep, "calmly as to a night of repose."

CHILDREN BY THE FIRST MARRIAGE.

953. Harriet Amelia, born Sept. 1, 1799; m. *Alvah Wheeler*, May 24, 1826.
954. Albert Rodney, " Oct. 14, 1802; m. *Delia Catharine Brown*, April, 1832.
955. Leander Wright, " Oct. 2, 1805; died July 28, 1820.
956. Hiram Worthington, " March 30, 1807; m. *Mary Jane Oliphant*, Dec. 10, 1834.
957. Sophia Adaline, " Oct. 20, 1808; m. *Benj. Franklin Hoxsey*, Sept., 1830.
958. Frances Emeline, " July 31, 1810; m. *George Clinton Wood*, Aug. 3, 1830.
959. Gurdon Henry, " March 27, 1812; m. *Susan Eliza Brown*, Dec. 4, 1834.
960. Aristarchus, " May 3, 1813; m. 1. *Mary Matilda Chamberlain*, March 27, 1834; 2. *Sarah E. Harrison*, Dec. 4, 1838.
961. Clarissa, " Jan. 15, 1816; m. *Hurlburt F. Fairchild*, Sept. 14, 1841.

962.	Ralph,	born April 9, 1817; m. *Mercy Briggs*, April, 1857.
963.	Dan Alonzo,	" Nov. 12, 1819; m. *Marietta Townsend*, Nov. 28, 1843.

CHILD BY THE SECOND MARRIAGE.

964.	Lucius Edwards,	born Jan. 17, 1824; m. *Mary King Tuthill*, May 17, 1852.

610.

GAD BULKELEY, son of John and Judith *Worthington* Bulkeley, born Feb. 20, 1779; married *Orra Barstow*, and settled in Canterbury, Conn.

CHILDREN.

965.	Adaline,	born
966.	John Worthington,	"
967.	Samuel Barstow,	"
968.	Simon Spalding,	"

611.

LYDIA BULKELEY, daughter of John and Judith *Worthington* Bulkeley, born April 25, 1781; was twice married: 1. To *John Worthington*; 2. To Dr. *William Mason*.

612.

DAN BULKELEY, son of John and Judith *Worthington* Bulkeley, born March 20, 1784; married *Phebe Burnett*.

613.

HARRIET BULKELEY, daughter of John and Judith *Worthington* Bulkeley, born Jan. 22, 1787; married *Samuel Mosely*.

620.

EUNICE BULKELEY, daughter of Daniel and Dorothy *Olmstead* Bulkeley, born April 14, 1772; married *Roger Foote*, May 26, 1790. Mr. Foote died June 10, 1823. Mrs. Eunice Foote died Jan. 22, 1846, aged 74.

CHILDREN.

969.	Eunice	*Foote*,	born May 12, 1791.
970.	Ezra	"	" Oct. 30, 1792; died July 29, 1793.
971.	Ezra	"	" June 7, 1795; m. *Sarah Louisa Bowler*.
972.	Dolly Olmsted	"	" March 3, 1797; m. *David Shepard*, of Genessee.
973.	Horace	"	" March 21, 1799; is an attorney at law, at Cleveland, Ohio.

BULKELEY FAMILY.   139

974.	Amelia	Foote,	born July 15, 1801; m. Ralph C. Foote, of Colchester.
975.	Carter	"	" June 10, 1804; resides at Perry, Ohio.
976.	Caroline	"	" Sept. 7, 1806; m. Luke Risley.
977.	David	"	" Aug. 15, 1809; m. Caroline Taylor.
978.	Marina	"	" Jan. 16, 1812.
979.	Linus	"	" July 12, 1813; Great Barrington, Mass.
980.	Charles	"	" July 1, 1817; Fort Wayne, Indiana.

622.

OLIVER BULKELEY, son of Daniel and Dorothy *Olmstead* Bulkeley, born July 24, 1776; married *Sophia Foote*, Nov. 2, 1797. He died Dec. 23, 1827, aged 62.

CHILDREN.

981.	William E.,	born Oct. 4, 1798.
982.	Daniel,	" May 16, 1800.
983.	Oliver,	" Jan. 4, 1802; died June 7, 1813.
984.	Lois,	" Aug. 9, 1803.
985.	Benjamin,	" June 13, 1806; died June 22, 1819.
986.	Sophia,	" Jan. 2, 1808.
987.	Salmon Cone,	" Feb. 23, 1810.
988.	Calvin Foote,	" Oct. 19, 1811.
989.	Dorothy L.,	" May 28, 1814.
990.	Betsey F.,	" April 27, 1816.
991.	Julia,	" June 27, 1819.
992.	Lucy,	" May 21, 1824.

637.

DAVID BULKELEY, son of David and Hannah *Beckwith* Bulkeley, born Sept. 24, 1780; married *Sally Chapman*, Dec. 26, 1805. She was born May 13, 1782.

CHILDREN.

993.	David Henry,	born Sept. 19, 1806.
994.	Anna,	" June 26, 1808.
995.	Jirah,	" July 16, 1810.
996.	George Chapman,	" Sept. 9, 1812.
997.	Sally Maria,	" April 11, 1815.
998.	Frances Jane,	" March 17, 1819.
999.	Richard,	" Feb. 17, 1824.

639.

ASA BULKELEY, son of Roger and Jerusha *Root* Bulkeley, born April 24, 1774; married *Sophia Loomis*, Dec. 12, 1796. She was born April 20, 1780. They resided in Colchester, Conn., where Mr. Bulkeley died, Dec. 24, 1804.

CHILDREN.
1000. Eliza L., born April 30, 1798; m. *John Witter*, April 30, 1817.
1001. Jerusha, " Jan. 26, 1800; died Jan. 6, 1804.
1002. John Adams, " Feb. 4, 1802; died in Alabama, unmarried, July, 1828.

642.

GEORGE BULKELEY, son of Roger and Jerusha *Root* Bulkeley, born March 8, 1780; married Sophia *Loomis* Bulkeley, widow of his deceased brother, Asa, Dec. 31, 1804. Mr. George Bulkeley died May 1, 1811; and his widow, Sophia, married *John White*, and died in Peoria, Illinois, Dec. 8, 1863.

CHILDREN OF GEORGE BULKELEY.
1003. Augustus Worthington, born Oct. 18, 1805.
1004. Caroline, " Nov. 4, 1807; m. *Thomas Lord*.
1005. Aurelia, " Oct. 12, 1810.

645.

GERSHOM BULKELEY, son of Roger and Jerusha *Root* Bulkeley, born May 14, 1788; married *Sally Babcock*, Oct. 12, 1809.

CHILDREN.
1006. Horatio Deming, born Dec. 8, 1810; died Sept. 28, 1823.
1007. Amelia Josephine Maria, " May 15, 1817; m. *Joseph McCall Goodwin*, Oct. 7, 1841.

648.

PRENTICE BULKELEY, son of Peter and Mary *Breed* Bulkeley, born June 11, 1772; married and had children, but the name of his wife has not been ascertained.

CHILDREN.
1008. Enoch, born Dec. 31, 1801.
1009. James, "

650.

LUCY BULKELEY, daughter of Peter and Mary *Breed* Bulkeley born March 9, 1778; married, about 1800, *John Breed*.

CHILDREN.
1010. John *Breed*, born ; died May 2, 1803.
1011. Lucy, " " ; died Dec. 30, 1821.

EIGHTH GENERATION.

666.

CLARISSA BULKELEY, daughter of Francis and Rhoda *Griswold* Bulkeley, born March 20, 1784; married *Charles Noyes*, of New

Canaan, N. Y., Dec. 31, 1807. No record of children has been received.

668.

FRANCIS BULKELEY, JUN., son of Francis and Rhoda *Griswold* Bulkeley, born Nov. 6, 1788; married *Content Mix*, of New Haven, Nov. 9, 1811. He died at sea, in 1817, on board the Brig Regent, off Cape Trafalgar, aged 29 years.

CHILDREN.

1012. Sarah A., born Nov., 1814; m. *Henry D. Field*, of Waterbury.
1013. Frances Henrietta, " Sept. 1817; m. *Matthew G. Elliot*.

672.

JAMES HENRY BULKELEY, son of Francis and Elizabeth *Fosdick* Bulkeley, born July 23, 1799; removed to Philadelphia, Penn., in 1814, and married *Adeline Alexander*, June 26, 1828.

CHILDREN.

1014. Anna Alexander, born April 13, 1829; m. *Henry S. Ogden*.
1015. Elisabeth Fosdick, " Jan. 4, 1831; died Sept. 16, 1867.
1016. Adeline Alexander, " May 8, 1832; unmarried.
1017. James Henry, Jun., " June 11, 1834; died Jan. 17, 1875. James Henry Bulkeley, Jun., was on board the Powhattan, Captain Mercer, as Captain's Clerk, when that ship was sent to Vera Cruz at the beginning of the Rebellion. Was also on the Wabash frigate, Capt. Mercer, cruising off Charleston, and in the battle or attack on Fort Hatteras, at the entrance of Roanoke Sound; afterwards with the army of Gen. McClellan, in the Commissary Department in Gen. McCall's command, above Georgetown, D. C., and at Harrison's landing, on the James river. After this he received an appointment as Paymaster, U. S. Navy, on the Guard Store Ship, West India squadron, Admiral Gardner; then on the Vicksburgh, in the attack on Fort Fisher. Then on the Monocacy, Captain Carter, Asiatic squadron, as Paymaster; remained in China and Japan seas four years; returned October, 1870, completely broken down in health; recovered somewhat, and was sent to Key West and Havana, on the Monitor Terror; came back in March, 1872, and died of consumption, Jan. 17, 1873.

1018.	Margaret Amelia,	born Feb. 5, 1836; m. *Edward McIntire.*
1019.	Helen Victoria,	" Dec. 24, 1837; died Dec. 12, 1869.
1020.	Mary Alrich,	" Aug. 1, 1839; died June 9, 1840.
1021.	William Alexander,	" July 2, 1841; m. *Mary A. Riley.*
1022.	Martha Wilson,	" July 8, 1843; died July 28, 1843.
1023.	Emily Cummings,	" June 22, 1845; died July 7, 1845.
1024.	Rosalie Augusta,	" Sept. 8, 1848; died April 29, 1839.

673.

CHARLES BULKELEY, son of Francis and Elizabeth *Fosdick* Bulkeley, born April 27, 1801, in Wethersfield, Conn.; removed from there to Philadelphia, in 1814, and married *Eliza Hunt*, of Boston, Mass., Sept. 2, 1828.

CHILDREN.

1025.	Eliza Hunt,	born Aug. 15, 1829; m. *Thomas C. Hill*, Jan. 19, 1856.
1026.	Ann Caroline,	" Nov. 11, 1831; m. *John Mickle.*
1027.	Frances Louisa,	" Nov. 4, 1833.
1028.	Sallie Prentiss,	" April 11, 1836; unmarried.
1029.	Charles,	" May 17, 1838.
1030.	Joseph Mackey,	" Oct. 30, 1839; died Aug. 4, 1841.

674.

HONOR FRANCIS BULKELEY, daughter of Edward and Diana *Bunce* Bulkeley, born in 1795; married *Joel Chapin*, in 1823.

CHILDREN.

1031.	Francis Leroy	Chapin.
1032.	Ann Wickham	"
1033.	Eliza	"
1034.	Elisabeth Stillman	"

676.

ELIZA BULKELEY, daughter of Edward and Diana *Bunce* Bulkeley, born in 1799; married *Richard Green*, and died without children, at Philadelphia, in 1852.

677.

EDWARD BULKELEY, son of Edward and Diana *Bunce* Bulkeley, born in Wethersfield, Conn., in 1801; was apprenticed to Edward Shepherd, of the same place. In 1821 he joined the Congregational church of that place. In 1822 he removed to New Haven. In 1825 he established himself in business in Orange street, New Haven; has continued in business in the same street to the present time. In 1828 he was married to *Lucy Mansfield*, by the Rev.

Nathaniel W. Taylor, D. D., Dwight Professor of Didactic Theology in Yale College; and formerly pastor of the Center church, of which his wife was a member. In 1832 he, with others, organized the Chapel Street Congregational church, now known as the Church of the Redeemer.

CHILDREN.

1035. Edward, born Oct. 30, 1828; died Feb. 19, 1831.
1036. John Francis, " May 15, 1831; died June 19, 1832.
1037. Edward, " May 15, 1833.

677½.

WEALTHY BULKELEY, daughter of Edward and Diana *Bunce* Bulkeley, born in 1804; married *Jesse St. John*.

CHILDREN.

1038. John Edward *St. John*.
1039. Francis "

683.

SUSAN WHITE, daughter of Joseph and Lucy *Bulkeley* White, born Feb. 6, 1783; married *Nathanael Eells*, of Whitestown, who died about 1825. She died in 1850, aged 67.

CHILD.

1040. Calvin *White*, born

684.

LUCY WHITE, daughter of Joseph and Lucy *Bulkeley* White, born July 22, 1784; was twice married. 1. To *Ornan Clark*, of Farmington, Conn., a farmer, who died Feb. 14, 1815. 2. To *Jesse Stanley*, of New Britain, Conn., a farmer, who died Aug. 19, 1827, aged 48.

CHILDREN BY HER FIRST HUSBAND.

1041. Henry White *Clark*, born Feb., 1807; m. *Emily Stanley*, in 1832.
1042. Sarah " " July 19, 1809; m. *Oren Stanley North*.
1043. Mervin " " July, 1812; m. *Caroline Guptil*.

CHILDREN BY SECOND MARRIAGE.

1045. A son, }   died in infancy.
                } twins, born Mch. 20, 1818.
1046. Almira *Stanley*, }   m. *George S. Cox*.
1047. Margaret "   " Nov. 26, 1820; m. *John E. Cowles*.
1048. Oliver Cromwell " " Feb. 23, 1823; m. *Charlotte Hine*.

686.

HENRY WHITE, son of Joseph and Lucy *Bulkeley* White, born Feb. 8, 1788; married *Julia Bidwell*, of Farmington. Feb. 7, 1815.

She was born Nov. 25, 1797. He engaged in farming in Whitestown, but resides now in Utica, N. Y. Mrs. Julia White died July 27, 1841, aged 43.

CHILDREN.

1049. Edward Bidwell *White*, born Dec. 4, 1815; died Aug. 17, 1828, aged 12.
1050. Harriet Maria " " Jan. 2, 1818; m. *E. G. Peckham*.
1051. Jane Amelia " " Mch. 26, 1824; m. *Henry Seymour Lansing*.
1052. Emily " " ; died in infancy.
1053. Abby " " ; died in infancy.
1054. Sarah Eliza " " Sept. 28, 1819; m. *Henry Malsom*.

687.

ABIGAIL WHITE, daughter of Joseph and Lucy *Bulkeley* White, born Aug. 26, 1789; married *Samuel Wilcox*, a farmer in Whitestown, N. Y.

CHILDREN.

1055. Julia Ann *Wilcox*, born Sept. 21, 1814.
1056. Lucy Bulkeley " " Dec. 9, 1816.
1057. George Chauncey " " Dec. 29, 1818.
1058. Susan Ells " " March 5, 1823.
1059. Henry White " " Feb. 14, 1826.
1060. Edward Lindsley " " Nov. 6, 1829.
1061. Samuel " " Sept. 6, 1832.

691.

THOMAS BULKELEY WHITE, son of Joseph and Lucy *Bulkeley* White, born Feb. 3, 1797; married and had a family. He lived for a few years in Michigan. He was a soldier in the Mexican war, and died in Texas or Mexico, about 1850. Nothing is known of his family.

692.

ELIZA WHITE, daughter of Joseph and Lucy *Bulkeley* White, born Nov. 7, 1798; married *Reuben Wilcox*, of Whitestown, and it is said, had four children, and died about 1825. Nothing further is known.

693.

MARY WHITE, daughter of Joseph and Lucy *Bulkeley* White, born in 1800; married *Henry Cooley*, of Auburn, N. Y., and died without issue, in 1836.

702.

CAROLINE BULKELEY, daughter of Stephen and Margaret N. Fanning Bulkeley, born in 1713; married *I. W. Stuart*, Esq., son of Prof. Moses Stuart, of Andover Theological Seminary, in the year 1834. They resided in Hartford, occupying the Charter Oak place, which Mrs. Stuart received by inheritance from her father. Mr. Stuart graduated at Yale, in the Class of 1828, with honors, and after graduation, devoted himself to literary pursuits until his death, which took place at Hartford.

CHILDREN.

1062. Ellen Margaretta.
1063. Isabella Winthrop.
1064. Grace Chetwood.

713.

GEORGE BULKELEY, son of Brownwell and Dolly *North* Bulkeley, born Nov. 20, 1814; married *Esther Pendleton*, and resides in Coventry, Chenango County, New York.

CHILDREN.

1065. Grace, born
1066. Robert, "

714.

FRANCIS BULKELEY, son of Brownwell and Dolly *North* Bulkeley, born April 16, 1819; married *Grace Joella Adams*. He graduated at Union College, Schenectady, N. Y., in 1838: afterwards became a planter of Richland, S. C. Mrs. Bulkeley died Oct. 18, 1858.

CHILDREN.

1067. Annie, born
1068. Francis, "
1069. Julia, " Sept. 9, 1823; m. *M. S. Converse.*

715.

MARY BULKELEY, daughter of Charles and Eunice *Robbins* Bulkeley, born April 8, 1785; married *Thomas Selden*, of East Haddam, Conn. She died August 13, 1853, and left no children.

717.

HENRY BULKELEY, son of Charles and Eunice *Robbins* Bulkeley, born March 7, 1789; married *Betsey Dodd*, of Hartford, who died April 15, 1872.

CHILDREN.

1070. Susan.
1071. Maria.
1072. Eunice.
1073. Elisabeth.
1074. Mary.
1075. Charles.

718.

ARCHIBALD BULKELEY, son of Charles and Eunice *Robbins* Bulkeley, born April 6, 1792, twin brother to Ashbel Bulkeley; married *Wealthy Ann Burr*, of Hartford, in September, 1815.

CHILDREN.

1076. Eliza.
1077. Maurice.
1078. Cornelia.
1079. Ann Augusta.
1080. Francis.
1081. Archibald B.

719.

ASHBEL BULKELEY, son of Charles and Eunice *Robbins* Bulkeley, twin brother to Archibald Bulkeley, born April 6, 1792; married *Eliza Fanning*, of Charleston, S. C., May 25, 1816.

CHILDREN.

1082. Charles H.
1083. Ashbel.
1084. Eliza.

720.

ERASTUS BULKELEY, son of Charles and Eunice *Robbins* Bulkeley, born Nov. 6, 1793; married *Mary Walbridge*.

CHILDREN.

1086.	Edwin Adolphus,	born Jan. 25, 1826, Charleston, S. C.; m. *Catharine F. Oakley*.
1087.	Theodore Augustus,	"	; m. *Harriet L. Skinner*.
1088.	Frederick Conrad,	"	; m. *Fanny Wilcox*.
1089.	Henry Deming,	"	; m. *Cara Byxbee*.
1090.	Reginald Walbridge,	"	; m. *Carrie A. Wilkinson*.
1091.	Mary Virginia,	"	; m. *Arthur F. Hanks*.

721.

EMELINE BULKELEY, daughter of Charles and Eunice *Robbins* Bulkeley, born Nov. 6, 1793, twin sister of Erastus Bulkeley; married *S. H. P. Hall,* May 14, 1826. Now of Binghamton, N. Y. She died Aug. 28, 1855, at Balston Spa, N. Y.

CHILDREN.

1092. Charles S., born May 20, 1827, at Binghamton; graduated at Yale, 1869; no children.
1093. William B., "   ; m. *Elisabeth S. J. Paddock.*
1094. Josephine E. M., "   ; m. *Hugh Allen;* one child, Jane E.
1095. Theodore Parsons, " ; m. *Alexandrine L. Godfrey;* graduated at Yale, 1857.
1096. Richard H., "   ; m., 1. *Hannah P. Trowbridge;* 2. *Kate E. Cresswell.*

733.

MARY BULKELEY WILLIAMS, daughter of Willis and Rhoda *Bulkeley* Williams, born June 16, 1806; married *John Edwards,* Dec. 7, 1836.

CHILD.

1097. Henry *Edwards.*

734.

LORENZO LEWIS WILLIAMS, son of Ralph Willis and Rhoda *Bulkeley* Williams, born April 24, 1808; married *Emeline Cook.*

CHILDREN.

1098. Rhoda B.   *Williams.*
1099. Emeline C. "
1100. Diana H.   "
1101. George C.   "
1102. Mary B.   "
1103. Elisabeth O. "
1104. A son, born after the making of his father's will.

736.

ALFRED NORTH, son of Dr. Nathan and Nancy *Bulkeley* North, born at Exeter, New Hampshire, March 10, 1807; married, 1. *Minerva Bryan,* of Fairfield, N. Y., June 7, 1835; sailed for Singapore, as Missionary of the A. B. C. F. M., July 20, 1835; returned to the United States in October, 1847. He married, 2. *Martha Bryan,* of Fairfield, N. Y., Jan. 15, 1851, and died at Chilton, Wisconsin, March 3, 1869.

CHILDREN.

1105. Edwin Barnes *North,* born January 29, 1837, at Singapore—sent to America in 1845; graduated at Marietta College in 1863, and died at Port Hudson, La., in 1864.

1106. Martha Bryan   North, born Jan. 5, 1839—sent to the U. S. in 1845; sailed from San Francisco for Pekin, as Missionary of the Women's Union Missionary Society, June 1, 1870.
1107. Anna Catharine   "   "   Dec 3, 1840, at Singapore; m. *Alvan D. Wilder*, of Sacramento, Cal., Nov., 1870. Lives at South Vallejo, Cal., and has two children.
1108. Thomas Hastings   "   "   Jan. 22, 1843, at Singapore. Served in the Federal army during the Rebellion; m. *Sarah Humphrey*, of Bachelder, Kansas, Feb. 29, 1868. Lives at Wakefield, Clay County, Kansas, and has four children.

CHILDREN BY SECOND MARRIAGE.

1109. Orlando Bryan   North, born Feb., 1852, at Trenton, N. Y. Lives at Springfield, Ill,
1110. William Whiteside   "   "   Oct., 1857, at Pittsford, N. Y. Lives at Springfield, Ill.

739.

THERESA ORNE BULKELEY NORTH, daughter of Dr. Nathan and Nancy *Bulkeley* North, born July 22, 1815; married *Ezra Sterling Ely*, Feb., 1843.

CHILD.

1111. Nathan North *Ely*,   born Sept., 1844, at Checktowaga, N. Y.; died Feb., 1861.

740.

GERRIT P. POST, son of John G. and Louisa *Bulkeley* Post, born Nov. 9, 1812; married *Ruth Keith*, of Newport, New York, Jan. 12, 1836.

CHILDREN.

1112. Julia Ward   Post, born Oct. 20, 1836, at Newport, N. Y.; m. *Frederick Fitch*.
1113. John Williams   "   "   June 17, 1841, at Boonville, N. Y.; died at Harper's Ferry, Va., Nov. 1, 1862.
1114. Margaret Louisa   "   "   March 23, 1846; m. *Frederick Fitch*, October 1, 1868.

747.

PETER BULKELEY POST, son of John G. and Louisa *Bulkeley* Post, born July 25, 1817; married *Elisabeth Smith*, of Bristol, Conn., Nov. 17, 1842. He died Oct. 2, 1862.

CHILDREN.

1115. Bertha Louisa   Post, born April 12, 1846; m. *Charles Allen Alger*.
1115½. Adrian Bulkeley   "   "   April 30, 1856, at Boonville, N. Y.

750.

GEORGE R. POST, son of John G. and Louisa *Bulkeley* Post, born May 1, 1824; married *Elizabeth Lee Whaples*, of New Britain, Conn., June 23, 1851.

CHILDREN.

1116.	Caroline Elizabeth *Post*,	born	April 15, 1854.
1117.	John Gerard	"	" Oct. 15, 1855; died Feb. 5, 1862.
1118.	George Curtis	"	" April 15, 1860; died Dec. 9, 1862.
1119.	May Lee	"	" April 12, 1865.
1120.	Gerritt Bulkeley	"	" July 26, 1867.

755.

CORNELIUS BULKELEY IRWIN, son of Peter and Lydia *Bulkeley* Irwin, born June 7, 1811; married *Maria North*, in 1835. Lives at New Britain, Conn.

755.

CHARLES NORTH BASS, M. D., son of Samuel and Belinda *Bulkeley* Bass, born Aug. 30, 1816; married *Juliette Burnham*, Aug. 29, 1841, of Leyden, N. Y., and died Aug. 31, 1865.

CHILDREN.

1121. Charles Samuel *Bass*, born July, 1847, at Leyden.
1122. Belinda Eliza   "   " Jan. 16, 1850, at Leyden; died April 13, 1853.

767.

JOSEPH EDMUND BULKELEY, son of Edmund and Nancey *Robbins* Bulkeley, born Feb. 9, 1812, at Rocky Hill; left his native place at the age of 13, and located as clerk in New York City. He early established himself as a wholesale leather merchant, where, by diligence and industry, he built up and sustained a very successful and lucrative business, which he has continued until the present time, having united his sons with him as co-partners in trade. This branch prefer to spell the name Bulkley.

He married Mrs. *Mary Lawrence Bicknell*, daughter of John Lawrence, of Newton, L. I., Oct. 23d, 1837.

CHILDREN.

1122½.	Elizabeth L., adopted daughter;		m. *George A. Welles*.
1123.	Edmund Williams,	born Oct. 2, 1838;	m. *Caroline J. Turner*.
1124.	Justus Lawrence,	" July 4, 1840;	m. *Laura E. Caldwell*.
1125.	Josephine,	" Dec. 13, 1841;	m. *Theodore M. Barnes*.
1126.	Mary L.,	" Aug. 24, 1843;	m. *Ferdinand S. Eutz*.
1127.	Marguerite,	" June 13, 1847.	

768

JUSTUS ROBBINS BULKELEY, son of Edmund and Nancey *Robbins* Bulkeley, born at Rocky Hill, March 9th, 1815; married at Augusta, Georgia, to *Mary K. Adams*, daughter of John M. Adams, May 1, 1851. He was a merchant in Augusta, Georgia, from 1834 to 1853. From 1855 to his death (at Rye, Dec. 30, 1862,) he was President of the New York and New Haven Railroad.

CHILDREN.

1128. Julius Huntington, born Feb. 22, 1852, at Augusta, Ga., died March 13th, 1855.
1129. Sarah Adams, " Sept. 20, 1853, at Ravenswood, L. I. Lost at sea on the Ville Du Havre, Nov. 22, 1873.

772.

MARTHA ROBBINS BULKELEY, daughter of Henry and Martha *Tucker* Bulkely, born Dec. 31, 1848; married *William Brown*, of Glastonbury, May 18, 1867.

CHILDREN.

1130. Martha Elizabeth, born Oct. 15, 1867.
1131. Willie Wallace, " Nov. 24, 1869.
1132. Eugene Augustus, " Mch. 27, 1871.
1133. A daughter. " Feb. 17, 1874.

779.

AMELIA BULKELEY, daughter of Walter Williams Bulkeley, born ———; married Rev. *Horace Williams*.

780.

SUSAN M. BULKELEY, daughter of Walter Williams Bulkeley, born ———; married *Hiram H. Webb*, of Rockingham, N. C., Oct. 8, 1855.

784.

MERCY MILLER, daughter of Caleb and Dorothy *Butler* Miller, and granddaughter of Nathaniel and Abigail *Bulkeley* Miller, born Nov. 28, 1796; married *Braddick G. Brand*, in Madison, Hamilton County, N. Y., April 27, 1815, a blacksmith by trade. She died in Lodi, Spencer County, N. Y., July 27, 1835. He was born in Hopkinton, R. I., June 8, 1792, and died Jan. 1, 1868.

CHILDREN.

1134. Amanda M. *Brand*, born August 21, 1821; never married.
1135. Abigail D., " June 18, 1830; never married.

788.

URBEN BUTLER MILLER, son of Caleb and Dorothy *Butler* Miller and grandson of Nathanael and Abigail *Bulkeley* Miller, born Dec. 31, 1800 ; married *Anna Rees*, of Sherburne, N. Y., May 23, 1822. He died at Fort Wayne, Indiana, March 31, 1861. He was a Baptist Clergyman.

CHILDREN.

1136. Kendrick B. *Miller*, born Oct. 1, 1825, at Berkshire, N. Y.; m. *Rose Hotchkiss*, at Medina, Mich., Jan. 23, 1853.
1137. Nathanael C. " " March 19, 1829, Virgil, N. Y.; m. *Margaret Embry*, Ft. Wayne, Indiana, Sept. 10, 1855.
1138. Claudius C. " " Dec. 30, 1832, at Hector, Tompkins County, N. Y.; m. *Mary Smith Huntington*, of Indiana, Nov. 12, 1863.
1139. Martha " " Sept. 10, 1834, at Farmersville, Seneca County, N. Y.; m. *Charles Philly*, of Fort Wayne, Indiana, Dec. 31, 1856.
1140. Mary J. " " July 16, 1836, at Geneva, Ontario County, m. Rev. *George A. Simonson*, of Indianapolis, Indiana, Jan. 30, 1860. She died Oct. 23, 1868.
1141. Mercy A. " " June 6, 1838, at Geneva, Ontario County, N. Y.; m. *Jacob Kees*, of Adamsville, Mich., Dec. 23, 1862.
1142. Jacob R. " " May 14, 1841, at Waterloo, Seneca County, N. Y.; m. a lady in Topeka, Kansas, Nov. 12, 1873. He was 8 years in service of the U. S. government.
1143. Ulrick Urben " " April 20, 1846, at Edwardsburg, Mich.
1144. Anna E. " " June 30, 1848, at Phelps, N. Y.; m. *Warren T. Bush*, of Fabius, N. Y., Feb. 20, 1867.

787.

SOLOMON BULKELEY MILLER, son of Caleb and Dorothy *Butler* Miller and grandson of Nathanael and Abigail *Bulkeley* Miller, born Sept. 12, 1803 ; married *Fanny Burton* in Hamilton, Madison County, N. Y., Dec. 26, 1828. She was born April 4, 1805, and died Dec. 11, 1865.

CHILDREN.

1145. Oscar F. *Miller*, born April 4, 1831, in Hamilton, Madison County, N. Y.; m. *Marion Walker* in Bath, N. Y., Oct. 28, 1856. Has been for several years a practicing physician ; was in the war of the rebellion, acting as Chief Apothecary nearly a year ; taken sick and discharged ; has four children.
1146. Josephine L. " " Dec. 4, 1832, in Hamilton, Madison County, N. Y.

1147. Jane Rebeccah *Miller*, born July 26, 1834, in Lodi, Seneca County, N. Y.
1148. Dorothy Esther   "   " April 13, 1836, in   "   "   "   "   ;
                                m. George Loomer March 6, 1859 ; one child,
                                Hettie, born April 23, 1865.
1149. Caleb Elijah   "   " March 5, 1838, at Lodi, Seneca County, N. Y.
1150. Amos Bulkeley   "   " Feb. 17, 1840, at   "   "   "   "
1151. Solomon Butler "   " Nov. 8, 1842, at   "   "   "   "
                                Died in the war of the rebellion.
1152. Lyman   "   " July 18, 1844, at Lodi, Seneca County, N. Y.

791.

THANKFUL BUTTON, daughter of George and Rebeccah *Miller* Button and granddaughter of Nathanael and Abigail *Bulkeley* Miller, born Aug. 18, 1800, married *William Knapp*, Jan. 27, 1820. He was born April 3, 1800.

CHILDREN.

1153. Edward Miller *Knapp*, born March 14, 1821.
1154. Anna B.   "   " March 15, 1825.
1155. Frances Angeline "   " Oct. 29, 1827.
1156. Thankful I.   "   " Feb. 26, 1830.
1157. George R.   "   " March 21, 1831.

793.

NANCY BUTTON, daughter of George and Rebeccah *Miller* Button and granddaughter of Nathanael and Abigail *Bulkeley* Miller, born July 8, 1807 ; married *Ariel T. Alderman*. He was born Oct. 6, 1803.

CHILDREN.

1158. Austin *Alderman*, born Aug. 31, 1829.
1159. Julia C.   "   " Aug. 8, 1831.
1159½. Denio T.   "   " Feb. 26, 1834.
1160. Homer M.   "   " April 24, 1843.

796.

AMANDA MILLER, daughter of Elijah Bulkeley and Ruth *Hall* Miller and granddaughter of Nathanael and Abigail *Bulkeley* Miller, born Feb. 15, 1809 ; married *Horace Hall*, Dec. 25, 1828.

CHILDREN.

1161. Sarah C. *Hall*, born Sept. 28, 1831.
1162. Helen M.   "   " Apr. 20, 1834.
1163. Charles V.   "   " Apr. 23, 1837.

798.

ADALINE C. MILLER, daughter of Elijah and Ruth *Hall* Miller and granddaughter of Nathanael and Abigail *Bulkeley* Miller, born Nov. 3, 1814; married Rev. *C. D. Burlingham*, Sept. 7, 1834.

CHILDREN.

1164.	Marion	*Burlingham,*	born	Sept. 29, 1837.
1165.	John Emory	"	"	Jan. 6, 1840.
1166.	Charles Herman	"	"	July 5, 1842.
1167.	William	"	"	1844.
1168.	Franklin	"	"	June 27, 1847.
1169.	Amos C.	"	"	Sept. 18, 1855.

799.

HANNAH H. MILLER, daughter of Elijah and Ruth *Hall* Miller and granddaughter of Nathanael and Abigail *Bulkeley* Miller, born Jan. 30, 1819; married *Charles Todd*, Oct. 13, 1844.

CHILDREN.

1170.	Ruth Maria	*Todd,*	born	Oct. 12, 1846.
1171.	George	"	"	Oct. 21, 1854.
1172.	Charles Herbert	"	"	Oct. 18, 1858.

800.

NATHANAEL W. MILLER, son of Elijah and Ruth *Hall* Miller, and grandson of Nathanael and Abigail *Bulkeley* Miller, born October 9, 1820; married *Juliaette Kenyon*, July 22, 1848.

CHILDREN.

1173. Elijah B., born May 18, 1850.
1174. Henry E., " April 29, 1855.
1175. Mary N., " September 6, 1856.

802.

HIRAM C. MILLER, son of Elijah and Ruth *Hall* Miller, and grandson of Nathanael and Abigail *Bulkeley* Miller, born June 25, 1834; married *Mary Canfield*.

803.

SARAH M. BULKELEY, daughter of James and Hannah *Myers* Bulkeley, born September 4, 1803; married *Sylvester Goodrich*. Mr. Goodrich is a farmer, and resides in Rocky Hill.

CHILDREN.

1176. Sarah *Goodrich*, born August 26, 1838.
1177. Charles A., " " December 22, 1839.
1178. Martha J., " " August 29, 1843.

804.

HARRIET BULKELEY, daughter of James and Hannah *Myers* Bulkeley, born November 30, 1805; married *Rodolphus Griswold*, son of Joel Griswold, of Simsbury. The following names of children were furnished by a relative from memory, without dates. They may not be named in their order:

CHILDREN.

1179. Augustus *Griswold*.
1180. Watson "
1181. Harriet "
1182. Mary "
1183. Laura "
1184. Emma Jane "
1185. Smith "
1186. George "
1187. Rodolphus "
1188. Eliza "
1189. Nancy "
1190. Sarah M. "

805.

JULIA BULKELEY, daughter of James and Hannah *Myers* Bulkeley, born July 3, 1807; married *Daniel Small*. They reside in the state of Rhode Island.

CHILDREN.

1191. Francis Hubbard *Small*, born August 25, 1838.
1192. Eliza Jane " " December 2, 1840.
1193. James B. " " 1845.
1194. Harriet M. " " 1850.

806.

JAMES BULKELEY, JR., son of James and Hannah *Myers* Bulkeley, born August 30, 1811; married *Julia Risley*.

CHILDREN.

1195. Walter, born
1196. Jane, "
1197. Ralph "

807.

GEORGE W. BULKELEY, son of James and Hannah *Myers* Bulkeley, born September 6, 1814; married *Lucy Sperry*, April 17, 1842. He was a machinist, and resided in Bloomfield, Conn. He died in 1874.

CHILDREN.

1198. Laura Ann, born February 14th, 1844.
1199. Eliza M., " May 15, 1849.

1200. Mary Elisabeth, born July 17, 1855.
1201. Carrie Emma,   "   September 27, 1860.
1202. Lydia Ida,   "   April 20, 1863.
1203. George Henry,   "   January 7, 1869.

808.

ELIZA BULKELEY, daughter of James and Hannah *Myers* Bulkeley, born December 15, 1816; married *Isaac Sperry*, April 8, 1840, and died March 17, 1848.

CHILD.

1204. Ellen Eliza, born April 7, 1842; married *Elisha J. Arnold*.

809.

NANCY BULKELEY, daughter of James and Hannah *Myers* Bulkeley, born June 2, 1818; married *Edward Risley*. Mr. Risley is a blacksmith, and resides in Rocky Hill.

CHILDREN.

1205. Jane E. *Risley*, born June 15, 1839; died January 22, 1856.
1206. Sarah M.   "   "   March 6, 1847; married Donald L. Vaughn.
1207. Martha W. "   "   March 5, 1848; married Frank Belden.
1208. Edwin J. "   "   March 6, 1849; died young.
1209. Edwin J. "   "   August 15, 1850; died young.
1210. Almira J. "   "   March 17, 1853; died August 24, 1854.
1211. Alice J. "   "   November 30, 1855.
1212. George B. "   "   November 18, 1858.
1213. Emma J.   "   "   October 5, 1859.

810.

JANE ELLEN BULKELEY, daughter of James and Hannah *Myers* Bulkeley, born April 7, 1822; married *Joseph S. Latham*, August 27, 1845, of Providence, R. I.

CHILDREN.

1214. James Alfred *Latham*, born April 9, 1849.
1215. Joseph Augustus "   "   December 6, 1850.
1216. Charles Bulkeley "   "   July 9, 1859.

811.

WILLIAM R. BULKELEY, son of James and Hannah *Myers* Bulkeley, born April 7, 1825; married *Emma L. Freeman*, January 6, 1850. He is a farmer and teamster, and resides in Rocky Hill.

CHILDREN.

1217. William F., born May 29, 1851.
1218. James H., "   February 14, 1854.
1219. Helen E., "   May 1, 1856.

1220. Emma M., born August 1, 1858.
1221. Charles E.,   "   April 5, 1863.
1222. Mary,   "   February 28, 1866.
1223. George G.,   "   February 4, 1871.

812.

MARIA BULKELEY, daughter of Justus and Mabel *Brandegee* Bulkeley, born   ; married *Lyman Wilson*. They are reported to have had three children, but no names have been returned.

814.

EDWIN BULKELEY, son of Justus Bulkeley and Mabel *Brandegee* Bulkeley, born   ; was twice married. Nothing further is known.

815.

MARY AMELIA BULKELEY, daughter of Justus and Mabel *Brandegee* Bulkeley; married *Francis Chambers*, Dec. 7, 1854.

CHILDREN.

1224. Agnes Bulkeley Chambers, born Dec. 3, 1855.
1225. Mary R.   "   "   Oct. 10, 1861.

816.

HARRIET BULKELEY, daughter of Justus and Mabel *Brandegee* Bulkeley; married Mr. ——— *Lester*.

820.

THOMAS STANLEY ROBBINS, son of Allen and Amelia *Bulkeley* Robbins, born Oct. 17, 1805; was twice married, 1. To *Martha C. Sears*, August 30, 1832. She was born June 5, 1810, and died Dec. 23, 1843. 2. To *Marabah McConner*, May 2, 1844. She died Jan. 15, 1849.

CHILDREN.

1226. Caroline A.,   born Aug. 7, 1833.
1227. Chloe M.,   "   Dec. 7, 1835.
1228. Martha U. B.,   "   March 8, 1838.
1229. Allen Austin,   "   Sept. 26, 1839; died Oct. 24, 1843.
1230. Mary Louise,   "   Sept. 10, 1841.
1231. Emeline E.,   "   Dec. 15, 1843; died Feb. 21, 1845.

CHILDREN BY THE SECOND MARRIAGE.

1233. Martha A.,   born May 20, 1846.
1234. Marabah M.,   "   Feb. 17, 1848; died Feb. 15, 1849.

821.

CHLOE W. ROBBINS, daughter of Allen and Amelia *Bulkeley* Robbins, born Jan. 9, 1808; married *Frederick Marsh*, of Montpelier, Vt. Had one child, died in infancy.

CHILD.

1235. An infant, born   ; died

822.

ALLEN A. ROBBINS, son of Allen and Amelia *Bulkeley* Robbins, born May 15, 1816; married *Abby Ann Goodrich*, Oct. 29, 1840.

CHILDREN.

1236. Thomas Hamlin *Robbins*, born Nov. 4, 1841; graduated at Yale 1868.
1237. Annie Amelia   "   " July 15, 1845; m. *Wm. G. Robbins.*

824.

ABIGAIL U. B. ROBBINS, daughter of Allen and Amelia *Bulkeley* Robbins, born Jan. 19, 1819; married Rev. *Joshua L. Maynard*, Oct. 14, 1840. She died May 11, 1845.

CHILDREN.

1238. Amelia Caroline *Maynard*, born June, 1842.
1239. Francis A.   "   "   1843.
1240. Joshua Bond   "   "
1241. Robert Leland   "   "

825.

EMILY WEBSTER ROBBINS, daughter of Allen and Amelia *Bulkeley* Robbins, born Jan. 14, 1825; married, Feb. 6, 1845, *Robert Sugden, Jr.*

CHILDREN.

1242. Robert Allen *Sugden*, born Sept. 8, 1847.
1243. Amelie M.   "   " Aug. 24, 1849.
1244. Abbie Lizzie   "   " March 26, 1852; died May 1, 1867.
1245. Emily Robbins   "   " Oct. 1, 1861.

826.

AMELIA ANN BULKELEY, daughter of John G. and Abigail *Hart* Bulkeley; married *Norman Butler*.

827.

URSULA BULL BULKELEY, daughter of John and Abigail *Hart* Bulkeley; married *Josiah Button*.

158 BULKELEY FAMILY.

CHILDREN.

1246. Catharine *Button.*
1247. Hosea B.   "
1248. John   "
1249. Abigail   "

820.

HOSEA BULKELEY, son of John G. and Abigail *Hart* Bulkeley, born   , 1819; married *Susan Petit* of Middletown.

CHILD.

1250. Mary, born June 12, 1842; m. *Edward S. Thompson* of Glastonbury.

831.

BENJAMIN G. BULKELEY, son of John G. and Abigail *Hart* Bulkeley, born Nov. 29, 1818; married *Emily Abigail Clark* of Meriden, Dec. 30, 1839. Resides in Meriden, Conn. She was born July 22, 1820.

CHILDREN.

1251. Sarah Gertrude,   born July 3, 1841; m. *Jasper E. Higby*, Dec. 19, 1863.
1252. Caroline Christine, " Nov. 18, 1843; m. *Wm. Henry Allen*, May 28, 1864.
1253. William Benjamin, " Sept. 15, 1845; m. *Hattie Moffit*, April 25, 1871.
1254. Ella May,   " Feb. 18, 1851.

830.

CAROLINE HART BULKELEY, daughter of John G. and Abigail *Hart* Bulkeley, born Aug. 8, 1812; married *Philip Butler* of Middletown, Nov. 25, 1834. They reside in the northern part of Cromwell.

CHILDREN.

1256. Richard Valentine *Butler,* born Nov. 9, 1838; died July 17, 1841.
1257. Susie L.   "   " June 3, 1842; m. *Benjamin Ranney.*
1258. Horace R. } twins, " " April, 1845; { m. *Cora Wilcox.*
1259. Henry R. }   { died Jan. 13, 1872.
1260. Carrie A.   "   " April 7, 1852.

832.

FRANCES BULKELEY, daughter of John G. and Abigail *Hart* Bulkeley, born   ; married *William Clark.* They reside in Meriden.

834.

WILLIAM BULKELEY, son of Dr. Sylvester and Mary *Johnson* Bulkeley, born   ; married *Lurania Belden*.

CHILD.

1261. William.

835.

MARY ANN BULKELEY, daughter of Dr. Sylvester and Mary *Johnson* Bulkeley, born   ; married *John Brandagee*.

CHILDREN.

1262. Mary   *Brandagee*, born
1263. William Sylvester   "

836.

MARTHA G. BULKELEY, daughter of Gershom and Laura *Goodrich* Bulkeley, born Dec. 11, 1826; married Lucius M. Beaumont, Nov. 27, 1845. She had four children, which are recorded under Head number 839.

837.

EDMUND BEAUMONT, son of Ira and Mabel *Bulkeley* Beaumont, born Sept. 2, 1812; married *Elisabeth Church* in the spring of 1835.

CHILDREN.

1264. Edmund Church, born
1265. Frank,   "
1266. Eumona,   "

838.

IRA O. BEAUMONT, son of Ira and Mabel *Bulkeley* Beaumont, born in 1814 ; married *Sarah Douglass*.

CHILD.

1267. Olive *Beaumont*.

839.

LUCIUS M. BEAUMONT, son of Ira and Mabel *Bulkeley* Beaumont, born Dec. 4, 1816; married *Martha G. Bulkeley*, daughter of Gershom and Laura *Goodrich* Bulkeley, Nov. 27, 1845. (Vide under head number 836.)

CHILDREN.

1268. Laura Mabel *Beaumont*, born Aug. 10, 1846 ; m. Frank Dickinson, Sept. 6, 1865.
1269. William L.   "   " Dec. 2, 1851.
1270. Paul   "   " April 11, 1857.
1271. Virginie   "   " March 22, 1863 ; died April 18, 1863.

840.

CHARLES G. BEAUMONT, son of Ira and Mabel *Bulkeley* Beaumont, born Dec. 24, 1818; married *Mary Pratt*, May 6, 1842.

CHILDREN.

1272. Lucius S. *Beaumont*, born June 22, 1843; m. Ellen Madigan.
1273. George E.   "   " June 17, 1845; m. Emma Ward, Oct. 31, 1867.
1274. Charles   "   " Nov. 27, 1848; died Feb. 19, 1855.
1275. Olive   "   " Dec. 14, 1850; m. William E. Pratt.
1276. Alfred   "   " Dec. 3, 1853.
1277. Charles   "   " July 17, 1856.
1278. Ira   "   " Nov. 24, 1858.
1279. John L.   "   " Feb. 23, 1861.
1280. Mary E.   "   " March 12, 1863.

841.

LAURA BEAUMONT, daughter of Ira and Mabel *Bulkeley* Beaumont, born March 31, 1821; married *Alfred Smith*. She died Oct. 24, 1849.

CHILDREN.

1281. Catharine *Smith*, born Jan. 14, 1848; m. Robert Scranton.
1282. Henry Lewis   "   " July 12, 1852; died Feb. 5, 1853.
1283. Mabel   "   " April 24, 1854.
1284. Edward   "   " Feb. 8, 1857.

843.

THOMAS BEAUMONT, son of Ira and Mabel *Bulkeley* Beaumont, born 1824; married *Josephine Peckwell*.

CHILDREN.

1285. Olive,   born.
1286. Mary,   "
1287. Thomas,   "
1288. Catharine, "

844.

EMELINE BEAUMONT, daughter of Ira and Mabel *Bulkeley* Beaumont, born about 1826; married *Joseph McFarland*.

CHILDREN.

1289. Ira Beaumont *McFarland*, born April, 1854; died in 3 weeks.
1290. Sarah   "   " June 23, 1855.
1291. Josephine   "   " July 27, 1858.
1292. Emeline   "   " June 17, 1860.
1293. Mabel   "   " Dec. 7, 1867.

845.

HARRIET L. BEAUMONT, daughter of Ira and Mabel *Bulkeley* Beaumont, born Feb. 15, 1831; married *John W. Lockwood*, May 4, 1848.

CHILDREN.

1294.	John G.	*Lockwood*, born April 30, 1849.
1295.	Anna M.	"	" Aug. 18, 1851; m. Raymond Claghorne.
1296.	Josephine H.	"	" May 22, 1853; m. Col. James Forney.
1297.	Harriet B.	"	" May 17, 1855; m. Albert F. Mills, Oct. 1873; died April 24, 1875.
1298.	Seth R.	"	" March 30, 1858; died young.
1299.	Sarah S.	"	" Oct. 15, 1860.

849.

ABIGAIL R. SMITH, daughter of Davis and Abigail S. Smith, born Nov. 7, 1821; married *Moses W. Williams*, Oct. 30, 1841. Mr. Williams is a farmer, and they reside in Rocky Hill.

CHILDREN.

1300. Henry Chapman *Williams*, born March 9, 1844; m. *Cornelia Neff*.
1301. Catharine Louise " " Feb. 20, 1847; died Aug. 3, 1852.
1302. Ella Frances " " Dec. 13, 1853; m. *Stephen Francis Churchill*.
1303. Margaret Smith, " " Aug. 4, 1856; died March 3, 1870.

852.

MARY J. SMITH, daughter of Davis and Abigail S. *Bulkeley* Smith, born Nov. 4, 1823; married *Ambrose Wolcott*, Feb. 4, 1853. They reside in Wallingford, Conn. Mr. Wolcott is a farmer.

CHILDREN.

1304. Francis *Wolcott*, born July 12, 1854; died Aug. 18, 1854.
1305. Charles " " May 2, 1856.
1306. Carrie " " Sept. 4, 1859.
1307. George " " May 12, 1861.
1308. Ida " " Nov. 23, 1863.

855.

HENRY HORACE SMITH, son of Davis and Abigail S. *Bulkeley* Smith, born Dec. 1, 1829; married *Phillippa G. Hubbard*, May 7, 1854. They reside in Middletown, Ct.

CHILDREN.

1309. Arthur Davis *Smith*, born June 29, 1855.
1310. Sarah Collins " " April 7, 1859.
1311. Georgianna " " Nov. 29, 1861.
1312. Jerome Collins " " Oct. 24, 1869.
1313. Harry Hilliard " " Nov. 16, 1871.

856.

MARTHA AMELIA SMITH, daughter of Davis and Abigail S. Bulkeley Smith, born Feb. 11, 1832; married *Walter S. Wilcox*, Nov. 12, 1856. They reside in Hartford, Conn., where he is a foreman of blacksmithing at Colt's factory.

CHILDREN.

1314. Alfred Davis   *Wilcox*, born May 17, 1859; died Jan. 17, 1867.
1315. Henry Williams   "   "   July 9, 1868.

860.

EBENEZER BULKELEY, son of Allen and Eliza *Riley* Bulkeley, born ———; married *Anastasia Crittenden*. No record of children has been furnished.

861.

HARRIET ABBOT BULKELEY, daughter of Allen and Eliza *Riley* Bulkeley, born ———; married *Henry Roberts*.

863.

MARY JANE BULKELEY, daughter of Allen and Eliza *Riley* Bulkeley, born   ; married *William Spear*.

866.

JANE BULKELEY, daughter of Frederick and Nancey *Riley* Bulkeley, born Jan. 2, 1819; married *Walter Edwards*, Nov. 15, 1843.

CHILDREN.

1316. Elizabeth,   born Oct. 29, 1844; m. *Edward M. Frances*, March 24, 1870. Children—Everett M., born Sept. 26, 1872; Bernice, born June 14, 1874.
1317. Fanny Maria,   " Aug. 28, 1846; died Sept. 3, 1849.
1318. Frederick Bulkeley,   " Oct. 14, 1850.
1319. Frank Daniel,   " Feb. 12, 1853.

870.

HENRY W. BULKELEY, son of Burrage and Caroline *Miller* Bulkeley, born Sept. 25, 1853; married *Ellen M. Butler*.

CHILD.

1320. Herbert,   lived six months.

874.

JOSEPH A. BULKELEY, son of Burrage and Caroline *Miller* Bulkeley, born Nov. 3, 1843; married *Emma Jane Whitmore*, daughter of Lewis Whitmore, Dec. 31, 1856. He died November, 1872.

CHILDREN.

1321. An infant daughter, born   1867; died in infancy.
1322. Bertha,   "   July 31, 1868.
1323. Harry Grant,   "   Nov. 28, 1871.

875.

CARRIE M. BULKELEY, daughter of Burrage and Caroline *Miller* Bulkeley, born March 4, 1846; married *Franklin E. Davenport*.

CHILD.

1324. Frank Bulkeley *Davenport*, born July 15, 1871.

885.

LUCY BULKELEY, daughter of Prescott and Penelope *Tryon* Bulkeley, born June 17, 1823; married *Hamilton Horton*, of Glastonbury.

CHILDREN.

1325. Herbert   *Horton*, born May 23, 1845; unmarried.
1326. Henry P.   "   "   July 17, 1848.
1327. Frederick   "   "   April 6, 1853.
1328. Infant daughter   "   "   March 4, 1855; died March 21, 1855.
1329. Edward Trumbull   "   "   Oct. 10, 1858; died Feb. 3, 1860.
1330. George Bulkeley   "   "   Aug. 26, 1861.

886.

LAURA BULKELEY, daughter of Prescott and Penelope *Tryon* Bulkeley, born   ; married *George Smith*.

CHILDREN.

1331. George Mason *Smith*, born
1332. Eliza Jane   "   "
1333. Earl   "   "
1334. Agnace   "   "
1335. Carlos   "   "

887.

MARTHA EDWARDS BULKELEY, daughter of Prescott and Penelope *Tryon* Bulkeley, born Jan. 8, 1827; married *William Tyler*, of Glastonbury, Dec. 29, 1850.

BULKELEY FAMILY.

CHILDREN.
1336. William Prescott Tyler, born March 9, 1853.
1337. John Sweet " " Dec. 25, 1855.
1338. Rosa Isora Islington " " July 25, 1857.
1339. Byron Bulkeley " " July 25, 1866.

867.

NANCY R. BULKELEY, daughter of Frederick and Nancy *Riley* Bulkeley, born December 30, 1822; married *Benjamin H. Turner*, January 3, 1865. They reside at Fort Wayne, Indiana.

868.

STEPHEN BULKELEY, son of Frederick and Nancy *Riley* Bulkeley, born May 6, 1825; married *Prudence Warner*, January 23, 1850. They reside in Wethersfield.

CHILDREN.
1340. Fannie Rebecca, born November 2, 1850; m. *John Hanmer*, January 28, 1874; 1 child.
1341. Alice, " April 9, 1852.
1342. Prudence Warner, " January 25, 1854; died April 2, 1860.
1343. Frederick, " February 8, 1856.
1344. Stephen, " January 4, 1861.
1345. Charles, } twins, " March 25, 1864;
1346. Chester, } died October 27, 1867.
1347. Robert Riley, " September 6, 1866.

869.

KATE E. BULKELEY, daughter of Frederick and Nancy *Riley* Bulkeley, born April 23, 1834; married *John Warner*, November 20, 1872.

CHILD.
1348. Kittie *Warner*, born October 11, 1873.

891.

WALTER BULKELEY, son of Prescott and Penelope *Tryon* Bulkeley, born   ; married *Electa Hunt*, in 1852.

CHILDREN.
1349. Della, born September 5, 1854.
1350. Ida Lawrence, born January or February, 1857.

892.

ELLEN LOUISE BULKELEY, daughter of Prescott and Penelope *Tryon* Bulkeley, born   ; married *Samuel Abby*, May 15, 1866.

CHILD.
1351. Ruth *Abby*, born February 15, 1867.

803.

HARRIET GRISWOLD BULKELEY, daughter of Prescott and Penelope Tryon Bulkeley, born   ; married *Lyman Killam*, September 25, 1865.

CHILDREN.

1352. Walter Bulkeley *Killam*, born September 30, 1869.
1353. Arthur   "   "   August 29, 1873.

804.

ABBY JANE BULKELEY, daughter of Prescott and Penelope *Tryon* Bulkeley, married *Henry D. Hutchinson*, June 10, 1863.

CHILD.

1354. Nellie Bulkeley *Hutchinson*, born December 11, 1864.

909.

CHARLES EDWIN BULKELEY, son of John Charles and Sally *Taintor* Bulkeley, born October 16, 1799. He was twice married, 1, to Mary Isham, May 4, 1829; 2, to Widow *Julia Worthington*.

CHILDREN BY THE FIRST MARRIAGE.

1355. Mary, born   ; died young.
1356. Charles Edwin, born

CHILDREN BY THE SECOND MARRIAGE.

1357. Charles Edwin.
1358. Robert John.
1359. George Denison.

910.

JOHN T. BULKELEY, son of John Charles and Sally *Taintor* Bulkeley, born October 3, 1801; married *Clarissa P. Bulkeley*, daughter of Elijah Bulkeley. They reside at Colchester, where he has held the office of deputy sheriff a long series of years.

CHILDREN.

1360. A son, died young, without name.
1361. Sarah Taintor, born August 29, 1835; m. *Gurdon Waterman*.
1362. Frank,   " January 6, 1839; m. *Lottie J. Talcott*.
1363. Robert,   " September 22, 1842. He was killed at the storming of Port Hudson in the war of the rebellion.
1364. John T.,   " November 23, 1845; died in 1858, aged 13.

911.

ELIPHALET ADAMS BULKELEY, son of John Charles and Sally *Taintor* Bulkeley, born January 20, 1803; married *Lydia S. Morgan*, of Colchester, March 31, 1830, and died in 1872. The following biographical sketch of Judge Bulkeley appeared in the columns of the *Hartford Courant* at the time of his decease:

"On Tuesday, the 6th instant, Judge Bulkeley, while seated in the office of the Ætna Life Insurance Company, of which he was president, was stricken with paralysis. During that day and the day following he was, at intervals, able to converse, but afterwards was wholly unconscious up to the time of his death, which occurred at his residence in Washington Street, at a quarter before seven o'clock last evening. For the past few years he has been almost wholly deprived of sight, and that affliction, which made it difficult for him to get about, gave him the appearance of being much more feeble in body than he really was.

"Judge Bulkeley was born in Colchester on the 20th of June, 1803, and was therefore sixty-nine years of age. He graduated at Yale College in the class of 1824, and after his graduation studied law in the office of William P. Williams, in Lebanon. In 1830 he was married to Lydia S. Morgan, of Colchester, who survives him, and at about that time he removed to East Haddam. He practiced law in that place, and was also president of the East Haddam Bank. He represented the town in the General Assembly, and was twice a member of the Senate from the nineteenth district. In 1847 he removed to Hartford, and filled the office of School Fund Commissioner. For several years he held official positions, and was a leading man in politics. In 1857 he was elected with Nathaniel Shipman to the legislature, from Hartford, and was chosen Speaker of the House of Representatives by the Union Republicans. He was originally a Whig, and joined the republican party at its formation. In the practice of law here he formed a partnership with the late Judge Henry Perkins, the firm being Bulkeley and Perkins. His later years have been devoted to the business of life insurance. He was the first president of the Connecticut Mutual Company, which he assisted in organizing, and subsequently, in 1850, organized the Ætna Life Company, taking its presidency at the start, and holding it to the time of his death. He was largely interested in all the Ætna moneyed corporations, banking and insurance, fire and life, and was also a director in the Willimantic Linen Company, and other concerns, besides being a leading stockholder in very many profitable business enterprises. Out of them he accumulated a handsome fortune, approximating a million of dollars.

"Judge Bulkeley's habits of life were very regular. He was especially prompt in all his engagements, making it a duty to be present at meetings where his presence was expected. It is said of him that for eighteen years he has never failed, until during his last sickness, to attend and preside over the meetings of the Pearl Street Ecclesiastical Society, to which he belonged. When he lived in Church Street his regularity of attendance at school meetings in the first district was a matter of remark, and since he removed to Washington Street he has been equally punctual at all the meetings of the south district. At all gatherings, whether religious, political, or otherwise, in which he took an interest he was never tardy. His regularity and promptness were not exceeded by any other citizen, probably. And he was especially faithful to all his political obligations. It was not enough that he should vote on election day, but he urged others to do so. He never neglected his duty as a citizen. One marked characteristic of the man was his wonderfully retentive memory as to individuals and dates. His knowledge in this respect enabled him to give, with surprising accuracy, many genealogical facts relating to families, whose own members were in ignorance. Few men have lived in the state who have possessed such general information with regard to individual associations. In other respects his knowledge was quite extensive, accurate, and valuable."

CHILDREN.

1365. Mary Morgan, born October 21, 1833; died June 20, 1835.
1366. Charles Edwin, " December 16, 1835; graduated at Yale College in 1856; lawyer at Hartford; captain of artillery in the civil war, and died in the service, December, 1864, while in command of Fort Garesche, near Washington.
1367. Morgan Gardner," December 26, 1837.
1368. William Henry, " March 2, 1840; m. *Emma Guerney.*
1369. Mary Jerusha, " September 27, 1843; m. *Leverett Brainard.*
1370. Eliphalet Adams," July 11, 1847; died December 17, 1848.

912.

Dr. J. E. A. BULKELEY, son of Jonathan and Elizabeth *Simons* Bulkeley, born Nov. 16, 1823; married *Clara C. Stark.* Resides at Wilkesbarre, Penn.

913.

FRANCES BULKELEY, daughter of Jonathan and Elizabeth *Simons* Bulkeley, born March 10, 1832; married *A. R. Brundage*, Esq., attorney-at-law in Wilkesbarre, Penn., Sept. 22, 1853.

BULKELEY FAMILY.

CHILDREN.
1371. Richard Bulkeley *Brundage*, born June 22, 1854.
1372. Elizabeth Mary   "   ". Feb. 22, 1857; died July, 1858.
1373. Mary Gillett.

924.

Roxy Bulkeley, daughter of John and Theodora *Foote* Bulkeley; married *James M. Goodwin* of East Hartford, Dec. 21, 1809.

CHILDREN.

1374. James M.,   born Oct. 1, 1810; m. { 1. *Julia Dunham.*
                                              { 2. *Charlotte Boyd.*
1375. Frederick,   " July 24, 1812.
1376. Mary,   " Jan. 26, 1818.
1377. Henry Wheaton,   " April 26, 1823.
1378. William Alfred, " Feb. 14, 1831.

926.

Henry Bukeley, son of William and Mary *Champion* Bulkeley, born June 16, 1791; married   , and resided in Middle Haddam.

928.

Mary Bulkeley, daughter of William and Mary *Champion* Bulkeley, born July 13, 1793; married *Charles Hurd* of Middle Haddam, Conn. They had no children.

930.

William Bulkeley, son of Gershom and ——— *Noble* Bulkeley. Married and had one child at Kinderhook, N. Y. Nothing further is known.

CHILD.

1379. William.

933.

Judith Bulkeley, daughter of Gershom and ——— *Noble* Bulkeley, born   ; married Platt Talcott of Lanesboro, Mass.

936.

Richard Bulkeley, son of Elijah and Pamelia *Loomis* Bulkeley, born Dec. 26, 1787; married *Aurel Chapman*, Dec. 23, 1813.

CHILDREN.
1380. Guy Richard,   born Sept. 14, 1816.
1381. Clarissa Pamelia, " April 30, 1819; died 1844.

937.

CELINDA BULKELEY, daughter of Elijah and Pamelia *Loomis* Bukeley, born Aug. 23, 1793; was twice married: 1. To *Alanson Porter* of Williamstown, Mass. 2. To *Russel Chapman* of Colchester, Conn. She died childless, Dec. 1, 1867.

938.

EMELINE U. BULKELEY, daughter of Elijah and Pamelia *Loomis* Bulkeley, born Sept. 12, 1806; married *Pomeroy Hall*, a merchant of Colchester, Oct. 5, 1823. He was born May 8, 1796, and died July 9, 1865.

1382.	Edwin Bulkeley	*Hall*, born Feb. 5, 1826; died in infancy.		
1383.	Cornelia Pomeroy	"	"	May 18, 1828; m. Rev. *Bradford M. Dinsmore*, Nov. 20, 1852.
1384.	Jane Elisabeth	"	"	Jan. 20, 1830; m. *Daniel Kellog* of Colchester, May 25, 1850.
1385.	Frances Emeline	"	"	Aug. 22, 1833.
1386.	Charles Edwin	"	"	Oct. 10, 1835; died in infancy.
1387.	Samuel Loomis	"	"	Oct. 20, 1837; died in infancy.
1388.	Sarah Pamelia	"	"	Jan. 26, 1839; m. *Ira N. Dinsmore*.
1389.	Alonzo Pomeroy	"	"	April 5, 1841; died in infancy.
1390.	Edward	"	"	Aug. 10, 1843; died in infancy.
1391.	Catharine	"	"	Dec. 29, 1844; died in infancy.
1392.	James Dow	"	"	May 3, 1846; m. *Sarah J. Chappell*, Sept. 20, 1867.

939.

CLARISSA PAMELIA BULKELEY, daughter of Elijah and Pamelia *Loomis* Bulkeley, born May 8, 1809; married *John T. Bulkeley*, by whom she had four children. (For her children *vide* Head No. 910.)

940.

SOPHIA MARIA BULKELEY, daughter of Elijah and Pamelia *Loomis* Bulkeley, born Nov. 15, 1811; married *Jonathan Chappell*. They had no children.

942.

JOHN A. TAINTOR, son of Roger and Abigail *Bulkeley* Taintor, married *Delia Crook*, and had—

CHILDREN.

1393.	Louisa *Taintor*, born July 28, 1832; m. *Charles Kneeland*.
1394.	Alice	"	"	Dec. 29, 1835.

943.

CLARISSA BULKELEY, daughter of Joshua Robbins and Sally *Taintor* Bulkeley, born ; married *Job Pierson*.

944.

MARY BULKELEY, daughter of Joshua Robbins and Sarah *Taintor* Bulkeley, born ; married *Parker Hall*.

947.

ADALINE BULKELEY, daughter of Gad and Orra *Barstow* Bulkeley, born ; married *Jared Warner Fitch*.

948.

JOHN WORTHINGTON BULKELEY, son of Gad and Orra *Barstow* Bulkeley, born 1811; married three times: 1. To *Adelaide Hilliard*. 2. To *Eliza Tracy*. 3. To Widow *Helen Reynolds*.

949.

SAM BARSTOW BULKELEY, son of Gad and Orra *Barstow* Bulkeley, born Jan. 21, 1813; married *Mary Elisabeth Roath*, Sept. 30, 1839. Mr. Bulkeley is a druggist in Norwich, Conn.

CHILDREN.

1395. Mary Worthington, born Nov. 6, 1840.
1396. Emma Roath, " May 25, 1844.

953.

HARRIET AMELIA BULKELEY, daughter of Gurdon and Fanny *Wright* Bulkeley, born Sept. 1, 1799; married Dr. *Alvan Wheeler*, May 24, 1826. They lived successively at Great Barrington, Mass., Greenbush and Binghamton, N. Y., and with their oldest son, Gurdon Bulkeley Wheeler, in Delaware, where Dr. Wheeler died Oct. 12, 1868. Mrs. Wheeler now resides at Upsonville, Penn., with her oldest daughter, Fannie Adeline, wife of Franklin F. Smith. Dr. Alvan Wheeler graduated at Williams College, where he was tutor for two years; took his professional diploma at Pittsfield Medical Institution; practiced medicine successfully at Great Barrington, Mass., till forced by asthma to desist; taught a classical school two years at Greenbush, N. Y.; then became a farmer at Binghamton, N. Y., where for several years he was a prominent member of the Presbyterian church session. He was a man of extensive reading, correct taste, and active piety.

CHILDREN.

1397.	Gurdon Bulkeley	Wheeler,	born Aug. 15, 1829; m. *Cynthia L. Knight.*
1398.	Benjamin	"	" May 15, 1831; died May 7, 1843.
1399.	Fanny Adaline	"	" Aug. 25, 1833; m. *F. F. Smith.*
1400.	Edmund	"	" May 5, 1835; m. *Nellie Cutting.*
1401.	Samuel Porter	"	" Jan. 12, 1839; m. *Catharine F. E. Goss.*
1402.	Hattie	"	" April 19, 1845.

955-1.

ALBERT RODNEY BULKELEY, son of Gurdon and Fanny *Wright* Bulkeley, born Oct. 14, 1802; married *Delia Catharine Brown*, April, 1832, and have had one child.

956.

REV. HIRAM WORTHINGTON BULKELEY, son of Gurdon and Fanny *Wright* Bulkeley, born March 30, 1807; was for three years a member of Williams College, in the class of 1831; taught as principal of the academy at North Granville, N. Y.; studied theology at the Auburn Seminary; preached a short time at North Adams, Mass.; bought in 1836 Dr. Wheeler's interest in the school at Greenbush, N. Y.; removed the school in 1839 to Ballston, N. Y., of which he is still the proprietor. He married *Mary Jane Oliphant*, Dec. 10, 1834.

CHILDREN.

1403.	Mary Elisabeth,	born	April 25, 1836; m. *Samuel Thomas Black*, May 7, 1861.
1404.	Robert Worthington,	"	July 17, 1837; died Jan. 1, 1838.
1405.	Robert Burrage,	"	Oct. 22, 1838; died Feb. 26, 1843.
1406.	Fannie,	"	May 21, 1841; m. *James F. Doolittle*, June 5, 1869.
1407.	Mansfield,	"	Dec. 4, 1844; died May 24, 1847.
1408.	Charles,	"	July 24, 1847.
1409.	Emma,	"	Feb. 13, 1849; m. *Frank H. Morris*, June 18, 1874.
1410.	John Scudder,	"	Dec. 9, 1850; m. *Alice Earl*, Dec. 17, 1873.
1411.	Susie,	"	May 13, 1853.
1412.	William Fairchild,	"	Aug. 26, 1854.
1413.	Worthington,	"	April 12, 1856.

957.

SOPHIA ADALINE BULKELEY, daughter of Gurdon and Fanny *Wright* Bulkeley, born October 20, 1808; married *Benjamin Franklin Hoxsey* in September, 1830, and died without issue, April 4, 1832. Rev. Benjamin F. Hoxsey graduated at Williams College, and at Auburn Theological Seminary, became a home missionary in Missouri, was a sincere and earnest preacher, and died early.

958.

FRANCES EMELINE BULKELEY, daughter of Gurdon and Fanny *Wright* Bulkeley, born July 31, 1810; married Rev. George Clinton Wood, who graduated at Williams College, and at Auburn Theological Seminary, became a home missionary in Missouri, where he labored for many years with zeal and success. He now resides at Jacksonville, Ill.

959.

GURDON HENRY BULKELEY, son of Gurdon and Fanny *Wright* Bulkeley, born March 27, 1812; married *Susan Eliza Brown*, December 4, 1834. He invented and patented a process for drying grain and lumber for exportation by superheated steam, without pressure, which has proved extensively useful.

960.

ARISTARCHUS BULKELEY, son of Gurdon and Fanny *Wright* Bulkeley, born May 3, 1813. He has been twice married—1, to *Mary Matilda Chamberlain*, March 27, 1834. who died February 16, 1836; 2, to *Mary E. Harrison*, December 24, 1838, and died March 11, 1872.

961.

CLARISSA BULKELEY, daughter of Gurdon and Fanny *Wright* Bulkeley, born June 15, 1816; married *Hurlburt F. Fairchild*, September 14, 1841. Mr. Fairchild pursued classical studies at Williams College, practiced law in Arkansas, became judge of Supreme Court, and resigned during the civil war. He was a distinguished jurist, and for his calm good sense and general affability was loved and honored by all who knew him.

962.

RALPH BULKELEY, son of Gurdon and Fanny *Wright* Bulkeley, born April 9, 1817; married *Mercy Briggs*, in April, 1857.

963.

DON ALONZO BULKELEY, son of Gurdon and Fanny *Wright* Bulkeley, born November 12, 1819; married *Marietta Townsend*, November 28, 1843. He is known to the agricultural societies of several states as the man to whom the country is indebted as the originator of several of our choicest varieties of potatoes, among which are the "Monitor," the "Bulkeley Seedling," the "Berkshire," &c. He resides on the paternal Stone Hill Farm in Williamstown, Mass.

CHILDREN.

1414. Alice Amelia, born February 20, 1845; m. *Daniel Jay Sweet*, January 13, 1869.
1415. William Alonzo, born May 20, 1848; m., 1, *Henrietta C. Pearl*, Dec. 16, 1869, who died; 2, *Mary Elenor Beckstern*, April 7, 1873.
1416. Caroline Frances, born January 20, 1850; m. *Alfred D. Hubbard*, December 13, 1871.

964.

LUCIUS EDWARDS BULKELEY, son of Gurdon and Nancy *Porter* Bulkeley, born January 17, 1824, graduated at Williams College, studied law with Judge Cady, of Albany, practiced for several years in New York City, and more recently at San Francisco, possesses great energy, and is an earnest and successful advocate. He married *Mary King Tuthill*, May 17, 1852.

CHILD.

1417. Lucius, born March 10, 1854.

971.

EZRA FOOTE, son of Roger and Eunice *Bulkeley* Foote, born June 7, 1795; married *Sarah Louisa Bowles*, October 22, 1818. They settled in Painesville, Ohio.

CHILDREN.

1419. Mary Ann *Foote*, born September 14, 1819; m. Rev. Henry Tulledge.
1420. Charles Bowles " September 10, 1821.
1421. Caroline Amelia " October 12, 1823; m. *Edward Killam*.
1422. Sarah L. " April 26, 1826, died October 3, 1826.
1423. Edward Augustus " October 27, 1827.
1424. Sarah Louisa " January 23, 1830; died January 25, 1831.
1425. Robert B. " June 4, 1832.

977.

DAVID FOOTE, son of Roger and Eunice *Bulkeley* Foote, born August 15, 1809; married *Caroline Taylor*, daughter of Joseph and *Esther Taylor*, and settled at Great Barrington, Mass.

CHILDREN.

1426. Edward *Foote*, born March 10, 1836.
1427. Sarah E. " " June 26, 1838.

1004.

CAROLINE BULKELEY, daughter of George and Sophia *Loomis* Bulkeley, born November 4, 1807; married *Thomas Durphy Lord*, July 16, 1825.

CHILDREN.

1428.	William Lucas	*Lord,*	
1429.	Ann Eliza	"	
1430.	Robert Augustus	"	
1431.	Aurelia Bulkeley	" born December 1st, 1832; m. William H. Haskell.
1432.	Josephine Caroline	"	" August 31, 1835.
1433.	George Washington	"	"

1005.

AURELIA BULKELEY, daughter of George and Sophia *Loomis* Bulkeley, born October 12, 1810, married, 1, to *Albert H. Quimby*, March 20, 1842. He died June 10, 1842. 2, To *John Dredye*, of Peoria, Ill., September 11, 1850. He died September 18, 1869. They had no children.

NINTH GENERATION.

1012.

SARAH A. BULKELEY, daughter of Francis and Content *Mix* Bulkeley, born November, 1814; married Henry D. Field, of Waterbury. Nothing farther is known.

1013.

FRANCES HENRIETTA BULKELEY, daughter of Francis and Content *Mix* Bulkeley, born September, 1817; married *Matthew G. Elliot*. No record of children has been furnished.

1014.

ANNA ALEXANDER BULKELEY, daughter of James H. and Adaline *Alexander* Bulkeley, born April 13, 1829; married *Henry S. Ogden*, July 3, 1853.

CHILDREN.

1434.	Henry A.	*Ogden,*	born July 17, 1856.
1435.	Frances	"	" Feb. 28, 1860; died Jan. 8, 1861.
1436.	Rosalie Adaline	"	" June 9, 1863.
1437.	Helen Agnes	"	" March 26, 1866.

1018.

MARGARET AMELIA BULKELEY, daughter of James II. and Adaline *Alexander* Bulkeley, born Feb. 5, 1836; married *Edward McIntire*, Oct. 12, 1865.

CHILDREN.

1438.	Edward Harding	*McIntyre*,	born Sept. 26, 1866.
1439.	Alexander Reed	"	" May 19, 1869.
1440.	Henry Bulkeley } twins,	"	
1441.	Clarissa Stanley }	"	" Oct. 10, 1872.

1021.

WILLIAM ALEXANDER BULKELEY, son of James II. and Adaline *Alexander* Bulkeley; married *Mary A. Riley*, Feb. 14, 1863. He was in the U. S. Army during the Rebellion, as Hospital Steward, at Satterlie, Philadelphia, and at Port Royal, S. C., and has lately been appointed Superintendant of the New House of Correction.

CHILDREN.

1442. Mary Adaline,   born March 26, 1866; deceased May 13, 1866.
1443. William Alexander,   " May 13, 1867.

1025.

ELIZA HUNT BULKELEY, daughter of Charles and Eliza *Hunt* Bulkeley, born Aug. 15, 1829; married *Thomas C. Hill*, Jan. 19, 1856.

CHILDREN.

1444. Sophia Perry *Hill.*
1445. Charles   "
1446. Helen Hunt   "

1026.

ANN CAROLINE BULKELEY, daughter of Charles and Eliza *Hunt* Bulkeley, born Nov. 11, 1831; married *John Mickle*.

CHILDREN.

1447. Sarah Prentiss *Mickle.* Died in infancy.
1448. John   "

1027.

FRANCES LOUISA BULKELEY, daughter of Charles and Eliza *Hunt* Bulkeley, born Nov. 4, 1833; married *Stephen Brock*, of St. Louis, Missouri.

1029.

CHARLES BULKELEY, JUN., son of Charles and Eliza *Hunt* Bulkeley, born May 17, 1838; married *Sarah Tudor*.

CHILD.

1449. William Tudor.

1037.

DR. EDWARD BULKELEY, JUN., born in New Haven, in 1833; received the degree of Dr. of Medicine from the Medical Department of Yale College, in July, 1856. Entered the volunteer army as a medical officer, 6th Regiment Connecticut Volunteer Infantry, commission dated Sept. 2, 1861. Served in South Carolina, Florida, and Virginia, and was mustered out by expiration of term of service, in Virginia, September, 1864. Served as A. A. Surgeon, U. S. A., in Washington, D. C., from November, 1864, to July, 1865. Since that time has continued to practice medicine in New Haven. He married *Grace Caroline Bishop*, of New Haven, May, 1867.

CHILDREN.

1450. Jane Bouticon, born May, 1868.
1451. Lucy Mansfield, " March, 1870.
1452. Grace Chetwood, " November, 1872.
1452½. Edward, " March 12, 1875.

1069.

JULIA BULKELEY, daughter of Francis and Grace J. *Adams* Bulkeley, born Sept. 3, 1823; married *M. S. Converse*, A. M., of Otsego, N. Y. Now living at Elmira, Chemung County, N. Y.

CHILDREN.

1453. Georgiana *Converse*, born Oct. 12, 1850.
1454. Helen " " May 25, 1856.

1086.

REV. EDWIN ADOLPHUS BULKELEY, D. D., son of Erastus and Mary *Walbridge* Bulkeley, born at Charleston, S. C., Jan. 25, 1826; graduated at Yale College, in the Class of 1844, and at the Union Theological Seminary of New York, in 1847: was pastor of the Congregational Church of Geneva, N. Y., from 1847 to 1850. Pastor of the Congregational Church of Groton, Mass., from 1850 to 1864: was installed pastor of the Presbyterian Church of Plattsburgh, N. Y., in 1864. where he still resides. He received the degree of S. T. D., from the University of Vermont, in 1868. He is the author of a number of printed sermons, two of which, "Wars and Rumors of Wars." at the breaking out of the Rebellion in 1861, and "The Uncrowned Nation," on the death of President Lincoln, in 1865. attracted considerable notice at the time, and have been widely circulated. He married *Catharine F. Oakley*, of Huntington, L. I. They have had eight children, three only of whom are living.

CHILDREN.
Names received too late to be mentioned in regular order.

(1.)	Theodore Meier,	born at Groton, Mass.,	Aug. 26, 1849;	died July 29, 1860.
(2.)	Charles Henry,	" "	June 16, 1851;	died June 28, 1871.
(3.)	Mary Virginia,	" "	Oct. 13, 1853.	
(4.)	Catharine Frederica Kunze,	" "	Feb. 1, 1856; died July 11, 1860.	
(5.)	Helen Muhlenberg,	" "	Jan. 22, 1861.	
(6.)	Edwin,	" "	Sept. 10, 1862.	
(7.)	Arthur Hanks,	born at Plattsburgh, N. Y..	Nov. 19, 1864;	died Nov. 7, 1865.
(8.)	Eliza Jaffray,	" "	Jan. 15, 1867;	died July 31, 1869.

1087.

THEODORE AUGUSTUS BULKELEY, son of Erastus and Eunice *Robbins* Bulkeley, born   ; married *Harriet Lockwood Skinner*, August 26, 1851. They had no children.

1088.

FREDERICK CONRAD BULKELEY, son of Erastus and Eunice *Robbins* Bulkeley, born   ; married, Oct. 2. 1855. *Fannie M. Wilcox*.

CHILDREN.

1455.	Jennie Wilcox,	born Feb. 4, 1862.
1456.	Mary Walbridge,	" Sept. 22, 1863.
1457.	Minnie Adele,	" Jan. 30, 1866; died Sept. 27, 1869.

1089.

HENRY DEMING BULKELEY. son of Erastus and Eunice *Robbins* Bulkeley. born   ; married *Carra A. Bybee*, Dec. 15, 1856. They have had seven children, of whom only four survive.

CHILDREN.

1458. Maggie Adair, born July 16, 1858.
1459. Henry Walbridge, " Dec. 13, 1860.
1460. Joseph Norman, " Sept. 17, 1868.
1460¼. Nellie Witherspoon, " June 25, 1870.

1090.

REGINALD WALBRIDGE BULKELEY, son of Erastus and Eunice *Robbins* Bulkeley, born   ; married *Carrie A. Wilkinson*, Have had two children, of whom only one survives. Mr. Bulkeley died June 1, 1873.

CHILDREN.

1461. Erastus Woodbridge, born Feb. 6, 1853.
1461½. Edward Wilkinson, " May 22, 1861; died July 28, 1862.

1091.

MARY VIRGINIA, daughter of Erastus and Mary *Walbridge* Bulkeley, born   ; married *Arthur F. Hanks*, of Hartford, Conn., and they have no children.

1092.

CHARLES S. HALL, son of S. H. P. and Emeline *Bulkeley* Hall, born June 23, 1824; graduated at Yale College in the class of 1849; married *Mary Harris*, of Ballston, New York; residence, Binghamton, N. Y.

CHILDREN.

1461¾. Louise H.   *Hall*, born March 17, 1858; died Sept. 4, 1858.
1462. Charles H.   "   "   March 19, 1860.
1463. Arnold H.   "   "   May 5, 1863.
1464. Samuel Holden Parsons   "   "   Oct. 10, 1868.

1093.

WILLIAM B. HALL, son of S. H. P. Hall, born July 15, 1829; married *Elizabeth S. I. Paddock*, March, 1851. He died Jan. 27, 1856. She died Jan. 12, 1867, leaving no children.

1094.

JOSEPHINE E. M. HALL, daughter of S. H. P. and Emeline *Bulkeley* Hall, born March 17, 1831; married *Hugh Allen*, of New York, May 17, 1853; and died Jan. 12, 1857.

CHILD.

1465. Josephine E. A. *Allen*, born Dec. 25, 1856.

1095.

THEODORE PARSONS HALL, son of S. H. P. and Emeline *Bulkeley* Hall, born Dec. 15, 1835; graduated at Yale in 1857, and married Jan. 11, 1860, *Alexandrine Louise Godfrey*, and resides at Detroit, Michigan. She was born May 4, 1836.

CHILDREN.

1466. Maria Stella Holden *Hall*, born December 26, 1860.
1467. Josephine E. " " June 5, 1862.
1468. Samuel Holden Parsons " " June 30, 1864; died Dec. 15, 1864.
1468½. Nathalie Heloise " " June 1, 1866.
1469. Corinne Alexandrine " " Feb. 11, 1868; died Feb. 2, 1869.
1470. Alexandrine Eugenie " " Dec. 4, 1869.
1470½. Maria Archange Naverre " " Sept. 7, 1872.

1096.

RICHARD H. HALL, son of Samuel H. P. and Emeline *Bulkeley* Hall, born Oct. 28, 1839; was twice married. 1. To *Hannah P. Trowbridge*, of New York, Oct. 28, 1861. She died Dec. 30, 1863. 2. To *Kate E. Cresswell*, Oct. 30, 1867. Mr. Hall died Oct. 7, 1872.

CHILD.

1471. Edwin Trowbridge *Hall*, born Dec. 16, 1863.

1107.

ANNA CATHARINE NORTH, daughter of Alfred and Minerva *Bryan* North, born Dec. 3, 1840; married *Alva D. Wilder*, of Sacramento, Cal., Nov. 1870; lives at South Vallejo.

CHILDREN.

1472. Edwin Milton *Wilder*, born Oct. 1871.
1473. Frank " " Oct. 1873.

1108.

Rev. THOMAS HASTINGS NORTH, son of Alfred and Minerva *Bryan* North, born Jan. 22, 1843, at Singapore; married *Sarah Humphrey*, Feb. 29, 1868. Resides at Wakefield, Kansas.

CHILDREN.

1474. Laura Minerva *North*, born May 23, 1869.
1475. Martha Caroline " " Jan. 14, 1871.
1476. Alfred Myron " " June 9, 1872.
1477. An infant son (not named), " May 12, 1875.

1112.

JULIA WARD POST, daughter of Gerrit P. and Ruth *Keith* Post, born Oct. 20, 1836; married *Frederick Fitch*, of Lexington, Kentucky, June 13, 1861. He married her sister, *Margaret L.*, Oct. 1, 1868.

CHILDREN.

1476.	John Gerrit	*Fitch*, born April 5, 1863; died Jan. 10, 1869.
1477.	Ellen Pauline	"	" May 4, 1864.
1478.	Julia Post	"	" May 17, 1866; died June 16, 1866.

1114.

MARGARET LOUISA POST, daughter of Gerrit P. and Ruth *Keith* Post, born March 23, 1846; married *Frederick Fitch*, of Lexington, Kentucky, Oct. 1, 1868.

CHILDREN.

1479. Frederick Keith *Fitch*, born May 26, 1871.
1480. Maurice " " Oct. 24, 1873.

1115.

BERTHA LOUISA POST, daughter of Peter Bulkeley and Elisabeth *Smith* Post, born April 12, 1846; married *Charles Allen Alger*, Oct. 20, 1870.

CHILDREN.

1481. Lucy Elizabeth *Alger*, born July 23, 1871.
1482. John Post " " Dec. 7, 1872.

1122¼.

ELISABETH LAWRENCE BULKELEY, adopted daughter of Joseph E. Bulkeley; married *George A. Welles*, January 10, 1860.

CHILDREN.

1. Mary Lawrence *Welles*, born Nov. 5, 1861.
2. Edmund Bulkeley " " Jan. 31, 1863.
3. George Augustus " " April 5, 1865.
4. Elizabeth M. " " April 2, 1867.

1123.

EDMUND WILLIAMS BULKELEY, son of Joseph Edmund and Mary L. Bulkeley, born Oct. 2d, 1838; married *Caroline J. Turner*, March 16, 1870. He died May 7, 1875, without issue. He was engaged with his father and younger brother at the time of his decease in the wholesale leather business.

1124.

JUSTUS LAWRENCE BULKELEY, son of Joseph Edmund and Mary L. Bulkeley, born July 4, 1840; married *Laura E. Caldwell*, Feb. 15, 1871. Is in the wholesale leather business in New York with his father.

CHILD.

1483. Josephine, born August 12, 1872.

1125.

JOSEPHINE BULKELEY, daughter of Joseph Edmund and Mary L. Bulkeley, born Dec. 13, 1841; married *Theodore M. Barnes*, April 25, 1867.

CHILDREN.

1484. Catharine Moore *Barnes*, born May 7, 1868.
1485. Joseph Bulkeley " " July 22, 1869.
1486. Theodore M. " " Dec. 13, 1874.

1126.

MARY BULKELEY, daughter of Joseph Edmund and Mary L. Bulkeley, born Jan. 24, 1843; married *Ferdinand S. Entz*, June 8, 1865.

CHILDREN.

1487. Justus Bulkeley *Entz*, born June 16, 1867.
1488. Marian Wood " " Sept. 25, 1869.
1489. Theodore Barnes " " Nov. 10, 1871.
1489. Marguerite Bulkeley " " Jan. 11, 1873.

1145.

OSCAR F. MILLER, son of Solomon Bulkeley and Fanny *Burton* Miller, born April 4, 1831; married *Marion Walker*.

CHILDREN.

1491. Fay *Miller*, born May 11, 1858.
1492. Cora " " Oct. 20, 1862.
1493. Willie " " June 11, 1870.
1494. Robert " " June 22, 1873.

1148.

DOROTHY ESTHER MILLER, daughter of Solomon and Fanny *Burton* Miller, born April 13, 1836; married *George Loomer*, March 6, 1859.

CHILD.

1494½. Hettie *Loomer*, born April 23, 1865.

1206.

SARAH M. RISLEY, daughter of Edward and Nancy *Bulkeley* Risley, born March 6, 1847; married *Donald Le Vaughn*, Dec. 7, 1865.

CHILDREN.

1494. Ida *Le Vaughn*, born September, 1867.
1495. Edward   "   " October, 1869.

1207.

MARTHA W. RISLEY, daughter of Edward and Nancy *Bulkeley* Risley, born March 5, 1848; married *Frank Belden*, May 16, 1866.

CHILD.

1496. Frank *Belden*, born August 3, 1868.

1209.

EDWIN J. RISLEY, daughter of Edward and Nancy *Bulkeley* Risley, born August 15, 1850; married *Alice Belden*, March 9, 1873.

1226.

CAROLINE A. ROBBINS, daughter of Thomas and Martha C. *Sears* Robbins, born August 7, 1833; married *Woodruff Dunham*.

CHILDREN.

1497. A son *Dunham*. Died young.
1498. Mary   "

1227.

CHLOE M. ROBBINS, daughter of Thomas and Martha C. *Sears* Robbins, born Dec. 7, 1835; married *Chester C. Robbins*, in 1854.

CHILDREN.

1499. Frederick S.
1500. Samuel A.
1501. Eliza May.
1501½. Fannie Louise.
1502. Franklin.
1503. Caroline.

1237.

ANNIE AMELIA ROBBINS, daughter of Allen A. and Abby Ann *Goodrich* Robbins, born July 15, 1845; married *William G. Robbins*, August 24, 1870. Mr. Robbins is a farmer in Rocky Hill.

CHILDREN.

1504. Julia Amelia, born May 5, 1872; died April 2, 1874.
1505. Allen Williams, " February 16, 1874.

1250.

MARY BULKELEY, daughter of Hosea and Susan *Petit* Bulkeley, born April 12, 1842, in Wethersfield, Illinois; married *Edward S. Thompson*, of Glastonbury, July 8, 1866. Mr. Thompson is a merchant by occupation, and resides at South Glastonbury.

CHILDREN.

1506. Helen Thompson, born March 20, 1871.
1507. Susie May, " May 5, 1873.

1251.

SARAH GERTRUDE BULKELEY, daughter of Benjamin G. and Emily Abigail *Clark* Bulkeley, born July 3, 1841; married *Jasper E. Higby*, Dec. 19, 1863.

1252.

CAROLINE CHRISTINE BULKELEY, daughter of Benjamin G. and Emily Abigail *Clark* Bulkeley, born Nov. 18, 1843; married *William Henry Allen*, May 28, 1864.

1253.

WILLIAM BENJAMIN BULKELEY, son of Benjamin G. and Emily Abigail *Clark* Bulkeley, born Sept. 15, 1845; married *Hattie Moffet*, April 25, 1871.

1257.

SUSIE L. BUTLER, daughter of Philip and Caroline *Hart Bulkeley* Butler, born June 3, 1842; married *Benjamin Ranney*, of Middletown, Nov. 1, 1865. Mrs. Susie L. Ranney died Oct. 27, 1867.

CHILDREN.

1508. Gaston *Ranney*, born July, 1865; died Nov. 2, 1865.
1509. Charles " " June, 1867.

1258.

HORACE R. BUTLER, son of Philip and Caroline *Hart Bulkeley* Butler, born April, 1845; married *Cora Wilcox*, April 1, 1869.

CHILD.

1510. Barnard Butler, born October 8, 1870.

1268.

LAURA M. BEAUMONT, daughter of Lucius and Martha G. *Bulkeley* Beaumont, born Aug. 10, 1846; married *Frank Dickinson*, Sept. 6, 1865.

CHILD.
1511. Frank Beaumont *Dickinson*, born June 8, 1866.

1272.

LUCIUS S. BEAUMONT, son of Charles G. and Mary *Pratt* Beaumont, born June 22, 1843; married *Ellen Madigan*. They have no children.

1273.

GEORGE E. BEAUMONT, son of Charles and Mary *Pratt* Beaumont, born June 17, 1845; married *Emma Ward*, Oct. 31, 1867.

CHILDREN.

1512.	William Ward	*Beaumont*,	born August 21, 1868.
1513.	Schuyler Colfax	"	" March 4, 1870.
1514.	George E.	"	" May 6, 1872.

1275.

OLIVE BEAUMONT, daughter of Charles and Mary *Pratt* Beaumont, born Dec. 14, 1850; married *William E. Pratt*, of Essex, Conn.

1281.

CATHARINE SMYTH, daughter of Laura and Alfred Smyth, born ——; married *Robert Scranton*, 1870.

CHILDREN.

1515.	Laura	*Scranton*,	born April 10, 1872.
1516.	Anna Lockwood	"	" October 25, 1874.

1295.

ANNIE M. LOCKWOOD, daughter of John and Harriet L. Beaumont Lockwood, born Aug. 18, 1851; married *Raymond Clayhorn*.

CHILD.
1517. Mabel.   Died at six months old.

1296.

JOSEPHINE H. LOCKWOOD, daughter of John and Harriet L. Beaumont Lockwood, born May 22, 1853; married Col. *James Forney*.

1297.

HARRIET B. LOCKWOOD, daughter of John and Harriet L. Beaumont Lockwood, born May 17, 1855; married *Albert F. Mills*, Oct., 1873, and died at Philadelphia, April 24, 1875.

CHILD.

1518. Lockwood *Mills*, born April 21, 1875; died July 28, 1875.

1300.

HENRY CHAPMAN WILLIAMS, son of Moses W. and Abigail S. Smith Williams, born March 9, 1844; married *Cornelia Neff*.

1302.

ELLA FRANCES WILLIAMS, daughter of Moses W. and Abigail S. Smith Williams, born December 13, 1853; married *Stephen Francis Churchill*.

1316.

ELISABETH EDWARDS, daughter of Walter and Jane *Bulkeley* Edwards, born October 29, 1844; married *Edward M. Francis*, March 24, 1870.

CHILDREN.

1521. Everett *Francis*, born September 26, 1872.
1522. Bernice E. "   "   June 16, 1874.

1340.

FANNIE REBECCA BULKELEY, daughter of Stephen and Prudence *Warner* Bulkeley, born November 2, 1850; married *John Hanmer*, January 28, 1874.

CHILD.

1523. Alice Elisabeth *Hanmer*, born November 4, 1874.

1361.

SARAH TAINTOR BULKELEY, daughter of John T. and Clarissa P. Bulkeley, born August 29, 1835; married *Gurdon Waterman*, in 1854, and in less than two years were both lost at sea.

1362.

FRANK BULKELEY, son of John T. and Clarissa P. Bulkeley, born January 16, 1839; married *Charlotte J. Talcott*, October 4th, 1868. She died July 16, 1872.

CHILD.

1524. Alice Talcott, born June 25, 1870.

1368.

WILLIAM HENRY BULKELEY, son of Eliphalet Adams and Lydia S. *Morgan* Bulkeley, born March 2, 1840; married *Emma Gurney*, of Brooklyn, N. Y., September 8, 1863. He is president of The Kellogg & Bulkeley Co., lithographers, Hartford, Conn.

CHILDREN.

1525. Mary Morgan, born June 21, 1864.
1526. William Eliphalet, " February 19, 1868.
1526¼. Charles Branford, " July 24, 1869; died August 13, 1869.
1526½. Grace Chetwood, " June 25, 1870.
1526¾. John Charles, " September 24, 1871.

1369.

MARY JERUSHA BULKELEY, daughter of Eliphalet Adams and Lydia S. *Morgan* Bulkeley, born September 27, 1843; married *Leverett Brainard*.

CHILDREN.

1527. Mary Lydia *Brainard*, born November 14, 1867.
1528. Charles Edwin, " December 10, 1869.
1529. Lucy Morgan, " January 22, 1872.
1530. Robert Leverett, " March 31, 1874.

1383.

CORNELIA POMEROY HALL, daughter of Pomeroy and Emeline U. *Bulkeley* Hall, born May 18, 1828; married Rev. *Bradford M. Dinsmore*, November 25, 1852.

CHILDREN.

1531. Jennie E. *Dinsmore*, born August 3, 1854; died October 11, 1858.
1532. Edward Arthur, " July 13, 1856; died January 5, 1858.
1533. Grace Chetwood, " October 29, 1861.

1384.

JANE ELISABETH HALL, daughter of Pomeroy and Emeline U. *Bulkeley* Hall, born January 20, 1830; married *Daniel Kellog*, of Colchester.

CHILDREN.

1534. Charles Edward *Kellog*, born December 14, 1852; died June 17, 1853.
1535. Edward Browning " December 4, 1856.
1536. Samuel Herbert " April 13, 1861.

1388.

SARAH PAMELIA HALL, daughter of Pomeroy and Emeline U. *Bulkeley* Hall, born January 26, 1839; married *Ira A. Dinsmore*, of Colchester. July 10, 1867.

1392.

JAMES DOW HALL, son of Pomeroy and Emeline U. *Bulkeley* Hall, born May 3, 1846; married *Sarah J. Chappel*, of New London, September 20, 1867.

1393.

LOUISE TAINTOR, daughter of John A. and Delia *Crook* Taintor, born July 28, 1832; married *Charles Kneeland*, May 11, 1854.

CHILDREN.

1537. Adele *Taintor*, born April 26, 1856.
1538. Alice,   "   "   November 23, 1860.

1397.

GURDEN BULKELEY WHEELER, son of Dr. Alvan and Harriet Amelia *Bulkeley* Wheeler, born August 15, 1829; married *Cynthia L. Knight*.

1399.

FANNY ADALINE WHEELER, daughter of Dr. Alvan and Harriet Amelia *Bulkeley* Wheeler, born August 25, 1833; married *F. F. Smith*.

1400.

EDWARD WHEELER, son of Dr. Alvan and Harriet Amelia *Bulkeley* Wheeler, born 1835; married *Nellie Cutting*.

1401.

SAMUEL PORTER WHEELER, son of Alvan and Harriet Amelia *Bulkeley* Wheeler, born January 12, 1839; married *Catharine F. E. Goss*, at Kalamazoo, Mich., January 11, 1860. She was born at Parsonsfield, Me., January 26, 1840. Mr. Wheeler was educated at the academy at Binghamton, in the classics; was admitted to the bar, December 9, 1859, and immediately thereafter entered upon the practice of law in Cairo, Ill., where he still resides.

CHILDREN.

1539. Alvan Goss *Wheeler*, born May 19, 1861; died June 12, 1861.
1540. Charles Everett " " September 20, 1862; died May 23, 1864.
1541. Katie " " August 30, 1864; died June 9, 1865.
1542. Edith " " October 27, 1865.
1543. Abbie " " August 31, 1868.
1544. Bessie " " April 23, 1871.
1545. Hattie " " August 15, 1872.
1546. Carrie " " October 11, 1873.
1547. Samuel Porter " " October 31, 1874.

1403.

MARY ELISABETH BULKELEY, daughter of Hiram Worthington and Mary Jane *Oliphant* Bulkeley, born April 25, 1836; married *Samuel Thomas Black*, May 7, 1861.

1406.

FANNIE BULKELEY, daughter of Hiram Worthington and Mary Jane *Oliphant* Bulkeley, born May 21, 1841; married *James F. Doolittle*, June 5, 1869.

CHILD.

1548. Millie F. *Doolittle*, born August 6, 1872.

1409.

EMMA BULKELEY, daughter of Hiram Worthington and Mary Jane *Oliphant* Bulkeley, born Feb. 13, 1849; married *Frank H. Morris*, June 18, 1874.

1410.

JOHN SCUDDER, son of Hiram Worthington and Mary Jane *Oliphant* Bulkeley, born Dec. 9, 1850; married *Alice Earl*, Dec. 17, 1873.

1415.

WILLIAM ALONZO BULKELEY, son of Dan. Alonzo, born May 20, 1848; was twice married: 1. To *Henrietta C. Pease*, Dec. 16, 1869. 2. To *Mary Eleanor Beckstern*, April 7, 1873.

CHILD.

1549. Alice, born March 25, 1871.

1118.

AURELIA BULKELEY LORD, daughter of Thomas Durphy and Caroline *Bulkeley* Lord, born Dec. 7, 1832; married at Canton, Ill., to *Wm. H. Haskell*, Nov. 2, 1851. He was born Jan. 4, 1828, at Troy, N. Y. Now publishing The Amboy, Illinois, Journal.

CHILDREN.

1550.	Henrietta Aurelia *Haskell*,	born Aug. 6, 1853, at Canton, Ill.
1551.	Josephine C.	"	" June 30, 1856.
1552.	William Lord	"	" April 20, 1858.
1553.	Mary Willis	"	" Jan. 17, 1864.

1419.

JOSEPHINE CAROLINE LORD, daughter of Thomas Durphy and Caroline *Bulkeley* Lord, born Aug. 31, 1835; married, in Canton, Ill., *Charles Smith*, April 16, 1856. Mr. Smith is a Cotton Manufacturer, at Worcester, Mass.

CHILDREN.

1554.	John Lord	*Smith*,	born Aug. 1, 1857.
1555.	Charles Worcester	"	" Oct. 7, 1860.
1556.	William Lord	"	" Feb. 9, 1863.
1557.	Frank Loomis	"	" Aug. 25, 1864.
1558.	Henry Witter	"	" Nov. 5, 1865.
1559.	Caroline Bulkeley	"	" Nov. 20, 1867.
1560.	Josephine Caroline	"	" March 9, 1870.

SECOND GENERATION.

17.

PETER BULKELEY, youngest son of Rev. Peter and Grace *Chetwood* Bulkeley, was born June 12, 1643. He came to Fairfield, Conn., with his mother; married and settled there, and was by profession a physician. The name of his wife has not been ascertained. She probably died before him. He made his will March 25, 1691, in the 19th year of his age. In said will he names his two oldest daughters, Grace and Margaret, and son Peter, 7½ years old. From the will of his brother Gershom, of Wethersfield, we find that he had other children, as Gershom and Dorothy, to whom his brother Gershom makes legacies. Gershom's will is some twenty years later than that of Peter. Peter's will commits three children, Margaret, Grace, and Peter, to the care of his brother Gershom, of Wethersfield, which would lead to the inference that they were the youngest.

The following is a copy of his will, taken from the Fairfield Probate Record.

"I Peter Bulkeley, in the 49th year of my age, now ready to go the way of all flesh, do die in the faith of that doctrine which has been preached among us. I give my soul to God that gave it. As to my small estate, my two feather beds with the bedding and linen, I would have them divided between my two oldest daughters, Grace and Margaret. As to that flock bed that is at Hannah Sherman's, there let it remain; or if young James Bennett have it, it shall be only upon courtesy, doing my executor's pleasure, as he may see cause, in the room of other clothing; and when Peter shall come to be bound let two indentures be written interchangeably, wherein the said James shall be engaged to teach him the art of weaving both lining and wooling to the best of his capacity, being bound to him 'till he become one and twenty, being now this day seven years and a quarter old. The mare that is now at Daniel Silliman's, the man that I had her of is to have her again, being so agreed upon between me and his agent Bradley, to be delivered at New Haven, together with a Bill of Nathaniel Chittenden for New Haven; the other horse must go into the estate. All the other estate I leave it wholly to my executor, whether physick or other household stuff, and as above so the house and land. I shall leave it wholly to my executor, he knowing all the concerns about it, and the writing being tyed safe in the trunk. I do here make my beloved brother, Gershom Bulkeley, my sole executor, to do and act in all things as occasion shall require. That this is my last will and testament is hereby declared by setting to my hand and seal this 25th of March, 1691.

PETER BULKELEY.

Witnesses.
JOHN BULKELEY.
WILLIAM HALL.

An Inventory follows this will, and was exhibited to the court July 7, 1691.

It seems he left Margaret and Peter, minors, to be clothed out of the estate, unless they shall be provided for by Mr. Gershom

Bulkeley. The persons appointed to see to this are John and Joseph Bulkeley. There was some difficulty involved, and the court appointed Thomas Jones to adjust the matter."

CHILDREN.

1561. Gershom.
1562. Dorothy.
1563. Margaret.
1564. Grace.
1565. Peter, born Dec. 25, 1683.

THIRD GENERATION.

1561.

GERSHOM BULKELEY, son of Peter Bulkeley, was admitted to full communion of the church in Fairfield, under Mr. Wells, June 13, 1731. He married *Rachel Talcott*.

CHILDREN.

1566.	Eunice,	baptized	Jan. 14, 1701–2.
1567.	Rachel,	"	March 3, 1706.
1568.	Gershom,	"	March 27, 1709.
1569.	Grace,	"	May 27, 1711.
1570.	Hezekiah,	"	Nov. 2, 1713.
1571.	Peter,	"	Feb. 5, 1715; died May 14, 1803.
1572.	Jonathan,	"	May 18, 1718.
1573.	Grace,	"	Feb. 2, 1720; m. *John Burr*, Nov. 9, 1741.
1574.	Talcott,	"	Aug. 23, 1724.

1565.

PETER BULKELEY, son of Peter Bulkeley, of Fairfield, and grandson of Rev. Peter Bulkeley, of Concord, Mass.; was a weaver—admitted to full communion Aug. 5, 1733. He married *Hannah Ward*, daughter of Samuel Ward, of Mill Plain. He had administration on his estate granted Dec. 9, 1752, and distribution Feb. 16, 1754. His will was probated Dec. 31, 1771, and he left to each of his nine children £112–13–4, the value of their portion of land.

CHILDREN.

1575.	David,	baptized	March 9, 1711.
1576.	Sarah,	"	Dec. 14, 1712; died young.
1577.	Sarah,	"	Nov. 2, 1713; m. *Joseph Perry*, Nov. 11, 1713; one son, Joseph.
1578.	Peter,	"	Oct. 9, 1715.
1579.	Andrew,	"	Oct. 6, 1717.
1580.	Gershom,	"	Aug. 13, 1721; died May 17, 1797.
1581.	Jabez,	"	Aug. 4, 1723.
1582.	Olive,	"	July, 1725; died Aug. 28, 1812.
1583.	Hannah,	"	Oct. 17, 1726; m. *Eleazer Osborne*.
1584.	Moses,	"	July 9, 1727.
1585.	James,	"	Aug. 3, 1729; died 1803.
1586.	Mary,	"	Oct. 17, 1731; m. Feb. 6, 1755, *Thomas Osborne*.

FOURTH GENERATION.

1568.

GERSHOM BULKELEY, son of Gershom and Rachel *Talcott* Bulkeley, married *Sarah Banks*, daughter of James Banks, May 17, 1736.

CHILDREN.

1587.	Amelia,	born Oct. 19, 1738; died May 27, 1754.
1588.	Joseph,	" Nov. 2, 1741; died April 22, 1742.
1589.	Gershom,	" Sept. 19, 1751; m. *Amelia Bradley*, May 3, 1776.

1570.

HEZEKIAH BULKELEY, son of Gershom and Rachel *Talcott* BULKELEY; married *Catharine Hill*, Jan. 4, 1739.

CHILDREN.

1590.	Ann,	born Sept. 13, 1739.
1591.	Hezekiah,	" Oct. 17, 1749.

1571.

PETER BULKELEY, son of Gershom and Rachel *Talcott* Bulkeley, born Feb. 5, 1715; died May 4, 1808. He married *Anna Hill*, July 9, 1740. She was born 1719, and died April 11, 1795.

CHILDREN.

1592.	William,	born	Feb. 17, 1741 ; died March 7, 1787.
1593.	Abigail,	"	April 12, 1743 ; m. *Daniel Burr*, April 20, 1769.
1594.	Grace,	"	April 7, 1745 ; died April, 1766.
1595.	Elizabeth,	"	Dec. 13, 1746 ; m. *Peter Morehouse*.
1596.	Gershom,	"	May 9, 1748.
1597.	Rachel,	"	March 30, 1750; m. *Robert and Peter Scudder*.
1598.	Jonathan,	"	Nov. 15, 1751.
1599.	Eunice,	"	April 9, 1753 ; m. *David Meeker*.
1600.	Abraham,	"	June 15, 1755.
1601.	Jerusha,	"	Jan. 26, 1757 ; m. *John Osborne*, May 16, 1780.
1602.	Eleanor,	"	July 21, 1759 ; m. *Lovel Chapman*, Dec. 30, 1779.
1603.	Anne,	"	Aug. 17, 1761 ; m. *Increase Burr*.

1574.

TALCOTT BULKELEY, son of Gershom and Rachel *Talcott* Bulkeley, born Aug. 23, 1724; married *Esther Bradley*, June 19, 1753.

CHILDREN.

1604.	Esther,	baptized	Sept. 10, 1754.
1605.	Molly,	"	Feb. 6, 1755 ; m. Dec. 19, 1774, *Joseph Morehouse*.
1606.	Amelia,	"	June 12, 1757.
1607.	Talcott,	"	Feb. 24, 1759.
1608.	Abigail,	"	Aug. 2, 1761 ; m. *Josiah Bradley*, of Greenfield, Jan. 28, 1779.
1609.	Happy,	"	June 19, 1763 ; m. *Gad Aldersman*, of Simsbury, June 18, 1783.
1610.	Bradley,	"	Jan. 20, 1765; died young.
1611.	Ruhamah,	"	Aug. 26, 1767.
1612.	Bradley,	"	May 7, 1769.

1575.

DAVID BULKELEY, son of Peter and Hannah *Ward* Bulkeley, baptized March 9, 1711; married *Sarah Beers*, of Fairfield, Conn.; removed with his brother Moses to Nine Partners, N. Y., when the war came on. He died in Weston, Conn., in 1804, aged 93. In his youth he was a weaver, farmer, deacon of the church, and a good man. He also was quite a poet. Not being comfortable at Nine Partners, his son David brought him to his home in Weston, where he died.

CHILDREN.

1613.	Eunice,	baptized	Aug. 28, 1737 ; died young.
1614.	Eunice,	"	Oct. 5, 1740; married *Daniel Godfrey*, of Weston.
1615.	Sarah,	"	June 6, 1742 ; m. *Benjamin Whittier*, Nov. 17, 1764.
1616.	David,	"	July 1, 1744 ; died Aug. 3, 1819.
1617.	Hannah,	"	June 5, 1746 ; m. *William Downes*.

1618.	Ward,	baptized	March 13, 1747-8.
1619.	Lois,	"	May 27, 1750 ; m. *Jonathan Cole*, May 15, 1770.
1620.	Isaac,	"	1753 ; died 1770.
1621.	Grace,	"	April 22, 1753 ; m. *Thaddeus Perry*, Jan. 19, 1774.
1622.	Joseph,	"	May 1, 1755 ; died June 4, 1813.

1577.

SARAH BULKELEY, daughter of Peter and Hannah *Ward* Bulkeley, baptized Nov. 2, 1713; married *Joseph Perry*, son of Joseph Perry, Nov. 11, 1736, died Aug. 20, 1753.

CHILDREN.

1623.	Peter	*Perry*,	born Feb. 4, 1738.
1624.	Joseph	"	" April 11, 1741 ; died May 9, 1743.
1625.	Sarah	"	" July 25, 1744.
1626.	Joseph	"	" Aug. 4, 1748.

1578.

PETER BULKELEY, son of Peter and Hannah *Ward* Bulkeley, baptized Oct. 9, 1715; was a sea captain from Black Rock, Conn., to the West Indies. He married for his first wife, *Sarah Turney*, daughter of Thomas Turney, Jan. 1, 1740-41; for his second, *Hannah Sherwood*, of Newtown, Feb. 14, 1760.

CHILDREN BY THE FIRST WIFE.

1627.	Elizabeth,	born Aug. 27, 1741 ; m.	*McInster*.
1628.	Andrew,	" Nov. 27, 1743.	
1629.	Peter,	" May 13, 1745.	
1630.	Aaron,	" Feb. 22, 1748.	
1631.	Sarah,	" Dec. 22, 1750 ; m.	*Meeker*.
1632.	Gershom,	" Feb. 6, 1753.	
1633.	Turney,	" June 9, 1755.	
1634.	Nathan,	" Feb. 16, 1757 ; died 1837.	

CHILD BY THE SECOND WIFE.

1635. Hannah, born Jan. 12, 1761.

1579.

ANDREW BULKELEY, son of Peter and Hannah *Ward* Bulkeley, born Oct. 6, 1717; married *Abigail*   , who died, Nov. 11, 1815, aged 76.

CHILD.

1636. Abigail,   baptized Nov. 8, 1771.

1581.

JABEZ BULKELEY, son of Peter and Hannah *Ward* Bulkeley, baptized Aug. 4, 1723; married *Elizabeth Osborne*, Nov. 5, 1747.

CHILDREN.

1637. Elisabeth *Osborne,* baptized Nov. 26, 1750.
1638. Lydia   "   " March 18, 1753, m. *Jonathan Bulkeley,* son of Gershom Bulkeley.
1639. Sarah   "   " April 2, 1758; m. *Ebenezer Sturgis.*

1583.

HANNAH BULKELEY, daughter of Peter and Hannah *Ward* Bulkeley, baptized Oct. 11, 1726; married *Eleazer Osborne,* June 29, 1738. She died May 22, 1788.

CHILDREN.

1640. Eleazer *Osborne,* born April 11, 1739.
1641. Sarah   "   " May 27, 1741.
1642. David   "   " Sept. 3, 1743.
1643. Gershom   "   " April 23, 1746.
1644. Hannah   "   " Nov. 11, 1748.
1645. Grezzel   "   " March 24, 1751.
1646. Ellen   "   " Dec. 18, 1754.
1647. Ebenezer   "   "

1584.

MOSES BULKELEY, son of Peter and Hannah *Ward* Bulkeley, born at Southport, July 9, 1727; married *Abigail Sturgis,* Aug. 29, 1758. They settled at Nine Partners, Washington, Dutchess County, New York.

CHILDREN.

1648. Jabez,   baptized Aug. 12, 1760.
1649. Ellen,   " May 30, 1762.
1650. Elizabeth,   " Nov. 25, 1764.
1651. Sturgis,   " June 14, 1767.
1652. Moses,   " Aug. 21, 1769.

1585.

JAMES BULKELEY, son of Peter and Hannah *Ward* Bulkeley, born Aug. 3, 1729; married *Elizabeth Whitehead,* Jan. 16, 1738; died June 27, 1809.

CHILDREN.

1653. Mary,   born April 3, 1757.
1654. Eunice,   " April 15, 1759.
1655. Abigail,   " Dec. 5, 1760; m. *Josiah Beardsley,* July 20, 1779.
1656. Eleazer,   " Feb. 2, 1763; died Feb. 5, 1843.
1657. Mabel,   " May 24, 1765; m. *Nathan Wheeler;* died Dec. 14, 1827.
1658. James,   " Aug. 27, 1768; died Sept. 15, 1805.

1659.	Elisabeth,	born June 14, 1772; died April 5, 1847; m. *Richard Bangs.*
1660.	Honkin,	" April 7, 1770; died Dec. 1, 1819.
1661.	Andrew,	" Sept. 4, 1774; died July, 1795.
1662.	Moses,	" Oct. 27, 1776; died July, 1795.
1663.	Mary,	" July 28, 1779; m. *Joab Squire.* Removed to Ohio in 1817.

1586.

MARY BULKELEY, daughter of Peter and Hannah *Ward* Bulkeley, born Oct. 17, 1731; married *Howes Osborne*, son of John Osborne, Feb. 6, 1755.

CHILD.

1664. John *Osborne,* born June 24, 1756.

FIFTH GENERATION.

1589.

GERSHOM BULKELEY, son of Gershom and Sarah *Banks* Bulkeley, born September 19, 1751; married *Amelia Bradley*, March 3, 1776.

CHILDREN.

1665. Amelia, born March 24, 1776; married *Lyman Hall*, October 22, 1797, and died in 1814.
1666. Bradley, " September 24, 1780; died October 5, 1781.
1667. Gershom, " June 28, 1784; died June 23, 1830.
1668. Timothy, " September 23, 1787; married *Susannah Osborne*, October 19, 1823; died October 12, 1857.

1591.

HEZEKIAH BULKELEY, son of Hezekiah and Catharine *Hill* Bulkeley, born October 17, 1749; married *Abigail Blackman*, February 23, 1775.

CHILDREN.

1669. Zalmon, born 1782; died March 2, 1842.
1670. Abigail, " September 28, 1790; married *Jesse Bradley.*
1671. Clarissa, " September 13, 1794; married *Squire Disbrow.*
1672. Huldah, "   ; married *David Oysterbanks*, and had one child, Ann Bulkeley; died November 3, 1805, aged 3.

1592.

WILLIAM BULKELEY, son of Peter and Ann *Hill* Bulkeley, born February 17, 1741; married *Elizabeth Burr*, who died in 1805, aged 62. He was one of the largest property holders of the borough of Southport. He built the house in which Miss Emily Meeker resides, and owned all the land east side of the bridge, including the woods to the water's edge; also the land where Mr. George Bulkeley now resides; the Congregational Church; the railroad station and all the land east of it to the main road. He died in 1787, aged 41.

CHILDREN.

1673. William, born 1768; died in 1808.
1674. Grace,   ; married April 27, 1788, 1, *Peter Whitney;* 2, *Ephraim Robbins.*
1675. Burr,   " July 24, 1777; married *Sarah Conklin.*
1676. Hill,   "
1677. Talcott,   "   of Greenfield.
1678. Elisabeth, "   ; married *Samuel Higgins,* September 24, 1804.
1679. Eunice,   " 1776; died in 1798.
1680. Anne Hill, " 1778; died unmarried, and left property.

1596.

GERSHOM BULKELEY, son of Peter and Ann *Hill* Bulkeley, born May 9, 1748; married. 1. *Elizabeth Chapman,* who died in 1795, aged 44. He removed from Sasco, Fairfield County, in the beginning of the century, first to Rye. N. Y., afterwards to Harrison, Westchester County, N. Y. Elizabeth Chapman, his first wife, had two sisters, one married Simon Couch, the other Talcott Banks, of the parish of Green's Farms. Her father was a clergyman, the Rev. Daniel Chapman, and preached at Green's Farms. Her brother, Lovell Chapman, lived and died at Green's Farms. James Chapman lived, near Muddy Brook, very secluded, (almost a hermit). He was a weaver. David Chapman removed to the state of Delaware. Denny Chapman went to Ballston, Saratoga County, N. Y. The younger Denny Chapman, the Protestant Methodist clergyman, lived at Plainfield, N. J. The Chapmans were once considered the "big guns" of the nation. Many of them went to the Susquehanna Country, and became thrifty farmers. He married, 2. *Widow Platt,* whose maiden name was *Raymond;* 3, *Mary Osborne,* widow of David, April 20, 1804. Her maiden name was *Bertram.*

CHILDREN.

1681. Mary,   married May 27, 1799, *Abijah Wakeman.*
1682. Elisabeth,   married February 5, 1797, *John Alvord.*

1683. Peter, born November 25, 1774; died June 27, 1840.
1684. Charles," April 5, 1786; died in 1794.
1685. Lovel, ⎫
       ⎬ twins,   died young.
1686. Desire, ⎭
1687. William,
1688. Gershom,

CHILDREN BY THE SECOND MARRIAGE.

1689. Caroline, baptized May 20, 1798.
1690. Abby Jane, born May 7, 1802; died May, 1838.

CHILDREN BY THE THIRD MARRIAGE.

1691. Ann,   married *Rev. E. Platt.*
1692. Jane,

There were five families of children dwelling as one in that patriarchal household, and it was a family of harmony and love. Neither before nor after his death was there any thing but the best of feeling between all its different branches. So great was the attachment that two marriages took place between the step children and his own children.

1598.

JONATHAN BULKELEY, son of Peter and Ann *Hill* Bulkeley, born November 15, 1751; married *Lydia Bulkeley*, daughter of Jabez, December 12, 1776.

CHILDREN.

1693. Barzilla, a minister settled in Flushing, L. I.; married *Mary Green.*
1694. Anna,
1695. Jonathan,   married *Ann Osborne.*
1696. Sarah,
1697. William, minister; married *Miss Battelle;* died at Santa Cruz.
1698. Anna,   married, 1, *Mr. Lane;* 2, *Mr. Leach.*
1699. Clarissa, ⎫
1700. Lydia,   ⎬   died young of consumption.
1701. Sarah,   ⎭

1600.

ABRAHAM BULKELEY, son of Peter and Anna *Hill* Bulkeley, born June 15, 1755; married *Jane* ———.

CHILDREN.

1702. Rachel, born May 21, 1784; died October 21, 1819; married *Stephen Osborne,* November 17, 1799.
1703. Francis, " January 30, 1786; died September 17, 1818.
1704. Esther, " July 13, 1789; married *Levi Downes,* January 14, 1816; died November 28, 1861.
1705. Charlotte," October 24, 1791; m. *David Jennings,* 1832; died May, 1874.
1706. Joel Burr," July 7, 1798; married *Priscilla Sturges.*

CAROLINE BULKELEY OSBORNE.

1612.

BRADLEY BULKELEY, son of Talcott and Esther Bulkeley, born May 7, 1769; married *Mollie Burr*, July 13, 1791.

CHILDREN.

1707. Harriet, baptized June 10, 1798.
1708. Abigail, " September, 1803.
1709. Mary Bradley, " October 20, 1805.

1617.

DAVID BULKELEY, son of David and Sarah *Beers* Bulkeley, born July 1, 1744. He married *Sarah*   , born in 1755; died in 1813. He died August 3, 1813.

CHILDREN.

1710. David Ward, born 1783; married *Rebeccah Gregory*, May 11, 1789.
1711. Aaron, " 1788; married *Anna* ———.
1712. Nehemiah, " 1791. He is now (1875) about 83 years of age
1713. Moses, " August, 1802; died in 1872, by an accident, aged 70.
1714. Sarah, " married *David Gallfray*.
1715. Lois, " married *Stephen Perry*.
1716. Eunice, " married *John Gilbert*.

1620.

ISAAC BULKELEY, son of David and Sarah *Beers* Bulkeley, born in Green's Farms, Conn., 1753; married November 8, 1762, *Deborah Couch*, who died October 31, 1816, aged 78.

CHILDREN.

1717. Deborah, born July 24, 1763; married *Abel Turney*, of Fairfield, December 26, 1784.
1718. Molly, " June 24, 1764; married, 1, *Abel Turney*; 2, *Aaron Cable*, February 23, 1806.
1719. Isaac, " 1766.
1720. Levi, baptized May 29, 1768; died young.
1721. David, born May 23, 1770; died in Waterbury, October 11, 1860, aged 90.

1622.

JOSEPH BULKELEY, son of David and Sarah *Beers* Bulkeley, born in Weston, Conn., May 1, 1755; married *Grizzel Thorp*, July 27, 1777.

CHILDREN.

1722. Isaac,   } m. *Mehetabel Simmons*.
                       } twins, born November 13, 1778;
1723. Clarissa,   } m. *Peter Sturgis*, July 7, 1799.
1724. Ward, " November 29, 1782; died March 8, 1862.
1725. Sarah, " July 9, 1784; m. *David Bradley*, Dec. 31, 1815.
1726. Eunice, " July 3, 1786; m. *Aaron Morehouse*, Oct. 25, 1807.

1727. Anna,   born December 22, 1787; died young.
1728. Anna,   "   October 30, 1789; died young.
1729. David,   "   August 1, 1791; m. *Deborah* ———; no children.
1730. Anna,   "   March 1, 1793; m. *Aaron Bulkeley*, Nov. 28, 1816.
1731. Joseph, ⎫   died in 1837.
               ⎬ twins," July 3, 1795;
1732. Benjamin,⎭   died January 26, 1872.
1733. Lois,   "   October 31, 1797; m. *Ebenezer Morehouse*.

1629.

PETER BULKELEY, son of Peter and Sarah *Turney* Bulkeley, born May 3, 1745; married May Green. He resides in Redding, Conn.

CHILDREN.

1733½. Peter, born about 1764.
1734. Mary,   "   1767.
1735. Sarah,   "   1770.
1736. Elisabeth," 1773.
1737. Phebe,   "   February 9, 1776; m. *Micajah Nash*; died Dec. 11, 1781.
1738. Gershom, "   July 29, 1779; died November 28, 1849.
1739. Lucy,   "   November 14, 1783; died November 9, 1864.
1740. Andrew, "   1785; m. *Damaris Wheeler*; died in 1860.
1741. Ebenezer G., born December 30, 1787; died February 11, 1871.
1742. Daniel S.,   "   December 17, 1790; died **August 28, 1872**.

1633.

TURNEY BULKELEY, son of Peter and Sarah *Turney* Bulkeley, born June 9, 1795; married Esther Johnson.

CHILDREN.

1743. William, born June 7, 1787; died, April, 1869.
1744. David,   "   1793; died January 24, 1823.
1745. Eunice, "   ; m. *Aaron Grey*.
1746. Sarah,   "   March 21, 1779; m. *David Burr*, November 24, 1803.
1747. Lucy,   "   ; m. *David Lyons*.
1748. Lois,   "   1784; m. *Washington Hall*, of Newtown, Conn.
1749. Eliza,   "   ; m. November, 1824, *Eli Hawley*. They live in Bethel, Conn.
1750. Arrety, "   ; m. November 27, 1819, *Morris Burr*, of Greenfield.
1751. Amelia, "   ; m. *Marcus Noble*.

1634.

NATHAN BULKELEY, son of Peter and Sarah *Turney* Bulkeley, born February 16, 1757. He removed from Fairfield to Danbury, Conn., in 1800, and preached in the First Baptist Church until his death, June 9, 1837. He married, 1, a *Jennings*; 2, *Anna* ———, who died February 1, 1817.

CHILDREN BY THE FIRST MARRIAGE.

1752. Sarah, married Marsh, of New Milford.
1753. Gershom, settled in New Milford.
1754. Deacon Nathan, born November 1, 1787; died April 11, 1858.
1755. Esther.

1856.

ELEAZER BULKELEY, son of James and Elisabeth Whitehead Bulkeley, born February 2, 1763; married Mary Ogden, daughter of Jonathan Ogden, December 22, 1785, of Mill Plain, Conn. The following historical sketch has been furnished by one of his descendants:

Eleazer Bulkeley was born February 2, 1763. His father, James, was a weaver, "and intended," he says in his narrative, "that I should learn the same trade, for which I had a great dislike. From eight to ten, at intervals, I was at school, and attending to my father's calls. From ten until twelve I was of some assistance to him, earning in the summer months twenty shillings a month. At twelve I inclined to follow a seafaring life, and at the close of the year 1774 left my home in Mill River, for New York, on a market boat. At the close of the month of April, 1775, the inhabitants were panic-struck at the news, by a messenger on horseback, of the battle of Lexington. The battle of Bunker Hill occurred soon after, and the people were now making every effort to put themselves into a common defense, both by sea and land.

"At the commencement of the year 1776 the Defense, an armed vessel, was fitted out at New Haven by the state of Connecticut. A goodly number of men, and boys too, enlisted in her from Fairfield, I among the latter, after receiving (reluctantly) my father's permission. We were taken from Black Rock, to the vessel then lying in New Haven Harbor, on the 13th of March, 1776, and returned in the Defense to Black Rock, when we learned of the evacuation of Boston by the British. We proceeded to Boston. Our first encounter was with a sloop and brig, and after a close contest both surrendered. The loss on their side was thirty-nine killed and wounded; on ours none killed, and a few only wounded. Colonel Campbell (captain) was taken prisoner. He was afterwards exchanged for Colonel Ethan Allen, then in England a prisoner. After this action we sailed for New London, where we were put on another vessel, to which the name of our old one was given, and in June started on a cruise. When ten or twelve days out I espyed a sail. On coming up to it we found it a British ship from Jamaica

We took off her crew, put a prize master on board, and ordered her back to New London. Early one morning in the last of September we left Holmes Hole for New London. For two months we remained in New London. While here I was severely bitten by a squirrel, and nearly lost my life by a fall. My skull was fractured, and it was some time before I recovered. In December our captain resigned for a more important charge, and, under command of another, we sailed for the West Indies. Through the winter we cruised about the islands, captured four prizes, which safely arrived at the several ports to which they were sent. In the following spring we returned to New Bedford, when I and a number of others applied for a discharge. Some time after this the Defense was ordered to Boston, to be cut in two and lengthened. We were discharged, and in the early summer I returned to my parents, after an absence of thirteen months, and for the services rendered in the Defense at this early age I am now receiving a pension.

"After remaining at home three or four months I found a number of my associates were joining a company in Fairfield, to go to New London to a privateer that was being fitted out, and I resolved at once to go. I knew my parents would not willingly give their consent to my going, so in the evening I bundled up a few clothes and threw them to the ground from the chamber window, mingled again with the family, and as opportunity offered walked out, took up my clothes and went to Fairfield, where I joined the company and repaired to Black Rock, thence to New London. We soon went to sea, and, as we fell in with no vessels, concluded to repair to the Western Islands and intercept vessels bound for Quebec. Shortly after we captured a British vessel bound for this port, and ordered her back to New Bedford. I was one of the crew put on board. It was thirty-nine days before we made land, and for thirteen days were in want of provisions, subsisting mostly on English damaged biscuit boiled in beer. (The arrival of the brig safely seemed almost a miracle, after passing by all the British ports, and not meeting with a single British sail.) Shortly after this I took passage in a privateer sloop for New London. Having arrived here, and ashamed to go home, having earned nothing, I enlisted in the Brig Nancy, and sailed, on the first of November, for the West Indies. After cruising for some time without success we sailed for Cayenne, on the Surinam coast. Much time was spent here. We, however, resumed the cruise on the first of January. Off Antigua we were run down by what we supposed was a British vessel, but which proved to be the American privateer, Bunker Hill, from Boston. This unlucky mistake broke up our cruise, and we bore up for home, arriving at New London in about fifteen days, after a cruise of five months. Here we found the Defense, bound for Fairfield, and I with a number of our crew took passage in her for Black Rock, not, however, to reach the latter place in this vessel, for we went back to New London. The ship brought up on a reef and was lost, and again I started for home in a galley. Arriving at Black Rock I gathered up my clothes and started for home, with a full determination to follow some other business beside privateering for the future. I was joyfully welcomed, notwithstanding my two last years had given my parents so much trouble and anxiety. My time now was mostly employed in going to school, and taking vacancies to keep guard.

"At the beginning of the year 1779, I enlisted with a company of forty men under command of Capt. E. Thorp. The guard was stationed close to the beach on the east side of Kinsey's Point; night only required close watch. But on the 7th of July, standing alone on the place now occupied by Oliver Perry, Esq., I saw two hundred British land on the hill opposite. They at once commenced the burning of Fairfield.

"At the opening of the year 1780 my time expired, and for this land service I am receiving a pension (1841) which, with my year's sea service, is termed a full pension. In April, 1780, I sailed for Nantucket with Capt. Stephen Thorp, where I with his consent, enlisted for a cruise to the West Indies. At Providence we found our vessel ready for sea. We sailed the 20th of April for the island of Cuba. About the middle of May, when approaching our destination, the ship brought suddenly on a sunken reef, but by the Captain's stratagem was saved, and we again made sail for Hispaniola, entering in two or three days the harbor of St. Francis. Here we repaired damages. This incessant labor caused much sickness. I was brought very low with intermittent fever. Capt. Gardiner was very kind to me, showing a father's solicitude for me. I still grew weaker, and all hopes of recovery were given up. I thought if I could be at home, I should die content, but the idea of breathing my last in a foreign land, was most painful. A physician brought on board by the Captain, left a vial with my attendant, telling him to give me a few drops in water every half hour. Upon taking the first spoonful, it seemed to me like fire through my whole system, giving new life and animation, and I recovered slowly from that very hour, and in two or three weeks could walk about deck with assistance. On the first of July we sailed for Philadelphia, and on the morning of the fifteenth arrived off Cape Henlopen. All were in high spirits, expecting to be in Philadelphia that night. While waiting for a pilot we were boarded and taken possession of by two schooners of New York. The captors offered our crew their liberty if they would assist in getting the "Sally" afloat, (for she had been aground on a place called the Sheer,) they gladly accepted the proposal. Being still feeble, I lay in my berth. One of the Refugees ordered me on deck; as I was ascending the companion way slowly the ruffian aimed a blow at me with a lynch staff which just grazed my side. About sun-down, I, with the rest of the sick, were put in a boat and shoved off from the "Sally," and landed on Cape Henlopen beach; dragging our boat across the beach into Lewiston Creek, we rowed up to Lewiston, where we arrived at 10 o'clock at night. In the morning a sailor kindly gave me a straw hat, which was very acceptable, as I had nothing to screen my head from the scorching sun. I went across the street on to an eminence, to see if I could discover any signs of the "Sally" and her captors; not one of them was to be seen. I learned afterwards, that after getting the "Sally" afloat, the refugees violated their promise to liberate the crew, confined them in a prison ship in New York, where nearly all of them died.

"As I stood upon the hill looking for my lost comrades, my feelings can be better imagined than described. It was a beautiful morning, about wheat harvest, the level fields covered with grain as far as the eye could reach, the birds singing, the quails whistling, and all nature seemed joyous; I alone was miserable, enfeebled by my long sickness, without friends or money, far from home, my shipmates all gone, despair overcame me, and I burst into tears. Recovering my spirits after a while, I returned to the village; the landlady gave me a bowl of bread and milk, the first food I had tasted since leaving the ship. The pilot who brought us ashore took me with him to Cape May, where was his home, and brought me to the Pilots' hotel, kept by Mr. Buck, making known to him my circumstances. Mr. Buck welcomed me with much kindness, telling me to stay with him till I was fully recovered. I remained with him nearly three weeks, and being now quite well again, I determined to return to Philadelphia. On taking leave of Mr. Buck and his family, I expressed my fears that I might never be able to make him any return for his kindness and attention to me. He replied, "You may yet become a useful member of society, if you do, and you meet a person in distress, relieve him, and in that way you will recompense me." Some months afterwards I bought in St. Thomas, a set of China, as a present for Mrs. Buck. I sent it by one of our crew, who proved to be a thief, and never delivered it. While in Philadelphia I agreed to go with Capt. Mathews in his market boat, and made three trips with him. When being fully recovered in health, I shipped in Brig Joanna for St. Thomas, for $40 the run. After a short passage, we arrived at St. Thomas. Our return cargo was salt; each of the crew had the privilege of 4 bags (8 bushels) to be sold for their benefit in Philadelphia. After a passage of six or seven weeks we reached Philadelphia, and on discharging the cargo my bags of salt were missing. This was a serious loss to me, as it cost little, and then sold for four dollars a bushel. I afterwards learned that the same rascal to whom I entrusted the set of China for Mrs. Buck, had stolen my bags of salt, and sold them in the night. I received the wages for my last voyage, deducting the physician's bill at St. Thomas, and after a few days shipped on a brig for Havana. With what I had saved and a month's advance, I laid out $40 for flour, cheese, and apples, on my own account. In 15 days we anchored in Havana. Our cargo was in great demand; flour $20 per barrel, cheese 75 cents a pound, and other articles in proportion. I bought from a boat having such articles for sale, a powder-horn made in the "Moro Castle," on which was a representation of the Spanish Crown, the Castle, and vessels going in and out of the harbor of Havana, which I gave to my grand-daughter, Mary Josephine Bulkeley, in 1841, having owned it myself sixty years. We sailed from Havana, and on the 20th of February, after an absence of three months, arrived in Philadelphia. On settling up my voyage I found myself in possession of over $100. After providing myself with necessary clothing, still having $80 in silver, I turned my thoughts homewards. At Kings Ferry, fifty miles above New York, on my way home, I met an old acquaintance, Gershom Bulkeley, whom I accompanied to Mill River, arriving at home on the first of April, after an absence of a year. Remaining two weeks at home, I went to Boston with Capt. Peters. discharged cargo, and returned to Middletown, when I took my discharge, and walked to Black Rock in one day. Through the summer of 1781, I was engaged on a small Brig owned by the inhabitants of "Mill River."

"Early in 1782, I went with Capt. Stephen Thorp to Rhode Island, and continued in the same vessel through the summer. In the autumn I visited my uncle Moses Bulkeley, who lived back in the country, and bought of him the land on which I now live, (1841,) for fifty dollars. In December I joined one of the boats from Fairfield, in a projected expedition to take some British forts on Long Island. From this time until peace was declared in the following spring, I was engaged in no affair of particular moment.

"In April, 1783, news of peace arrived, which caused great rejoicing. Everybody was anxious to visit New York, which had been in possession of the enemy seven years. I went in April. While there, I engaged to go to New Providence in a small sloop owned by George Brown. We arrived safely in New Providence, disposed of our cargo, took in a return cargo, and started again for New York. I was now put in charge of the sloop, and sailed for Nova Scotia, taking with me Capt. Brown and wife, and a number of his friends. A part of my passengers, and himself and wife landed at Granville, and put up temporary houses. Afterward Capt. Brown laid out a town at Beaver's Harbor, and urged me to take a lot. I declined at first, but he insisting, I accepted one, and gave James Tucker a power of attorney with ten dollars to take care of it for me, but I never went there again to claim it. In September we sailed for Boston, remained there a few days, and in October sailed again for Nova Scotia. Here the sloop was laid up for the winter, but thinking it would not do to be idle long, I made a voyage to Boston, returning to Nova Scotia in 1784, the beginning of the year. I remained three months, visiting the families I had brought here. May following made a voyage to Boston, and in July one to New York. In August, after a monthly visit in the Bay, I sailed again for New York, taking with me Capt. Brown and his family, who had sold out in Nova Scotia. We arrived in October. We sailed the same month for Jamaica; a few days out experienced severe weather. Coming up with Turks Island, as I was asleep in the cabin, I dreamed that I saw land and reefs of rocks ahead. Waking suddenly, visibly impressed with my dream, I hurried on deck, and found the vessel running directly for the land and reefs just as they had appeared in my dream. She would undoubtedly have run ashore in a few minutes had I not in this singular manner been warned of our danger. Arriving safely at Kingston, we discharged our cargo in three weeks, and in November cleared for New York, arriving there the 5th of January, 1785. On settling with the owners for my services there was due me for the last nineteen months $200, which Capt. Brown paid me in gold, one of which pieces I have always retained. I now returned home, where I remained six weeks, but not contented to remain longer idle, I engaged as mate with Capt. Joseph Bartram, and made a voyage in a sloop to North Carolina; returned home in April. I was now solicited by Miah Perry to take part of a vessel with him, which I concluded to do. On one occasion, when Mr. Perry and I were in Marblehead with a cargo of flax, we were swindled out of about $100 worth of it by one whom we thought would help us sell it. We felt quite sore at our loss, as it was the commencement of our coasting business. I continued in the same business during the summer of 1785, between Mill River, New York, and New Haven. In the autumn of this year I was married to Mary Ogden, daughter of Jonathan Ogden, who died in 1775, when she was only five years old. He would often call her to him and say, 'My poor Polly, what will become of you?'

"In the spring of 1786 I built a house, which is still standing near where I now live. In the autumn Mr. Perry and I dissolved all further connection in the way of business. Unaccustomed to idle habits, I went as mate in a brig to Point Peter, about sixty miles from Cape Francis. We lay here three months, returning to Black Rock in April, 1787. In the spring of this year I bought out Miah Perry's part of the sloop, and continued in the coasting trade the next year; sold out soon after, and bought part of another vessel. Continuing this business for a time I increased my vessel property as means would allow, and as my sons grew up placed them in business with myself, and so have continued, father and sons being equally united."

Thus originated the shipping firm of E. Bulkeley & Sons, of New York, which has continued from that date (1788) until the present time—nearly a century. He died February 5, 1843, and for his benevolence and goodness of heart those can testify who knew him best. His mind was ever active. As a patriot and republican of the "old school" he took a lively interest in the perpetuity and welfare of his country, the independence of which he had in some small measure contributed to establish. After the close of the war he was actively engaged in commercial business with his sons until his death.

CHILDREN.

1756. Jonathan, born November 26, 1786.
1757. Andrew, " December 13, 1789.
1758. Lot, " July 13, 1794.
1759. Moses, " September 18, 1796.
1760. George, " February 2, 1800.
1761. Charles, " January 5, 1804.

1657.

MABEL BULKELEY, daughter of James and Elisabeth *Whitehead* Bulkeley, born May 24, 1765; married *Nathan Wheeler*, of Greenfield, Conn.; died December 14, 1827.

CHILDREN.

1762. Nathan *Wheeler*, a farmer in Greenfield, Conn.
1763. Sanford   "   "   "   "
1764. Howkin   "   now living, about 80 years of age.
1765. Moses   "   lived with William on Long Island.
1766. William   "   a prominent physician near Babylon, L. I.

1658.

JAMES BULKELEY, son of James and Elisabeth *Whitehead* Bulkeley, born in Southport, Conn., August 27, 1768; married Miss *Jarvis*, and died in Norfolk, Va., September 15, 1805.

CHILDREN.

1767. Stephen, born in 1794; died January, 1864, unmarried.
1768. Walter, "
1769. Julia Ann, baptized December 15, 1798; m. *Philo Smith*, August 7, 1825.
1770. James, " January 8, 1802.
1771. George Jarvis, born Nov. 16, 1812; m. Miss *Chapman*. No children.
1772. Rosalie, " May 9, 1815.

1660.

HOWKIN BULKELEY, son of James and Elisabeth *Whitehead* Bulkeley, born April 7, 1770; married—1, *Catharine Judson;* 2, *Elisabeth Lee.* He died December 1, 1819.

CHILDREN BY THE FIRST MARRIAGE.

1773. Styles, born October 19, 1795.
1774. Tuzar, " October 21, 1798.
1775. Catharine, born in 1800; m. *Moses Bulkeley.* She died in 1832.
1776. Hiram, " 1805.
1777. Elisabeth, " 1808.

CHILDREN BY THE SECOND MARRIAGE.

1779. Amanda.
1780. George.

1659.

ELISABETH BULKELEY, daughter of James and Elisabeth Whitehead Bulkeley, born June 14, 1772; married, 1, *Richard Bangs*, Dec., 1793; he died April 5, 1847. 2, *Levi Perry*.

CHILDREN.

1781. Jonathan *Bangs*.
1782. Eliza   "   m.   *Jennings*.

1663.

MARY BULKELEY, daughter of James and Elisabeth *Whitehead* Bulkeley, born July 28, 1779; married *Joab Squire*, July 31, 1800. Removed to Florence, Ohio, about 1816.

CHILDREN.

1783.	Ruth	*Squire*.	
1784.	Adeline	"	
1785.	Munson	"	
1786.	George	"	
1787.	Virgil } twins,	"	a merchant banker in Ohio.
1788.	Mary }	m.	*Tillinghast*, of Ohio.
1789.	William	"	
1790.	Charles	"	a politician. He was elected to the State Senate of Ohio, but died before taking the seat. He was a fluent speaker, and a promising young man.

SIXTH GENERATION.

1667.

GERSHOM BULKELEY, son of Gershom and Amelia Bulkeley, born June 28, 1784; married *Esther Morehouse*, December 10, 1808.

CHILDREN.

1791. Gershom, born August 17, 1809; died July 31, 1826.
1792. Mary,   "   October 10, 1811; m. *Jessup Sherwood*, May 31, 1829.
1793. Sarah B., "   March 10, 1814; m. *Daniel Crossman*, February 28, 1835.
1794. William Timothy, born May 13, 1817; died July 24, 1818.
1795. Amelia,   "   June 30, 1819; m. *Seth Bulkeley*, Sept. 12, 1843.
1796. Emily,   "   March 31, 1822; m. January 1, 1845, *Isaac Chidsey*, of Boston; died in 1852.
1797. Gershom, "   October 14, 1827.

27

1668.

TIMOTHY, son of Gershom and Amelia Bulkeley, born September 23, 1787; married, 1, *Susannah Osborne*, October 19, 1823; 2, *Abigail Bulkeley*, January 23, 1830. She was born in 1802.

CHILDREN.

1798. Timothy Wakeman, born November 18, 1832.
1799. Sereno Bradley, " October 14, 1842.

1669.

ZALMON BULKELEY, son of Hezekiah and Abigail *Blackman* Bulkeley, born in 1782; married *Eleanor Meeker*, November 24, 1801.

CHILDREN.

1800. Abigail, born April 25, 1802.
1801. Caroline, " June 8, 1803; m. *Joseph Osborne*, November 22, 1819; died September 21, 1864.
1802. Seth, " April 29, 1805.
1803. Julia, " June 3, 1807.
1804. Hezekiah, " September 22, 1809.
1805. Wakeman Burt, born March 12, 1812; died in 1833.
1806. William, " March 9, 1815; died in infancy.
1807. William, " December 2, 1816.
1808. Esther, " November 9, 1818.

1673.

WILLIAM BULKELEY, son of William and Elisabeth *Burr* Bulkeley, born in 1768, and inherited the paternal homestead. It was not burned during the revolutionary war. He built the store, now improved, occupied by W. B. Meeker, keeping a country supply store, sending market boats to New York City. Upon a business visit to the city he was taken ill with yellow fever, brought home, and died in 1808, aged 40. He married *Sarah Redfield*, who died in 1842, aged 76.

CHILDREN.

1809. William, baptized May 12, 1790; m. *Charlotte Clark*.
1810. Polly, " July 16, 1792.
1811. Althea, " October 15, 1794; m. *Nathaniel Ward* in 1830, who died in 1839.
1812. Henrietta, " December 3, 1797; m. *Samuel Perry;* died in 1873.
1813. Eunice, " March 8, 1800; m. *John Rider* in 1844; died in 1856.
1814. Huldah Burritt, baptized May 9, 1802; died young.
1815. Elihu, " August 8, 1804; died October 15, 1821.

1674.

GRACE BULKELEY, daughter of William and Elisabeth Bulkeley, born   ; married twice—1, to *Peter Whitney*; 2, to *Ephraim Robbins*.

CHILDREN BY THE FIRST MARRIAGE.

1822. Betsey *Whitney*,
1823. Peter,

1675.

BURR BULKELEY, son of William and Elisabeth *Burr* Bulkeley, born July 27, 1777; married *Sarah Conklin*, who was born March 28, 1783. She died February 17, 1867. He died October 2, 1828.

CHILDREN.

1816. Amelia, born Feb. 20, 1809; m. *George B. Alvord*; died August 6, 1854.
1817. Oliver K., "   December 29, 1810.
1818. Elisabeth," January 6, 1814; died September 6, 1843.
1819. Abel C.,   "   January 12, 1817.
1820. William, "   April 2, 1821.
1821. Sarah A.," June 20, 1823.

1682.

ELISABETH BULKELEY, daughter of Gershom and Elisabeth *Chapman* Bulkeley; married *John Alvord*, February 5, 1797.

CHILDREN.

1824. Eliza *Alvord*, m.   Ware, of Lexington Avenue and Thirty-Fourth Street, New York City.
1825. C. T.   "   of Manhattan Savings Institution, N. Y.

1687.

WILLIAM BULKELEY, son of Gershom and Elisabeth *Chapman* Bulkeley, born   ; married *Maria B. Osborn*, daughter of Daniel Osborn, of Sasco, Conn.; died August 29, 1860, aged 73, and was buried at Rye, N. Y.

CHILDREN.

1826. Mary, died unmarried, May 12, 1843, aged 23.
1827. Daniel, born April 5, 1814.
1828. Clara,   "   m. *James Morgan*, of Mount Vernon, Ind.
1829. Mary Caroline, wife of S. M. Studwell, has two children, Frederick B., and Albert L.
1830. Philemon C., born December 15, 1828; m. June 13, 1855.

1688.

GERSHOM BULKELEY, son of Gershom and Elisabeth *Chapman* Bulkeley, born   ; married *Mary G. Brush*, of New

York, February 9, 1799. He resides in Port Chester, N. Y. In 1811 he traveled abroad, visiting Wales, the residence of the Bulkeley family at the island of Anglesia. He was coming from New York, when about ten or twelve years of age, with Captain Ella Bulkeley, son of James Bulkeley, and accidentally got overboard. Captain Bulkeley got outside and hung his feet overboard, and he took hold of them, and so he saved his life. When they came to tea at night he said, "You would have looked very pretty with the eels eating you up," so he saved his life by a miracle.

CHILDREN.

1831. Charles Seymour, a successful engineer, and some incidents of his life would be interesting.
1832. Edward,
1833. Helen A., born, February, 1827; m. *W. D. Harrison*, of Port Chester.
1834. Susan S., " March 10, 1828; died July 20, 1828.
1835. Gilbert Brush, born October 10, 1831. Unmarried.
1836. Gershom, " September 29, 1834; died January 19, 1841.
1837. George A., " October 20, 1838; died January 22, 1842.

1695.

JONATHAN BULKELEY, son of Jonathan and Lydia Bulkeley, born ; married *Ann Osborn*, and died in 1870. By a second wife he had a daughter.

CHILD.

1837. Lydia, married *Shelton*.

1703.

FRANCIS BULKELEY, son of Abraham and   Bulkeley, born January 30, 1786; married, 1, *Sarah Morehouse*, February 25, 1816; 2, *Esther Bulkeley*.

CHILDREN.

1838. John Francis, born September 5, 1816.
1839. Hester, " July 30, 1820.
1840. Peter, " May 23, 1821.
1841. Maria, " April 4, 1824.
1842. Gershom, " October 29, 1826. Unmarried.
1843. Mary Jane, " May 24, 1829.
1844. Sarah, " 1830; m. *John Ward*, November 18, 1818.
1849. Abraham, " 1832.

1706.

JOEL BURR, son of Abraham and Jane Bulkeley, born July 7, 1798; married *Priscilla Sturgis*.

CHILDREN.

1850. Edward S., born December 5, 1825; died September 20, 1826.
1851. Edward S , " August 22, 1827; m. *Emily Merwin*, June 5, 1824.
1852. Elisabeth, " April 19, 1831.
1853. Jane Burr, " December, 1834.
1854. Charles F., " January 11, 1839.
1855. Susan F., " March 30, 1841.

1710.

DAVID WARD BULKELEY, son of David and Sarah Bulkeley, born in Easton, Conn., in 1783; married *Rebecca Gregory*, who was born May 11, 1789.

CHILDREN.

1856. Matthew, born Aug. 27, 1811; died, aged 61.
1857. David Ward, " Feb. 2, 1815.
1858. Eunice, " Jan. 27, 1817.
1859. George, " March 15, 1820.
1860. Sarah Ann, " May 3, 1825; m. *Andrew Smith*.
1861. Rebecca Jane, " June 7, 1831; m. *Martin Rowland*.

1711.

AARON BULKELEY, son of David and Sarah Bulkeley, born in 1788, in Easton, Conn.; married *Anna* ———.

CHILDREN.

1862. Benjamin Franklin, born Dec., 1819.
1863. Angeline, " 1824; m. *George W. Gorham*.
1864. Moses Aaron, " 1833; m. *Elisabeth Wakeman*.

1712.

NEHEMIAH BULKELEY, son of David and Sarah Bulkeley, born in Easton, Conn., in 1791; married, Oct. 3, 1819, 1, *Sarah Beers*, 2, *Ellen Fillio*, in 1872.

CHILDREN BY THE FIRST WIFE.

1865. Minerva, born 1821; died Nov. 15, 1836.
1866. Columbus, " Jan. 22, 1822; m. *Eliza J. Smith*.
1867. Mary, " 1825; m. *James Andrews*—one child, Mary Eliza.

1713.

MOSES BULKELEY, son of David and Sarah Bulkeley, born Aug., 1802; married, but the name of his wife is not known.

CHILDREN.

1867. Eliza, born 1827; m. *Ransom Hammond*.
1868. George Washington, " 1829.
1869. Sarah, " 1832; m. *Bradley Brown*.

1717.

Deborah Bulkeley, son of Isaac and Deborah *Couch* Bulkeley, born in Green's Farms, July 24, 1763; married, Dec. 26, 1784, *Abel Turney*, son of Stephen Turney.

CHILDREN.

1870.	Andrew	*Turney*,	born Feb. 6, 1786.
1871.	Ellen	"	" May 28, 1789.
1872.	Levi	"	" May 16, 1791.
1873.	Esther	"	" June 6, 1793.
1874.	Samuel	"	" Oct. 3, 1795.
1875.	Mary	"	" Sept. 8, 1797.
1876.	Hannah	"	" Dec. 8, 1799.
1877.	William	"	" Oct. 6, 1802.
1878.	Eunice	"	" March 28, 1805.

1719.

Isaac Bulkeley, son of Isaac and Deborah *Couch* Bulkeley, born in Green's Farms, in 1766; married *Abigail Turney*, July 13, 1797.

CHILDREN.

1879. Anson.
1880. Jane.
1881. Catharine.
1882. Nancy,   m. *William Harold.*
1883. Isaac.
1884. Abby.
1885. Eliza.

1721.

David Bulkeley, son of Isaac and Deborah *Couch* Bulkeley, born in Easton, Conn., May 23, 1770; married *Mary L. Sturgis Morehouse*. She was born Dec. 30, 1775. He died in Waterbury, Conn., Oct. 11, 1860. She died March 26, 1861.

CHILD.

1886. Sturgis,   born Oct. 12, 1799; died July 9, 1857, in Waterbury—a skillful physician.

1722.

Isaac Bulkeley, son of Joseph and Grizzel *Thorp* Bulkeley, born Nov. 13, 1778; married, in 1799, *Mehitable Simmons*, of Newburgh. She was born March 18, 1779, and died April 9, 1869. He died Nov. 16, 1861.

CHILDREN.

1887.	Joseph,	born May 26, 1800; died April, 1847.
1888.	Caleb,	" Dec. 25, 1801. He removed to Poughkeepsie, N. Y.
1889.	Ward,	" Aug. 2, 1803; died Oct. 30, 1819.
1890.	Rachel,	" April 24, 1805.
1891.	David,	" Aug. 18, 1807; died Nov. 5, 1819.
1892.	John S.,	" Aug. 20, 1809; died Oct. 30, 1819.
1893.	Sarah,	" May 18, 1810.
1894.	Isaac,	" May 17, 1812.
1895.	William,	" Oct. 8, 1814.
1895½.	Sally Ann,	" June 8, 1817.
1896.	Cornelius,	" June 5, 1819; died Dec. 5, 1819.
1897.	Cornelius S.,	" Sept. 1, 1821; died Oct. 5, 1835.
1898.	Elizabeth,	" Feb. 12, 1823.

1724.

WARD BULKELEY, son of Joseph and Grizzel *Thorp* Bulkeley, born Dec. 29, 1782; died March, 1862. He married *Mary Beers*, June 6, 1808, who died Feb. 9, 1848, aged 61.

CHILDREN.

1899.	Henry,	born Sept. 30, 1810.
1900.	Amanda,	" June 6, 1813; m. *Thomas Brown*, March 1, 1840; died Sept. 30, 1857.
1901.	George,	" Sept. 1, 1816; died March 23, 1864.
1902.	Frederick,	" July 18, 1818.
1903.	Andrew,	" Aug. 25, 1821.
1904.	Malvina,	" Feb. 12, 1825; m. Rev. *Levi Burt Stimson*, Dec. 27, 1853.
1905.	Mary E.,	" Nov. 10, 1828.

1725.

SARAH BULKELEY, daughter of Joseph and Grizzel *Thorp* Bulkeley, born July 9, 1784; married *David Bradley*, Dec. 3, 1815.

CHILDREN.

1906.	David	*Bradley*.
1907.	William Henry	"

1731.

JOSEPH BULKELEY, son of Joseph and Grizzel *Thorp* Bulkeley, born in Southport, July 13, 1795; married *Charlotte Mason*, June 7, 1829.

CHILDREN.

1908.	Charles,	born 1831; a carpenter.
1909.	David,	" 1833.

1732.

BENJAMIN BULKELEY, son of Joseph and Grizzel *Thorp* Bulkeley, born July 13. 1795; married *Rebeccah Davis*, March 15, 1818.

CHILDREN.

1910. Francis, born Jan. 30, 1819; m. *Mary Nichols*, daughter of Peter Nichols, June 6, 1842.
1911. Mary, " 1823; m. *Samuel Bunnell*, of Southport.

1737.

PHEBE BULKELEY, daughter of Peter and Mary *Greene* Bulkeley, born Feb. 9, 1796; married *Micajah Nash*, March 2, 1819. He was born Jan. 23, 1774, and died December 11, 1851.

CHILDREN.

1912. John, born Jan. 7, 1803; died Sept. 10, 1841; m. twice, and left children.
1913. Freelove, " April 10, 1804; died May 17, 1835; m. *Charles Peck*.
1914. Elisabeth L., " Nov. 6, 1805; died Dec. 9, 1826.
1915. Mary P., " July 3, 1809; died Aug. 4, 1829.
1916. Sarah T., " Oct. 8, 1810; died July 13, 1837.
1917. Julia R., " Sept. 10, 1812; m. *Anson Smith*.
1918. Peter M., " Nov. 1, 1814; m. *Avis Briscoe*.
1919. Dennis W., " June 10, 1818; m., 1. *Betsey Lawrence*, in 1844. She died in 1853. He m., 2. *Catharine Lawrence*, in 1854, and had one child.

1738.

GERSHOM BULKELEY, son of Peter and Mary *Greene* Bulkeley, born July 29, 1779; married *Damaris Wheeler*, who was born in Weston, Dec. 30, 1777, and died in Danbury, July 1, 1865. He died November 28, 1849.

CHILDREN.

1920. Orphelia, m. *Ira Benedict*.
1921. Martha, m. *Edwin Hoyt*, of Danbury, Conn., and had four children, who are married and have children.
1922. Peter V., born May 6, 1811; died Oct. 15, 1858.
1923. Lucy A., m. *Hiram Shepard*.

1740.

ANDREW BULKELEY, son of Peter and Mary *Greene* Bulkeley, born Nov. 14, 1785; married *Sally Mallory*; and died in 1860. They reside at Corning, Steuben County, N. Y.

CHILDREN.
1924. Andrew, born July 5, 1805; died May 27, 1854.
1925. Barzilla.
1926. Peter Beach.
1927. Alonzo.
1928. Charlotte.
1928½. Clara

1741.

EBENEZER G., son of Peter and Mary Greene Bulkeley, born Dec. 30, 1787; married, 1. Sophia Greene, Nov., 1814, who was born October, 1793, and died March 28, 1833. 2. Emilie Toue. He died, Feb. 11, 1871. They reside at Rockford, Ill.

CHILDREN BY THE FIRST WIFE.
1929. Priscilla S., born April 2, 1815; m. *Joseph Van Alstine*, in 1852.
1930. Peter G., " April 28, 1817.
1931. Mary A., " April 26, 1819; m. *Joseph VanAlstine* in 1850, and died Nov., 1851.
1932. Orrin, " July 4, 1821; died July 14, 1821.
1933. Clarissa, " July 27, 1823; m. *William Forbes*, Feb. 11, 1858.
1934. Eliza, " Sept. 8, 1824; died Oct., 1849.
1935. Andrew, " April 17, 1827.
1936. Edwin E., " April 26, 1829.

CHILDREN BY THE SECOND WIFE.
1938. Haran D., born June 10, 1834; m. ; lives in Philadelphia; 3 children.
1939. Sophia, " Sept. 19, 1836; m. *Wm. H. Forbes, jr*, Sept., 1861; one child, Mary, born April 20, 1862. She died 1865.
1940. William, " June 26, 1838; died July, 1863.
1941. Lucy A., " Feb. 10, 1841; died Nov. 10, 1863; m. *Farewel Slafter*, 1857.
1942. Emeret, " Nov. 24, 1842; m. Oct. 1, 1865, *Robert F. Sedam*.
1943. Elon G., " March 3, 1844; died 1848.

1742.

DANIEL S. BULKELEY, son of Peter and Mary Greene Bulkeley, born Dec. 27, 1790; married *Miriam Peck*, April 13, 1834; died Aug. 28, 1872.

CHILDREN.
1944. Charles S., born March 21, 1836; died Feb. 17, 1838.
1945. Mary E., " Sept. 6, 1837; m. *Edwin E. Bulkeley*, March 31, 1872.
1946. Phebe L., " March 22, 1839.

1743.

WILLIAM, son of Turney and Esther Morehouse Bulkeley, born June 7, 1787; married *Jane Morehouse*, who was born in 1807.

CHILDREN.

1947.	Esther Jane,	born	June 25, 1828; m. Feb. 10, 1847. 1. *Ward Perry;* 2. *Jas. Golden:* 3. *Sterling Edwards.*
1948.	Eleanor Burr,	"	Dec. 4, 1830; m. March, 1857, 1. *Albert G. Talmadge:* 2. March 10, 1869, *James Bailey,* of Middletown, Conn.
1949.	William Turney,	"	Dec. 27, 1833; m. *Frances Brown.*
1950.	David Burr,	"	July 27, 1835; m. *Emily Blakeman.*
1951.	Augustus,	"	Feb. 14, 1838; m. *Emily Williams.*
1952.	Mary Eliza,	"	Aug. 20, 1840; m. *Sterling Wilson,* of Norwalk, Conn.
1953.	Sarah Maria,	"	1842; died 1860, aged 18.
1954.	Nathan,	"	1846; died 1864, aged 18. He went to the war in the 2d Conn. Artillery, and died on the way out to New Orleans, of measles.
1955.	Amelia Frances,		died June 11, 1849.

1744.

DAVID BULKELEY, son of Turney and Esther *Morehouse* Bulkeley, born 1793; married *Lucy* ———; died Jan. 4, 1823.

CHILDREN.

1956.	Clarrissa,	m. ——— *Curtis,* of Trumbull.
1957.	Lucy Ann,	m. *Gershom Wakeman.*
1958.	David Burr.	
1959.	Nathan,	born 1822; died Feb. 17, 1848, aged 26. He was a young physician, and studied with Dr. Blakeman, of Greenfield, Conn.

1753.

GERSHOM BULKELEY, son of Nathan and ——— *Jennings* Bulkeley, married and settled in New Milford, and had six children, five sons and one daughter. The sons all died after arriving at maturity, within a year and a half of each other.

1754.

DEACON NATHAN BULKELEY, son of Nathan and ——— *Jennings* Bulkeley, born Nov. 1, 1787; died April 16, 1855. He married *Phebe Barnum,* who died April 25, 1869. She was born March 6, 1787.

CHILDREN.

1960.	Sarah,	born Feb. 21, 1804; died Jan. 11, 1828.
1961.	Anna,	" May 30, 1809; died Nov. 9, 1839.
1962.	Turney,	" June 30, 1818.
1963.	Mary,	" Aug. 6, 1821; died April 14, 1859.

1756.

JONATHAN, son of Eleazer and Mary *Ogden* Bulkeley, born in Southport, Conn., July 9, 1786; died Jan. 16, 1859. He married,

Respectfully yours,
Andrew Berkley

April 15, 1810, *Miranda Thorp*. She died Aug. 22, 1815. He always lived in his native place, and was active in all public matters. He served in the war of 1812, and received a pension. He was several times a member of the State Legislature, and was one of the committee for superintending government works in Southport harbor. He was associated with his father and brothers in commercial business until his death.

CHILDREN.

1964.	Mary Frances,	born June 13, 1811; died Sept. 7, 1812.
1965.	Henry Thorp,	" June 23, 1813; m. *Rebekah W. Pomeroy*, of Stonington, Conn., Feb. 12, 1862.
1966.	Ann Eliza,	" March 15, 1815; m. June 20, 1831, *Francis Perry*, of Southport, Conn.
1967.	Augustus,	" March 12, 1817.
1968.	Mary Frances,	" July 4, 1823.

1757.

ANDREW BULKELEY, son of Eleazer and Mary *Ogden* Bulkeley, born at Southport, Conn., May 23, 1789, and died March 18, 1867. He married, August 11, 1815, *Sally Dimon*, of Southport, Conn. She died Dec. 28, 1868, aged 86. Thrice in middle life he represented his town in the State Legislature, and manifested, during a long life, a most lively interest in the affairs of his town, State, and country. He was associated with his brothers in commercial business.

CHILDREN.

1969.	Edwin,	born Dec. 2, 1817; m. *Helen Perry*, daughter of Gurdon and Abby Sherwood Perry.
1969½.	Julia Perry,	died young.
1970.	Mary Josephine,	" 1819; m. *Hon. Benjamin Pomeroy*, of Stonington (dec.). June 7, 1848.
1971.	Lewis Dimon,	" 1821; m. *Julia F. Wakeman*, of Southport (dec.)
1972.	Louisa Dimon,	" 1821; m. *Wm. Boardman Leonard*, of Owego, N. Y., July 5, 1847.

1758.

LOT BULKELEY, son of Eleazer and Mary *Ogden* Bulkeley, born July 13, 1794; married *Emeline Jennings*, March 8, 1830. He died Oct. 3, 1847. He was associated with his brothers in commercial business until his death.

CHILDREN.

1973.	Franklin,	born March 13, 1831.
1974.	George,	" Feb. 10, 1836. A graduate of Yale in 1855.
1975.	Arthur,	" July 26, 1837; died young.
1976.	Eleazer,	" Sept. 11, 1838; died Sept. 13, 1847.
1977.	Milton,	" July 14, 1840; died Jan. 25, 1872.

1978. Emeline,   born Dec. 19, 1841.
1979. Peter,   "   Oct. 27, 1844.
1980. Lot,   "   Aug. 8, 1843; died Nov., 1874.

1759.

MOSES BULKELEY, son of Eleazer and Mary *Ogden* Bulkeley, born in Southport, Conn., Sept. 18, 1796, and died Nov. 13, 1868. He went to sea at an early age, and for many years followed this profession with activity and energy, and, in association with his father and brothers, soon attained a respectable position in the commerce of the country. A conscientious member of the church, her welfare was ever near his heart, and by his example and liberality he was ready at all times to promote her interests. Benevolent and kind, he especially endeared himself to all those with whom he became acquainted. He married *Catherine Bulkeley*, daughter of Howkin Bulkeley, of Stratford, Conn. She was born Dec. 18, 1800, and died Oct. 17, 1837.

CHILDREN.
1981. Oliver,   born 1826.
1982. Frederick, "   1828; died March 11, 1872; unmarried.

1760.

GEORGE, son of Eleazer and Mary *Ogden* Bulkeley, born in Southport, Conn., Feb. 2, 1800; was married, July 22, 1840, to *Elizabeth Andrews*, daughter of Benjamin Andrews, of New York. She was born May 24, 1817. He was an active member of the firm of E. Bulkeley & Sons, and lived in New York for many years, where he had the principal management of the business. In 1860 he retired from business, and removed to Southport, Conn., where he now resides. This and others of the Fairfield family spell the name—Bulkley.

CHILDREN.
1983. James Eleazer, born April 25, 1841. Died from injuries received by an accident on the New Haven Railroad, October 18, 1864, aged 23. He graduated at Yale in the class of 1863, and spent the following summer abroad. On his return he entered the Columbia Law School in the fall of 1863.
1984. Mary Ogden,   " January 3, 1843; m. *Charles M. Gilman*, June 19, 1867.
1985. Eliza Andrews,   " Dec. 24, 1844; died April 3, 1846.
1986. Eliza Andrews,   ⎫
                        ⎬ twins, born July 11, 1848.
1987. Benjamin Andrews, ⎭
1988. Frances Virginia, born September 25, 1850; m. September 23, 1874, *John H. Perry*, of Southport, Conn.
1989. Georgie Augusta, born January 26, 1853.

1762.

CHARLES BULKELEY, son of Eleazer and Mary *Ogden* Bulkeley, born at Southport, Conn., January 5, 1804. He was associated with his father and brothers in commercial business. He married *Elisabeth Beers*, daughter of Abel Beers, of Mill Plain, Conn., January 4, 1831. She was born September 14, 1812. He died Oct. 13, 1875.

CHILDREN.

1990. Mary Elisabeth, born July 10, 1832; m. *Isaac Jennings*, October 9, 1855.
1991. Elisabeth Whitney, born August 18, 1834; m. *Rev. Frederick Hyde*, Oct. 12, 1870.
1992. Charles Eleazer, " September 1, 1836; died January 28, 1837.
1993. Georgianna, " April 23, 1838; m. *W. B. Nichols*, Oct. 20, 1857.
1994. Catharine, " November 10, 1840; died April 21, 1875.
1995. Charles Henry, " March 22, 1844; died Sept. 10, 1874, in Paris, France.

1768.

WALTER BULKELEY, son of James and Miss —— *Jarvis* Bulkeley, born in Southport, Conn.; married *Betsey Smith*, December 24, 1816; died November 5, 1851.

CHILDREN.

1996. Theodore, baptized March 1, 1818; lost at sea in 1850.
1997. Horatio, " July 30, 1820; died in Matura, Cuba, August 5, 1858.
1998. John Henry, " September 16, 1821; died April 10, 1827.
1999. Walter, " April 4, 1824; died August 9, 1825.
2000. Frederick Payson, 1826; died May 14, 1828.
2001. John Henry, June 15, 1828; lost at sea 1850.
2002. Edgar, July 5, 1835; lost at sea on a passage with his brothers, from Bordeaux, France, to New Orleans.
2003. Sarah Elizabeth, baptized at Southport, Conn., June, 1833; m. *Edward Alvord*, of Southport, Conn., June 15, 1859.

1770.

JAMES BULKELEY, son of James and Miss —— *Jarvis* Bulkeley, born in Southport, Conn., January 28, 1812; married *Ellen Sherwood*, November 6, 1825. He died December 27, 1843.

CHILDREN.

2004. Benjamin Sherwood, baptized October 29, 1826.
2005. James, " June 20, 1828.

1772.

GEORGE JARVIS, son of James and —— Jarvis Bulkeley, was born Nov. 16, 1812. He married *Miss Chapman*. (No children.)

1773.

STYLES BULKELEY, son of Howkin and Catharine *Judson* Bulkeley, born in Southport, October 19, 1795; married *Catharine Judson*, January 15, 1826.

CHILDREN.

2009. Charles Judson, born in 1827.
2008. Henry, " 1829.

1776.

HIRAM BULKELEY, son of Howkin and Catharine *Judson* Bulkeley, born in Southport, Conn.; married, but the maiden name of his wife is not known. Address, Brighton, Canada.

CHILDREN.

2009. Styles,
2010. William,
2011. Mary, m. *Thomas Webb*.

1774.

TUZAR BULKELEY, son of Howkin and Catharine *Judson* Bulkeley, born at Southport, Conn., October 21, 1798; married in 1829, *Frances M. Upson*, of Southington, Conn.

CHILDREN.

2013. Edward, born in 1830; died, May, 1849.
2014. James, " 1832; died in 1849.
2015. Henry, " 1835; m. *Caroline Comfort*.
2016. Elisabeth, " 1837; m. *Charles H. Daly*.
2017. Tuzar, " 1844; died November 25, 1867. He was a graduate of Yale College in 1865, studied law, and died of consumption, at Catskill, shortly after finishing his studies.
2018. Mary, " 1844.
2019. Florence, " 1847; married *William Koitz*, of Catskill, N. Y.; died March 17, 186-.

SEVENTH GENERATION.

1791.

GERSHOM BULKELEY, son of Gershom and Esther *Morehouse* Bulkeley, born August 17, 1807; married *Mary Elisabeth Gillett*, November 9, 1851.

CHILD.

2020. Charles Edwin, born October 18, 1852.

1798.

TIMOTHY WAKEMAN BULKELEY, son of Timothy and Abigail Bulkeley, born in Greenfield, Conn., November 18, 1832; married

Charlotte Lucretia Sterling, June 7, 1865, and lives in Scranton, Penn.

1799.

SERENO BRADLEY BULKELEY, son of Timothy and Abigail Bulkeley, born in Greenfield, Conn., in 1842; married Mary Josephine Meeker, December 23, 1867, and lives in Scranton, Penn.

1802.

SETH BULKELEY, son of Zalmon and Eleanor Bulkeley, of Southport, born April 20, 1805; married, 1. *Mary Ogden*, July 15, 1835; 2. *Amelia Bulkeley*, Sept. 12, 1843.

CHILDREN.

2021. Walter Ogden, born in 1837; died in infancy.
2022. Mary Ogden, " September 3, 1842; m., 1, *E. T. Hall*, of Southport, Conn.
2023. Zalmon, " September 2, 1844; died December 21, 1866.

1804.

HEZEKIAH BULKELEY, son of Zalmon and Eleanor Bulkeley, born in Southport, Sept. 22, 1819; married *Dolly Bartlett*, and died June 27, 1860.

CHILDREN.

2024. Hezekiah Ripley.
2025. Elethea, m. *Charles Knapp*.
2026. David, died in infancy.
2027. Thomas.
2028. Mary Ann, born in 1851.

1807.

WILLIAM BULKELEY, son of Zalmon and Eleanor Bulkeley, born in Southport, Conn., Dec. 2, 1816; married *Martha J. Nichols*, January 14, 1845.

CHILDREN.

2029. Eleanor, born Jan. 2, 1847.
2030. George W., " Feb. 19, 1850.
2031. Frederick W., " March 21, 1857.
2032. William, " Feb. 8, 1861.
2033. Henry, " June 1, 1863.

1809.

WILLIAM BULKELEY, son of William and Sarah *Redfield* Bulkeley, born in Southport, Conn.; baptized May 12, 1790; married *Charlotte Clark*, of Boston, in 1818. He died May 8, 1868, aged 78 years.

CHILDREN.

2034. William Clark, baptized Jan. 26, 1820.
2035. Mary Ann Farmer, m. *Emanuel Currant*, of Boston, Sept. 10, 1848.

2036. Thomas Aubin, m. *Harriet F. Lamb*, of Newark, N. J.
2037. Charlotte Malvina.
2038. Edward M.
2039. Sarah Maria, died in 1851, aged 21.
2040. Julia Howard, m. in 1860, *Victor Moreau Randolph*, branch of Richmond, Va.

1811.

ALATHEA BULKELEY, daughter of William and Sarah *Redfield* Bulkeley, born in Southport, Conn., Oct. 15, 1794; married *Nathanael Wood*, of Danbury, Conn., in 1830. He died in 1839.

CHILDREN.
2041. William Augustus, resides in Bridgeport, Conn.
2042. David Nathaniel, died in 1858, in New Mexico, while on a pleasure trip.

1812.

HENRIETTA BULKELEY, daughter of William and Sarah *Redfield* Bulkeley, born at Southport, Conn., Dec. 3, 1797; married *Samuel Perry*, of Fairfield, Conn.

CHILDREN.
2043. Emily, m. *George Ryder*, of Danbury, Conn.
2044. Henrietta, died in 1849, aged 21.
2045. Sarah, m. *Daniel Marsh Redfield*, of Port Chester, in 1866. She has three children, Annetta, George Perry, Walter Marsh.

1816.

AMELIA BULKELEY, daughter of Burr and Sarah *Conklin* Bulkeley, born Feb. 20, 1809; married *George B. Alvord*, in 1831. He was born September 8, 1798.

CHILDREN.
2046. Caroline E. *Alvord*, born Dec. 8, 1832; m. *Abraham C. Hyatt* May 21, 1851.
2047. George B. "   " Sept. 16, 1834; m. *Margaret Horan* Jan. 3, 1856.
2048. Amelia "   " Dec. 12, 1836; m. *Timothy Cornwell* Aug. 28, 1855.
2049. James O. "   " July 12, 1839; died May 12, 1843.
2050. Banks C. "   " May 19, 1842; unmarried.
2051. Edwin P. "   " March 26, 1846; m. *Mary G. Dunn* Feb. 10, 1869.
2052. Charles F. "   " Dec. 8, 1850; died March 14, 1851.

1817.

OLIVER K. BULKELEY, son of Burr and Sarah *Conklin* Bulkeley, born Dec. 29, 1810; married, 1. *Frances M. Penny*. 2. *Martha Webb*.

CHILDREN BY FIRST MARRIAGE.
2053. George P., m. *Harriet Young*.
2054. Alonzo C., m. *Mary P. Griffith*.
2055. Sarah E., m. *John L. Terry*.

1819.

ABEL C. BULKELEY, son of Burr and Sarah *Conklin* Bulkeley, born Jan. 12, 1817; married *Ann G. Penny*, Jan. 14, 1846.

CHILDREN.

2056. Mary Matilda, born Jan. 10, 1847; m. *Albert G. Bassett*, May 22, 1867.
2057. Edwin Fillmore, " Aug. 29, 1848; died July 30, 1862.
2058. Caroline Amelia, " Sept. 7, 1849.
2059. Anna Louisa, " Feb. 2, 1853.
2060. William Conklin, " Aug. 16, 1856.
2061. Charles Abel, " Sept. 29, 1858.

1820.

WILLIAM BULKELEY, son of Burr and Sarah *Conklin* Bulkeley, born April 2. 1821; m. *Lavinia T. Townsend*. March 1. 1843.

CHILDREN.

2062. William, born June 29, 1844; unmarried.
2063. George A., " Sept. 29, 1846; m. *Etta Bright*, July, 1873.
2064. Isaac H., " March 7, 1849; deceased.
2065. Emma T., " Aug. 4, 1851.
2066. Ella A., " June 5, 1853.
2067. Amelia A., " Sept. 6, 1855; m. *Wm. T. Andrews*, Jan. 4, 1875.

1821.

SARAH A. BULKELEY, daughter of Burr and Sarah *Conklin* Bulkeley, born June 20, 1823; married, May 7, 1844. *William R. Starkweather*, of New York City.

CHILDREN.

2068. William B., born Feb. 13, 1846.
2069. S. Hume, " Feb. 7, 1848.
2070. Mary E., " Dec. 29, 1850.
2071. Henry R., " July 14, 1853.
2072. James A., " Aug. 12, 1856.
2073. Olivia H., " June 29, 1859.
2074. A. Lathrop, " March 3, 1862.

1827.

DANIEL BULKELEY, son of William and Maria *Osborne* Bulkeley, born in Harrison, New York, April 5, 1814; married *Caroline Kellog Benedict*, daughter of Trowbridge Benedict, of West Norwalk, Conn., Sept. 19, 1837. She was born in New Canaan. Feb. 11, 1816. They emigrated to Illinois in 1839, arriving in Albion Nov. 28, and have resided in that State ever since. His health was so poor in New York that the physicians advised a change, which has proved entirely beneficial to him.

CHILDREN.

2075. Abbe Maria, born Jan. 9, 1839; died Aug. 28, 1846, at Grayside, Ill.

2076. William Trowbridge, born June 28, 1841; m. Nov. 11, 1869, *Eliza Kellet*, daughter of Thomas Kellet, an Englishman, who came to Illinois in 1818.
2077. Mary Caroline, " Dec. 17, 1843; m. June 20, 1866, at Port Chester, *Earnest William Kohlsaat*, son of Riner Kohlsaat, a German, who went to Illinois in 1839, and married Miss Sarah Hall. At the time of his death he was Agent of the American Bible Society in Chicago. He had three children.
2078. Egbert James, " Dec. 15, 1846.
2079. Daniel Richards, " April 8, 1849.
2080. Jesse Benedict, " May 28, 1851.
2081. Emily Kate, " Aug. 23, 1854.
2082. Henry Philemon, " Sept. 3, 1856.
2083. Clarence Edward, " Nov. 23, 1858; died May 8, 1872.

1828.

CLARA BULKELEY, daughter of William and Maria B. *Osborne* Bulkeley; married *James Morgan*, of Mt. Vernon, Indiana.

CHILDREN.

2084. Carrie B., m. *Stephen Post*.
2085. Maria B.

1829.

MARY CAROLINE BULKELEY, daughter of William and Maria B. *Osborne* Bulkeley; married *M. L. Studwell*.

CHILDREN.

2086. Frederick B. *Studwell*.
2087. Albert C. "

1830.

PHILEMON C. BULKELEY, son of William and Maria B. *Osborne* Bulkeley, born Dec. 15, 1828; married *J. Moody*, of New Rochelle. June 13, 1855. Resides at Luca Av., St. Louis, Missouri.

CHILDREN.

2088. Mary E., born Nov. 12, 1856.
2089. William M., " Nov. 5, 1858.
2090. Louis Carlton, " Sept. 19, 1862.

1831.

CHARLES SEYMOUR BULKELEY, son of Gershom and Mary G. *Brush* Bulkeley.

1838.

JOHN FRANCIS BULKELEY, son of Francis and Sarah *Morehouse* Bulkeley, born September 5, 1816; married *Fanny Murray*, May 27, 1846.

CHILDREN.

2091.	Sereno F.,	born March 5, 1848; died June 21, 1852.
2092.	Sarah M.,	" May 18, 1851; died Sept. 23, 1852.
2093.	Francis M.,	" Jan. 18, 1854.
2094.	John S.,	" March 21, 1858.

1840.

PETER BULKELEY, son of Francis and Sarah *Morehouse* Bulkeley, born May 23, 1821; married, but the maiden name of his wife has not been received.

CHILDREN.

2095.	Henry A.,	born Oct. 4, 1857.
2096.	Sarah G.,	" Sept. 28, 1859.
2097.	Mary S.,	" Jan. 26, 1862.
2098.	Albert F.,	" May 23, 1866.
2099.	Anne A.,	" Sept. 5, 1866.

1849.

ABRAHAM BULKELEY, son of Francis and Sarah *Morehouse* Bulkeley, born in 1832; married May 24, 1866, *Anna Pike*, daughter of Samuel Pike, of Southport, Conn.

1851.

EDWARD S. BULKELEY, son of Joel Burr and Priscilla *Sturges* Bulkeley, born Aug. 22, 1827; married *Emily Merwin*, June 5, 1856. (He died Dec., 1874.) After her death he married a second time. Her name is *Thompson*.

CHILDREN BY THE FIRST WIFE.

2100.	William M.,	born Jan. 10, 1856.
2101.	Emily G.,	" July 11, 1858.
2102.	Frederick E.,	" October, 1860.

CHILDREN BY THE SECOND WIFE.

2104.	Adelaide,	born December, 1871.
2105.	Everet Sturges,	" August, 1873.

1856.

MATTHEW BULKELEY, son of David Ward and Rebeccah *Gregory* Bulkeley, born Aug. 27, 1811; married *Ellen Sturges*.

CHILD.

2106. Mary, m. August 20, 1867, *Andrew James*, Principal of the Boys' Military School of Weston, Conn.

1859.

GEORGE BULKELEY, son of David Ward and Rebeccah *Gregory* Bulkeley, born at Weston, Conn., March 15, 1820; married, but to whom is not known.

CHILDREN.

2107. Eugene,   born July 7, 1851.
2108. Mary Eliza,   "   Aug. 13, 1852.
2109. Daniel Ward,   "   Dec. 22, 1854.
2110. George Gregory, "   March 15, 1857.
2111. Charles P.,   "   June 26, 1860.
2112. Carrie Maria,   "   Oct. 22, 1862.
2113. Rebecca,   "   Sept. 19, 1865.

1862.

BENJAMIN FRANKLIN BULKELEY, son of Aaron and Anna Bulkeley, born Dec., 1819; married *Frances Belden*.

CHILD.

2114. Benjamin Belden.

1864.

MOSES AARON BULKELEY, son of Aaron and Anna Bulkeley, born in 1833; married *Elisabeth Wakeman*. He died June 26, 1865.

CHILDREN.

2115. Anna Belle,   born April, 1861
2116. Moses Aaron,   "   January, 1865.

1866.

COLUMBUS BULKELEY, son of Nehemiah and Sarah *Beers* Bulkeley, born Jan. 22, 1822; married *Eliza J. Smith*.

CHILD.

2117. Mary Smith.

1867.

MARY BULKELEY, daughter of Nehemiah and Sarah *Beers* Bulkeley, born in 1825; married *James Andrews*.

CHILD.

2118. Mary Eliza *Andrews*.

1886.

STURGES BULKELEY, son of David and Mary *Morehouse* Bulkeley, born Oct. 12, 1799; married, June 30, 1824, *Nancy Shelton*, daughter of James Shelton, of Huntington, a descendant of Daniel Shelton, one of the first settlers of Stratford, and his wife Elisabeth, grand-daughter of Thomas Welles, Governor of Connecticut, one of the earliest settlers of Hartford. He was a physician. He died July 9, 1857.

CHILDREN.

2119. Frances Shelton, born March 5, 1826; m. Dec. 20, 1848, *John Deacon*, M. D., of New Orleans, La., and died in Waterbury, June 4, 1850.
2120. Cornelia H., " Nov. 26, 1827; Sept. 8, 1859; m. *Samuel Towner Rogers*, M. A., of Yale, 1844, and afterward Professor in Washington College, Charlestown, Maryland.
2121. Sarah J., " June 29, 1830; died Oct. 17, 1848.

1887.

JOSEPH BULKELEY, son of Isaac and Mehetabel *Simmons* Bulkeley, born May 26, 1800; married
No record of children has been received.

1888.

CALEB BULKELEY, son of Isaac and Mehetabel *Simmons* Bulkeley, born December 25, 1801. He removed to Poughkeepsie, N. Y., and married, but the name of the lady is not known.

CHILDREN.

2122. Ann Eliza.
2123. Caleb.

1894.

ISAAC BULKELEY, son of Isaac and Mehetabel *Simmons* Bulkeley, born in Southport, May 17, 1812; married *Mary A. Vandyne*, who was born January 12, 1822.

CHILDREN.

2124. William H., born September 25, 1840.
2125. Harriet, " March 28, 1843.
2126. Dillie, " December 29, 1845.
2127. Mary F., " September 17, 1848.
2128. Garrett, " October 5, 1852.
2129. Josephine M.," April 26, 1856.
2130. Herbert, " August 26, 1862.

1899.

HENRY BULKELEY, son of Ward and Mary *Beers* Bulkeley, and resides in New Haven, Conn. He was born in Southport, September 31, 1810; married, but the names of his wife and children are not returned.

1900.

AMANDA BULKELEY, daughter of Ward and Mary *Beers* Bulkeley, born at Southport, Conn., June 6, 1813; married *Thomas Brown*, of the same place, March 1, 1840, and had one son.

CHILD.

2131. William *Brown*.

1903.

ANDREW BULKELEY, son of Ward and Mary *Beers* Bulkeley, born in Southport, Conn., August 25, 1821; married *Maria L. Hubbel*.

CHILDREN.

2132. Maria L.,   born January 6, 1845; died August 21, 1845.
2133. Harriet W.,   " March 18, 1850; died January 18, 1873.
2134. Mary Ella,   " March 9, 1853.

1908.

CHARLES BULKELEY, son of Joseph and Charlotte *Mason* Bulkeley, born in Fairfield, Conn., in 1831; married *Julia B. Northrop*.

CHILDREN.

2135. Charles, born in 1853.
2136. William, "   1868.

1909.

DAVID BULKELEY, son of Joseph and Charlotte *Mason* Bulkeley, born in Fairfield, Conn., in 1853; married *Mary Baker*, October 25, 1855.

CHILD.

2137. David, born, June, 1857; died December 28, 1857, aged 6 months.

1910.

FRANCIS BULKELEY, son of Benjamin and Rebecca *Davis* Bulkeley, born in Southport, January 30, 1819; married June 28, 1842, *Mary Nichols*, daughter of Peter Nichols.

CHILDREN.

2138. Benjamin, born in 1848.
2139. Kate,   "   1852.

1922.

PETER W. BULKELEY, son of Gershom and Damaris *Wheeler*

Bulkeley, born in Danbury, May 6, 1816; married *Clara Henry*, and died October 15, 1858.

CHILDREN.
2140. Nathan A.
2141. Emily N., married *Frank Peck*, and has one child.

1930.

PETER G. BULKELEY, son of Ebenezer G. and Sophia *Green* Bulkeley, born April 28, 1817; married in Rockford, Ill., 1, *Marietta Landers*; 2. *Mary Peck*; 3. *Clarissa King*.

CHILD.
2142. Byron, who died young.

1935.

ANDREW BULKELEY, son of Ebenezer G. and Sophia *Green* Bulkeley, born April 17, 1827; married *Ann Maria Hobart* in 1854.

CHILDREN.
2143. Helen M., born, June, 1855.
2144. Clara M., " March, 1858.

1936.

EDWIN E. BULKELEY, son of Ebenezer G. and Sophia *Green* Bulkeley, born April 26, 1829; married March 31, 1872, Mary E. Bulkeley, daughter of Daniel and Miriam *Peck Bulkeley*, who has rendered very essential assistance in gathering statistics for this work. They removed from Newtown, Conn., to Rockford, Ill., in the fall of 1873.

1938.

HARAN D. BULKELEY, son of Ebenezer and Emilia *Tone* Bulkeley, born June 10, 1834; married and lives in Philadelphia. He has three children.

1949.

WILLIAM TURNEY BULKELEY, son of William and Jane *Morehouse* Bulkeley, born at Greenfield Hill, Conn., December 27, 1833. He is a farmer, and married *Frances Brown*.

CHILDREN.
2145. Mary Jane.
2146. William.
2147. Elmer.

1951.

AUGUSTUS BULKELEY, son of William and Jane *Morehouse* Bulkeley, born at Greenfield Hill, Conn., February 4, 1838; married *Emily Williams*. They now reside in Norwalk, Conn.

CHILDREN.

2148. Elisabeth.
2149. George.
2150. Caroline.

1962.

TURNEY BULKELEY, son of Nathan and Phebe *Barnum* Bulkeley; married *Lucy Sherman*, who was born June 23, 1814; died September 22, 1843; 2, June 29, 1844, *Olive Warren*, who was born December 2, 1820. He died, after a short illness, in October, 1874.

From the Bridgeport Standard of November, 1874.

"Turney Bulkeley died last week in South Norwalk, and his remains were taken to Danbury for interment, where his wife was buried only three weeks before. Mr. Bulkeley had been a freighter on the Danbury and Norwalk Railroad from the first running of the trains on that road, and had also established a business on the Shepaug Road. He built up a large business, was often called to New York, and was widely known throughout the country. He was pleasant and agreeable in his manner, and having been an active man for many years, a large circle of friends will regret his death and mourn his loss."

CHILDREN.

2151. Julia Ellen, born April 25, 1845.
2152. Phebe Anna, " December 25, 1846.
2153. Eudora Eugenia, " November 5, 1850.
2154. Nathan Turney, " December 29, 1852.

1965.

HENRY THORP BULKELEY, son of Jonathan and Miranda *Thorp* Bulkeley, born in Southport, Conn., June 23, 1813; married *Rebecca Williams Pomeroy*, daughter of Benjamin Pomeroy, of Stonington, Conn. They now reside at Southport, Conn.

1966.

ANN ELIZA BULKELEY, daughter of Jonathan and Miranda *Thorp* Bulkeley, born March 15, 1815; married *Miah Perry*, of Southport, Conn. No further returns have been made.

1967.

MARY FRANCES BULKELEY, daughter of Jonathan and Miranda T. Bulkeley, born in Southport, Conn., July 4, 1823; married Rev. *S. J. M. Merwin*, of New Haven, Conn., January 20, 1846. She died March 28, 1859.

CHILD.

2155. Miranda Bulkeley Merwin, born in 1847, in Southport, Conn., and resides in Wilton, Conn.

1968.

AUGUSTUS BULKELEY, son of Jonathan and Miranda T. Bulkeley, born in Southport, Conn., March 12, 1817; married March 8, 1855, *Julia M. Perry*, daughter of Charles Perry, of Southport. She died February, 1869.

1969.

EDWIN BULKELEY, son of Andrew and Sarah *Dimon* Bulkeley, born in Southport, Conn., December 2, 1817; married July 7, 1846, *Helen Perry*, daughter of Gurden Perry, of Southport, Conn. He is actively engaged in the paper business in New York City.

CHILDREN.

2156. Helena Perry, born July, 1849.
2157. Andrew, baptized September 15, 1850.
2158. Moses, born in 1852.
2159. Theodora, " 1864.
2160. Sarah Camillia, born in 1858.
2161. Jonathan, " 1860.
2162. Grace Alice, " 1864.
2163. Estella, deceased.

1970.

LEWIS BULKELEY, son of Andrew and Sarah *Dimon* Bulkeley, born in Southport in 1821; married November 2, 1852, *Julia Francis Wakeman*, daughter of Jessup Wakeman, of Southport.

CHILDREN.

2164. Ida Frances.
2165. Lewis, died June 23, 1867.
2165½. Luella.

1971.

LOUISA BULKELEY, daughter of Andrew and Sarah *Dimon* Bulkeley, born in Southport, Conn., in 1821; married July 5, 1847, *William B. Leonard*. They now reside in Brooklyn, L. I.

CHILDREN.

2166. William Andrew, born in 1848. He is now rector of a church in Brooklyn. He married March, 1873, *Sarah Sullivan*, daughter of Thomas Sullivan, of Brooklyn, L. I.
2167. Lewis Heman, " 1850; married in 1872, Elisabeth Robinson, daughter of Jeremiah Robinson, of Brooklyn.
2167½. Louisa, " March, 1853.

1972.

MARY JOSEPHINE BULKELEY, daughter of Andrew and Sarah *Dimon* Bulkeley, born in Southport, Conn., in 1823; married June 7. 1848, *Benjamin Pomeroy*, of Stonington, Conn., who died in 1867.

CHILDREN.

2168. Benjamin *Pomeroy*, born in 1852.
2169. Josephine Bulkeley *Pomeroy*, born in 1855; died October, 1868.
2170. Mary Frances   "   "   1869.

1979.

MILTON BULKELEY, son of Lot and Emeline *Jennings* Bulkeley, born in Southport, Conn., July 14, 1840, graduated at Yale College in 1861, and commenced studying medicine with Dr. Parker, of New York. He sailed from New York on the 10th of May, 1862, on the Steamer Daniel Webster, for Fortress Monroe, and was stationed on the Sanitary Commission Steamer Knickerbocker, at White House, Va., as assistant surgeon, May 27, 1862. He returned home sick, and sailed for San Francisco, Cal., for the benefit of his health, where he was engaged for a time in the shipping business, in the firm of Sherwood, Bulkeley & Co. He married February 12, 1868, *Kate A. Wheaton*, of San Francisco, Cal., and died January 25, 1872.

CHILD.

2171. Milton, born February 11, 1869.

1979.

LOT BULKELEY, son of Lot and Emeline *Jennings* Bulkeley, born in Southport, Conn., August 8, 1843; married October 24, 1865, *Fanny B. Thorp*, daughter of Henry Thorp, of Mill Plain, Conn.; died November 4, 1874.

CHILDREN.

2172. Louisa Lenox, born February 8, 1867; died February 11, 1873.
2173. Elsie Alden,   " October 14, 1869.

1981.

OLIVER BULKELEY, son of Moses and Catherine Bulkeley, born in Southport, Conn., in 1826; married in 1859, *Amelia Gilbert*, daughter of Stephen Gilbert, of New Haven, Conn.

CHILDREN.

2174. Moses, born in 1860.
2175. Katie Amelia, born in 1864.
2176. Gilbert Allen,   " 1866; died in 1868.
2176½. Annie Louise,   " 1871.

1984.

MARY OGDEN BULKELEY, daughter of George and Elisabeth *Andrews* Bulkeley, born January 2, 1844; married June 19, 1867, Charles M. *Gilman*, son of Benjamin Ives Gilman, of Monticello, Ill.

CHILD.

2177. Benjamin Ives, born September 4, 1871.

1990.

MARY ELISABETH BULKELEY, daughter of Charles and Elisabeth *Beers* Bulkeley, born in Southport, Conn., and baptized in 1839; married October 9, 1855, *Isaac Jennings*, of Fairfield, Conn.

CHILDREN.

2180.	Mary Eliza	born April 14, 1859; died Feb. 17, 1871.
2181	Charles,	" Oct. 20, 1865.

1991.

ELIZABETH WHITNEY BULKELEY, daughter of Charles and Elisabeth *Beers* Bulkeley, born in Southport, Conn., and baptized, in 1841; married, October 12, 1870, *Rev. Frederick Hyde*. They reside at present, at Lockport.

CHILD.

2182. Frederick Bulkeley *Hyde*, born June 17, 1873.

1993.

GEORGIANNA BULKELEY, daughter of Charles and Elizabeth *Beers* Bulkeley, born in Southport, Conn.; married, Oct. 20, 1857, *William Nichols*, of Greenfield, Conn.

CHILDREN.

2183.	George Banyer	*Nichols*,	born Feb. 15, 1859.
2184.	Elisabeth Bulkeley	"	" Aug. 11, 1860.
2185.	Annie Ward	"	" Feb. 7, 1864.
2186.	William Banyer	"	" March 18, 1866.
2187.	Albert	"	" Aug. 1, 1873.

1995.

CHARLES HENRY BULKELEY, son of Charles and Elisabeth *Beers* Bulkeley, born in Southport, Conn., in 1843; married, Sept. 4, 1866, *Emma Brainerd*, daughter of Henry Brainerd, of Portland, Conn. He died in Paris, France, Sept. 10, 1874.

CHILDREN.

2188.	Annie Emery,	born Sept. 20, 1867.
2189.	Erastus Brainerd,	" May 15, 1869.
2190.	Grace Emma,	" July 17, 1871.

2003.

SARAH ELISABETH BULKELEY, daughter of Walter and Betsey *Smith* Bulkeley, born in Southport, Conn., and baptized in 1833; married June 15, 1859, *Edward Alvord*, a lawyer, of Southport, Conn.

CHILD.

2191. Edward, deceased.

2004.

BENJAMIN SHERWOOD BULKELEY, son of James and Ellen *Sherwood* Bulkeley, baptized Oct. 29, 1826, in Southport, Conn.; married, Sept. 3, 1861, *Eliza Ann Burr.*

CHILDREN.

2192. Ellen S., born July 15, 1862.
2193. Benjamin S., " Sept. 26, 1865.
2194. James Osborne, " ———; died in infancy.

2005.

JAMES BULKELEY, son of James and Ellen *Sherwood* Bulkeley, born in Southport, Conn.; baptized June 20, 1828; married *Sarah E. Burr.* No children.

2008.

HENRY BULKELEY, son of Tuzar and Frances *Upson* Bulkeley, born in 1835; married *Caroline Comfort.*

CHILD.

2195. Julia, born in 1866.

2023.

MARY OGDEN BULKELEY, daughter of Seth and Mary *Ogden* Bulkeley, born Sept. 3, 1842; married *E. T. Hall*, of Southport, Conn.; has four children; their names have not been furnished the writer.

2034.

WILLIAM CLARK BULKELEY, son of William and Charlotte *Clark* Bulkeley, baptized Jan. 26, 1820; married *Mary A. Cobb*, of New Braintree, Conn., in 1849. They now reside in Lebanon, N. H.

CHILDREN.

2195. William Howard, preparing for the University.
2196. Clarendon Cobb, at College.

2035.

MARY ANN FARMER BULKELEY, daughter of William and Charlotte *Clark* Bulkeley; married *Emanuel Currant*, of Boston, Mass., Sept. 10, 1848. They now reside at Richmond, Va.

CHILDREN.

2197. William Bulkeley *Currant*, born in 1850; died in 1854, aged 4 years.
2198. Sarah Maria   "   died in 1867, aged 1 month.
2199. Charlotte Farmer   "
2200. Alice B.   "   resides at Richmond, Va.

2036.

THOMAS AUBIN BULKELEY, son of William and Charlotte *Clark* Bulkeley, born ———; married *Harriet F. Lamb*, of Newark, N. J. He was a merchant in Richmond, Va., where he died in 1864, aged 42.

CHILDREN.

2201. Ada Virginia.
2202. Julia Florence,   died in 1862, aged 3.
2203. Charles Howard.
2204. Lillian May,   died in 1862, aged 1.

2038.

EDWARD M. BULKELEY, son of William and Charlotte *Clark* Bulkeley; married, 1. *Urania S. Alvord*, of Southport, in 1850, and died in 1865, aged 36. 2. *Mary E. Haddock*, of Newbury, Vt.

CHILDREN BY THE FIRST WIFE.

2205. Clinton Alvord,   born
2206. Ella Morton,   "   in 1855; m. Oct. 8, 1874, Mr. *Watkins*, of Savannah, Georgia.
2207. Charlotte Elisabeth, " in 1860; died in 1868, aged 8.
2208. Edward Clifton.

CHILDREN BY THE SECOND WIFE.

2210. William Norton.
2211. Richard Haddock.

2040.

JULIA HOWARD BULKELEY, daughter of William and Charlotte *Clark* Bulkeley, born in Southport, Conn.; married *Victor M. Randolph Branch*, of Richmond, Va., in 1860.

CHILDREN.

2212. William Randolph.
2213. Aubin Bulkeley.
2214. Charlotte Stannard,   died at Richmond, Va., aged 14 months.

20-45.

SARAH PERRY, daughter of Samuel and Henrietta *Bulkeley* Perry; married *Daniel Marsh Redfield.*

CHILDREN.

2215. Annetta   *Redfield.*
2216. George Perry   "
2217. Walter Marsh   "

20-46.

CAROLINE G. ALVORD, daughter of George B. and Amelia *Bulkeley* Alvord, born Dec. 8, 1832; married May 21, 1851, *Abram C. Hyatt.*

CHILDREN.

2218. Caroline A. *Hyatt,*   born Jan. 16, 1856.
2219. Charles C.   "   " Aug. 30, 1858.
2220. Milton A.   "   " April 19, 1861.
2221. William C.   "   " Oct. 29, 1863.
2222. Irene M.   "   " May 9, 1866.

20-47.

GEORGE B. ALVORD, son of George B. and Amelia *Bulkeley* Alvord, born Sept. 16, 1834; married *Margarett Horan,* Jan. 3, 1856.

CHILDREN.

2223. George Alonzo *Alvord,*   born Oct. 11, 1858.
2224. John Henry   "   " July 25, 1863.

20-48.

AMELIA ALVORD, daughter of George B. and Amelia *Bulkeley* Alvord, born Dec. 12, 1826; married *Timothy Cornwell,* August 28, 1855.

CHILDREN.

2225. Amelia   *Cornwell,*   born May 9, 1846; m. *Willard Candie,* March 26, 1874.
2226. Mary H.   "   " Sept. 28, 1858.
2226½. Annie J.   "   " May 21, 1860.
2227. Jennie K.   "   " Dec. 6, 1863.
2228. Carrie G.   "   " Aug. 6, 1866.
2229. Willie R.   "   " June 2, 1868; died July 5, 1869.
2230. Susan D.   "   " April, 1870.
2231. Edith   "   " Aug. 1872; died July, 1873.
2232. Solita   "   " September, 1874.

2051.

EDWIN P. ALVORD, son of George B. and Amelia *Bulkeley* Alvord, born March 26, 1846; married *Mary Dunn,* Feb. 10, 1859. No children.

2876.

WILLIAM TROWBRIDGE BULKELEY, son of Daniel and Caroline *Trowbridge* Bulkeley, born in Grayville, Ill., June 28, 1841; married Nov. 11, 1869, *Eliza Kellet*, daughter of Thomas Kellet. He entered the United States service August 13, 1862, Company B, 87th Regiment, Illinois Volunteers, Col. John E. Whitney. Was at the siege and capture of Vicksburg; was detailed as messenger at Gen. Banks' Headquarters, Department of the Gulf, at New Orleans, about August 17, 1873. Appointed clerk of the same department, June, 1864. He was discharged from service July 3, 1865. Since that time has been living on his father's farm, two miles from Grayville, Ill.

CHILDREN.

2233. Thomas Kellet, born Sept. 7, 1870.
2234. Mary Ellen, " July 24, 1872.

ADDENDA.

The following names should be connected with No. 310½, page 90, and were received too late to be inserted in their regular order.

310½.

JOHN BULKELEY, son of Peter, and grandson of Gershom Bulkeley, and great-grandson of Rev. Peter Bulkeley, the emigrant settler, and of the fourth generation, born about 1687; married *Deborah Shipman*, of Saybrook, in the then Parish of Chester, May, 1714, and has two children recorded on the Saybrook Records.

CHILDREN.

1. John, born March 3, 1715.
2. Job, " Feb. 23, 1719.

FIFTH GENERATION.

1.

JOHN BULKELEY, son of John and Deborah *Shipman* Bulkeley, born March 3, 1715; married *Ruth Sanford*, of Saybrook, but no children are found on the records. He may have had children who removed from Saybrook.

2.

JOB BULKELEY, son of John and Deborah *Shipman* Bulkeley, born Feb. 23, 1719; married *Dorcas Conkling*, of Saybrook, February, 1837.

CHILDREN.

3. Job, born July 18, 1739.
4. Conkling, " June 17, 1741.

5. Mary,   born June 5, 1743.
6. Anne,   "   May 24, 1745.
7. William,   "   June 22, 1747.
8. Abraham,   "   August 5, 1749.
9. Daniel,   "   Sept. 14, 1751.
10. Joel,   "   Aug. 8, 1754; never married.
11. Dorcas,   "   Jan. 24, 1757; married and had 2 children.

SIXTH GENERATION.

3.

JOB BULKELEY, son of Job and Dorcas *Conkling* Bulkeley, born July 18, 1739; married *Jemima Utter*, Nov. 30, 1768.

CHILDREN.

12. Jemima,   born Sept. 6, 1770.
13. Job,   "   Jan. 5, 1772.
14. Mary,   "   April 30, 1773.
15. Ezra,   "   Oct. 7, 1774.
16. Dorcas,   "   Sept. 6, 1776.
17. Temperance, "   Dec. 9, 1778.
18. Joseph,   "   Jan. 7, 1781.
19. Chloe,   "   April 8, 1784.
20. Washington, "   Sept. 26, 1785.

4.

CONKLING BULKELEY, son of Job and Dorcas *Conkling* Bulkeley, born June 14, 1741.

CHILDREN.

21. Conkling,   born Oct. 20, 1768.
22. John,   "   March 26, 1770.
23. Barach,   "   March 20, 1772.
24. Sarah,   "   July 14, 1774.
25. Jerusha,   "   Oct. 14, 1776.
26. Hannah,   "   May 14, 1779.
27. Ashur,   "   March 20, 1782.
28. Joel,   "   June 26, 1785.
29. Rebecca,   "   Nov. 14, 1788.

7.

WILLIAM BULKELEY, son of Job and Dorcas *Conkling* Bulkeley, born June 22, 1747; married *Mary Chapman*, daughter of Nathanael Chapman, Sept. 3, 1772.

CHILDREN.

30. Mary, born August 2, 1773.
31. Ann Conkling, " Feb. 12, 1775.
32. Clara Dorcas, " April 6, 1777.
33. Phebe Anna, }
   } twins, " Feb. 26, 1779.
34. Polly Fanny, }
35. William Worthington, " March 22, 1781; died Aug. 12, 1792.
36. Betsy Saba, " Feb. 16, 1783.
37. Abisha Chapman, " Dec. 28, 1784; died August 24, 1785.
38. Vashti Yoma, " June 18, 1786.
39. Lotty Mershons, " Sept. 8, 1788.
40. Abisha Chapman, 2d, " Aug. 15, 1790.
41. William Worthington, 2d, " Jan. 3, 1792.
42. John Ely, " May 13, 1794.
43. Lucy Mary Ann, " July 31, 1796.

8.

ABRAHAM BULKELEY, son of Job and Dorcas *Conkling* Bulkeley, married and had eight children. The name of his wife and date of marriage are unknown to the compiler. Neither are the dates of the children's births known.

CHILDREN.

44. Abram.
45. Isaac.
46. Jacob.
47. Ebenezer.
48. Thankful.
49. Nancy.
50. Ruth.
51. Daniel.
52. Martha.

9.

DANIEL BULKELEY, son of Job and Dorcas *Conkling* Bulkeley, born September 14, 1751. The following facts in regard to him were communicated by a granddaughter, Mrs. Mary J. Law:

"He served in the revolutionary war as messenger, at one time, for General Washington; was in several engagements; was slightly wounded in a skirmish on Long Island; was with the army when they crossed to New Jersey through the fog on that memorable occasion mentioned in history. Afterwards he served as a recruiting agent to the close of the war. He settled in Somers. He was thrice married, 1, to *Mary Parsons*, in 1783, who died May 14, 1797; 2, to *Anna Howard*, of Rocky Hill, February 6, 1798, who died November 10, 1806; 3, to *Rhoda Preston*, October 6,

1807. He died November 3, 1830, aged 79. He removed from Somers to Ellington in 1806 or 1807, and remained there until his death.

CHILDREN BY HIS FIRST WIFE.

53. Walter, born September 14, 1782. He was never married.
54. Fanny, " January 29, 1787.
55. Daniel, " February 4, 1791.
56. Laura, " . Probably died young.

CHILDREN BY THE SECOND MARRIAGE.

58. Nelson, born June 6th, 1799.
59. Elisha, " September 28, 1801.
60. Mary Ann, born June 25, 1805.

SEVENTH GENERATION.

But few of this generation are known to the writer, as they became widely scattered. I give a few of them.

28.

JOEL BULKELEY, son of Conklin Bulkeley, born June 16, 1785; married, 1, *Temperance Bushnell*, daughter of Francis Bushnell; 2, *Hannah Maria Bushnell*, the sister of his first wife.

CHILDREN.

61. Temperance A., born December 3, 1814; m. *Ezra Moore*.
62. Charles Frederick," July 4, 1816.
63. Samuel Socrates, "
64. Wealthy M., "   m. *Frank Tiffany*.

CHILDREN BY THE SECOND MARRIAGE.

65. Ann Jeanett,   m. *Jonathan Lay*.
66. William A.,   m. *Sarah C. Chapman*, widow of Frederick W. Chapman, Jr., and daughter of *Alvin Spencer*.
66½. Jerome A.,   m. *Victoria Clarke*.
67. Ellen A.,   Unmarried.

50.

ELISHA BULKELEY, son of Daniel and Anna *Howard* Bulkeley, born September 28, 1801. He was married to *Anna Sexton*, of Somers, September 27, 1840.

CHILDREN.

67½. Mary Jane, born December 5, 1843.
68. Nancie Ann, " April 14, 1847.
69. Angenetta Rebecca, born October 11, 1852.

ADDENDA. 245

EIGHTH GENERATION.

61.

TEMPERANCE A. BULKELEY, daughter of Joel and Temperance *Bushnell* Bulkeley, born December 3, 1814; married *Ezra Moore*, December 13, 1840. They reside at Deep River, Conn.

CHILDREN.
70. Newton S., born February 5, 1842; died May 24, 1863.
71. Charles Winfield, born July 31, 1843.
72. Josephine E., " May 8, 1845.
73. Aurelia T., " September 20, 1846.
74. Emily J., " February 8, 1852.

62.

CHARLES FREDERICK BULKELEY, son of Joel and Temperance *Bushnell* Bulkeley, born July 4, 1816. He was twice married, 1, to *Louisa Platts;* 2, to *Emeline Buell*.

CHILDREN.
75. Adelbert.
76. Francis.
77. Nellie.
78. Sarah.
79. Elmer.

67½.

MARY JANE BULKELEY, daughter of Elisha and Anna *Sexton* Bulkeley, born December 5, 1843; married *James C. Law*, of Hazardville (Enfield). He is a manufacturer of kegs and canisters for powder.

CHILDREN.
80. Jesse May Law.
81. Bertha Adella.

APPENDIX.

THE LIFE OF REV. PETER BULKLY.

BY THE REV. COTTON MATHER, D. D., F. R. S.

Ipse Aspectus Boni viri delectat.—*Sen.**

§ 1. It has been a matter of some reflection that among the pretended successors of Saint Peter there never was any Pope that would pretend unto the name of Peter; but if any of them had been christened by that name at the font, they afterwards changed it when they came unto the chair. No doubt, as Raphael Urbine, the famous painter, being taxed for making the face in the picture of Peter too red, replied, He did it on purpose, that he might represent the apostle *blushing in heaven* to see what successors he had on *earth:* so these infamous apostates might blush to hear themselves called Peter, while they are conscious unto themselves of their being strangers to all the vertues of that great apostle. But the denomination of Peter might be with an everlasting agreeableness claimed by our eminent Bulkly, who, according to the spirit and counsel of Peter, "fed the flock of God among us, taking the oversight thereof not by constraint, but willingly; not for filthy lucre, but of a willing mind."

§ 2. He was descended of an honourable family in Bedfordshire, where for many successive generations the names of Edward and Peter were alternatively worn by the heirs of the family. His father was Edward Bulkly, D. D., a faithful minister of the gospel; the same whom we find making a supplement unto the last volume of our books of martyrs. He was born at Woodhil, (or Odel,) in Bedfordshire, January 31st, 1582.

---

* The very looks of a good man are a source of pleasure.

His education was answerable unto his original; it was learned, it was genteel, and, which was the top of all, it was very *pious:* at length it made him a Batchellor of Divinity, and Fellow of Saint John's Colledge in Cambridge, the colledge whereinto he had been admitted about the sixteenth year of his age; and it was while he was but a *junior batchellor* that he was chosen a fellow.

§ 3. When he came abroad in the world a good benefice befel him, added unto the estate of a gentleman, left him by his father, whom he succeeded in his ministry at the place of his nativity, which one would imagine *temptations* enough to keep him out of a *wilderness.*

Nevertheless, the concern which his *renewed soul* had for the *pure worship* of our Lord Jesus Christ, and for the planting of *evangelical churches* to exercise that worship, caused him to leave and sell *all*, in hopes of gaining the "pearl of great price" among those that first peopled New-England upon those glorious ends. It was not long that he continued in conformity to the ceremonies of the church of England; but the good Bishop of Lincoln connived at his non-conformity, (as he did at his father's,) and he lived an unmolested non-conformist until he had been three prentice-ships of years in his ministry. Towards the *latter end* of this *time* his ministry had a notable success in the conversion of many unto God; and this was one occasion of a *latter end* for this *time.* When Sir Nathanael Brent was Arch-Bishop Laud's General, as Arch-Bishop Laud was *another's*, complaints were made against Mr. Bulkly for his non-conformity, and he was therefore silenced.

§ 4. To New-England he therefore came, in the year 1635; and there having been for a while at Cambridge, he carried a good number of planters with him, up further into the *woods*, where they gathered the *twelfth church* then formed in the colony, and called the town by the name of Concord.

Here he *buried* a great estate, while he *raised* one still for almost every person whom he employed in the affairs of his husbandry. He had many and godly servants, whom, after they had lived with him a fit number of years, he still dismissed with bestowing *farms* upon them, and so took others after the like manner, to succeed them in *their* service and *his* kindness. Thus he cast his bread both upon the waters and into the earth, not expecting the return of this his charity to a religious plantation until "after many days."

§ 5. He was a most excellent scholar, a very well-read person, and one who, in his advice to young students, gave demonstrations that he knew what would go to make a scholar. But it being essential unto a *scholar* to love a scholar, so did he; and in token thereof endowed the library of Harvard-Colledge with no small part of his own.

And he was therewithal a most exalted Christian, full of those devotions which accompany a "conversation in heaven;" especially, so exact a Sabbath-keeper, that if at any time he had been asked "whether he had strictly kept the Sabbath?" he would have replied, "*Christianus sum, intermittere non possum.*"* And *conscientious*, even to a degree of *scrupulosity*. That scrupulosity appeared particularly in his avoiding all *novelties* of apparel, and the *cutting of hair* so close, that of all the famous namesakes he had in the world, he could have least born the *sir-name* of that well known author, Petrus Crinitus.†

§ 6. It was observed that his neighbours hardly ever came into his company, but whatever *business* he had been talking of, he would let fall some holy, serious, divine, and useful sentences upon them, ere they parted: an example many ways worthy to be imitated by every one that is called a minister of the gospel.

In his ministry he was another FAREL, *Quo Nemo tonuit fortius.*‡ He was very *laborious*, and because he was, through some infirmities of body, not so able to visit his flock, and instruct them from house to house, he added unto his other publick labours on the Lord's days, that of constant catechising; wherein, after all the unmarried people had answered, all the people of the whole assembly were edified by his expositions and applications.

His first sermon was on Rom. i. 16: "I am not ashamed of the gospel of Christ." At Odel he preached on part of the prophecy of Isaiah, and part of Jonah, and a great part of the gospel of Matthew, and of Luke, the Epistles to the Philippians, and of Peter, and of Jude, besides many other scriptures. At Concord he preached over the illustrious truths about the *person*, the *natures*, the *offices of Christ;* [what would he have said if he had lived unto this evil day, when 'tis counted good advice for a minister of the gospel "not to preach much on the person of Christ?"] the greatest part of the book of Psalms; the conversion of Zacheus; Paul's commission, in Acts xxvi. 18. His death found him handling the

---

* I am a Christian; I cannot swerve from duty.
† Peter the Long Haired.
‡ Than whom no one thundered louder.

commandments, and John xvi. 7, 8, 9. He expounded Mr. Perkins his *six principles*, whereto he added a *seventh*, and examined the young people, what they understood and remembered of his exposition.

Moreover, by a sort of winning, and yet prudent *familiarity*, he drew persons of all ages in his congregation to *come* and sit with him when he could not *go* and sit with them; whereby he had opportunity to do the part of a faithful pastor in considering the state of *his flock*.

Such was his pious conduct that he was had much in reverence by his people; and when at any time he was either *hasty* in *speaking* to such as were about him, whereto he was disposed by his bodily pains, or *severe* in *preaching* against some things that others thought were no way momentous, whereto the great exactness of his piety inclined him; yet those little *stinginesses* took not away the interests which he had in their hearts; they "knowing him to be a just man, and an holy, observed him."

And the *observance* which his own people had for him was also paid him from all sorts of people throughout the land; but especially from the ministers of the country, who would still address him as a *father*, a *prophet*, a *counsellor*, on all occasions.

§ 8. Upon his importunate pressing a piece of *charity*, disagreeable to the will of the *ruling elder*, there was occasioned an unhappy *discord* in the church of *Concord;* which yet was at last healed by their calling in the help of a *council*, and the ruling elder's abdication. Of the temptations which occurred on these occasions, Mr. Bulkly would say, "He thereby came—1, To know more of God; 2, To know more of himself; 3, To know more of men." *Peace* being thus restored, the *small things* in the beginning of the church there increased in the hands of their faithful Bulkly, until he was translated into the regions which afford nothing but *concord* and *glory*, leaving his well-fed "flock in the wilderness" unto the pastoral care of his worthy son, Mr. Edward Bulkly.

§ 9. It is remarked that a man's *whole religion* is according to his acquaintance with the *new covenant*. If, then, any person would know what Mr. Peter Bulkly was, let him read his judicious and savoury treatise of the *gospel covenant*, which has passed through several editions with much acceptance among the people of God. Quickly after his first coming into this country he preached many sermons on Zech. ix. 11: "The blood of thy covenant." The importunity of his congregation prevailed with him to preach this doctrine of the covenant over again in his lectures, and fit it for the press. He did accordingly; and of that book the well known Mr. Shepard, of Cambridge, has given this testimony: "The church of God is bound to bless God for the holy, judicious and learned labours of this aged, experienced, and precious servant of Jesus Christ, who hath taken much pains to discover, and that not in words and allegories, but in the demonstration and evidence of the spirit, the great mystery of godliness wrapt up in the *covenant;* and hath now fully opened many knotty questions concerning the same, which happily have not been brought so full to light until now, which cannot but be of singular and seasonable use to prevent apostasies from the simplicity of the covenant and gospel of Christ."

§ 10. Having offered this particular account of a *book* which is to be reckoned among the *first-born* of New-England, I may not forbear doing my country the service of extracting from it one paragraph, which we may reckon the dying charge of a Moses to an Israel in a wilderness:

"And thou, New-England, which art exalted in priviledges of the gospel above many other people, know thou the 'time of thy visitation,' and consider the great things the Lord hath done for thee. The gospel hath *free passage* in all places where thou dwellest; Oh! that it might be *glorified* also by thee! Thou enjoyest many faithful witnesses, which have testified unto thee the gospel of the grace of God. Thou hast many bright stars shining in thy firmament, to give thee the 'knowledge of salvation from on high, to guide thy feet in the way of peace.' Be not *high-minded* because of thy priviledges, but *fear* because of thy danger. The more thou hast committed unto thee, the more thou must account for. No people's account will be heavier than thine, if thou do not walk worthy of the means of thy salvation. The Lord looks for more from thee than from other people—more *zeal* for God, more *love* to his truth, more *justice* and equity in thy ways. Thou shouldest be a *special* people, an *only* people, none like thee in all the earth. Oh! be so, in loving the gospel, and the ministers of it, having them in 'singular love for their work's sake.'

"Glorifie thou the *word* of the Lord, which has glorified *thee.* Take heed, least for neglect of either, God 'remove thy candlestick' out of the midst of thee; lest being now 'as a city upon an hill, which many seek unto, thou be left 'like a beacon upon the top of a mountain,' desolate and forsaken. If we walk unworthy of the gospel brought unto us, the greater our *mercy* hath been in the enjoying of it, the greater will our *judgment* be for the contempt."

§ 11. His first wife was the daughter of Mr. Thomas Allen, of Goldington, a most vertuous gentlewoman, whose nephew was the Lord Mayor of London, Sir Thomas Allen. By her he had nine sons and two daughters. After her death he lived eight years a widdower, and then married a vertuous daughter of Sir Richard Chitwood, by whom he had three sons and one daughter.

Age at length creeping on him, he grew much afraid of out-living his *work;* and his fear he thus expressed in a short epigram, composed March 25, 1657:

> Pigra senectutis jam venit inutilis ætas,
> Nil aliud nunc sum quam fere pondus iners.
> Da tamen, Alme Deus, dum vivam, vivere laudi
> Æternum sancti Nominis usque Tui.
> Ne vivam (moriar potius!) nil utile Agendo:
> Finiat opto magis, mors properata Dies.
> Vel doceam in Sancto Cætu tua verba salutis,
> Cælestive canam Cantica sacra Choro;
> Seu vivam, moriarve, tuus sim, Christe, quod uni
> Debit mea est, debita morsque tibi.*

He was *ill* as well as *old* when he writ these verses, but God granted him his desire. He recovered, and preached near two years after this, and then expired, March 9, 1658–9, in the seventy-seventh year of his age.

§ 12. The epigram newly mentioned invites me to remember that he had a competently good stroke at Latin poetry, and even in his old age affected sometimes to improve it. Many of his composures are yet in our hands. One was written on his *Birth-day*, June 31st, 1654:

> Ultimus iste Dies Mensis, mihi primus habetur;
> Quo cœpi lucem cernere primus erat.
> Septuaginta duos Annos exindè peregi.
> Atque tot Annorum est Ultimus iste Dies.
> Præterito Veteri jum nunc novus incipit Annus
> O utinam mihi sit mens nova, vita nova.†

---

* I've reached the evening of my mortal day;
A sluggish mass of clay is this my frame;
Yet grant, O God, that while I live, I may
Live to the glory of Thy holy name.
And if in life I may not honour Thee,
From such dishonour may Death set me free.

Whether within Thy holy courts below
I preach salvation unto dying men—
Or in Thine Upper Temple, with the flow
Of angel-quirings blend my raptured strain—
Living or dying, Thine I still would be:
My life and death alike are due to Thee.

† This *last* day of the month is *first* to me,
For with it dawning life began to be.
Nor have its mild returns been slow or few:
Of seventy-two long years this is the last;
A new year now begins, the old year passed;
Oh may my heart and life be also new!

Another of them was written on an earthquake, October 29, 1653:

> Ecce Dei nutu tellus pavefacta tremescit,
> Terra Tremens mota est sedibus ipsa suis,
> Nutant Fulcra Orbis, mundi compago saluta est;
> Ex vultu irati contremit ille Dei.
> Contremuit tellus, imis concussa Cavernis,
> Ponderibus quanquam sit gravis illa suis.
> Evomit ore putres magno cum murmure ventos,
> Quos in visceribus clauserat ante suis.
> Ipsa tremit Tellus scelerum gravitate vivorum,
> Sub sceleris nostri pondere Terra tremit.
> O nos quam duri! Sunt ferrea pectora nobis;
> Non etenim gemimus cum gemit omne solum.
> Quis te non metuit, metuit quem Fabrica munda
> Quemque timent cæli, terraque tota tremit.
> Motibus à Tantis nunc tandem terra quiescat,
> Sed cessent potius crimina nostra precor.*

The rest we will bury with him, under this

EPITAPH.

> Obiit jam qui jamdudum abierat *Bulklæus;*
> Nec Patriam ille mutavit, nec pæne vitam;
> Eò ivit, quò ire consueverat, et ubi jam erat.†

---

* The solid earth, before an angry God,
Shakes at the terrors of His awful nod.
The balance of the mighty world is lost—
Its vast foundations, in confusion toss'd,
Through all the hollows of its deepest caves
Rock like a vessel foundering in the waves.
Volumes of sulphurous air, with booming sound,
Burst through the gorges of the parted ground.
The earth doth heave with groanings of distress,
Beneath the weight of human sinfulness.
Shall not our eyes drop penitential rain,
When all creation travaileth in pain?
GREAT GOD! who shall not fear Thee in the hour
When heaven and earth are trembling at thy power!
FATHER, to nature's tumult whisper peace,
And bid the wickedness of man to cease!

† BULKLY hath left us for a happier shore—
Nay, rather lingers where he was before.
He ne'er hath slept beneath this humble sod,
For both in life and death he was with GOD.

INDEX

TO THE

DESCENDANTS OF REV. PETER BULKELEY,

THE SETTLER.

IN TWO PARTS.

PART I.

CHRISTIAN NAMES OF DESCENDANTS BEARING THE SURNAME OF BULKELEY.

[The figures in the left-hand column designate the number of the individual, and in the right-hand column the date of birth.]

A

Number.		Birth.	Number.		Birth.
1630.	Aaron,	1748	1655.	Abigail,	1760
1711.	Aaron,	1788	1670.	Abigail,	1790
136.	Abel,	1789	1708.	Abigail,	1803
1819.	Abel C.,	1817	1800.	Abigail,	1802
946.	Abby,		559.	Abigail S.,	1799
1884.	Abby,		194.	Ada,	
196.	Abby H.,		2201.	Ada V.,	
894.	Abby J.,		141.	Adad,	
1690.	Abby F.,	1812	217.	Adad,	1816
122.	Abigail,	1781	947.	Adaline,	
126.	Abigail,	1769	965.	Adaline,	
135.	Abigail,	1787	2114.	Adelaide,	1871
320.	Abigail,	1720	1811.	Alathea,	1794
366.	Abigail,	1743	872.	Albert,	1838
469.	Abigail,	1769	2187.	Albert,	
478.	Abigail,	1770	217.	Albert H.,	
558.	Abigail,	1795	1086.	(7) Arthur H.,	1864
1593.	Abigail,	1743	954.	Albert R.,	1802
608.	Abigail,	1761	2098.	Albert T.,	1866
1636.	Abigail,	1771	261.	Alford,	1849

Number.		Birth.	Number.		Birth.
597.	Alfred,	1766	1079.	Ann A.,	
599.	Alfred,	1769	1966.	Ann E.,	
1341.	Alice,	1852	2122.	Ann E.,	
1849.	Alice,	1871	1694.	Anna,	
1414.	Alice A.,	1845	1698.	Anna,	
1524.	Alice T.,	1870	1961.	Anna,	1809
567.	Allen,	1786	423.	Anna,	1747
2054.	Alonzo C.,		437.	Anna,	1753
1779.	Amanda,		994.	Anna,	1808
1900.	Amanda,	1821	1727.	Anna,	
551.	Amelia,	1782	2115.	Anna B.,	1861
1587.	Amelia,	1738	211.	Anna L.,	1826
1606.	Amelia,	1757	2059.	Anna L.,	1853
1665.	Amelia,	1776	287.	Anna R.,	
1795.	Amelia,	1819	1603.	Anne,	1761
1816.	Amelia,	1809	2188.	Anne E.,	1867
826.	Amelia A.,		1680.	Anne H.,	1778
1957.	Amelia F.,	1849	1067.	Annie,	
1007.	Amelia J. M.,	1815	2176½.	Annie L.,	
179.	Andrew,		1879.	Anson,	
192.	Andrew,		718.	Archibald,	1792
1628.	Andrew,	1743	1081.	Archibald B.,	
1661.	Andrew,	1774	961.	Aristarchus,	1813
1740.	Andrew,	1785	1978.	Arthur,	1837
1757.	Andrew,	1789	639.	Asa,	1744
1903.	Andrew,	1821	719.	Ashbel,	1792
1924.	Andrew,		1083.	Ashbel,	
1935.	Andrew,	1827	716.	Augustus,	1787
1863.	Angeline,		170.	Augustus,	1814
256.	Ann,	1836	1957.	Augustus,	1838
421.	Ann,	1758	1968.	Augustus,	1825
1691.	Ann,		1003.	Augustus W.,	1805

B

1693.	Barzillai,		2004.	Benjamin S.,	1868
1925.	Barzillai,		2193.	Benjamin S.,	
349.	Benjamin,		1322.	Bertha,	1868
463.	Benjamin,	1761	484.	Betsy,	
481.	Benjamin,	1784	540.	Betsey,	1793
1732.	Benjamin,	1795	547.	Betsey,	1781
2138.	Benjamin,	1848	990.	Betsey F.,	1816
1987.	Benjamin A.,	1848	1675.	Burr,	1777
2114.	Benjamin B.,		397.	Burrage,	1767
831.	Benjamin G.,		570.	Burrage,	1805
2161.	Benjamin P.,	1852	871.	Burrage,	1836
638.	Benjamin R.,	1772	2142.	Byron,	
640.	Benjamin R.,	1776			

C

Number.		Birth.	Number.		Birth.
1888.	Caleb,		2135.	Charles,	1853
2123.	Caleb,		2181.	Charles,	1865
220.	Caroline,	1823	1526½.	Charles B.,	1861
257.	Caroline,	1837	909.	Charles E.,	1799
1004.	Caroline,	1807	1221.	Charles E.,	1863
1689.	Caroline,	1798	1357.	Charles E.,	1836
1801.	Caroline,	1803	1992.	Charles E.,	
2150.	Caroline,		2020.	Charles E.,	1852
1058.	Caroline A.,	1849	1854.	Charles F.,	1839
1252.	Caroline C.,	1843	1082.	Charles H.,	
1416.	Caroline F.,	1850	1086.	(2) Charles H.,	1851
830.	Caroline H.,		1995.	Charles H.,	1844
215.	Caroline L.,	1813	2203.	Charles H.,	1827
1201.	Carrie E.,	1860	2009.	Charles H.,	
875.	Carrie M.,	1846	2111.	Charles P.,	1860
2112.	Carrie M.,	1862	1994.	Charles S.,	1836
294.	Catharine,	1660	1705.	Charlotte,	1791
354.	Catharine,		1928.	Charlotte,	
564.	Catharine,	1778	441.	Chauncey,	1741
1795.	Catharine,	1800	546.	Chauncey,	1782
1881.	Catharine,		669.	Chauncey,	1790
1994.	Catharine,	1840	671.	Chauncey,	1798
199.	Catharine A.,	1815	491.	Chester,	1781
1886.	(4) Catharine F. K.,	1856	1346.	Chester,	1864
937.	Celinda,	1793	536.	Chesterfield,	
181.	Charity,	1804	1828.	Clara,	
36.	Charles,	1719	2083.	Clarence E.,	
296.	Charles,	1663	181.	Clarissa,	1804
311.	Charles,	1703	539.	Clarissa,	1791
327.	Charles,	1710	666.	Clarissa,	1784
350.	Charles,		943.	Clarissa,	
425.	Charles,	1753	961.	Clarissa,	1816
432.	Charles,	1763	1671.	Clarissa,	1794
485.	Charles,	1760	1699.	Clarissa,	
673.	Charles,	1801	1723.	Clarissa,	1778
1075.	Charles,		1956.	Clarissa,	
1029.	Charles,	1838	937.	Clarissa P.,	1809
1082.	Charles,		2205.	Clinton A.,	
1345.	Charles,	1864	1866.	Columbus,	1822
1408.	Charles,	1847	2120.	Cornelia H.,	1827
1684.	Charles,	1786	1896.	Cornelius,	1819
1761.	Charles,	1803	1897.	Cornelius S.,	1821
1908.	Charles,	1831			

258   INDEX.

D

Number.		Birth.	Number.		Birth.
612.	Dan,	1784	1616.	David,	1744
963.	Dan A.,	1819	1729.	David,	1791
9.	Daniel,	1625	1891.	David,	1807
45.	Daniel,	1668	1909.	David,	1832
53.	Daniel,	1680	2026.	David,	
64.	Daniel,	1718	2137.	David,	1857
132.	Daniel,	1785	1950.	David B.,	1835
214.	Daniel,		1958.	David B.,	
417.	Daniel,	1744	993.	David H.,	1806
470.	Daniel,	1772	710.	David W.,	1783
488.	Daniel,	1770	1857.	David W.,	1815
618.	Daniel,	1766	1686.	Desire,	
982.	Daniel,	1800	2126.	Dillie,	1845
1827.	Daniel,	1814	298.	Dorothy,	1662
2079.	Daniel R.,	1849	318.	Dorothy,	1716
1742.	Daniel S.,	1790	325.	Dorothy,	1700
2109.	Daniel W.,	1854	396.	Dorothy,	1766
419.	David,	1749	621.	Dorothy,	1774
468.	David,	1766	624.	Dorothy,	1780
637.	David,	1780	1562.	Dorothy,	
1575.	David,	1711	989.	Dorothy L.,	1814

E

Number.		Birth.	Number.		Birth.
2002.	Edgar,	1835	1602.	Eleanor,	1759
518.	Edmund,	1787	2029.	Eleanor,	1847
1123.	Edmund W.,	1338	1948.	Eleanor B.,	1830
2.	Edward,	1614	1256.	Eleazer,	1763
22.	Edward,	1669	1976.	Eleazer,	1838
298.	Edward,		2025.	Elethea,	
465.	Edward,	1767	15.	Eliezer,	1638
677.	Edward,	1801	1815.	Elihu,	1804
876.	Edward,		604.	Elijah,	1766
1035.	Edward,	1828	411.	Eliphalet,	1746
1037.	Edward,	1833	592.	Eliphalet,	1782
1452½.	Edward,	1875	911.	Eliphalet A.,	1803
1832.	Edward,		1370.	Eliphalet A.,	1847
2013.	Edward,	1830	2173.	Elsie A.,	1869
1850.	Edward L.,	1825	144.	Elisabeth,	
1857.	Edward S.,	1827	265.	Elisabeth,	
814.	Edwin,		271.	Elisabeth,	
1086.	(6) Edwin,	1862	275.	Elisabeth,	
1866.	Edwin A.,	1826	283.	Elisabeth,	
1936.	Edwin E.,	1829	291.	Elisabeth,	
2059.	Edwin F.,	1848	312.	Elisabeth,	
2098.	Egbert J.,	1846	487.	Elisabeth,	
386.	Eleanor,	1747	657.	Elisabeth,	

Number.		Birth.	Number.		Birth.
984.	Elisabeth,		1978.	Emeline,	1841
1073.	Elisabeth,		721.	Emeline M.,	1798
1595.	Elisabeth,	1746	938.	Emeline U.,	1806
1627.	Elisabeth,	1741	1942.	Emeret,	1842
1650.	Elisabeth,	1764	234.	Emily,	1838
1659.	Elisabeth,	1772	1796.	Emily,	1852
1678.	Elisabeth,		1023.	Emily C.,	1845
1682.	Elisabeth,	1797	2101.	Emily G.,	1858
1736.	Elisabeth,	1773	2081.	Emily K.,	1854
1818.	Elisabeth,	1814	2141.	Emily N.,	
1852.	Elisabeth,	1831	409.	Emma,	1849
1898.	Elisabeth,	1823	1220.	Emma M.,	1858
2016.	Elisabeth,	1837	1396.	Emma R.,	1844
2148.	Elisabeth,		1008.	Enoch,	
2015.	Elisabeth F.,	1831	927.	Epaphroditus,	1791
276.	Elisabeth J.,	1842	720.	Erastus,	1798
222.	Elisabeth L.,	1807	2138.	Erastus B.,	1869
1122½.	Elisabeth L.,		2163.	Estella,	
1372.	Elisabeth M.,	1857	47.	Esther,	
1637.	Elisabeth O.,	1750	73.	Esther,	1713
1034.	Elisabeth S.,		87.	Esther,	1746
1991.	Elisabeth W.,	1834	93.	Esther,	
676.	Eliza,	1799	103.	Esther,	1763
808.	Eliza,		109.	Esther,	
1033.	Eliza,		111.	Esther,	1755
1076.	Eliza,		155.	Esther,	
1084.	Eliza,		1604.	Esther,	1754
1085.	Eliza,		1704.	Esther,	1789
1749.	Eliza,	1824	1755.	Esther,	
1867.	Eliza,	1827	1808.	Esther,	1818
1855.	Eliza,		1947.	Esther J.,	1828
1934.	Eliza,	1824	2153.	Eudora E ,	1850
1985.	Eliza A.,	1846	2107.	Eugene,	1851
1986.	Eliza A.,	1848	418.	Eunice,	1747
1025.	Eliza H.,	1829	489.	Eunice,	1774
1086.	(8) Eliza J.,	1867	620.	Eunice,	1672
1000.	Eliza L.,	1798	1556.	Eunice,	1701
1199.	Eliza M.,	1849	1599.	Eunice,	1753
2066.	Ella A.,	1858	1613.	Eunice,	1837
1254.	Ella M.,	1851	1614.	Eunice,	1840
2206.	Ella M.,	1855	1654.	Eunice,	1759
156.	Ellen,	1779	1679.	Eunice,	1776
1649.	Ellen,	1762	1716.	Eunice,	
892.	Ellen L.,		1726.	Eunice,	1786
281.	Ellen R.,	1850	1745.	Eunice,	
2192.	Ellen L.,	1862	1813.	Eunice,	1800
1943.	Elon G.,	1844	1858.	Eunice,	1817
193.	Emeline,				

F

Number.		Birth.	Number.		Birth.
1406.	Fannie,	1841	1068.	Francis,	
497.	Fanny,	1781	1080.	Francis,	
573.	Fanny,	1781	1703.	Francis,	1786
594.	Fanny,	1787	2073.	Francis M.,	1854
680.	Fanny,		224.	Francis L.,	1811
832.	Frances,		1362.	Frank,	1839
915.	Frances,	1832	1973.	Frank,	1831
958.	Frances E.,	1810	258.	Frederick,	1840
1013.	Frances H.,	1817	390.	Frederick,	1755
998.	Frances J.,	1819	1343.	Frederick,	1856
1027.	Frances L.,	1833	1902.	Frederick,	1818
462.	Francis,	1757	1982.	Frederick,	1828
668.	Francis,	1788	1088.	Frederick C.,	
709.	Francis,	1818	2102.	Frederick E.,	1860
714.	Francis,	1819	2031.	Frederick W.,	1857

G

610.	Gad,	1779	51.	Gershom,	1796
8.	George,	1623	70.	Gershom,	1696
190.	George,		313.	Gershom,	1714
642.	George,	1780	326.	Gershom,	1709
678.	George,		373.	Gershom,	1746
713.	George,	1814	555.	Gershom,	1789
1186.	George,		603.	Gershom,	1763
1760.	George,	1800	643.	Gershom,	1783
1780.	George,		645.	Gershom,	1788
1859.	George,	1820	931.	Gershom,	
1901.	George,	1816	1561.	Gershom,	1561
1974.	George,	1836	1568.	Gershom,	1709
2114.	George,		1580.	Gershom,	1721
1993.	Georgianna,	1838	1589.	Gershom,	1751
2064.	George A.,	1846	1596.	Gershom,	1748
991.	George C.,	1812	1632.	Gershom,	1753
1359.	George D.,		1643.	Gershom,	1746
2006.	George D.,	1812	1667.	Gershom,	1784
230.	George F.,		1688.	Gershom,	
1223.	George G.,		1738.	Gershom,	1779
2110.	George G.,	1857	1753.	Gershom,	
1203.	George H.,	1869	1791.	Gershom,	1809
1771.	George I.,	1812	1797.	Gershom,	1827
661.	George W.,		1842.	Gershom,	1826
807.	George W.,	1814	2176.	Gilbert A.,	1866
1868.	George W.,	1826	1835.	Gilbert B.,	1831
2030.	George W.,	1850	59.	Grace,	1711
14.	Gershom,	1636	1065.	Grace,	
44.	Gershom,	1665	1564.	Grace,	

INDEX.   261

Number.		Birth.	Number.		Birth.
1573.	Grace,	1720	1064.	Grace C.,	
1594.	Grace,	1745	1526½.	Grace C.,	1869
1621.	Grace,	1753	609.	Gurden,	1777
674.	Grace,	1788	614.	Gurden,	1764
2112.	Grace A.,	1864			

H

Number.		Birth.	Number.		Birth.
42.	Hannah,	1648	717.	Henry,	1789
48.	Hannah,		926.	Henry,	1791
117.	Hannah,	1768	1899.	Henry,	1810
128.	Hannah,	1773	2015.	Henry,	1835
185.	Hannah,		2033.	Henry,	1863
204.	Hannah,	1825	846.	Henry B.,	1825
309.	Hannah,		1089.	Henry D.,	
480.	Hannah,	1775	272.	Henry L.,	
649.	Hannah,	1775	2082.	Henry P.,	1836
817.	Hannah,		2071.	Henry R.,	1853
1583.	Hannah,	1726	129.	Henry S.,	1773
1617.	Hannah,	1746	1965.	Henry T.,	1813
1635.	Hannah,	1761	1771.	Henry W.,	1847
1876.	Hannah,	1799	870.	Henry W.,	
1938.	Haran D.,	1834	218.	Henrietta,	1817
1609.	Happy,	1763	2044.	Henrietta,	1849
1707.	Harriet,	1803	1320.	Herbert,	
272.	Harriet,		175.	Hester,	
543.	Harriet,	1801	1839.	Hester,	1820
667.	Harriet,	1786	471.	Hettie,	1781
804.	Harriet,	1805	1895½.	Hetty A.,	1817
816.	Harriet,		228.	Hettie J.,	1821
1181.	Harriet,		1570.	Hezekiah,	1713
861.	Harriet A.,		1591.	Hezekiah,	1749
953.	Harriet A.,	1799	1804.	Hezekiah,	1809
286.	Harriet E.,		2024.	Hezekiah R.,	
2133.	Harriet W.,	1850	1676.	Hill,	
233.	Hattie,	1835	1776.	Hiram,	1805
1454.	Helen,	1856	562.	Honor,	1774
1833.	Helen A.,	1827	674.	Honor F.,	1795
1219.	Helen E.,	1856	1660.	Honkin,	1770
2143.	Helen M.,	1855	305.	Horace,	1779
1086.	(5) Helen M.,	1861	1997.	Horatio,	1820
1019.	Helen V.,	1837	1006.	Horatio D.,	1810
284.	Henry,		305.	Hosea,	1799
652.	Henry,		475.	Huldah,	1764
681.	Henry,	1791	1814.	Huldah B.,	1802

I

Number.		Birth.	Number.		Birth.
260.	Ira,	1848	1222.	Isaac,	1978
619.	Ichabod,	1769	1883.	Isaac,	
2164.	Ida F.,		1894.	Isaac,	1812
896.	Imogene L.,	1851	2065.	Isaac II.,	1849
304.	Isaac,	1701	1063.	Isabella W.,	
1620.	Isaac,	1753	431.	Israel,	1762
1719.	Isaac,	1766			

J

Number.		Birth.	Number.		Birth.
10.	Jabez,	1626	39.	John,	1642
65.	Jabez,	1719	57.	John,	1701
68.	Jabez,	1729	71.	John,	1701
1581.	Jabez,	1723	105.	John,	
1648.	Jabez,	1760	121.	John,	1778
429.	James,	1757	133.	John,	1788
476.	James,	1766	183.	John,	1805
530.	James,		299.	John,	
806.	James,	1811	324.	John,	1705
1585.	James,	1725	347.	John,	1728
1658.	James,	1768	409.	John,	1742
1770.	James,	1802	415.	John,	1738
2005.	James,	1828	422.	John,	1744
2014.	James,		458.	John,	1750
130.	James C.,		517.	John,	1785
1983.	James E.,	1842	601.	John,	1759
1017.	James H.,	1834	686.	John,	1783
1218.	James H.,	1854	776.	John,	1855
2194.	James O.,		819.	John,	
282.	James S.,	1852	828.	John,	1818
21.	Jane,		945.	John,	
866.	Jane,	1819	1002.	John A.,	1802
1692.	Jane,		675.	John B.,	
1880.	Jane,		1526¾.	John C.,	1772
145.	Jane B.,	1868	1838.	John F.,	1816
1853.	Jane B.,	1834	853.	John G.,	1785
223.	Jane M.,		1998.	John H.,	1821
372.	Jehiel,	1745	1410.	John S.,	1850
262.	Jerome,	1852	1892.	John S.,	1809
438.	Jerusha,	1758	2094.	John S.,	1858
1001.	Jerusha,	1800	910.	John T.,	1801
1601.	Jerusha,	1757	1364.	John T.,	1845
2080.	Jesse B.,	1851	935.	John W.,	1788
995.	Jirah,	1810	948.	John W.,	
1706.	Joel B.,	1798	966.	John W.,	
6.	John,	1620	80.	Jonathan,	1731
0.	John,		125.	Jonathan,	1767
37.	John,	1748	319.	Jonathan,	1718

INDEX.

Number.		Birth.	Number.		Birth.
389.	Jonathan,	1753	1030.	Joseph M.,	1839
392.	Jonathan,	1759	1125.	Josephine,	1841
590.	Jonathan,		1483.	Josephine,	1872
1572.	Jonathan,	1718	85.	Josiah,	1743
1695.	Jonathan,		416.	Joshua,	1741
1756.	Jonathan,	1786	606.	Joshua R.,	1771
2181.	Jonathan,	1860	608.	Judith,	1775
11.	Joseph,		933.	Judith,	
34.	Joseph,	1715	209.	Julia,	1818
40.	Joseph,	1644	596.	Julia,	
54.	Joseph,	1682	707.	Julia,	
75.	Joseph,	1709	805.	Julia,	1807
88.	Joseph,	1848	865.	Julia,	1819
91.	Joseph,	1759	916.	Julia,	1837
261.	Joseph,		991.	Julia,	1819
279.	Joseph,	1840	1803.	Julia,	1807
333.	Joseph,	1722	2195.	Julia,	1866
365.	Joseph,		1769.	Julia A.,	1798
440.	Joseph,	1740	2151.	Julia E.,	1852
519.	Joseph,	1789	2202.	Julia F.,	
774.	Joseph,	1851	769.	Julius C.,	1815
862.	Joseph,		1128.	Julius H.,	1852
1588.	Joseph,	1741	370.	Justus,	1752
1731.	Joseph,	1795	541.	Justus,	1795
1887.	Joseph,	1800	1124.	Justus L.,	1840
874.	Joseph A.,	1843	768.	Justus R.,	1813
767.	Joseph E.,	1812			

K

Number.		Birth.
869.	Kate,	1834

L

Number.		Birth.	Number.		Birth
507.	Laura,	1784	1748.	Lois,	1784
679.	Laura,		508.	Louisa,	1786
778.	Laura,	1856	2090.	Louisa C.,	1862
886.	Laura,	1825	1970.	Louisa D.,	1821
958.	Leander W.,	1805	2172.	Louisa L.,	1867
213.	Leona L.,	1827	1758.	Lot,	1794
646.	Leonard,		1779.	Lot,	1848
172.	Levi,	1768	1685.	Lovell,	
919.	Lewis,		200.	Lucina,	1817
1970.	Lewis,	1821	1417.	Lucius,	1854
2165.	Lewis,		964.	Lucius E.,	1824
2204.	Lillian M.,	1862	331.	Lucy,	1720
1619.	Lois,	1750	475.	Lucy,	1760
1715.	Lois,		650.	Lucy,	1778
1733.	Lois,	1797	705.	Lucy,	

264   INDEX.

Number.		Birth.	Number.		Birth.
878.	Lucy,		417.	Lydia,	1839
885.	Lucy,	1825	509.	Lydia,	1788
992.	Lucy,	1824	611.	Lydia,	1781
1011.	Lucy,		1638.	Lydia,	1753
1739.	Lucy,	1783	1700.	Lydia,	
1957.	Lucy A.,		1837.	Lydia,	
2165¼.	Luella,		1202.	Lydia J.,	1863
393.	Lydia,	1761	1152.	Lyman,	1844

M

92.	Mabel,	1768	1653.	Mary,	1757
374.	Mabel,	1792	1663.	Mary,	1779
1657.	Mabel,	1765	1681.	Mary,	1799
1458.	Maggie,		1734.	Mary,	1767
118.	Maltbie,		1792.	Mary,	1811
1407.	Mansfield,	1844	1826.	Mary,	
1904.	Malvine,	1825	1911.	Mary,	1823
1563.	Margaret,		1963.	Mary,	1821
1018.	Margaret A.,	1836	2011.	Mary,	
1127.	Margaretta,	1847	2018.	Mary,	1844
3.	Mary,	1615	2106.	Mary,	
7.	Mary,	1621	1820.	Mary A.,	1839
120.	Mary,	1775	1931.	Mary A.,	1519
163.	Mary,	1861	2028.	Mary A.,	1857
189.	Mary,		2035.	Mary A. F.,	
259.	Mary,	1846	1709.	Mary B.,	1805
308.	Mary,	1710	1820.	Mary C.,	1843
353.	Mary,		2077.	Mary C.,	1843
403.	Mary,	1740	873.	Mary D.,	1872
410.	Mary,	1743	1905.	Mary E.,	1828
486.	Mary,	1764	1945.	Mary E.,	1837
514.	Mary,	1778	1952.	Mary E.,	1840
607.	Mary,	1774	1990.	Mary E.,	1832
654.	Mary,	1793	2070.	Mary E.,	1850
715.	Mary,	1785	2180.	Mary E.,	1852
773.	Mary,	1850	2134.	Mary E.,	1853
877.	Mary,		2180.	Mary E.,	1859
888.	Mary,		2234.	Mary E.,	1840
889.	Mary,		2118.	Mary E. A.,	
928.	Mary,	1793	1964.	Mary F.,	1811
934.	Mary,		1967.	Mary F.,	1823
944.	Mary,		2127.	Mary F.,	1848
1074.	Mary,		2171.	Mary F.,	1859
1126.	Mary,	1843	2226.	Mary H.,	1858
1222.	Mary,	1866	1369.	Mary J.,	1843
1250.	Mary,		1843.	Mary J.,	1829
1355.	Mary,		1972.	Mary J.,	1823
1586.	Mary,	1731	2145.	Mary J.,	

Number.		Birth.	Number.		Birth.
201.	Mary M.,	1819	2085.	Maria B.,	
1525.	Mary M.,	1864	2132.	Maria L.,	1845
2056.	Mary M.,	1847	232.	Marion,	1831
1984.	Mary O.,	1844	1856.	Matthew,	1811
2022.	Mary O.,	1842	1877.	Maurice,	
711.	Mary S.,	1812	212.	Miranda,	1822
2097.	Mary S.,	1862	2155.	Miranda B.,	1847
2117.	Mary S.,		1977.	Milton,	1840
1395.	Mary W.,	1840	2171.	Milton,	1869
1456.	Mary W.,		2220.	Milton A.,	1861
1091.	Mary V.,		1605.	Molly,	1755
1086.	(8) Mary V.,	1853	1718.	Molly,	1764
66.	Martha,	1721	140.	Morehouse,	
84.	Martha,	1740	216.	Morehouse,	1815
479.	Martha,	1773	267.	Morehouse,	
533.	Martha,		1367.	Morgan G.,	1837
864.	Martha,	1815	395.	Moses,	1764
1921.	Martha,		1584.	Moses,	1727
887.	Martha E.,	1827	1652.	Moses,	1769
772.	Martha R.,	1848	1662.	Moses,	1776
1022.	Martha W.,	1839	1713.	Moses,	1802
142.	Medad,		1759.	Moses,	1796
187.	Maria,		1765.	Moses,	
812.	Maria,		2153.	Moses,	1852
1071.	Maria,		2174.	Moses,	1866
1841.	Maria,	1824	2116.	Moses A.,	1865

N

578.	Nabby,	1782	221.	Nathanael S.,	1828
615.	Nabby,	1769	490.	Nancy,	1777
74.	Nathan,	1718	506.	Nancy,	1781
101.	Nathan,	1757	584.	Nancy,	
106.	Nathan,		809.	Nancy,	1818
173.	Nathan,		1882.	Nancy,	
1634.	Nathan,	1757	710.	Nancy H.,	1822
1754.	Nathan,	1787	867.	Nancy R.,	1822
1954.	Nathan,	1846	67.	Nehemiah,	1724
1959.	Nathan,	1822	1712.	Nehemiah,	1791
2140.	Nathan A.,		1460½.	Nellie,	
2154.	Nathan T.,	1852	895.	Noah E.,	1843
1762.	Nathan W.,		1460.	Norman,	

O

57.	Olive,		983.	Oliver,	1802
557.	Olive,	1794	1817.	Oliver K.,	1810
330.	Oliver,	1717	595.	Orlando,	1793
367.	Oliver,	1744	1932.	Orrin,	1821
622.	Oliver,	1776			

P

Number.		Birth.	Number.		Birth
17.	Peter,	1643	1733½.	Peter,	1797
18.	Peter,	1641	1840.	Peter,	1821
35.	Peter,		1980.	Peter,	1844
124.	Peter,	1765	1926.	Peter B.,	
297.	Peter,	1664	1930.	Peter G.,	1817
215.	Peter,	1711	1918.	Peter M.,	1814
316.	Peter,	1712	1922.	Peter W.,	1811
426.	Peter,	1744	138.	Polly,	1794
647.	Peter,	1770	1810.	Polly,	1792
1565.	Peter,	1683	647.	Prentice,	1772
1571.	Peter,	1715	352.	Prescott,	1749
1578.	Peter,	1715	579.	Prescott,	1797
1629.	Peter,	1745	1342.	Prudence W.,	1854
1683.	Peter,	1774			

R

Number.		Birth.	Number.		Birth
58.	Rachel,	1706	999.	Richard,	1824
498.	Rachel,	1783	506.	Rodney,	1784
1569.7	Rachel,	1706	576.	Rodney,	
1597.	Rachel,	1750	1066.	Robert,	
1890.	Rachel,	1805	1363.	Robert,	1842
516.	Ralph,	1783	1404.	Robert B.,	1838
962.	Ralph,	1817	1358.	Robert J.,	1842
1195.	Ralph,		1347.	Robert R.,	1866
41.	Rebecca,	1646	1404.	Robert W.,	1837
82.	Rebecca,	1737	420.	Roger,	1751
83.	Rebecca,	1739	641.	Roger,	1778
2113.	Rebecca,	1865	644.	Roger,	1786
1861.	Rebecca J.,	1831	1024.	Rosalia A.,	1848
1090.	Reginald W.,		1436.	Rosalia A.,	1863
496.	Rhoda,	1776	1611.	Ruhamah,	1767
515.	Rhoda,	1781	94.	Ruth,	1773
572.	Rhoda,	1788	180.	Ruth,	1800

S

Number.		Birth.	Number.		Birth
131.	Sally,		104.	Sarah,	1768
529.	Sally,		110.	Sarah,	1749
548.	Sally,	1783	119.	Sarah,	1773
577.	Sally,	1787	355.	Sarah,	
997.	Sally M.,	1815	414.	Sarah,	1735
1028.	Sally P.,	1836	443.	Sarah,	1745
46.	Sarah,		616.	Sarah,	1779
56.	Sarah,	1694	1576.	Sarah,	1712
69.	Sarah,	1694	1577.	Sarah,	1713
77.	Sarah,	1729	1615.	Sarah,	1742

INDEX.

Number.		Birth.	Number.		Birth.
1696.	Sarah,		987.	Sophia A.,	1808
1701.	Sarah,		940.	Sophia M.,	1811
1725.	Sarah,	1784	33.	Silence,	1705
1746.	Sarah,	1779	1085.	Smith,	
1844.	Sarah,	1830	1853.	Susan F.,	1841
1893.	Sarah,	1810	780.	Susan M.,	
196.	Sarah,	1804	1834.	Susan S.,	1828
2045.	Sarah,	1866	1411.	Susie,	1857
197.	Sarah A.,	1812	554.	Sylvester,	1787
1129.	Sarah A.,	1853	1651.	Sturges,	1769
1821.	Sarah A.,	1823	1886.	Sturges,	1799
593.	Sarah C.,	1784	201.	Styles,	
2160.	Sarah C.,	1858	1773.	Styles,	1795
2003.	Sarah E.,	1833	134.	Stephen,	
2055.	Sarah E.,		186.	Stephen,	
1251.	Sarah G.,	1841	477.	Stephen,	1768
2096.	Sarah G.,	1859	563.	Stephen,	1776
2121.	Sarah J.,	1830	566.	Stephen,	1783
1953.	Sarah M.,	1842	868.	Stephen,	1825
2092.	Sarah M.,	1851	1344.	Stephen,	1861
803.	Sarah M.,	1855	1767.	Stephen,	1794
1361.	Sarah T.,	1835	210.	Stephen E.,	1824
535.	Sophia,	1782	269.	Stephen R.,	
682.	Sophia,		1773.	Styles.	1795
986.	Sophia,	1808			

T

1086.	(1) Theodore M.,	1849	1633.	Turney,	1755
4.	Thomas,	1617	1962.	Turney,	1818
52.	Thomas,	1678	1774.	Tuzar,	1798
127.	Thomas,	1771	2017.	Tuzar,	1844
2027.	Thomas,		1574.	Talcott,	1724
2036.	Thomas A.,		1607.	Talcott,	1759
1668.	Timothy,	1787	1677.	Talcott,	

U

157.	Uriah,	1782

V

1789.	Virgil,	

W

813.	Walter,		1865.	Wakeman B.,	1812
891.	Walter,		2100.	Wallace M.,	1856
1999.	Walter,	1824	1618.	Ward,	1747
2021.	Walter O.,	1837	1724.	Ward,	1782
521.	Walter W.,	1797	1889.	Ward,	1803

Number.		Birth.	Number.		Birth.
1080.	Watson,		2010.	William,	
677½.	Wealthy,	1804	2032.	William,	1861
12.	William,		2062.	William,	1844
205.	William,		2136.	William,	1868
271.	William,		2146.	William,	
376.	William,	1754	1021.	William A.,	1841
460.	William,	1754	1443.	William A.,	1867
494.	William,	1773	1253.	William B.,	1845
550.	William,	1781	2186.	William B.,	1866
602.	William,	1761	2032.	William C.,	1861
655.	William,		2062.	William C.,	1856
665.	William,	1781	981.	William E.,	1798
818.	William,		1526.	William E.,	1868
825¼.	William,		705.	William F.,	1816
834.	William,		1217.	William F.,	
930.	William,		1412.	William F.,	1854
1379.	William,		2195.	William H.,	
1592.	William,	1741	189.	William H.,	1796
1673.	William,	1768	2124.	William H.,	1840
1687.	William,		227.	William H.,	1819
1697.	William,		1368.	William H.,	1840
1743.	William,	1787	1907.	William H.,	
1766.	William,		2089.	William M.,	1858
1806.	William,	1815	2210.	William N.,	
1807.	William,	1816	811.	William R.,	1825
1809.	William,	1790	158.	William S.,	1786
1820.	William,	1821	1794.	William T.,	1817
1877.	William,	1802	1947.	William T.,	1833
1895.	William,	1814	1413.	Worthington,	
1940.	William,	1838			

Z

| 1669. | Zalmon, | 1782 | 2023. | Zalmon, | 1844 |

PART II.

DESCENDANTS HAVING OTHER NAMES THAN THAT OF BULKELEY.

[The figures in the left-hand column contain the number of each individual, and those in the right-hand column the respective date of birth.]

A

Number.		Birth.	Number.		Birth.
1357.	Abby, Ruth,	1867	2052.	Alvord, Charles T.,	1850
1158.	Alderman, Austin,	1829	1825.	Alvord, C. T.,	
1159½	Alderman, Denice,		2191.	Alvord, Edward,	
1160.	Alderman, Homer M.,	1843	2050.	Alvord, Edwin P.,	1846
1159.	Alderman, Julia C.,	1831	1824.	Alvord, Eliza,	
1482.	Alger, John P.,	1872	2223.	Alvord, George A.,	1858
1481.	Alger, Lucy E.,	1871	2047.	Alvord, George B.,	1834
2048.	Alvord, Amelia,	1836	2049.	Alvord, James O.,	1839
2050.	Alvord, Banks C.,	1842	2224.	Alvord, John H.,	1863
2046.	Alvord, Caroline G.,	1832	2107.	Andrews, Mary E.,	

B

1782.	Bangs, Eliza,		1279.	Beaumont, John L.,	1861
1781.	Bangs, Jonathan,		841.	Beaumont, Laura,	1820
1484.	Barnes, Catharine M.,	1868	1268.	Beaumont, Laura M.,	1846
1485.	Barnes, Joseph B.,	1869	839.	Beaumont, Lucius M.,	1816
1486.	Barnes, Theodore M.,	1874	1272.	Beaumont, Lucius L.,	1843
755.	Bass, Charles N.,	1816	1286.	Beaumont, Mary,	
754.	Bass, Louisa B.,	1812	1280.	Beaumont, Mary E.,	1863
1276.	Beaumont, Alfred,	1852	842.	Beaumont, Olive,	1822
1274.	Beaumont, Charles,	1848	1264.	Beaumont, Olive,	
1277.	Beaumont, Charles,	1856	1285.	Beaumont, Olive,	
1840.	Beaumont, Charles G.,	1818	1270.	Beaumont, Paul,	1857
1288.	Beaumont, Catharine,		1513.	Beaumont, Schuyler Colfax,	1870
837.	Beaumont, Edmund,	1812			
1264.	Beaumont, Edmund C.,		843.	Beaumont, Thomas,	
844.	Beaumont, Emeline,		1287.	Beaumont, Thomas,	
1266.	Beaumont, Emmona,		1871.	Beaumont, Virginie,	1863
1265.	Beaumont, Frank,		1869.	Beaumont, William L.,	1851
1273.	Beaumont, George E.,	1845	1512.	Beaumont, William W.,	1868
1314.	Beaumont, George E.,	1872	1496.	Belden, Frank,	1868
845.	Beaumont, Harriet L.,		1906.	Bradley, David,	
1278.	Beaumont, Ira,	1858	1907.	Bradley, Wm. H.,	
838.	Beaumont, Ira O.,	1814	1528.	Brainard, Charles E.,	

Number.		Birth.	Number.		Birth
1529.	Brainard, Lucy M.,		758.	Butler, Cornelia,	1812
1527.	Brainard, Mary L.,		405.	Butler, Dorathy,	1768
1530.	Brainerd, Robert L.,		920.	Butler, Edward,	
1262.	Brandagee, Mary,		923.	Butler, Ellen,	
1263.	Brandagee, William L.,		759.	Butler, Eunice R.,	1814
1010.	Breed, John,		921.	Butler, Frances,	
1011.	Breed, Lucy,		919.	Butler, George,	
659.	Brown, Austin,		922.	Butler, Gertrude,	
45.	Brown, Daniel,	1663	1259.	Butler, Henry R.,	1845
43.	Brown, Eleazer,		1158.	Butler, Horace R.,	1845
1132.	Brown, Eugene A.,	1870	404.	Butler, John,	1766
661.	Brown, George W.,		760.	Butler, Joseph H. B.,	1818
44.	Brown, Gershom,	1665	757.	Butler, Juliana,	1809
660.	Brown, John,		756.	Butler, Mary W.,	1806
1130.	Brown, Martha E.,	1867	764.	Butler, Nancy,	1820
658.	Brown, William,		1256.	Butler, Richard N.,	1838
2131.	Brown, William,		403.	Butler, Stephen,	1764
1131.	Brown, Willie W.,	1869	1257.	Butler, Susie L.,	1842
1372.	Brundage, Elizabeth M.,	1854	1249.	Button, Abigail,	
1373.	Brundage, Mary G.,		1246.	Button, Catharine,	
1371.	Brundage, Richard B.,		795.	Button, Elijah,	
1169.	Burlingham, Amos C.,	1855	789.	Button, Emery,	
1166.	Burlingham, Charles H.,	1842	794.	Button, Emy,	
1168.	Burlingham, Franklin,	1847	792.	Button, Fanny,	
1165.	Burlingham, John E.,	1840	791.	Button, George,	
1164.	Burlingham, Marion,	1837	1247.	Button, Horace B.,	
1167.	Burlingham, William,	1844	1248.	Button, John,	
1510.	Butler, Barnard,	1870	793.	Button, Nancy,	
1260.	Butler, Carrie A.,	1852	790.	Button, Thankful,	

C

1032.	Chapin, Ann W.,		2232.	Cornwell, Solita,	1874
1033.	Chapin, Eliza,		2030.	Cornwell, Susan D.,	1870
1034.	Chapin, Elisabeth S.,		2229.	Cornwell, Willie R.,	1868
1031.	Chapin, Francis L.,		1453.	Converse, Georgianna,	1850
847.	Chapman, Amelia M.,	1827	1454.	Converse, Helen,	1856
846.	Chapman, Henry B.,	1825	2200.	Currant, Alice B.,	
848.	Chapman, Sarah J.,	1829	2199.	Currant, Charlotte F.,	
1517.	Claghorn, Mabel,		2198.	Currant, Sarah M.,	
1041.	Clark, Henry W.,	1807	2197.	Currant, William B.,	
1043.	Clark, Mervin,	1812	381.	Curtis, Charles,	1746
1042.	Clark, Sarah,	1809	379.	Curtis, Dorothy,	1741
2225.	Cornwell, Amelia,	1856	384.	Curtis, Eleazer,	1753
2226½.	Cornwell, Anne J.,	1860	380.	Curtis, Josiah,	1744
2228.	Cornwell, Carrie G,	1861	385.	Curtis, Mary,	1755
2231.	Cornwell, Edith,	1872	382.	Curtis, Rachel,	1748
2227.	Cornwell, Jennie K.,	1863	383.	Curtis, Wait,	1757
2226.	Cornwell, Mary H.,	1858			

D

Number.		Birth.	Number.		Birth.
1324.	Davenport, Frank B.,	1871	1548.	Doolittle, Millie F.,	1872
340.	Deming, Deliverance,	1746	247.	Donelson, Anne,	
336.	Deming, Katharine,	1753	250.	Donelson, Catherine,	
339.	Deming, Mabel,	1743	249.	Donelson, Frederick,	
338.	Deming, Rebecca,	1738	248.	Donelson, Harry,	
341.	Deming, Richard,	1755	243.	Donelson, Jeanett,	
337.	Deming, Samuel,	1755	245.	Donelson, William,	
335.	Deming, Sarah,	1730	241.	Downer, George,	
334.	Deming, Treat,	1727	240.	Downer, Henry,	
1532.	Dinsmore, Edward A.,	1856	242.	Downer, John M.,	
1533.	Dinsmore, Grace C.,	1861	243.	Downer, Martha,	
1531.	Dinsmore, Jennie E.,	1854	1498.	Dunham, May,	

E

1316.	Edwards, Elisabeth,	1844	27.	Emerson, Edward,	
1317.	Edwards, Fanny M.,	1846	28.	Emerson, Joseph,	
1319.	Edwards, Frank D.,	1853	26.	Emerson, Peter,	
1318.	Edwards, Frederick B.,	1850	1487.	Entz, Justus B.,	1867
1097.	Edwards, Henry,		1488.	Entz, Marian W.,	1869
1040.	Eells, Calvin W.,		1490.	Entz, Marguerite B.,	1873
1111.	Ely, Nathan M.,	1844	1489.	Entz, Theodore B.,	1871

F

263.	Fairchild, Mary E.,	1856	933.	Foote, Horace,	1797
264.	Fairchild, Sarah J.,	1858	979.	Foote, Linus,	1813
289.	Fishback, Ella M.,	1869	978.	Foote, Marie,	1812
290.	Fishback, William B.,	1871	1419.	Fitch, Mary A.,	1819
1477.	Fitch, Ellen P.,	1864	1425.	Fitch, Robert B.,	1852
1479.	Fitch, Frederick K.,	1871	1427.	Fitch, Sarah E.,	1838
1476.	Fitch, John G.,	1863	1422.	Fitch, Sarah L.,	1826
1478.	Fitch, Julia,	1866	1424.	Fitch, Sarah L.,	1830
1480.	Fitch, Maurice,	1873	700.	Francis, Albert,	1808
974.	Foote, Amelia,	1801	1522.	Francis, Bernice E.,	1874
976.	Foote, Caroline,	1806	694.	Francis, Caroline,	1794
1421.	Foote, Caroline A.,	1823	1502.	Francis, Everett M.,	1872
975.	Foote, Carter,	1804	695.	Francis, Huldah,	1796
980.	Foote, Charles,	1817	697.	Francis, James B.,	1799
1420.	Foote, Charles B.,	1821	696.	Francis, John,	1797
977.	Foote, David,	1809	732.	Francis, Roxa,	
972.	Foote, Dolly O.,	1797	731.	Francis, Selah,	
1426.	Foote, Edward,	1834	699.	Francis, Stephen,	1802
1423.	Foote, Edward A.,	1827	698.	Francis, William,	1801
969.	Foote, Eunice,	1791	734.	Frisbie, Elihu,	
970.	Foote, Ezra,	1792	738.	Frisbie, Fanny,	
971.	Foote, Ezra,	1795			

G

Number.		Birth.	Number.		Birth.
2177.	Gilman, Benjamin I.,	1871	345.	Goodrich, Gershom,	1717
1179.	Griswold, Augustus,		880.	Goodrich, Henry B.,	1824
1188.	Griswold, Eliza,		730.	Goodrich, Jerusha,	1815
1184.	Griswold, Emma J.,		728.	Goodrich, Martha E.,	1809
1186.	Griswold, George,		1178.	Goodrich, Martha J.,	1843
1181.	Griswold, Harriet,		879.	Goodrich, Mary E.,	1822
1183.	Griswold, Laura,		726.	Goodrich, Oliver B.,	1834
1182.	Griswold, Mary,		343.	Goodrich, Richard,	1712
1189.	Griswold, Nancy,		346.	Goodrich, Richard,	1719
1187.	Griswold, Rudolphus,		344.	Goodrich, Sarah,	1715
1190.	Griswold, Sarah M.,		1176.	Goodrich, Sarah,	1838
1185.	Griswold, Smith,		1375.	Goodwin, Frederick,	1812
1180.	Griswold, Watson,		1377.	Goodwin, Henry W.,	1823
342.	Goodrich, Ann,	1710	1374.	Goodwin, James M.,	1810
1177.	Goodrich, Charles A.,	1839	1376.	Goodwin, Mary,	1818
729.	Goodrich, Eli,	1811	1378.	Goodwin, William A.,	1831
727.	Goodrich, George W.,	1806			

H

2218.	Hyatt, Caroline A.,	1856	2220.	Hyatt, Milton A.,	1861
2219.	Hyatt, Charles C.,	1858	2221.	Hyatt, William C.,	1863
2222.	Hyatt, Irene M.,	1866	2182.	Hyde, Frederick B.,	1873

I

597.	Isham, Alfred,	1766	600.	Isham, Sarah,	1771
599.	Isham, Alfred,	1769	755.	Irwin, Cornelius B.,	1811
598.	Isham, David,	1767			

J

2181.	Jennings, Charles,	1865	2180.	Jennings, Mary E.,	1859

K

1534.	Kellog, Charles E.,	1852	1538.	Kneeland, Alice F.,	1860
1535.	Kellog, Edward B.,	1856	1154.	Knapp, Anna B.,	1825
1536.	Kellog, Samuel H.,	1861	1153.	Knapp, Edward M.,	1821
1353.	Killum, Arthur,	1873	1155.	Knapp, Francis A.,	1827
1352.	Killum, Walter B.,	1869	1157.	Knapp, George R,	1831
1537.	Kneeland, Adele,	1856	1156.	Knapp, Thankful,	1830

L

781.	Lamb, Abigail,		1216.	Latham, Charles B.,	1859
782.	Lamb, Bushrod,		1814.	Latham, James A.,	1849
783.	Lamb, Melinda,		1215.	Latham, Joseph A.,	1850
288.	Laribee, John A. S.,		2167.	Leonard, Lewis H.,	1850

Number.		Birth.	Number.		Birth.
2169.	Leonard, Louise,	1853	444.	Lord, Epaphras,	1743
2166.	Leonard, William A.,	1848	453.	Lord, Eunice,	1756
1295.	Lockwood, Anna M.,	1851	627.	Lord, Eunice,	1773
1297.	Lockwood, Harriet B.,	1855	1438.	Lord, George W.,	
1294.	Lockwood, John G.,	1849	629.	Lord, Gershom,	1777
1296.	Lockwood, Josephine H.,	1853	457.	Lord, Ichabod,	1762
1299.	Lockwood, Sarah S.,	1860	438.	Lord, Jerusha,	1755
1298.	Lockwood, Seth R.,	1858	449.	Lord, Jerusha,	1749
1494½.	Loomer, Hattie,	1865	635.	Lord, Jervis,	1794
433.	Lord, Abigail,	1744	452.	Lord, John,	1754
456.	Lord, Abigail,	1761	1432.	Lord, Josephine C.,	1835
625.	Lord, Abigail R.,	1770	448.	Lord, Luce,	1748
632.	Lord, Alfred,	1785	628.	Lord, Lucy,	1775
437.	Lord, Anna,	1753	439.	Lord, Lydia,	1756
1429.	Lord, Ann E.,		455.	Lord, Lydia,	1759
631.	Lord, Amasa,	1783	434½.	Lord, Mary,	1748
1431.	Lord, Amelia B.,		636.	Lord, Ogden.	1794
450.	Lord, Bulkeley,	1751	634.	Lord, Oliver,	1792
454.	Lord, Caroline,	1758	439.	Lord, Patience,	1746
446.	Lord, Dorothy,	1746	633.	Lord, Ralph,	1790
451.	Lord, Dorothy,	1752	143.	Lord, Robert A.,	
445.	Lord, Elisha,	1745	435	Lord, Sarah,	1749
626.	Lord, Elisha,	1773	447.	Lord, Theodoret,	1747
436.	Lord, Elisabeth,	1757	1428.	Lord, William L.,	

M

583.	Marsh, Abigail,	1784	1440.	McIntyre, Henry B.,	1872
581.	Marsh, Ann,	1778	2155.	Merwin, Miranda B.,	1847
580.	Marsh, Ebenezer,	1777	1448.	Mickle, John,	
585.	Marsh, John,	1788	1447.	Mickle, Sarah P.,	
401.	Marsh, John,	1753	523.	Miller, Abigail,	
584.	Marsh, Lydia,	1786	1135.	Miller, Abigail D.,	1830
582.	Marsh, Mary,	1782	798.	Miller, Adaline C.,	1814
399.	Marsh, Mary,	1749	785.	Miller, Amanda,	1798
400.	Marsh, Martha,	1751	796.	Miller, Amanda,	1809
402.	Marsh, Rebecca,	1755	1134.	Miller, Amanda M.,	1821
1238.	Maynard, Amelia C.,	1842	525.	Miller, Amos,	1769
1239.	Maynard, Frances A.,	1843	1144.	Miller, Amos E.,	1843
1240.	Maynard, Joshua B.,		1150.	Miller, Amos B.,	1840
1241.	Maynard, Robert S.,		1144.	Miller, Anna E.,	1843
1292.	McFarland, Emeline,	1860	524.	Miller, Caleb,	1767
1289.	McFarland, Ira B.,	1852	1149.	Miller, Caleb E.,	1838
1291.	McFarland, Josephine,	1858	801.	Miller, Charles V.,	1825
1293.	McFarland, Mabel,	1867	1138.	Miller, Claudius C.,	1832
1290.	McFarland, Sarah,	1855	1492.	Miller, Cora,	1862
1439.	McIntyre, Alexander R.,	1869	1148.	Miller, Dorothy E.,	1836
1441.	McIntyre, Clarissa S.,	1872	528.	Miller, Elijah B.,	1783
1438.	McIntyre, Edward H.,	1856	1173.	Miller, Elijah B.,	1850

274   INDEX.

Number.		Birth.	Number.		Birth.
1491.	Miller, Fay,	1858	1141.	Miller, Mercy A.,	1838
799.	Miller, Hannah H.,	1819	526.	Miller, Nathanael,	1771
797.	Miller, Harriet,	1812	1137.	Miller, Nathanael C.,	1829
1174.	Miller, Henry E.,	1855	800.	Miller, Nathanael W.,	1820
802.	Miller, Hiram C.,	1834	1145.	Miller, Oscar F.,	1831
1842.	Miller, Jacob R.,	1841	527.	Miller, Rebeccah,	1776
1147.	Miller, Jane R.,	1834	1494.	Miller, Robert,	1873
1146.	Miller, Josephine L.,	1832	787.	Miller, Solomon B ,	1813
1136.	Miller, Kendrick B.,	1825	1151.	Miller, Solomon B.,	1842
1152.	Miller, Lyman,	1844	788.	Miller, Sylvester,	1806
1139.	Miller, Martha,	1834	1143.	Miller, Ulrick U.,	1846
1175.	Miller, Mary A.,	1856	876.	Miller, Urben B.,	1800
1140.	Miller, Mary J.,	1836	1493.	Miller, Willie,	1870
522.	Miller, Mercy,		1518.	Mills, Lockwood,	1875
784.	Miller, Mercy,	1796	664.	Mygatt, Thomas,	

N

1919.	Nash, Dennis W.,	1818	740.	North, Laura B.,	1818
1914.	Nash, Elisabeth L.,	1805	1474.	North, Laura M.,	1869
1913.	Nash, Freelove,	1804	741.	North, Lydia,	1820
1912.	Nash, John,	1803	1102.	North, Martha B.,	1837
1917.	Nash, Julia R.,	1812	1475.	North, Martha C.,	1871
1915.	Nash, Mary P.,	1807	1109.	North, Orlando B.,	1852
1918.	Nash, Peter M.,	1814	739.	North, Theresa O. B.,	1823
1916.	Nash, Sarah T.,	1810	1108.	North, Thomas H.,	1843
736.	North, Alfred,	1807	1110.	North, William W.,	1857
1746.	North, Alfred M.,	1872	2187.	Nichols, Albert,	1873
1107.	North, Anna C.,	1840	2185.	Nichols, Annie M.,	1864
742.	North, Anna L.,	1823	2184.	Nichols, Elisabeth B.,	1860
738.	North, Charles,	1813	2183.	Nichols, George B.,	1859
1105.	North, Edwin B.,	1837	2186.	Nichols, William B.,	1866
737.	North, Henry,	1811			

O

1435.	Ogden, Francis,	1860	1647.	Osborne, Ebenezer,	1759
1437.	Ogden, Helen A.,	1866	1643.	Osborne, Gershom,	1746
1434.	Ogden, Henry A.,	1856	1645.	Osborne, Grizzel,	1751
1436.	Ogden, Rosalie A.,	1863	1644.	Osborne, Hannah,	1745
1642.	Osborne, David,	1743	1664.	Osborne, John,	1779
1647.	Osborne, Ebenezer,		89.	Osborne, Mary,	1742
90.	Osborne, Ebenezer,	1747	1641.	Osborne, Sarah,	1741
1646.	Osborne, Ellen,	1744			

P

239.	Parish, Carrie,		170.	Peabody, Augustus,	1814
735.	Parker, Ebenezer,		160.	Peabody, Catharine M.,	1796
94.	Peabody, William H.,		168.	Peabody, Charles A.,	1810

Number.		Birth.	Number.		Birth.
162.	Peabody, Charlotte,	1799	1115½.	Post, Adrian P.,	1856
171.	Peabody, Frederick G.,	1818	1115.	Post, Bertha L.,	1846
167.	Peabody, George,	1807	1116.	Post, Caroline E.,	1854
161.	Peabody, Henry B.,	1797	1118.	Post, George C.,	1860
169.	Peabody, John B.,	1812	750.	Post, George R.,	1824
164.	Peabody, Lucy,	1803	1120.	Post, Gerritt B ,	1867
163.	Peabody, Mary,	1801	746.	Post, Gerritt P.,	1812
2043.	Perry, Emily,		1117.	Post, John G.,	1860
2044.	Perry, Henrietta,		749.	Post, John W ,	1841
1624.	Perry, Joseph,	1741	1112.	Post, Julia W.,	1836
1626.	Perry, Joseph,	1748	745.	Post, Louisa B.,	1811
1623.	Perry, Peter,	1738	1114.	Post, Margaret L.,	1846
1625.	Perry, Sarah,	1744	744.	Post, Mary A.,	1809
2044.	Perry, Sarah,		1119.	Post, Mary L.,	1865
2169.	Pomeroy, Benjamin,	1852	747.	Post, Peter B.,	1817
2170.	Pomeroy, Josephine B.,	1855	748.	Post, Sophia,	1820
2171.	Pomeroy, Mary F.,	1859			

R

1509.	Ramsey, Charles,	1867	1226.	Robbins, Caroline A.,	1833
1508.	Ramsey, Gaston,	1865	1503.	Robbins, Caroline,	
2215.	Redfield, Amietta,		1227.	Robbins, Chloe M.,	1835
2216.	Redfield, George P.,		821.	Robbins, Chloe W.,	1808
2217.	Redfield, Walter M.,		1501.	Robbins, Eliza M.,	
1211.	Risley, Alice J.,	1855	1231.	Robbins, Emeline E.,	1848
1210.	Risley, Almira J.,	1853	825.	Robbins, Emily W.,	1823
1208.	Risley, Edwin J.,	1849	1501½.	Robbins, Fannie L.,	
1209.	Risley, Edwin J.,	1850	1504.	Robbins, Franklin,	
1213.	Risley, Emma J.,	1859	1499.	Robbins, Frederick S.,	
1212.	Risley, George B.,	1858	1504.	Robbins, Julia A.,	1872
1205.	Risley, Jane E ,	1859	1134.	Robbins, Marabah M.,	1854
1209.	Risley, Martha W.,	1848	1233.	Robbins, Martha A.,	1846
1206.	Risley, Sarah M.,	1847	1228.	Robbins, Martha U. B.,	1838
824.	Robbins, Abigail U. B.,	1819	822.	Robbins, Mary A.,	1810
823.	Robbins, Allen A.,	1816	1230.	Robbins, Mary L.,	1841
1239.	Robbins, Allen A.,	1839	820.	Robbins, Thomas S.,	1805
1505.	Robbins, Allen W.,	1874	1237.	Robbins, Thomas H.,	1841
1237.	Robbins, Annie A.,	1845			

S

1516.	Scranton, Anna L.,	1874	849.	Smith, Abigail G.,	1819
1515.	Scranton, Laura,	1872	850.	Smith, Abigail R.,	1821
1192.	Small, Eliza J.,	1840	1335.	Smith, Carlos,	
1191.	Small, Francis H.,	1838	1559.	Smith, Caroline B.,	1867
1194.	Small, Hattie M.,	1850	858.	Smith, Caroline E.,	1838
1193.	Small, James B ,	1845	1281.	Smith, Catharine,	1848
1334.	Smith, Agnace,		1555.	Smith, Charles W.,	1860
1309.	Smith, Arthur D.,	1855	1833.	Smith, Earl,	

Number.		Birth.	Number.		Birth.
364.	Smith, Edward,		362.	Smith, Nathaniel,	1741
1284.	Smith, Edward,	1857	1310.	Smith, Sarah C.,	1859
359.	Smith, Elisabeth,	1733	853.	Smith, Sarah J.,	
1332.	Smith, Eliza J.,		251.	Smith, Stanley,	
1557.	Smith, Frank L.,	1864	1204.	Sperry, Ellen E.,	1842
1311.	Smith, Georgianna,	1861	1784.	Squire, Adeline,	
1331.	Smith, George M.,		1790.	Squire, Charles,	
854.	Smith, Henry D.,	1827	1786.	Squire, George,	
855.	Smith, Henry H.,	1829	1788.	Squire, Mary,	
1333.	Smith, Henry H.,	1871	1785.	Squire, Monson,	
1282.	Smith, Henry L.,	1852	1783.	Squire, Ruth,	
1858.	Smith, Henry W.,	1865	1787.	Squire, Virgil,	
358.	Smith, James,	1730	1789.	Squire, William,	
1312.	Smith, Jerome C.,	1869	1046.	Stanley, Almira,	1818
361.	Smith, John,	1738	1047.	Stanley, Margaret,	1820
1554.	Smith, John L.,	1857	1048.	Stanley, Oliver C.,	1823
360.	Smith, Joseph,	1736	2074.	Starkweather, A. L.,	1862
363.	Smith, Joseph,		1071.	Starkweather, Henry R.,	1853
1560.	Smith, Josephine.	1871	2072.	Starkweather, James A.,	1856
1283.	Smith, Mabel,	1854	2072.	Starkweather, Mary E.,	1850
857.	Smith, Margaret N.,		2073.	Starkweather, Oliver H.,	1859
357.	Smith, Martha,	1728	2069.	Starkweather, L. Ann,	1848
856.	Smith, Martha A.,		1736.	Starkweather, Wm. B.,	1846
851.	Smith, Martha G.,			Stevens, Frederick N.,	1824
552.	Smith, Mary Q.,				

T

1394.	Taintor, Alice,	1835	301.	Treat, Richard,	1694
1418.	Taintor, Alice,		307.	Treat, Sarah,	1707
951.	Taintor, Bulkeley,		303.	Treat, Thomas,	1699
941.	Taintor, Clarissa,	1790	1870.	Turney, Andrew,	1786
952.	Taintor, Henry G.,		1871.	Turney, Ellen,	1789
942.	Taintor, John A.,	1800	1873.	Turney, Esther,	1793
1393.	Taintor, Louise,		1878.	Turney, Eunice.	1805
1506.	Thompson, Helen,	1871	1876.	Turney, Hannah,	1799
1507.	Thompson, Susie May,	1873	1872.	Turney, Levi,	1791
1172.	Todd, Charles H.,	1855	1875.	Turney, Mary,	1797
1171.	Todd, George,	1854	1874.	Turney, Samuel,	1795
1170.	Todd, Ruth M.,	1846	1877.	Turney, William,	1802
302.	Treat, Charles,	1796	1339.	Tyler, Byron B,	1866
305.	Treat, Dorotheus,	1704	1337.	Tyler, John L.,	1855
306.	Treat, Dorothy,	1704	1388.	Tyler, Rosa I. G.,	1857
304.	Treat, Isaac,	1701	1336.	Tyler, William P.,	
308.	Treat, Mary,	1710			

W

1348.	Warner, Kittie,	1873	901.	Watrous, John C.,	1800
897.	Watrous, David E.,	1792	902.	Watrous, John C.,	1801
899.	Watrous, Frederick A.,	1795	903.	Watrous, Mary J.,	1803

Number.		Birth.	Number.		Birth.
900	Watrous, Nancy B.,	1797	1051.	White, Jane A.,	1822
904.	Watrous, Nathaniel H.,	1808	690.	White, Joseph,	1794
244.	Way, Ella,		684.	White, Lucy,	1784
512.	Webb, Abigail,	1766	693	White, Mary,	1800
513.	Webb, Martha,	1769	1054.	White, Sarah E.,	1829
511.	Webb, William,	1765	683.	White, Susan,	1783
1122¼.	(1) Welles, Edmund B.,	1863	690.	White, Thomas B.,	1797
1122½.	(2) Welles, Elisabeth M.,	1867	1822.	Whitney, Betsey,	
1122¾.	(3) Welles, George A.,	1865	1823.	Whitney, Peter,	
1122⅞.	(4) Welles, Mary L.,	1861	1314.	Wilcox, Alfred D.,	1859
723.	Wetherell, Harriet,	1787	1060.	Wilcox, Edward L.,	1829
724.	Wetherell, Polly,	1789	1057.	Wilcox, George C.,	1818
1539.	Wheeler, Abbie,	1868	1059.	Wilcox, Henry W.,	1826
1543.	Wheeler, Alvan G.,	1861	1315.	Wilcox, Henry W.,	1868
1398.	Wheeler, Benjamin,	1831	1055.	Wilcox, Julia A.,	1814
1544.	Wheeler, Bessie,	1871	1056.	Wilcox, Lucy B.,	1816
1546.	Wheeler, Carrie,	1873	1061.	Wilcox, Samuel,	1832
1540.	Wheeler, Charles E.,	1862	1058.	Wilcox, Susan E.,	1823
1542.	Wheeler, Edith,	1865	1472.	Wilder, Edwin,	1871
1400.	Wheeler, Edward,	1835	1473.	Wilder, Frank,	1873
1399.	Wheeler, Fanny A.,	1833	1301.	Williams, Catherine L.,	1847
1397.	Wheeler, Gurden B.,	1829	1100.	Williams, Diana H.,	
1402.	Wheeler, Hattie,	1845	1103.	Williams, Elisabeth P.,	
1545.	Wheeler, Hattie,	1872	1302.	Williams, Ella F.,	1853
1764.	Wheeler, Honkin,		1099.	Williams, Emeline C.,	
1541.	Wheeler, Katie,	1864	1101.	Williams, George C.,	
1765.	Wheeler, Moses,		731.	Williams, George L.,	1801
1762.	Wheeler, Nathan,		762.	Williams, George L.,	1801
1401.	Wheeler, Samuel R.,	1839	1300.	Williams, Henry C.,	1844
1547.	Wheeler, Samuel P.,	1874	734.	Williams, Lorenzo L.,	1808
1763.	Wheeler, Sanford,		765.	Williams, Lorenzo L.,	1808
1766.	Wheeler, William,		733.	Williams, Mary B.,	1805
62.	Whelpley, Joseph,		764.	Williams, Mary B.,	1805
61.	Whelpley, Rebeccah,		1102.	Williams, Mary B.,	
60.	Whelpley, Sarah,		732.	Williams, Ralph H.,	1803
687.	White, Abigail,	1789	766.	Williams, Ralph H.,	1803
1053.	White, Abbey,		735.	Williams, Ralph W.,	1811
688.	White, Bulkeley,	1791	764.	Williams, Ralph W.,	1811
689.	White, Bulkeley,	1793	1098.	Williams, Rhoda B.	
1049.	White, Edward B.,	1815	1042.	Wood, David N.,	
692.	White, Eliza,	1798	2041.	Wood, William A.,	
1052.	White, Emily,		907.	Worthington, Eliphalet,	1797
1050.	White, Harriet M.,	1818	906.	Worthington, Joseph,	1795
686.	White, Henry,	1788	908.	Worthington, Maria,	1800
685.	White, Huldah,	1786	905.	Worthington, Nancy,	1792

Z

129.	Zeller, Mary,	

INDEX

OF PERSONS CONNECTED WITH THE FAMILY BY MARRIAGE.

A

Number.		Date of Marriage	Number.		Date of Marriage.
892.	Abby, Samuel,	1866	2041.	Alvord, George B.,	
714.	Adams, Grace J.,		1682.	Alvord, John,	1797
768.	Adams, Mary K.,	1851	2038.	Alvord, Urania S.,	1850
1115.	Alger, Charles A.,	1870	793.	Alderman, Ariel T.,	
972.	Alexander, Adaline,		1609.	Alderman, Gad,	
1094.	Allen, Hugh,	1859	1760	Andrews, Elisabeth,	1840
1.	Allen, Jane,		1867.	Andrews, James,	
1252.	Allen, William H.,	1864	2068.	Andrews, Wm. T.,	1873
2046.	Alvord, Caroline G.,		817.	Arnold, Charles,	
2003.	Alvord, Edward,		766.	Arnold, Sarah,	1836
2051.	Alvord, Edwin P.,		328.	Avery, Lucy,	1742
1816.	Alvord, George B.,				

B

645.	Babcock, Sally,	1809	1472.	Beaumont, Lucius L.,	
237.	Bacon, Brennan P.,		1275.	Beaumont, Olive,	
1449.	Bailey, James,	1809	843.	Beaumont, Thomas,	
1793.	Baker, Mary,	1855	419.	Beckwith, Hannah,	1781
659.	Bangs, Richard,	1793	419.	Beckstern, Mary E.,	1781
1568.	Banks, Sarah,	1736	208.	Beebe, Henry E.,	
123.	Barnes, Ruth,		180.	Beech, Daniel,	1832
1125.	Barnes, Theodore M.,	1867	85.	Beers, Abigail,	
1754.	Barnum, Phebe,		1762.	Beers, Elisabeth,	1831
610.	Barstow, Orra,		40.	Beers, Martha,	
1814.	Bartlett, Dolly,		1724.	Beers, Mary,	1808
53.	Bartram, Harriet,		1212.	Beers, Sarah,	
755.	Bass, Charles,	1841	1575.	Beers, Sarah,	
510.	Bass, Samuel,	1841	1209.	Belden, Alice,	1873
2056.	Bassett, Albert G.,	1867	1862.	Belden, Frances,	
1697.	Bartlett, Miss,		1207.	Belden, Frank,	1866
839.	Beaumont, Charles G.,	1862	634.	Belden, Lurania,	
844.	Beaumont, Emeline,		317.	Belden, Thankful,	1743
1273.	Beaumont, George E.,	1867	305.	Benton, Hannah,	1754
845.	Beaumont, Harriet L.,	1848	1827.	Benedict, Caroline K.,	1837
556.	Beaumont, Ira,	1811	1920.	Benedict, Ira,	
838.	Beaumont, Ira C.,		207.	Bennet, Polly,	
841.	Beaumont, Laura,	1849	686.	Bidwell, Julia,	1815
1268.	Beaumont, Laura L.,	1865	769.	Bicknell, Mary L.,	1837
839.	Beaumont, Lucius,	1845	1037.	Bishop, Grace C.,	1867

Number.		Date of Marriage.	Number.		Date of Marriage
1591.	Blackman, Abigail,	1775	736.	Bryan, Minerva,	1835
1050.	Blakeman, Emily,		736.	Bryan, Martha,	1857
1403.	Black, Samuel T.,	1873	1739.	Beckley, Aaron.	1816
378.	Boardman, Frederick,	1790	1730.	Bulkeley, Ann,	1816
541.	Boardman, Mabel,		1668.	Bulkeley, Abigail,	
593.	Bolton, James,		202.	Bulkeley, Amelia,	
466.	Bostwick, Mr.		1759.	Bulkeley, Catharine,	
971.	Bowler, Larette L.,	1818	910.	Bulkeley, Clarissa P.,	
1374.	Boyd, Charlotte,		1703.	Bulkeley, Esther.	
516.	Bradford, Elisabeth,	1808	1945.	Bulkeley, Edwin,	1872
554.	Bradford, Mary,	1825	939.	Bulkeley, John C.,	
1725.	Bradley, David,	1815	1638.	Bulkeley, Jonathan,	
1574.	Bradley, Esther,	1753	1598.	Bulkeley, Lydia,	1776
1670.	Bradley, Jesse,		1936.	Bulkeley, Mary E.,	
1608.	Bradley, Josiah,	1779	642.	Bulkeley, Sophia L.,	1804
1995.	Brainerd, Eunice,		798.	Burlingham, C. D ,	1834
1369.	Brainard, Leverett,		218.	Burr, Wakeman,	
784.	Brand, Braddock G.,	1815	718.	Burr, Wealthy,	
204.	Branch, Victor M. R.,	1860	612.	Burnett, Phebe,	
835.	Brandagee, John,		491.	Buckerts, Hannah,	1806
426.	Breed, Hannah,	1768	465.	Bunce, Diana,	1796
428.	Breed, John		755.	Burnham, Juliaette,	1841
650.	Breed, John,		787.	Burton, Fanny,	1828
962.	Briggs, Mary,	1857	321.	Butler, Charles,	
2064.	Bright, Etta,	1873	524.	Butler, Dorothy,	1795
1918.	Briscow, Avis,		871.	Butler, Ellen M.,	
1927.	Brock, Stephen,		1258.	Butler, Horace L.,	1869
954.	Brown, Delia C.,	1832	514.	Butler, Joseph,	1803
38.	Brown, Eleazer,		827.	Butler, Josiah,	
1849.	Brown, Frances,	1834	826.	Butler, Norman,	
19	Brown, John,		830.	Butler, Philip,	1836
959.	Brown, Susan E.,		596.	Butler, Steuben,	
459.	Brown, Sylvanus,		1259.	Butler, Susie L.,	1868
1900.	Brown, Thomas,		527.	Button, George,	
772.	Brown, William,	1867	793.	Button, Mary,	
349.	Brown, Elisabeth,	1770	791.	Button, Thankful,	
915.	Brundage, A. B ,	1855	1089.	Bybee, Carrie A.,	1856
1688.	Brush, Mary G.,	1799			

C

354.	Cadwell, Mr.,		1392.	Chapel, Sarah J.,	1867
1224.	Caldwell, Laura E.,	1871	674.	Chapin, Joel,	1823
802.	Canfield, Mary,		956.	Chapman, Ansel,	1813
602.	Champion, Mary,	1788	589.	Chapman, Charles,	
427.	Champion, Polly,		1596.	Chapman, Elisabeth,	
960.	Chamberlain, Mary M.,	1834	1771.	Chapman, Miss,	
815.	Chambers, Francis,	1854	557.	Chapman, Revilo,	1823
940.	Chapel, Jonathan,		937.	Chapman, Russel,	

Number.		Date of Marriage.	Number.		Date of Marriage.
637.	Chapman, Sally,		693.	Cooley, Henry,	
2006.	Chapman, Miss,		2008.	Comfort, Caroline	
14.	Chauncey, Sarah,	1659	1675.	Conklin, Sarah,	
1.	Chetwood, Grace,		1069.	Converse, M. S.,	
837.	Church, Elisabeth,		734.	Cook, Emeline,	
1302.	Churchill, Stephen F.,		693.	Cooley, Henry,	
1295.	Claghorn, Raymond,		1620.	Couch, Deborah,	1762
1712.	Clark, Angeline A.,		1047.	Cowles, John E.,	
1899.	Clark, Charlotte,	1818	286.	Crane, William,	
1809	Clark, Charlotte,		1096.	Cresswell, Kate E.,	
835.	Clark, Emily A.,	1833	860.	Crittenden, Anastasia	
684.	Clark, Orman,		942.	Crook, Delia,	
832.	Clark, William,		370.	Culver, Mehetabel,	
2034.	Cobb, Mercy A.,	1849	2035	Currant, Emanuel,	1848
1046.	Coe, George L.,		316.	Curtis, Abigail,	1741
734.	Cook, Emma,		318.	Curtis, Thomas,	1741
1619	Cole, Jonathan,	1770			

D

416.	Day, Lois,	1761	1671.	Disbrow, Squire,	
656.	Dagget, Miss,		717.	Dodd, Betsey,	
2016.	Daly, Charles H.,		203.	Donelson, William,	
1732.	Davis, Rebeccah,	1818	1406.	Doolittle, James F.,	
875.	Davenport, Franklin E.,		838.	Douglass, Sarah A.,	
2119.	Deacon, John,		1701.	Downes, Levi,	
356.	Deming, James,		1617.	Downes, William,	
300.	Deming, Samuel,		1374.	Dunham, Julia,	
1268.	Dickinson, Frank,	1865	1226.	Dunham, Woodruff,	
1757.	Dimon, Sarah,	1815	2048.	Dunn, Mary,	
1383.	Dinsmore, Bradford M.,	1852	129.	Dunn, Sallie,	
1388.	Dinsmore, Ira A.,	1869			

E

1410.	Earl, Alice F.,	1873	683.	Eells, Nathaniel,	1825
562.	Edwards, Daniel,	1795	1013.	Elliot, Matthew G.,	
1316.	Edwards, Elisabeth,	1870	133.	Ellwood, Lucinda,	1813
733.	Edwards, John,	1836	739.	Ely, Ezra L.,	1843
764.	Edwards, John,		1137.	Embry, Margaret,	1858
392.	Edwards, Mary,	1787	23.	Emerson, Joseph,	1665
1947.	Edwards, Sterling,		1126.	Entz, Ferdinand L.,	1865
866.	Edwards, Walter,	1843	185.	Esterhazy, Enoch,	
565.	Edwards, Zenas,	1800			

F

961.	Fairchild, Hurlburt,	1841	719.	Fanning, Ann,	1816
212.	Fairchild, Samuel,	1853	97.	Faulkner, Everard,	
477.	Fanning, Margaret M.,		291.	Falkner, Edward,	

Number.		Date of Marriage.	Number.		Date of Marriage.
1012.	Field, Henry D.,		622.	Foote, Sophia,	1797
1712.	Fillio, Ellen,		600.	Foote, Theodore,	1787
280.	Fishback, John B.,		1933.	Forbes, William,	1858
1112.	Fitch, Frederick,	1861	170.	Forbes, William H.,	1861
1114.	Fitch, Frederick,	1868	462.	Fosdick, Elisabeth,	1797
947.	Fitch, Jared W.,		815.	Francis, Charles,	
21.	Flint, Ephraim,		1316.	Francis, Edward M.,	1870
977.	Foote, David,		475.	Francis, John,	1792
971.	Foote, Ezra,	1818	493.	Francis, Selah,	1763
974.	Foote, Ralph C.,		811.	Freeman, Emma L.,	1850
620.	Foote, Roger,	1790	497.	Frisbie, Elihu,	813

G

324.	Gardner, Mary,	1738	924.	Goodwin, James M.,	1809
302.	Gardner, Sarah,	1227	1007.	Goodwin, Joseph M.,	1841
1981.	Gilbert, Amelia,	1859	1947.	Golden, James,	
1716.	Gilbert, John,		228.	Gordon, Henry,	
1716.	Gillet, Elisabeth,	1851	1401.	Goss, Catharine F. E.,	
1984.	Gilman, Charles M,		401.	Grant, Ann,	1749
1095.	Godfrey, Alexander L.,		1629.	Green, Mary,	
1714.	Godfrey, David,		676.	Green, Richard,	1852
1614.	Godfrey, Daniel,		1741.	Green, Sophia,	1816
823.	Goodrich, Abby J.,	1840	1710.	Gregory, Rebecca,	1789
577.	Goodrich, Elisha,	1821	377.	Griswold, Abigail,	1776
657.	Goodrich, James,		350.	Griswold, Mary,	
490.	Goodrich, Joshua,	1800	462.	Griswold, Rhoda,	1781
555.	Goodrich, Laura,	1811	804.	Griswold, Rodolphus,	
310.	Goodrich, Richard,	1709	1043.	Guptil, Caroline,	
803.	Goodrich, Sylvester,		1368.	Guerney, Emma L.,	

H

2038.	Haddock, Mary E.,		2023.	Hall, E. T.,	
191.	Haines, Allen,		1385.	Hall, Frances E.,	1833
1470.	Hall, Alexandre E.,	1861	1162.	Hall, Helen M.,	1834
1389.	Hall, Alonzo P.,	1841	796.	Hall, Horace,	1825
1463.	Hall, Arnold H.,	1863	1392.	Hall, Jane D.,	1867
1391.	Hall, Catharine,	1844	138.	Hall, Jane E.,	
1570.	Hall, Catharine,	1739	1384.	Hall, Jane E.,	1830
1092.	Hall, Charles S.,	1827	1392.	Hall, James D.,	1846
1386.	Hall, Charles E.,	1835	1409.	Hall, Josephine C.,	1856
1462.	Hall, Charles H.,	1860	1094.	Hall, Josephine E.,	
1163.	Hall, Charles V.,	1837	1467.	Hall, Josephine E.,	1862
1469.	Hall, Corinne A.,	1868	1094.	Hall, Josephine F. M.,	1857
1383.	Hall, Cornelia P.,	1828	1461½.	Hall, Louisa H.,	1858
1390.	Hall, Edward,	1843	1466.	Hall, Maria S. H.,	1860
1382.	Hall, Edwin B.,	1826	1470½.	Hall, Marie A. N.,	1872
1471.	Hall, Edwin T.,	1863	944.	Hall, Parker,	

Number.		Date of Marriage.	Number.		Date of Marriage.
938.	Hall, Pomeroy,		73.	Hill, John,	1729
1096.	Hall, Richard H.,		100.	Hill, John,	1759
528.	Hall, Ruth,		99.	Hill, Joseph,	1752
1469.	Hall, Nathalie H.,	1866	97.	Hill, Sarah,	1742
1161.	Hall, Sarah C.,	1831	144.	Hill, Sophia P.,	
1398.	Hall, Sarah P.,	1867	1025.	Hill, Thomas G ,	1856
1464.	Hall, Samuel H. P.,	1868	948.	Hillard, Adelaide,	
1468.	Hall, Samuel H. P.,	1864	1048.	Hine, Charlotte,	
1387.	Hall, Samuel L ,	1837	1935.	Hobart, Ann M ,	1854
721.	Hall, S. H. P.,	1826	2047.	Horan, Margaret,	1856
1095.	Hall, Theodore P.,	1860	885.	Horton, Hamilton,	1844
1748.	Hall, Washington,		1329.	Horton, Edward T.,	1858
1092.	Hall, Wm. B.,		1327.	Horton, Frederick,	1851
1093.	Hall, Wm. D.,		1330.	Horton, George B.,	1861
476.	Hallam, Caroline,		1326.	Horton, Henry P.,	1848
1665.	Hallet, Lyman,	1797	1325.	Horton, Herbert,	1845
1340.	Hanmer, John,	1874	1136.	Hotchkiss, Rose,	1853
1524.	Hanmer, Alice E.,	1874	1921.	Hough, Edwin,	
1091.	Hanks, Arthur F.,		190.	Howland, Eunice,	
1882.	Harold, William,		957.	Hoxey, Benjamin,	
553.	Hart, Abigail,	1804	83.	Hoyt, Hannah,	1762
546.	Hart, Nancy,	1805	29.	Hubbard, Joseph,	
220.	Harding, Mr.,		1416.	Hubbel, Alfred D.,	1871
482.	Harkin, Eliza P.,	1814	139.	Hubbel, Chloe,	1812
1092.	Harris, Mary,		217.	Hubbel, Harriet,	
960.	Harrison, Sarah E.,	1838	91.	Hubbel, Ellen,	
1550.	Haskell, Henrietta A.,	1853	1403.	Hubbel, Maria S.,	
1551.	Haskell, Josephine C.,	1856	355.	Hubbard, Philippa,	
1553.	Haskell, Mary W.,	1864	58.	Hubbard, Mary,	1830
1418.	Haskell, Wm. H.,	1857	93.	Hull, Chapman,	
1552.	Haskell, William W.,	1864	1108.	Humphrey, Sarah,	1868
324.	Hastings, Abigail,	1751	1349.	Hunt, Della,	
1108.	Hastings, Thomas,		891.	Hunt, Electa,	
1749.	Hawley, Eli,		673.	Hunt, Eliza,	1828
76.	Henry, Beulah,	1754	1350.	Hunt, Ida L.,	1857
1922.	Henry, Clara,	1858	30.	Hunt, Samuel,	
1251.	Higby, Jasper E.,	1863	373.	Huntington, Hope,	1863
1678.	Higgins, Samuel,	1804	1138.	Huntington, May,	
1571.	Hill, Ann,	1740	928.	Hurd, Charles,	
1445.	Hill, Charles,		408.	Hurlburt, George B.,	
96.	Hill, Esther,	1735	894.	Hutchinson, Henry,	1763
66.	Hill, Hannah.		1354.	Hutchinson, Nellie B.,	1864
1446.	Hill, Helen H.,		1991.	Hyde, Frederick,	1870
98.	Hill, Isaac,	1745			
755.	Irwin, Cornelius B.,		414.	Isham, Joseph,	1765
509.	Irwin, Peter,	1805	909.	Isham, Mary,	1829

J

Number.		Date of Marriage.	Number.		Date of Marriage.
2108.	Jarvis, Andrew,		1634.	Jennings, Miss,	
1658.	Jarvis, Miss,		1633.	Johnson, Esther,	
23.	Jeffreys, Silence,		554.	Johnson, Mary,	
1791.	Jennings, David,	1832	4.	Jones, Sarah,	
1757.	Jennings, Emeline,	1830	1660.	Judson, Catharine,	
1990.	Jennings, Isaac,	1855	103.	Judson, Daniel,	

K

1141.	Kees, Jacob,	1862	349.	Kirby, Susannah,	1757
746.	Keith,	1836	2077.	Kohlseat, Ernest W.,	1839
2076.	Kellet, Eliza,	1869	2025.	Knapp, Charles,	
1384.	Kellog, Daniel,		791.	Knapp, William,	1820
800.	Kenyon, Juliaette,	1848	1393.	Keeland, Charles,	1854
893.	Killam, Lyman,	1865	1397.	Knight, Cyntha L.,	
1930.	King, Clarissa,				

L

478.	Lacy, Jasper,		88.	Lewis, Elisabeth,	1776
523.	Lamb, Asa,		1206.	LeVaughn, Dinah,	1865
2036.	Lamb, Harriet F.,		1971.	Leonard, Wm. B.,	
594.	Lamb, Henry,		1295.	Lockwood, Annie M.,	
412.	Lamb, John,		1297.	Lockwood, Harriet B.,	
1936.	Landers, Mariette,		845.	Lockwood, John W.,	
1698.	Lane, Miss,		1296.	Lockwood, Josephine,	
1051.	Lansing, Henry L.,		1148.	Loomer, George,	1859
810.	Latham, Joseph S.,	1845	2054.	Loomis, Harriet,	
327.	Latimer, Ann,	1741	420.	Loomis, Rhoda,	
407.	Latimer, Robert,		604.	Loomis, Pamela,	1787
278.	Larribee, John H.,		639.	Loomis, Sophia,	1796
1919.	Lawrence, Betsey,	1844	1418.	Lord, Amelia B.,	1857
1919.	Lawrence, Catherine,		331.	Lord, Epaphras,	
1698.	Leach, Maria,		329.	Lord, Ichabod,	1743
1660.	Lee, Elisabeth,		1004.	Lord, Thomas D.,	1825
227.	Lee, Sarah,		1747.	Lyon, David,	
816.	Lester, Mr.,				

M

1272.	Madigan, Ellen,		279.	Marshall, Agnes,	1872
172.	Mallory, Emily,	1805	1731.	Mason, Charlotte,	1829
1740.	Mallory, Sally,		611.	Mason, William,	
1054.	Malsom, Henry,		225.	May, Ann,	
78.	Maltbie, Hannah,		824.	Maynard, Joshua,	1840
677.	Mansfield, Lucy,	1828	820.	McConnor, Marabah,	1844
821.	Marsh, Frederick,		844.	McFarland, Joseph,	
320.	Marsh, John,	1749	1018.	McIntyre, Edward,	1865
387.	Marsh, Martha,		1627.	McIuster,	

284 INDEX.

Number.		Date of Marriage.	Number.		Date of Marriage.
1609.	Meeker, Eleanor,	1801	787.	Miller, Solomon B.,	1828
1631.	Meeker, Mr.,		788.	Miller, Urbane B.,	1822
1799.	Meeker, Mary J.,	1867	1297.	Mills, Albert F.,	1873
1851.	Merwin, Emily,		23.	Minot, Rebeccah,	1696
1967.	Merwin, S. J. M.,	1846	668.	Mix, Content,	1811
1026.	Mickle, John,		1253.	Moffit, Hattie,	1871
110.	Middleton, Ebenezer,	1749	1830.	Moody, J.,	1855
798.	Miller, Adaline C.,		27.	Moody, Mary,	
796.	Miller, Amanda,	1825	1726.	Morehouse, Aaron,	
1144.	Miller, Anna E.,	1867	183.	Morehouse, Catharine,	1836
570.	Miller, Caroline,		1733.	Morehouse, Ebenezer,	
1138.	Miller, Claudius C.,	1863	1667.	Morehouse, Esther,	1808
1148.	Miller, Dorothy E.,	1859	1743.	Morehouse, Jane,	
799.	Miller, Harriet H.,	1844	1605.	Morehouse, Joseph,	
802.	Miller, Hiram C.,		118.	Morehouse, Parthena,	
1136.	Miller, Kendrick B.,	1853	1595.	Morehouse, Peter,	
1139.	Miller, Martha,	1856	1703.	Morehouse, Sarah,	1816
1140.	Miller, Mercy,	1860	1828.	Morgan, James,	
784.	Miller, Mercy,	1815	911.	Morgan, Lydia S.,	1841
1141.	Miller, Mercy A.,	1862	613.	Mosely, Samuel,	
366.	Miller, Nathaniel,	1762	1409.	Morris, Frank H.,	1874
1157.	Miller, Nathaniel,	1855	532.	Myears, Hannah,	1809
800.	Miller, Nathaniel W.,	1848	189.	Myers, Orlando,	
1145.	Miller, Oscar F.,	1856	461.	Mygatt, John,	

N

1737.	Nash, Micajah,	1819	731.	North, Alfred,	
1301.	Neff, Cornelia,		1107.	North, Anna C.,	1870
232.	Nelson, Joseph,		483.	North, Dolly,	
328.	Newton, Susannah,	1756	755.	North, Maria,	1835
93.	Nichols, Gould,		506.	North, Nathan,	1805
1807.	Nichols, Martha J.,	1845	1042.	North, Oren L.,	
1910.	Nichols, Mary,		739.	North, Theresa O. B.,	
223.	Nichols, Rufus,		1108.	North, Thomas H.,	1868
1993.	Nichols, William,	1857	1908.	Northrop, Julia B.,	
1751.	Noble, Marcus,		207.	Northrop, Lord,	
603.	Noble, Widow,		666.	Noyes, Charles,	

O

1086.	Oakley, Catherine F.,		1586.	Osborne, Howes,	1755
1014.	Ogden, Henry S.,	1858	63.	Osborne, John,	
1656.	Ogden, Mary,	1785	1687.	Osborne, Maria B.,	
1802.	Ogden, Mary,	1835	1596.	Osborne, May,	1804
956.	Oliphant, Mary J.,	1834	1702.	Osborne, Stephen,	1799
417.	Olmsted, Dorothy,	1764	1668.	Osborne, Susannah,	1823
1695.	Osborne, Ann,		1596.	Osborne, Widow,	
1583.	Osborne, Eleazer,	1738	1672.	Oysterbank, David,	
1581.	Osborne, Elisabeth,	1747			

P

Number.		Date of Marriage.	Number.		Date of Marriage.
1093.	Paddock, Elisabeth S. I.,	1857	1621.	Perry, Thaddens,	1774
199.	Parish, Townsend,		829.	Petit, Susan,	
501.	Parker, Ebenezer,	1812	1139.	Philly, Charles,	1856
155.	Patchen, David,		943.	Pierson, Job,	
711.	Peabody, Abigail,		1849.	Pike,	1866
1415.	Pease, Henrietta G.,	1869	1996.	Platt, Widow,	
1913.	Peck, Charles,		1972.	Pomeroy, Benjamin,	1848
2141.	Peck, Frank,		1964.	Pomeroy, Rebecca W.,	
1930.	Peck, Mary,		351.	Pomeroy, Rachel,	1771
1742.	Peck, Miriam,	1834	937.	Porter, Alanson,	
1050.	Peckham, E. G.,		609.	Porter, Nancy,	1820
843.	Peckwell, Josephine,		710.	Pool, Joshua H.,	
713.	Pendleton, Esther,		1115½.	Post, Adrian B.,	1857
144.	Penfield, Elisabeth,		1115.	Post, Bertha L.,	1870
1819.	Perry, Ann G.,	1846	744.	Post, Gerrit B.,	1836
1817.	Perry, Frances M.,		508.	Post, John G.,	1806
1966.	Perry, Francis,		1112.	Post, John W.,	1861
1963.	Perry, Helen,		1114.	Post, Margaret,	1868
1969.	Perry, Helen,		747.	Post, Peter B.,	1842
1577.	Perry, Joseph,	1756	2084.	Post, Stephen	
1968.	Perry, Julia M.,		840.	Pratt, Mary,	1842
1667.	Perry, Miah,		1275.	Pratt, Wm. E.,	1842
1988.	Perry, Oliver,		299.	Prentice, Patience,	1701
74.	Perry, Sarah,	1756	298.	Prescott, Dorothy,	
1812.	Perry, Samuel,		25.	Prescott, Jonathan,	1681
1715.	Perry, Stephen,				

Q

1005.	Quimby, Albert H.,	1842

R

1259.	Ranney, Benjamin L.,	1865	809.	Risley, Edward,	
216.	Raynor, Sarah,		1209.	Risley, Edwin J.,	1873
2045.	Redfield, Daniel M.,		806.	Risley, Julia,	
1673.	Redfield, Sarah,		1207.	Risley, Martha W.,	1866
786.	Rees, Anna,	1822	1206.	Risley, Sarah M.,	1865
948.	Reynolds, Helen,		949.	Roath, Elisabeth,	
2043.	Rider, George,		824.	Robbins, Abigail U. B.,	
1813.	Rider, John,		326.	Robbins, Abigail,	1733
227.	Riggs, Sarah L.,	1841	551.	Robbins, Allen,	1804
370.	Riley, Ackley,	1805	822.	Robbins, Allen A,	1841
567.	Riley, Eliza,		1237.	Robbins, Annie A.,	1870
1021.	Riley, Mary A.,	1863	1226.	Robbins, Caroline A.,	1226
568.	Riley, Nancy,	1814	1227.	Robbins, Chester,	1854
387.	Riley, Susan,	1805	1227.	Robbins, Chloe M.,	1854
976.	Risley, Luke,		821.	Robbins, Chloe,	

Number.		Date of Marriage.	Number.		Date of Marriage.
825.	Robbins, Emily W.,		1237.	Robbins, Wm. G.,	1870
1674.	Robbins, Ephraim,		861.	Roberts, Henry,	
485.	Robbins, Eunice,	1782	210.	Rockwell, Harriet,	
521.	Robbins, Lucy,	1830	2120.	Rogers, Samuel T.,	
372.	Robbins, Mary,	1775	272.	Roof, Milton,	
518.	Robbins, Nancy,	1811	420.	Root, Jerusha,	
820.	Robbins, Thomas S.,	1832	156.	Ruggles, Philo,	

S

472.	Sage, Bathsheba,		204.	Smith, William,	
311.	Sage, Mary,		807.	Sperry, Lucy,	1842
709.	Sanger, Mary F.,		868.	Sperry, Isaac J.,	1840
157.	Sayer, Jane,		863.	Spear, William,	
1281.	Scranton, Robert,	1870	1663.	Squire, Joab,	1800
820.	Sears, Martha C.,		708.	Stacy, Mary F.,	
181.	Seeley, Henry,		1041.	Stanley, Emily,	1832
144.	Sedam, Robert F.,		684.	Stanley, Jesse,	
715.	Selden, Thomas,		912.	Stark, Clara C.,	
1941.	Shafter, Farewell,	1857	821.	Starkweather, Wm. R.,	1844
1886.	Shelton, Nancy,		1798.	Sterling, Charlotte I.,	1865
1923.	Shepard, Hiram,		308.	Stevens, Joseph,	
1578.	Sherman, Hannah,	1760	578.	Stevens, Isaac,	1819
1962.	Sherman, Lucy,		276.	Stoddard, Frederick D.,	
1770.	Sherwood, Ellen,	1825	313.	Stow, Joseph,	
590.	Simons, Elisabeth,	1823	702.	Stuart, I. W.,	1834
1722.	Simmons, Mehetabel,	1799	1829.	Studwell, M. L.,	
1833.	Slawson, W. D.,		1584.	Sturges, Abigail,	1758
1087.	Skinner, Harriet L.,	1851	1639.	Sturges, Ebenezer,	
805.	Small, Daniel,		1856.	Sturges, Ellen,	
850.	Smith, Abigail R.,		1723.	Sturges, Peter,	1799
841.	Smith, Alfred,	1849	1706.	Sturges, Priscilla,	
758.	Smith, Benjamin,		2166.	Sullivan, Sarah,	1873
1768.	Smith, Betsey,	1816	884.	Stevens, George O.,	1835
1281.	Smith, Catharine,	1870	883.	Stevens, Joseph H.,	1828
355.	Smith, Cephas,	1756	881.	Stevens, Norman B.,	1820
1709.	Smith, Charles,	1856	1062.	Stuart, Ellen M.,	
316.	Smith, Christina,	1769	1064.	Stuart, Grace C.,	
559.	Smith, Davis,	1819	1063.	Stuart, Isabella W.,	
1866.	Smith, Eliza J.,		2087.	Studwell, Albert C.,	
747.	Smith, Elisabeth,	1842	2086.	Studwell, Frederick B.,	
1399.	Smith, F. F.,		1039.	St. John, Francis,	
886.	Smith, George,		677½.	St. John, Jesse,	
855.	Smith, Henry H.,	1854	1038.	St. John, Edward,	
312.	Smith, Joseph,	1726	1244.	Sugden, Abbie L.,	1852
856.	Smith, Martha A.,	1856	1243.	Sugden, Amelia M.,	1849
1852.	Smith, Mary J.,		1245.	Sugden, Emily R.,	1861
1769.	Smith, Philo,		1242.	Sugden, Robert,	1847

T

Number.		Date of Marriage.
1393.	Taintor, Louisa,	1854
605.	Taintor, Roger,	1769
588.	Taintor, Sally,	1798
606.	Taintor, Sally,	1793
608.	Taintor, Solomon,	
1362.	Talcott, Lottie J.,	
933.	Talcott, Platt,	
297.	Talcott, Rachel,	1687
1561.	Talcott, Rachel,	
1948.	Tallmadge, Albert,	
977.	Taylor, Caroline	
2055.	Terry, John S.,	
1250.	Thompson, Edward L.,	1866
1979.	Thorp, Fanny B.,	1865
1622.	Thorp, Grizzel,	1728
1756.	Thorp, Miranda,	1810
799.	Todd, Charles,	1844
1741.	Torr, Emilie,	
1820.	Townsend, Lavinie T.,	1843
963.	Townsend, Marietta,	1843

Number.		Date of Marriage
199.	Townsend, Parish,	
948.	Tracy, Eliza,	
308.	Treat, Dorothens,	1754
314.	Treat, Isaac,	1730
808.	Treat, Mary,	
294.	Treat, Richard,	1704
307.	Treat, Sarah,	1729
295.	Treat, Thomas,	1693
1096.	Trowbridge, Hannah P.,	1861
322.	Trumbull, Jonathan,	
307.	Tryon, Joseph,	179'
379.	Tryon, Penelope,	
520.	Tucker, Martha,	18
1029.	Tudor, Sarah,	
1123.	Turner, Caroline J.,	
1717.	Turney, Abel,	
1719.	Turney, Abigail,	1797
1578.	Turney, Sarah,	1740
964.	Tuthill, Mary K.,	1852
887.	Tyler, William,	1850

U

| 222. | Ufford, John, | |
| 1774. | Upson, Frances M., | |

V

931.	Van Alstine,	
189.	Vanderburgh, Henry,	
930.	Vandyne, Mary A.,	
192.	Vastres, Mary A.,	

W

1864.	Wakeman, Elisabeth,	
1959.	Wakeman, Gershom,	
97.	Wakeman, Joseph,	
197.	Wakeman, Joseph,	1834
1970.	Wakeman, Julia F.,	
186.	Wakeman, Sarah,	
196.	Walcott, Samuel,	
720.	Walbridge, Mary,	
1145.	Walker, Marion,	1856
196.	Walrath, Samuel,	
1947.	Ward, Benjamin,	
1273.	Ward, Emma,	1869
1565.	Ward, Hannah,	
811.	Ward, Nathaniel,	
869.	Warner, John,	1782
549.	Warner, Polly,	
868.	Warner, Prudence,	1850

1962.	Warren, Olive,	
586.	Watrous, Daniel,	
201.	Way, Silas,	
353.	Webb, David,	
780.	Webb, Hiram H.,	1855
1817.	Webb, Martha,	
479.	Webster, George,	
474.	Webster, Martha,	
1122½.	Wells, George A.,	1860
322.	Wells, John,	1738
329.	Wells, Sarah,	
486.	Wetherell, Elisha,	
750.	Whaple, Elisabeth S.,	1857
687.	White, Abigail,	
692.	White, Eliza,	
1050.	White, Harriet M.,	
686.	White, Henry,	1815

Number.		Date of Marriage.	Number.		Date of Marriage.
1057.	White, Jane A.,		692.	Wilson, Reuben,	
473.	White, Joseph,	1782	1952.	Wilson, Sterling,	
684.	White, Lucy,		1000.	Witter, John,	
693.	White, Mary,		113.	Williams, Diana,	
691.	White, Thomas B.,		1302.	Williams, Ella F.,	
1585.	Whitehead, Elisabeth,	1738	1951.	Williams, Emily,	
571.	Whitmore, Charlotte,		1301.	Williams, Henry C.,	
874.	Whitmore, Emma J.,		779.	Williams, Horace D.,	
1674.	Whitney, Peter,		352.	Williams, Lois,	1774
953.	Wheeler, Alvan,		734.	Williams, Lorenzo L.,	
1738.	Wheeler, Damaris,		368.	Williams, Martha,	1791
1400.	Wheeler, Edward,		365.	Williams, Mary,	1776
1399.	Wheeler, Fannie A.,		733.	Williams, Mary,	1836
1397.	Wheeler, Gurdon B.,		850.	Williams, Moses W.,	1841
1979.	Wheeler, Kate A.,	1868	376.	Williams, Olive,	1776
1657.	Wheeler, Nathan,		388.	Williams, Prudence,	1773
18.	Wheeler, Rebecca,	1667	515.	Williams, Wyllis,	1799
1401.	Wheeler, Samuel P.,	1860	958.	Wood, George C.,	
182.	Wheeler, Thomas,		301.	Woodbridge, Susanna,	1728
41.	Whelpley, Joseph,		480.	Woodruff, Amos,	
1258.	Wilcox, Cora,	1869	210.	Woodruff, Sarah,	
1088.	Wilcox, Fannie,	1835	481.	Woodruff, Sarepta,	
692.	Wilcox, Reuben,		852.	Wolcott, Ambrose,	1853
687.	Wilcox, Samuel,		611.	Worthington, John,	
856.	Wilcox, Walter L.,	1856	587.	Worthington, Joseph,	1791
1107.	Wilder, Alvan D.,	1870	415.	Worthington, Judith,	1757
812.	Wilson, Lyman,		909.	Worthington, Julia,	
1090.	Wilkinson, Carrie A.,		609.	Wright, Fanny,	
330.	Wills, Sarah,		458.	Wright, Sarah	

Y

484. Yale, Philo.

ERRATA.

On page 98, near the bottom, for .Etates read Ætatis.
Page 116, the 5th line from the bottom, for Chaping read Chapin ———.
Page 176, near the middle, for Jane Boutuon read Jane Bontuon.
Page 233, No. 2156, for date 1841 read 1847.
Page 233, No. 2159, for 1864 read 1854.
Page 233, No. 2167, for Heman read Homan.
Page 234, for head number 1972 read 1970.
Page 235, in second line, for Jan. 2 read Jan. 3.
Page 235, under head number 1990, for baptized in 1839 read born July 10, 1832.
Under head number 1991, for baptized in 1841 read born Aug. 18, 1834, at Lockport, N. Y.
Under head number 1993, after born add April 23, 1838.
Under head number 1993, for George read Georgie, Feb. 16, and for Ward read Maud.
Under head number 1995, after born read March 22, 1844.

———•••———

The following was received when the book was nearly printed :

On Page 198, No. 1689, read Caroline, born April 9, 1798, married John Hall Osborne, Jan. 23, 1820. He died July 27, 1841.

CHILDREN.

Deborah Jane,	born Nov. 11, 1820; died Aug. 24, 1855.
David Munson,	" Dec. 15, 1822.
Geo. Lewis,	" July 21, 1825; died 1867.
Barnabas Bertram,	" Nov. 30, 1827; died April 7, 1832.
Edgar Bulkeley,	" Nov. 13, 1829.
Edwin Forbes,	died Nov. 21, 1831.
John Henry,	born Aug. 24, 1832.
Francis Hall,	" Sept. 17, 1834; died Nov. 23, 1855.
Joseph Bradshaw,	" Sept. 1, 1836; died April 28, 1837.
Abbe Jane,	" July 29, 1838.
Caroline Bulkeley,	" July 1, 1840.

www.ingramcontent.com/pod-product-compliance
Lightning Source LLC
Chambersburg PA
CBHW032044230426
43672CB00009B/1460